D0651924

Personality
Psychology
in the Workplace

MRT-GEN
122

Personality
Psychology
in the Workplace

Edited by
**Brent W. Roberts and
Robert Hogan**

American Psychological Association
Washington, DC

Copyright © 2001 by the American Psychological Association. All rights reserved. Except as permitted under the United States Copyright Act of 1976, no part of this publication may be reproduced or distributed in any form or by any means, or stored in a database or retrieval system, without the prior written permission of the publisher.

Published by
American Psychological Association
750 First Street, NE
Washington, DC 20002
www.apa.org

DBN: 173403/

To order
APA Order Department
P.O. Box 92984
Washington, DC 20090-2984
Tel: (800) 374-2721, Direct: (202) 336-5510
Fax: (202) 336-5502, TDD/TTY: (202) 336-6123
Online: www.apa.org/books/
Email: order@apa.org

In the U.K., Europe, Africa, and the Middle East, copies may be ordered from
American Psychological Association
3 Henrietta Street
Covent Garden, London
WC2E 8LU England

Typeset in Berkeley Book by EPS Group Inc., Easton, MD

Printer: United Book Press, Baltimore, MD
Dust jacket designer: Naylor Design, Washington, DC
Technical/Production Editor: Jennifer Powers

The opinions and statements published are the responsibility of the authors, and such opinions and statements do not necessarily represent the policies of the American Psychological Association.

Library of Congress Cataloging-in-Publication Data
Personality psychology in the workplace / edited by Brent W. Roberts and Robert Hogan.
     p. cm.—(Decade of behavior)
   Includes bibliographical references.
   ISBN 1-55798-753-X (alk. paper)
     1. Psychology, Industrial.   2. Personality and occupation.   3. Personality.
 I. Roberts, Brent.   II. Hogan, Robert, 1937–   III. Series.

HF5548.8 .P3996 2001
158.7—dc21

HF
5548.8
·P3996
2001

00-050271

British Library Cataloguing-in-Publication Data
A CIP record is available from the British Library.

Printed in the United States of America
First Edition

APA Science Volumes

Attribution and Social Interaction: The Legacy of Edward E. Jones

Best Methods for the Analysis of Change: Recent Advances, Unanswered Questions, Future Directions

Cardiovascular Reactivity to Psychological Stress and Disease

The Challenge in Mathematics and Science Education: Psychology's Response

Changing Employment Relations: Behavioral and Social Perspectives

Children Exposed to Marital Violence: Theory, Research, and Applied Issues

Cognition: Conceptual and Methodological Issues

Cognitive Bases of Musical Communication

Cognitive Dissonance: Progress on a Pivotal Theory in Social Psychology

Conceptualization and Measurement of Organism–Environment Interaction

Converging Operations in the Study of Visual Selective Attention

Creative Thought: An Investigation of Conceptual Structures and Processes

Developmental Psychoacoustics

Diversity in Work Teams: Research Paradigms for a Changing Workplace

Emotion and Culture: Empirical Studies of Mutual Influence

Emotion, Disclosure, and Health

Evolving Explanations of Development: Ecological Approaches to Organism–Environment Systems

Examining Lives in Context: Perspectives on the Ecology of Human Development

Global Prospects for Education: Development, Culture, and Schooling

Hostility, Coping, and Health

Measuring Patient Changes in Mood, Anxiety, and Personality Disorders: Toward a Core Battery

Occasion Setting: Associative Learning and Cognition in Animals

Organ Donation and Transplantation: Psychological and Behavioral Factors

Origins and Development of Schizophrenia: Advances in Experimental Psychopathology

APA Decade of Behavior Volumes

Contents

PART 1: THE PERSONALITY–I/O INTERFACE

PART 2: MEASUREMENT AND ASSESSMENT ISSUES IN APPLIED PERSONALITY PSYCHOLOGY

PART 3: EMERGING THEMES IN APPLIED PERSONALITY PSYCHOLOGY

Contributors

Roy F. Baumeister, Department of Psychology, Case Western Reserve University, Cleveland, Ohio

Joyce E. Bono, Department of Management and Organizations, College of Business Administration, University of Iowa, Iowa City

Walter C. Borman, Department of Psychology, University of South Florida, and Personnel Decisions Research Institutes, Tampa, Florida

Tina Cook, Department of Experimental Psychology, Oxford University, England, United Kingdom

Nicholas Emler, Department of Social Psychology, The London School of Economics and Political Science, England, United Kingdom

Rhona Flin, Department of Psychology, University of Aberdeen, Scotland, United Kingdom

David C. Funder, Department of Psychology, University of California, Riverside

Adrian Furnham, Department of Psychology, University College London, England, United Kingdom

Robert Hogan, Department of Psychology, University of Tulsa, Oklahoma

Leaetta M. Hough, The Dunnette Group, LTD., St. Paul, Minnesota

Timothy A. Judge, Department of Management and Organizations, College of Business Administration, University of Iowa, Iowa City

Adelheid A. A. M. Nicol, Military Psychology Department, Royal Military College of Canada, Kingston, Ontario

Deniz S. Ones, Department of Psychology, University of Minnesota, Minneapolis

Louis A. Penner, Department of Psychology, University of South Florida, Tampa, Florida

Delroy L. Paulhus, Department of Psychology, University of British Columbia, Vancouver, British Columbia, Canada

Sampo V. Paunonen, Department of Psychology, The University of Western Ontario, London, Ontario, Canada

Brent W. Roberts, Department of Psychology, University of Illinois, Urbana-Champaign

Richard W. Robins, Department of Psychology, University of California, Davis

Chockalingam Viswesvaran, Department of Psychology, Florida International University, Miami, Florida

Michael J. Zickar, Department of Psychology, Bowling Green State University, Ohio

Foreword

In early 1988, the American Psychological Association (APA) Science Directorate began its sponsorship of what has become an exceptionally successful activity in support of psychological science—the APA Scientific Conferences program. This program has showcased some of the most important topics in psychological science, and the conference participants have included many leading figures in the field.

As we enter a new century, it seems fitting that we begin with a new face on this book series—that of the Decade of Behavior (DoB). The DoB is a major interdisciplinary initiative designed to promote the contributions of the behavioral and social sciences to address some of our most important societal challenges and will occur from 2000 to 2010. Although a major effort of the initiative will be related to informing the public about the contributions of these fields, other activities will be put into place to reach fellow scientists. Hence, the series that was the "APA Science Series" will be continued as the "Decade of Behavior Series." This represents one element in APA's efforts to promote the DoB initiative as one of its partner organizations.

Please note the DoB logo on the inside jacket flap and the full title page. We expect this logo will become a familiar sight over the next few years. For additional information about DoB, please visit http://www.decadeofbehavior.org.

As part of the sponsorship agreement with APA, conference organizers commit themselves not only to the conference itself but also to editing a scholarly volume that results from the meeting. This book is such a volume. Over the course of the past 12 years, we have partnered with 44 universities to sponsor 60 conferences on a variety of topics of interest to psychological scientists. The APA Science Directorate looks forward to continuing this program and to sponsoring other conferences in the years ahead.

We are pleased that this important contribution to the literature was supported in part by the Scientific Conferences program. Congratulations to the editors and contributors on their sterling effort.

Richard McCarty, PhD
Executive Director for Science

Virginia E. Holt
*Assistant Executive Director
for Science*

Preface

Beginning in the late 1980s and early 1990s, we noticed an interesting trend in I/O psychology: personality psychology was making a comeback. At a time when personality psychologists were still bashful about using the term "trait" and the field was focused on such concrete motivational constructs as personal strivings and life tasks, industrial psychologists were discovering that personality measures could be used to predict outcomes such as job performance and job satisfaction.

Although there was little direct contact between the personality and I/O guilds (the groups attend separate conferences and do not support interdisciplinary programs of research), personality psychologists became aware of the findings of I/O psychologists, and that information provided the final nail in the coffin of the person–situation debate, that, by then, had been staggering along for 30 years. The early meta-analyses in I/O psychology showed that personality measures didn't predict just simple behavior but predicted the behaviors that people and organizations cared very deeply about. So, despite the bad reputation of personality psychology, and especially the notion of a personality trait, scores on well-constructed personality measures were consistent across time and situation, and predicted behavior—so much for 30 years of hand wringing.

As the 1990s progressed, enthusiasm for the use of personality measures in I/O psychology grew and the field of personality psychology also appeared to be going through a genuine renaissance. We did, however, notice several disturbing trends. First, as is always the case, there was little or no information exchange between personality psychologists and I/O psychologists. Except for a few hardy souls, I/O psychologists read only I/O research and attended only I/O conferences and vice versa for personality psychologists. Thus, personality psychologists continued doing basic research and I/O psychologists developed a relatively narrow view of the field of personality psychology.

As the 1990s came to a close, we felt the time was right to improve the information exchange between personality psychologists and I/O psychologists so that both might profit from the advances made in their respective fields. We took a group of personality psychologists that had been toiling away on basic issues and put them together with a group of I/O psychologists that had been working on the interface of personality psychology and I/O psychology. With the support of the American Psychological Association's Science Directorate, we hosted the conference Applied Personality Psychology: The Intersection of

Personality and I/O Psychology at the University of Tulsa in May of 1999. It was hugely successful, suggesting that the potential for ongoing dialogue between the two fields is excellent. We hope you enjoy this book as much as we enjoyed the conference.

Acknowledgments

We acknowledge the support of the American Psychological Association, the College of Arts and Sciences, and the graduate school of the University of Tulsa. We are also grateful to the members of the Department of Psychology, Abby Hallford, and especially Lisa Mills. Without the combined support of these organizations and individuals neither the conference nor this book would have been possible.

Personality
Psychology
in the Workplace

CHAPTER 1

Introduction: Personality and Industrial and Organizational Psychology

Robert T. Hogan
Brent W. Roberts

Personality psychology concerns the nature of human nature—it is a view of human performance from a very broad vantage point. From a strategic perspective, some notion of what people are like would seem to be crucial to any effort to manage, guide, persuade, or recruit individuals or to understand the economic, political, and social behavior of a group of individuals. Moreover, every discipline in the social sciences—anthropology, criminology, economics, history, political science, sociology—depends on assumptions about human nature. Unfortunately, these assumptions are at times adopted without sufficient consideration of their development, application, or validity. In an important sense, personality psychology is what Nietzsche was referring to in his essay *Beyond Good and Evil* when he characterized psychology as the queen of the sciences.

What Is Personality?

Although many educated people outside of psychology understand the importance of the assumptions people make about human nature, within academic psychology, only a fraction of scholars and researchers are interested in personality. More important, these scholars and researchers not only are a minority in the psychological community, but they often are an embattled minority whose very existence is periodically threatened. Curiously, however, every important theoretical perspective in clinical, counseling, developmental, and organizational psychology depends on assumptions about human nature. Thus, despite its minority status, personality psychology serves as the intellectual underpinning of the larger discipline within which it is embedded.

When Personality Went Away

During the 1960s, personality psychology was attacked repeatedly by social psychologists and behaviorists such as Mischel (1968) and Peterson (1965). The close link between mainstream social psychology and traditional behaviorism often goes unrecognized. For example, B. F. Skinner frequently referred to E. E. Jones, perhaps the most prominent social psychologist of the past 30 years, as his "most famous student." Behaviorism and social psychology are united in the view that it is more parsimonious and closer to the data to assume that what people do depends on the circumstances in which they find themselves rather than on stable characteristics within them. Personality psychologists have always recognized that social action takes place in particular contexts, meaning that an adequate account of social behavior requires specifying the context, but behaviorists argue that social behavior is adequately explained in terms of contextual factors alone. For behaviorists, personality as it is generally understood is either not very important or actually irrelevant.

The behaviorists took this argument about the irrelevance of personality and derived a corollary. On the basis of an empirical review of the literature and the guiding assumptions of behaviorism, they proposed that there is no evidence for the validity and utility of personality assessment—presumably because there is no personality to assess. If there is nothing to assess, then measures of that nothing cannot be expected to predict anything important and, indeed, they do not, or at least not very well. For example, Mischel (1968) concluded, on the basis of his review of the assessment literature, that the upper limit of validity coefficients for personality measures is about .30. This conclusion became widely accepted in the academic community.

Meanwhile, in the world of applied psychology, personality was not faring any better. Ghiselli and Barthol (1953) and Guion and Gottier (1965) reviewed the literature on personality and occupational performance and concluded that there was very little evidence to support the use of personality measures for personnel selection. They based their conclusions on the fact that validity coefficients for personality measures were so low (below .30). The result of all this was that, in the early 1970s, it became nearly impossible to publish measurement-based personality research in American Psychological Association (APA) journals, and it was impossible to secure funding for measurement-based personality research from mainstream funding sources in general and the National Science Foundation in particular.

Real-World Views

Meanwhile, outside of academe, nonpsychologists still believed that the qualities and characteristics within individuals are crucial determinants of their behavior.

Political campaigns continued to be waged on the basis of character, not policy, issues, and sales of such questionable personality measures as the Myers–Briggs Type Indicator steadily increased, despite the conventional wisdom of professional psychology. In a persuasive demonstration of how ordinary individuals ignore academic psychology, Joyce Hogan subscribed to Sunday newspapers from eight regions of the United States for 4 months. She retrieved and content-analyzed 8,000 employment advertisements. Hogan's major finding concerned what those placing the advertisements said they were looking for in potential employees. Specifically, the advertisers said they wanted personality characteristics such as initiative, integrity, and people skills at least as often as they wanted experience and particular technical competencies. Individuals whose income depends on the performance of others understand that personality matters.

Why Personality Went Away

Although nonpsychologists intuitively understand the importance of personality as a determinant of everyday performance, personality psychologists historically have done a poor job of making the case for that role to their skeptical academic peers. There were three major reasons why personality psychology experienced such a decline: (a) lack of consensus regarding the conceptual underpinnings of the discipline; (b) lack of consensus regarding the purpose of personality assessment; and (c) lack of consensus regarding what to measure, even if there were some agreement regarding why it should be measured. Given the lack of consensus regarding these issues, it seems that the decline of personality psychology was justified and perhaps even inevitable.

Conceptual Underpinnings

Allport's and Stagner's 1937 textbooks were instrumental in establishing personality psychology as a discipline. Allport and Stagner approached personality from an empirical and pragmatic perspective, considering it part of everyday life. However, they were minority voices; the key conceptual perspectives that have dominated personality psychology—as exemplified by Freud, Jung, Adler, and Horney—are primarily concerned with understanding and treating psychopathology. These views suggest that the most important generalization that can be made about people is that everyone is somewhat neurotic and the most important problem in an individual's life is to overcome his or her neurosis. This view dominated the field of personality psychology until fairly recently, and it is still quite important. However, it suffers from two problems. First, it is empirically false. Everyone is not somewhat neurotic. To be neurotic is to be substantially impaired, that is, dysfunctional to the point of being nonfunctional. On the other hand, if all that is known about someone is that he or she is not neurotic, what is actually known about that person? Obviously, not much. Nonetheless, the legacy of clinical theory doomed personality psychology to irrelevance from the outset. Freud's and Jung's ideas are much more interesting than Allport's, and it is easy to see why the psychopathological perspective came to dominate the discipline.

Personality Assessment

Psychological assessment is psychology's major contribution to everyday life. The purpose of cognitive assessment is clear: to forecast educational or training outcomes. The purpose of vocational assessment is clear as well: to forecast the degree of individual–occupational fit. But what is the purpose of personality assessment? Under the clinical model, its purpose is to assess individual differences in psychopathology, and this explains why the Rorschach, the Thematic Apperception Test, and the Minnesota Multiphasic Personality Inventory (MMPI) are the most widely used personality measures in the world (see McAdams, 2001).

There are thousands of personality measures in the published literature, and an overwhelming number of them are designed to assess elements of psychopathology. The result of this is that when people think of personality assessment, they immediately associate it with clinical diagnosis. In addition, this orientation substantially limits the validity of personality assessment as measures of psychopathology will be poor predictors of, for example, leadership, creativity, or service orientation.

There was one major exception to this clinical focus for personality assessment. Led by Cattell, Eysenck, and Guilford, an influential alternative tradition argued that the purpose of personality assessment was "to measure traits," and factor analysis was the method by which this would be done. The literature on the factor analytic study of personality is reminiscent of the medieval fallacy of dogmatic methodism, which held that if one only applied the proper method, one would inexorably find truth. In this case, the right factor analysis would reveal the real factors underlying the structure of personality, which would be traits. Missing from the factor analytic tradition of personality research, however, is a discussion of what to do with those traits once they were measured. Most discussions concerned how many traits there might be and how well they had been measured.

What to Measure

Although there are a vast number of personality measures in the published literature, and although they are overwhelmingly oriented toward measuring aspects of psychopathology, this fact is not often recognized. So, for example, measures of locus of control, efficacy, self-esteem, manifest anxiety, narcissism, depression, ego control, ego resilience, identity, optimism, pessimism, and propensity to stress are considered to be quite different. Judge and Bono (chapter 5) provide data showing that these measures all target the same underlying construct, but this insight has so far eluded most personality researchers. In any case, personality psychology in the late 1960s was in conceptual disarray, with no overarching theoretical paradigm, and the subject matter was operationalized through a large number of poorly validated scales with different names.

The response set controversy that developed in the late 1950s and lingered for 20 years further damaged the credibility of personality assessment. This controversy, which was never resolved to its proponents' satisfaction, turned on the empirical fact that there is a substantial correlation between the judged social desirability of MMPI items and the frequency with which they are endorsed by test takers. Advocates of the response set concept argued that when individuals respond to MMPI items, they are responding to the social desirability of the items, not their content. The response set controversy added to the general confusion regarding the meaning and purpose of personality assessment.

Given the negative climate that existed in the 1970s, it is surprising that anyone continued to do personality research. Some continued because it was too late in their careers to change; others continued due to stubbornness or perhaps faith. However, there was a better reason to persist. We received our graduate training at the Institute of Personality Assessment and Research (IPAR) at the University of California, Berkeley. At that time, IPAR was founded in 1949 by Nevitt Sanford, Edward Tolman, and Robert Tryon, who were familiar with the U.S. Office of Strategic Services (OSS) assessment center research conducted during World War II. One of the major findings of that research (OSS, 1948) was that measures of psychopathology did not predict real-world performance. Some individuals who seemed to be very well adjusted were poor OSS agents and vice versa. IPAR was established with a Rockefeller Foundation Grant to study high-level effectiveness. The first IPAR staff members included Frank Barron, Richard Crutchfield, Erik Erikson, Harrison G. Gough, Robert E. Harris, Donald W. MacKinnon, Nevitt Sanford, and Ronald Taft, and their careers demonstrated that high-level effectiveness, not psychopathology, was *an* appropriate, if not *the* appropriate, area of focus for personality psychology.

There are two additional points about IPAR that are important for this discussion. First, much of the research conducted there, especially that concerning creativity, yielded very strong results (cross-validated multiple *r*s of approximately .58, cf. Hall & MacKinnon, 1969). Second, the California Psychological Inventory (CPI; Gough, 1957; Gough & Bradley, 1996) was developed at IPAR during the 1950s and 1960s. The CPI was the first well-developed measure of normal personality designed to predict high-level effectiveness in important areas of human performance (as contrasted with the factor analytic focus on measuring traits). Over the years, the CPI was repeatedly attacked by factor analysts and other advocates of classical test theory on the grounds that it did not measure traits efficiently. What these critics overlooked was that the CPI did what it was designed to do—that is, predict significant, positive, real-world outcomes—and it did this quite well (cf. Gough, 1965).

Our point is that those associated with IPAR and familiar with the CPI in the 1970s were confident of the potential of personality research to contribute to the solution of significant everyday problems such as personnel selection and development. They understood what the purpose of assessment should be, and they had evidence that that purpose could be fulfilled.

Why Personality Came Back

Starting about 1990, the field of industrial and organizational (I/O) psychology rediscovered personality. In particular, I/O psychology rediscovered the usefulness of personality measures in selection contexts. There were four major reasons for this rediscovery. First, other than the interview, the selection method of choice for I/O psychology is cognitive testing. This is due in large part to the belief that cognitive test results accurately predict performance in virtually every job. However, cognitive tests almost always result in adverse impact for protected classes of job seekers. The near inevitability of adverse effects created substantial pressure on employers to both find and develop equally valid but less discriminatory selection methods. Well-constructed personality measures are race and gender neutral, making them attractive alternatives to cognitive measures, regardless of the validity issue.

Second, the appearance of the Five-Factor Model (FFM), normally attributed to Tupes and Christal (1961), provided a way of organizing personality measurement. Briefly, the FFM suggests that the thousands of existing personality measures can be organized or categorized in terms of five broad dimensions: a) Extraversion, b) Agreeableness, c) Conscientiousness, d) Emotional Stability, and e) Openness (cf. Wiggins, 1996). This generally agreed-on taxonomy of personality variables can be used to organize the personality and job performance literatures.

Third, the results of Project A, a 1980s U.S. Army Research Institute project designed to develop a better selection system for entry-level Army jobs, persuaded many that personality measurement was too important to be overlooked (see Hough, Eaton, Dunnette, Kamp, & McCloy, 1990). Project A began with a construct-oriented review of criterion-related validities in each predictor domain. Leaetta M. Hough and John D. Kamp used the FFM to summarize the validities for the personality domain and found useful results. On the basis of a content analysis of these results, Hough proposed a nine-construct taxonomy for summarizing the validities. The results appeared in an influential monograph published in the *Journal of Applied Psychology* (Hough, Eaton, Dunnette, Kamp, & McCloy, 1990).

Fourth, meta-analytic reviews by Barrick and Mount (1991) and Tett, Jackson, and Rothstein (1991) further signaled to the applied research community that personality measures were more valid than generally believed. Since 1991, the number of personality papers presented at the annual conference of the Society of Industrial and Organizational Psychology (APA's Division 14) has skyrocketed, and there now may be more significant personality research going on in Division 14 than in Division 8 (Society of Personality and Social Psychology). There certainly is more applied research being conducted.

The Resurgence of Personality: The Good News and the Bad News

The good news is that personality is back with a significant presence; the bad news concerns what modern researchers seem to think it is. I/O psychologists and other applied researchers think about cognitive ability in terms of g, a "simple and sovereign" concept. This may be a mistake, but that is the way it is (cf. Schmidt & Hunter, 1981). In the same way, I/O psychologists think about personality in terms of conscientiousness or p, another simple and sovereign concept (cf. Ones, Viswesvaran, & Schmidt, 1993). Perhaps even worse, they want to believe that more p is better for every job. However, there is more to both personality and occupational performance than p or conscientiousness. Even those researchers who move beyond conscientiousness usually want to define personality in terms of the FFM. Our major point here is that despite the newfound enthusiasm for personality few researchers have spent much time thinking carefully about its definition.

The Intersection of Personality and Industrial/Organizational Psychology and the Person–Situation Debate

There are some interesting links among personality assessment, the so-called person–situation debate of the 1970s and 1980s, and the resurgence of personality in I/O psychology in the 1990s. For example, Hartshorne and May's (1928) study of honesty, the study that sparked the person–situation debate, typically is interpreted as showing that children are not honest across situations. This suggests, therefore, that honesty cannot be reliably assessed or used to predict future behavior (Mischel & Shoda, 1995). In contrast, modern I/O psychologists believe that integrity tests are one of the best supplements to tests of cognitive ability in predicting job performance in adults (Schmidt & Hunter, 1998). It seems that honesty not only can be assessed, but that simple self-report tests of integrity can be used to predict consequential social behaviors (see also Ones and Viswesvaran, chapter 4).

Curiously, many of the studies originally questioning the validity of personality assessment were based on samples of children (e.g., Hartshorne & May, 1928; Shoda, Mischel, & Wright, 1989). There now is formidable empirical evidence that children are substantially less consistent than adults (Roberts & DelVecchio, 2000), and it seems odd to question personality assessment using studies based on the least consistent population. In contrast, I/O psychology's emphasis on adult populations is a model that more personality psychologists should follow; that is, personality psychology should move beyond the study of children and adolescents (i.e., college students) to studying adult populations.

During the person–situation debate, one of Mischel's (1968) most infamous statements was that validity coefficients for personality tests rarely exceeded .30. Researchers now know that the effect size for personality tests often exceeds that .30 ceiling (see Hogan, Hogan, & Roberts, 1996). For example, Helson, Roberts, and Agronick (1995) reported that a simple self-report scale of creative temperament measured in college had a correlation of .49 with achievement in creative careers assessed 30 years later. It is also known that if composites of valid measures are formed, the predictive validity of personality tests can reach as high as .50 (Hogan & Hogan, 1995). Therefore, a correlation of .30 is not a barrier per se.

That said, meta-analytic estimates of the average effect size of personality measures on outcomes such as job performance have ranged from .10 to .40 (Barrick & Mount, 1991; Ones et al., 1993; Tett et al., 1991). That is, the predictive validity of these measures appears to still be hovering around Mischel's (1968) .30 mark. The question then is whether Mischel was correct. We think the answer is no and that the .30 "red herring" should be laid to rest, for several reasons.

First, the range of effect sizes (e.g., .10 to .40) usually reflects the use of single, homogenous measures to predict single behaviors (e.g., using a single measure of conscientiousness to predict a single measure of job performance). According to Ahadi and Diener (1989), single measures should not be expected to predict single behavioral outcomes at a level much higher than .40 because multiple factors contribute to the expression of any given behavior. Second, researchers have argued that the .30 effect size is small relative to the possible range of the correlation coefficient (i.e., from −1 to 1). This is the wrong scale by which to judge a .30 effect size or judge the merits of personality measures. For example, Schmidt and Hunter (1998) have shown that the best predictors of job performance barely pass .50 and that most fall below .40. On a scale of 0 to .50, .30 looks pretty good.

Another way to eliminate the .30 red herring concerns the "variance accounted for statistic," whereby one squares the correlation and concludes that personality tests account for between 0% and 16% of the criterion variance. Ozer (1986) argued that the variance accounted for statistic is biased and possibly inappropriate for evaluating the significance of assessment-based findings.

Alternative effect size scales abound (Cohen, 1992). For example, one could use Rosenthal and Rubin's (1982) binomial effect size display, in which a correlation coefficient is translated into the increase one would expect in a simple 2 × 2 contingency table in which the base rate expectation is 50:50. With a .20 correlation, the hit rate improves from 50:50 to 60:40. With a .40 correlation, the hit rate improves from 50:50 to 70:30. These are reasonable percentages.

The final reason to ignore the .30 red herring concerns the implicit assumption that the remaining 84% to 100% of the variance is accounted for by situations. In an unfortunately undercited reanalysis of the classic social psychological experiments of the 1950s, 1960s, and 1970s, Funder and Ozer (1983) showed that, in the best case, situations have effect sizes comparable to those of personality tests (e.g., 16% of the variance). What is significant is that critics of personality, alleging conspicuously low predictive validity for personality assessment, often have hidden in the seeming anonymity of *F* tests and *t* tests and provided no evidence of their own of the apparent effect size of situations or other variables. (This is not the case in I/O psychology, which tends to report correlation or regression coefficients.) Personality psychologists essentially have been criticized for doing something methodologically appropriate—that is, personality psychologists report their results in the form of correlation coefficients, which provide an indication of both statistical significance and effect size. It can only be hoped that researchers who focus on ambiguous tests of statistical significance will begin reporting effect sizes. It then will be apparent that most effect sizes in personality, I/O, and social psychology do range from .10 to .40.

Defining Personality

Following MacKinnon (OSS, 1948), the first director of IPAR, and consistent with what Goldberg (1993) called the lexical tradition, the word *personality* is used in two very distinct ways. Used one way, *personality* refers to the distinctive impression a person makes on others. This is personality from the perspective of the observer, and it is functionally equivalent to a person's reputation. Used the second way, *personality* refers to the structures inside a person that explain why he or she creates a particular impression on others. This is personality from the perspective of the actor, and it is functionally equivalent to a person's identity.

Allport (1937) argued that reputation was not part of personality, but he was clearly wrong. People care deeply about their reputations. Indeed, from a role-theoretical perspective (Mead, 1934), intentional social interaction is designed primarily to protect or enhance reputation. Moreover, reputation is easy to study using observer ratings. Finally, because the best predictor of future behavior is past behavior and because reputation is based on past behavior, personality as reputation is inherently valid. In our opinion, the FFM is primarily about reputation.

There is substantial agreement about the taxonomy of reputation. Matters are quite different concerning personality from the perspective of the actor, however. Identity is quite a bit more complex than reputation and includes values, goals, interests, abilities, narratives, and roles as well as dispositions. Given its intrinsic complexity, personality from the inside is endlessly fascinating—even if it is ineffable—and likely will continue to be a source of confusion and debate for a long time. Fortunately, self-reports of personality traits also can be organized according to the Big Five (Goldberg, 1993), thereby affording some organizational clarity to one small component of identity.

Overview of the Book

This book is organized in three parts around three themes: Part 1, The Personality–I/O Interface; part 2, Measurement and Assessment Issues in Applied Personality Psychology; and part 3, Emerging Themes in Applied Personality Psychology. Part 1 brings together four perspectives on the use of personality testing in applied settings from some of the top researchers in the field. Hough (chapter 2) provides an overview of the personality–I/O interface and makes a compelling argument that much of the recent progress in I/O psychology depends on methods long used in personality psychology. Specifically, Hough states that personality psychology has inspired more construct-oriented thinking in I/O psychology and that this enhanced conceptual and theoretical approach has improved I/O research in several concrete ways.

Borman and Penner's chapter on citizenship performance (chapter 3) is an excellent example of the construct-oriented approach described by Hough. Borman and Penner present a model of citizenship performance and discuss how this performance domain is different from task performance. They also detail the precursors to citizenship performance which, unlike task performance, are centered on individual differences in personality rather than cognitive ability. One of the most exciting aspects of Borman and Penner's chapter is the way they link citizenship performance to individual differences in motivation. This chapter shows that some researchers' views of personality go beyond the Big Five to include such classic personality psychology constructs as goals and motives. Ones and Viswesvaran (chapter 4) provide a thorough review of criterion-focused occupational personality scales (COPS). These are personality scales that predict individual differences in such characteristics and actions as customer service behaviors, employee theft, and the ability to withstand stressful work situations. Using meta-analytic techniques, Ones and Viswesvaran synthesize empirical evidence and show that COPS are excellent predictors of the criteria they are intended to measure (e.g., drug use) as well as strong predictors of overall job performance. Ones and Viswesvaran also show that most COPS scales can be subsumed under the Big Five. More specifically, COPS scales appear to be related to the Big Five domains of agreeableness, conscientiousness, and emotional stability. Similarly, Judge and Bono (chapter 5) argue that neuroticism, self-esteem, locus of control, and generalized self-efficacy are indicators of a common construct, core self-evaluation. In bringing together previously disparate literatures on these four traits, Judge and Bono provide evidence that these separate traits cohere as a unitary construct and that individual differences in core self-evaluation are related rather strongly to job satisfaction and performance.

Part 2 contains four chapters on measurement and assessment issues. Funder (chapter 6) describes the realistic accuracy model, in which he shows that claims that people are incapable of making accurate judgments of others were rash. According to Funder, (a) people can judge others, and (b) their judgments can predict real-world behaviors. He puts forth a theory concerning the moderators of accuracy that should help to inform the next generation of research on the accuracy of job performance ratings, which are of course, judgments made by people that often are quite important.

Zickar (chapter 7) presents an introduction into the next frontier of psychometric research on personality scales, that is, item response theory. He provides a primer on the basics of item response theory and describes how this measurement evaluation system can enhance researchers' understanding of the personality–I/O psychology interface.

Paunonen and Nicol (chapter 8) take on the thorny issue of the bandwidth–fidelity trade-off in prediction and show that homogeneous measures of personality traits are preferred predictors of work criteria and that broad aggregations of personality traits (e.g., the Big Five) can result in decreased predictive accuracy.

Robins and Paulhus (chapter 9) confront the ever-present flaw in self-reports, self-enhancement. In contrast to the earlier controversies surrounding response sets and biases, Robins and Paulhus provide a theoretical model for understanding why people self-enhance; evidence for the base rate of enhancement and diminishment (both low); and evidence for the fact that one type of self-enhancement, defensive self-enhancement, is strongly linked to the personality trait of narcissism. This last finding invites an interesting solution to the self-enhancement imbroglio: If an individual or employer is concerned with self-enhancement, why not deselect narcissists?

The final section, part 3 is dedicated to considering emerging trends in applied personality psychology. Furnham (chapter 10) claims that person–environment fit is an overlooked mediator and moderator of the personality–job performance relationship and reviews relevant literatures. Flin (chapter 11) provides an overview of the difficulties in using personality tests to select for the "right stuff," or high-level performance in dangerous occupations and hazardous work settings. Emler and Cook (chapter 12) present a fascinating analysis of the links between moral character and effective leadership. They make a strong case that current selection systems are blind to this critical individual difference in leadership behavior. Finally, Baumeister (chapter 13) resurrects an energy model of the self in personality, demonstrating that the ego can become depleted when overworked. One can see immediate applications of this research in occupations that call for vigilance and exertion, such as air traffic control and truck driving—jobs in which ego depletion can have life-threatening consequences.

References

Ahadi, S., & Diener, E. (1989). Multiple determinants and effect size. *Journal of Personality and Social Psychology, 56,* 398–406.

Allport, G. W. (1937). *Personality: A psychological interpretation.* New York: Holt.

Barrick, M. R., & Mount, M. K. (1991). The Big Five personality dimensions and job performance: A meta-analysis. *Personnel Psychology, 44,* 1–26.

Cohen, J. (1992). A power primer. *Psychological Bulletin, 112,* 155–159.

Funder, D. C., & Ozer, D. J. (1983). Behavior as a function of the situation. *Journal of Personality and Social Psychology, 44,* 107–112.

Ghiselli, E. E., & Barthol, R. P. (1953). The validity of personality inventories in the selection of employees. *Journal of Applied Psychology, 37,* 18–20.

Goldberg, L. R. (1993). The structure of phenotypic personality traits. *American Psychologist, 48,* 26–34.

Gough, H. G. (1957). *The California Psychological Inventory manual.* Palo Alto, CA: Consulting Psychologists Press.

Gough, H. G. (1965). Conceptual analysis of psychological test scores and other diagnostic variables. *Journal of Abnormal Psychology, 70,* 294–302.

Gough, H. G., & Bradley, P. (1996). *California Psychological Inventory manual* (3rd ed.). Palo Alto, CA: Consulting Psychologists Press.

Guion, R. M., & Gottier, R. F. (1965). Validity of personality measures in personnel selection. *Personnel Psychology, 18,* 135–164.

Hall, W. B., & MacKinnon, D. W. (1969). Personality correlates of creativity among architects. *Journal of Applied Psychology, 53,* 322–326.

Hartshorne, H., & May, M. A. (1928). *Studies in the nature of character, Studies in deceit* (Vol. 1). New York: Macmillan.

Helson, R., Roberts, B. W., & Agronick, G. (1995). Enduringness and change in creative personality and the prediction of occupational creativity. *Journal of Personality and Social Psychology, 69,* 1173–1183.

Hogan, J. (1995). *Interpersonal skills required at work.* Tulsa, OK: Hogan Assessment Systems.

Hogan, R., & Hogan, J. (1995). *The Hogan Personality Inventory.* Tulsa, OK: Hogan Assessment Systems.

Hogan, R., Hogan, J., & Roberts, R. W. (1996). Personality measurement and employment decisions. *American Psychologist, 51,* 469–477.

Hough, L. M., Eaton, N. L., Dunnette, M. D., Kamp, J. D., & McCloy, R. A. (1990). Criterion-related validities of personality constructs and the effect of response distortion on those validities [Monograph]. *Journal of Applied Psychology, 75,* 581–595.

McAdams, D. P. (2001). *The Person.* Orlando, FL: Harcourt.

Mead, G. H. (1934). *Mind, self, and society.* Chicago: University of Chicago Press.

Mischel, W. (1968). *Personality and assessment.* New York: Wiley.

Mischel W., & Shoda, Y. (1995). A cognitive–affective system theory of personality: Reconceptualizing situations, dispositions, dynamics, and invariance in personality structure. *Psychological Review, 102,* 246–268.

Ones, D. S., Viswesvaran, C., & Schmidt, F. L. (1993). Comprehensive meta-analysis of integrity test validities: Findings and implications for personnel selection and theories of job performance [Monograph]. *Journal of Applied Psychology Monograph, 78,* 679–703.

Ozer, D. (1986). *Consistency in personality: A methodological framework.* New York: Springer-Verlag.

Peterson, D. R. (1965). Scope and generality of verbally defined personality factors. *Psychological Review, 72,* 48–59.

Roberts, B. W., & DelVecchio, W. F. (2000). The rank-order consistency of personality from childhood to old age: A quantitative review of longitudinal studies. *Psychological Bulletin, 126,* 3–25.

Rosenthal, R., & Rubin, D. B. (1982). A simple general purpose display of magnitude of experimental effect. *Journal of Educational Psychology, 74,* 166–169.

Schmidt, F. L., & Hunter, J. E. (1981). Employment testing: Old theories and new research findings. *American Psychologist, 36*, 1128–1137.

Schmidt, F. L., & Hunter, J. E. (1998). The validity and utility of selection methods in personnel psychology. *Psychological Bulletin, 124*, 262–274.

Shoda, Y., Mischel, W., & Wright, J. C. (1989). Intuitive interactionism in person perception: Effects of situation–behavior relations on dispositional judgments. *Journal of Personality and Social Psychology, 56*, 41–53.

Stagner, R. (1937). *Psychology of personality*. New York: McGraw-Hill.

Tett, R. P., Jackson, D. N., & Rothstein, M. (1991). Personality measures as predictors of job performance: A meta-analytic review. *Personnel Psychology, 44*, 703–742.

Tupes, E. C., & Christal, R. E. (1961). Recurrent personality factors based on trait ratings. *Journal of Personality, 60*, 225–251.

U.S. Office of Strategic Services. (1948). *Assessment of men: Selection of personnel for the Office of Strategic Services*. New York: Rinehart.

Wiggins, J. S. (Ed.). (1996). *The Five-Factor Model of personality: Theoretical perspectives*. New York: Guilford Press.

PART 1

The Personality–I/O Interface

CHAPTER 2

I/Owes Its Advances to Personality

Leaetta M. Hough

The 1990s were the decade of personality psychology contributions to industrial and organizational (I/O) psychology. The impact of personality psychology on I/O psychology has been significant. Initially, personality variables, models, and theories were not welcomed; now they are accepted and widely included in performance models and theories. Several trends in the thinking and research methods of the field of I/O psychology can be traced to hypotheses, theories, and research with personality variables in organizational and work settings.

This chapter highlights several areas in which I/O psychology has advanced because of the introduction and use of personality variables in researchers' thinking and studies. One trend is construct-oriented (taxonomic) thinking for both predictors (individual differences) and criteria (job performance) that has led to greater understanding of important work-related variables and their relationships with each other. An expanded view of job performance has resulted in job/work analysis methods that attend more completely to areas that usually were ignored or dismissed as being not important to job performance. The concept of competence also has been expanded. Intellectual intelligence, social intelligence, and emotional intelligence are now all considered part of a broader view of competence in the workplace. These expanded views have resulted in greater accuracy in predicting job performance. Moreover, expanded concepts of the predictor and criterion domains have produced selection systems that typically have fewer adverse effects on protected employee groups. Successful affirmative action programs can be based on a more broadly defined concept of merit. These changes represent important advances in I/O psychology.

More Construct-Oriented Thinking

Psychological constructs and their nomological nets are not new. Cronbach and Meehl's (1955) classic article on construct validity in psychological tests was published almost 50 years ago. Of course, I/O psychology has not been without constructs, and many in the field have called for more construct-oriented thinking. For example, Guion (1961), Dunnette (1963), and Smith (1976) all have long argued for more sophisticated thinking, especially construct-oriented thinking, about variables in I/O psychology. Nonetheless, the field is replete with research and articles that confound measurement methods with constructs and merge constructs into grossly heterogeneous variables. Both have hampered understanding of important variables, and seriously impeding good model and theory building.

Constructs and Measurement Methods Confounded

An examination of several meta-analyses reveals that I/O psychologists often confound constructs and measurement methods. Hunter and Hunter (1984) summarized the validity of several predictors used in I/O psychology. Their results, average corrected validities rank ordered according to the magnitude of relationship with overall job performance, are shown in Table 2.1. Predictors included in the study were, for example, ability composites, biographical inventories, interviews, interests, and age. Abilities, interests, and age are individual difference variables, whereas biographical inventories and interviews are

TABLE 2.1

Average Corrected Mean Validities From Hunter and Hunter (1984)

PREDICTOR	OVERALL JOB PERFORMANCE[a]
Ability composite	.53
Job tryout	.44
Biographical inventory	.37
Reference check	.26
Experience	.18
Interview	.14
Training and experience ratings	.13
Academic achievement	.11
Education	.10
Interest	.10
Age	−.01

Note. From "Validity and Utility of Alternative Predictors of Job Performance," by J. E. Hunter and R. F. Hunter, 1984, *Psychological Bulletin, 96,* p. 90. Copyright 1984 by the American Psychological Association. Adapted with permission of the author. [a]Supervisory ratings, corrected for error of measurement.

measurement methods that measure or assess individual differences. It is interesting that personality variables were not even included in the list of predictors
in this 1984 meta-analysis, reflecting the low opinion of personality variables
then held by most I/O psychologists. Schmitt, Gooding, Noe, and Kirsch (1984)
similarly conducted a meta-analysis of validity studies and confused constructs
with measurement methods. Table 2.2 contains their results. Schmitt and colleagues compared uncorrected validity coefficients for assessment centers, work
samples, biodata, supervisor/peer evaluations, general mental ability, personality,
special aptitude, physical ability, and other predictors. They found that when
predicting performance ratings, the average validity for assessment centers was
higher than for all other predictors considered. This should not be a surprising
result: Assessment centers typically consist of several of the measurement methods and individual difference variables contained in the rest of the list. Assessment center scores thus represent a composite of other variables and provide
little information other than that an overall score is a better predictor of job
performance than are its individual component predictors. Also interesting is
that Schmitt and colleagues found that personality variables correlate .21 (uncorrected) with job performance ratings. This result is strikingly different from
Guion and Gottier's (1965) conclusion that personality variables have little or
no systematic relationship with job performance criteria. Schmitt et al.'s results
for general mental ability and personality variables are, however, remarkably
similar to Ghiselli's (1966), which are presented in Table 2.3.[1]

Meta-analyses reflect researchers' basic assumptions, that is, their thinking
about which variables are important. If understanding the nomological net of
the variables is a goal, then the results of most existing meta-analyses are not
particularly helpful. Empirical examination of evidence such as that provided
by meta-analysis is extremely valuable; however, confounding constructs with
measurement methods is not.

Confounded Constructs

I/O psychologists have been lax in attending to the taxonomic structure of their
variables, perhaps due partly to excessive empiricism, and perhaps partly the
result of pragmatic attention to an immediate, applied goal. The goal of most
prediction situations is accurate prediction. In the world of work, this often has
meant one predictor composite and one criterion composite. Decisions often
are about entry into an organization or, once in an organization, promotion

---

[1]It is interesting to note that results of both of these meta-analyses reflect a significantly
higher level of validity for personality as a predictor of overall job performance than
Barrick and Mount (1991). (See Table 2.7.)

TABLE 2.2
Uncorrected Mean Validities From Schmitt, Gooding, Noe, and Kirsch (1984)

				CRITERION			
PREDICTOR	PERFORMANCE RATING	TURNOVER	ACHIEVEMENT/ GRADES	PRODUCTIVITY	STATUS CHANGE	WAGES	WORK SAMPLE
Assessment center	.43	—	.31	—	.41	.24	—
Work sample	.32	—	.31	—	—	.44	.35
Biodata	.32	.21	.23	.20	.33	.53	—
Supervisor/peer evaluations	.32	—	—	—	.51	.21	—
General mental ability	.22	.14	.44	—	.28	—	.43
Personality	.21	.12	.15	—	.13	.27	—
Special aptitude	.16	—	.28	—	—	—	.28
Physical ability	—	.15	.28	—	.61	—	.42

Note. From "Metaanalyses of Validity Studies Published Between 1964 and 1982 and the Investigation of Study Characteristics," by N. Schmitt, R. Z. Gooding, R. A. Noe, and M. Kirsch, 1984, *Personnel Psychology, 37*, p. 417. Copyright 1984 by Personnel Psychology, Inc. Adapted with permission.

TABLE 2.3

Uncorrected Mean Validities From Ghiselli (1966)

		PREDICTOR			
JOB	INTELLECTUAL ABILITIES	SPATIAL/ MECHANICAL	PERCEPTUAL ACCURACY	PERSONALITY	INTEREST
Executives/administrators	.29	.18	.24	.27	.31
Foremen	.24	.23	.14	.15	.15
Clerks	.27	.20	.27	.24	.12
Sales clerks	−.10	—	−.05	.35	.34
Commission sales representatives	.31	.07	.21	.24	.31
Protective service workers	.23	.16	.17	.24	−.01
Personal service workers	.03	—	−.10	.16	—
Vehicle operators	.14	.20	.36	—	.26
Tradespeople/craftspeople	.19	.23	.22	.29	−.13
Industrial workers	.16	.16	.18	.50	.14
Median validity	.21	.19	.20	.24	.15

Note. Although Ghiselli also summarized validities for training performance, the criterion in this table is job proficiency. — = no data. From *The Validity of Occupational Aptitude Tests* (tables 3.1–3.8, pp. 34–56) by E. E. Ghiselli, 1966. New York: Wiley. Copyright 1966 by John Wiley & Sons. Adapted with permission.

into more senior-level jobs—yes/no-type decisions—hence, one predictor composite and one criterion composite.

Predictor Constructs

I/O psychology research and meta-analyses confound constructs, merging diverse constructs into overly heterogeneous variables. For example, McDaniel, Whetzel, Schmidt, and Maurer (1994) examined the relationship between interviews and overall job performance and found that design characteristics of the interview, such as amount of structure, moderated the validity of the interview. McDaniel et al.'s results and approach are shown in Table 2.4. Huffcutt and Arthur (1994; see Table 2.5) also found that amount of structure, defined according to both interview questions and response scoring, moderated an interview's validity for predicting job performance. Another possible moderator is construct measured. Neither the McDaniel et al. nor the Huffcutt and Arthur studies controlled for constructs measured in the interview even though the constructs measured undoubtedly varied across studies.

Reilly and Chao (1982) performed a meta-analysis of the validities of biodata inventories. Their results are reported in Table 2.6 according to type of occupation and criterion. As with the interview meta-analyses discussed above, predictor constructs undoubtedly differed in the biodata inventories, yet Reilly and Chao combined them. They reported results across predictor constructs, thereby making those results less useful than if they had been reported according to construct.

It is very likely that most of the original articles and reports that these meta-analyses summarized did not report results according to construct, thereby making comparisons according to construct across studies impossible. Meta-analyses can be little better than the research they summarize, and I/O psychologists have tended not to report their results according to construct.

It was not until meta-analyses using personality variables appeared that I/O psychologists summarized criterion-related validities according to predictor construct. Hough, Eaton, Dunnette, Kamp, and McCloy (1990); Barrick and Mount (1991); and Hough (1992), for example, examined the validity of relatively homogeneous personality constructs for predicting job performance. Table 2.7 shows the variables Barrick and Mount examined and the relationships they found among personality constructs and overall job performance for different types of jobs. These studies represent an important departure from previous meta-analyses in I/O psychology and continue to influence thinking in the field. This influence is apparent in Schmidt and Hunter's (1998) meta-analysis (see Table 2.8), in which two personality constructs, conscientiousness and integrity, were included. Although this study represented clear progress—that is, Schmidt and Hunter included two personality constructs—they, nonetheless, continued to confound measurement methods with constructs.

TABLE 2.4

Corrected Mean Validities for Interviews From McDaniel, Whetzel, Schmidt, and Maurer (1994)

VARIABLE	VALIDITY
All interviews	.37
Interview content:	
Situational	.50
Job related	.39
Psychological	.29
Interview structure:	
Structured	.44
Unstructured	.33
Criterion purpose:	
Administrative	.36
Research	.47
Job-related × structure:	
Structured	.44
Unstructured	.33
Job-related × criterion purpose:	
Administrative	.39
Research	.50
Job-related, structured × purpose:	
Administrative	.37
Research	.51
All interviews:	
Individual interviewer	.43
Board interview	.32
Individual interview × structure	
Structured	.46
Unstructured	.34
Board interview × structure	
Structured	.38
Unstructured	.33

Note. Corrections include corrections for range restrictions. Criterion is overall job performance. From "The Validity of Employment Interviews: A Comprehensive Review and Meta-Analysis," by M. A. McDaniel, D. L. Whetzel, F. L. Schmidt, and S. D. Maurer, 1994, *Journal of Applied Psychology, 79,* pp. 606–607. Copyright 1994 by the American Psychological Association. Adapted with permission of the author.

TABLE 2.5
Corrected Mean Validities for Interviews From Huffcutt and Arthur (1994)

INTERVIEW STRUCTURE	VALIDITY
All interviews	.37
Structure 1 (least)	.20
Structure 2	.35
Structure 3	.56
Structure 4 (most)	.57

Note. Criterion is supervisory ratings of overall job performance. Structure is defined according to both interview question and response scoring. From "Hunter and Hunter (1984) Revisited: Interview Validity for Entry-Level Jobs," by A. I. Huffcutt and W. Arthur, Jr., 1994, *Journal of Applied Psychology, 79,* p. 188. Copyright 1994 by the American Psychological Association. Adapted with permission by the author.

Differential psychology (the study of individual differences) is a critically important foundation for I/O psychology. Differential psychology illustrates that good taxonomies exist for many domains of psychological variables. For example, the specific abilities that make up general cognitive intelligence (g) are well researched and well known. Nonetheless, in I/O psychology, the immediate, applied goal of validating a selection method or system has often overshadowed the long-term goal of understanding the nomological net of the constructs. Hunter (1986) argued that g predicts job performance in a variety of jobs as effectively as do combinations of specific abilities. Part of this may be due to emphasizing overall job effectiveness as the criterion. Regardless of the reason, many I/O psychologists have felt it unnecessary, perhaps even inefficient, to study the relationships between specific abilities and various job performance constructs.

The situation is different for personality variables. Different personality constructs predict different criteria. Meta-analyses of personality variables and their relationship with work-related criteria have highlighted the importance of summarizing validities according to rather than across constructs. Personality differs from general cognitive ability in another way: There is no g in personality. Although some (e.g., J. Hogan & Ones, 1997; Mount & Barrick, 1995; Salgado, 1997, 1998) have argued that conscientiousness is a useful predictor for all types of work, others (e.g., Hough, 1995, 1998; Hough, Ones, & Viswesvaran, 1998; Robertson & Callinan, 1998) have demonstrated that conscientiousness is not a useful predictor for all types of work.

TABLE 2.6

Uncorrected Mean Cross-Validities for Biodata Inventories From Reilly and Chao (1982)

OCCUPATION		CRITERION				AVERAGE FOR OCCUPATION
	TENURE	TRAINING	RATING	PRODUCTIVITY	SALARY	
Clerical	.52	—	—	—	—	.52
Sales	—	—	.40	.62	—	.50
Scientific/engineering	.50	—	.32	.43	.43	.41
Management	—	—	.40	—	.23	.38
Other nonmanagement	.14	—	—	—	—	.14
Military	.30	.39	.25	—	—	.30
Average for criteria	.32	.39	.36	.46	.34	.35

Note. From "Validity and Fairness of Some Alternative Employee Selection Procedures," by R. R. Reilly and G. T. Chao, 1982, *Personnel Psychology, 35,* p. 7. Copyright 1982 by Personnel Psychology, Inc. Adapted with permission from the author.

TABLE 2.7

Corrected Average Validities From Barrick and Mount (1991)

JOB		PERSONALITY CONSTRUCT				
	EXTRAVERSION	EMOTIONAL STABILITY	AGREEABLENESS	CONSCIENTIOUSNESS	OPENNESS TO EXPERIENCE
Professionals	−.09	−.13	.02	.20	−.08
Police officers	.09	.10	.10	.22	.00
Managers	.18	.08	.10	.22	.08
Salespeople	.15	.07	.00	.23	−.02
Skilled/semiskilled workers	.01	.12	.06	.21	.01
CRITERION					
Job proficiency	.10	.07	.06	.23	−.03
Training proficiency	.26	.07	.10	.23	.25
Personnel data	.11	.09	.14	.20	.01
M	.13	.08	.07	.22	.04

Note. Corrected for range restriction, criterion unreliability, and sampling error and between-study differences in test unreliability. From "The Big Five Personality Dimensions and Job Performance: A Meta-Analysis," by M. R. Barrick and M. K. Mount, 1991, *Personnel Psychology, 44,* pp. 13, 15. Copyright 1991 by Personnel Psychology, Inc. Adapted with permission of the author.

TABLE 2.8

Corrected Mean Validities From Schmidt and Hunter (1998)

PREDICTOR	OVERALL JOB PERFORMANCE
Work sample tests	.54
General mental ability tests	.51
Employment interviews (structured)	.51
Peer ratings	.49
Job knowledge tests	.48
T & E behavioral consistency method	.45
Job tryout procedure	.44
Integrity tests	.41
Employment interviews (unstructured)	.38
Assessment centers	.37
Biographical data measures	.35
Conscientiousness measures	.31
Reference checks	.26
Job experience (years)	.18
T & E point method	.11
Education (years)	.10
Interests	.10
Graphology	.02
Age (years)	−.01

Note. T&E = training and experience. From "The Validity and Utility of Selection Methods in Personnel Psychology: Practical and Theoretical Implication of 85 Years of Research Findings," by F. L. Schmidt and J. E. Hunter, 1998, *Psychological Bulletin,* *124,* p. 265. Copyright 1998 by the American Psychological Association. Adapted with permission of the author.

Criterion Constructs

As mentioned above, I/O psychologists often have been interested in predicting overall job performance rather than considering individual constructs. Few researchers have concentrated on understanding job performance and its dimensions. There are some notable exceptions, however. Early on, Guion (1961), Dunnette (1963), and Smith (1976) wrote of the need to conceptualize job performance more clearly. More recently, Campbell (1990) and his colleagues (Campbell, McCloy, Oppler, & Sager, 1993; Campbell, Gasser, & Oswald, 1996); Borman and Motowidlo (1993, 1997); Motowidlo, Borman, and Schmit (1997); Motowidlo and Van Scotter (1994); Organ (1988, 1990, 1997); and Van Dyne, Cummings, and Parks (1995) have focused on job performance constructs, defining them and modeling the criterion space. This represents a significant change in the thinking of I/O psychologists.

Nonetheless, much of what is known about predicting job performance is at the overall performance level. Even the meta-analyses with personality constructs typically have been summaries of validities for predicting overall job performance. Some researchers have recognized that job type may moderate the relationship between predictor construct and overall job performance. Ghiselli (1966), Reilly and Chao (1982), and Barrick and Mount (1991), for example, examined validities according to job type (e.g., clerical, sales, and police; see Tables 2.3, 2.6, and 2.7). Many researchers, for example, Ghiselli (1966), Schmitt et al. (1984), Reilly and Chao (1982), and Barrick and Mount (1991), have recognized that different types of criteria, such as training performance, tenure, absenteeism, and academic success, are also needed. However, all have focused their research on type of criterion rather than on the dimensions or components (constructs) of job performance. Some researchers (e.g., Ones, Viswesvaran, & Schmidt, 1993) have examined a specific personality construct (e.g., integrity) and its relationship to different types of criteria (e.g., overall job performance, counterproductivity, self-report criteria, and external criteria). Organ and Ryan (1995) summarized validities of attitudinal and dispositional predictors of organizational citizenship behavior. A few researchers (Hough, 1992; Hough et al., 1990; Hough et al., 1998) have summarized validities according to predictor constructs and job performance constructs (e.g., creativity, teamwork, irresponsible behavior) as well as according to criterion type (e.g., training performance, educational success, salary). Table 2.9 shows Hough's (1992) results. As shown, different personality constructs correlate differently with different job performance constructs as well as with different criterion types.

Acceptance of personality constructs as useful predictors of job performance constructs also requires the realization that overall job performance is an insufficient criterion for I/O psychologists interested in predicting job performance. Much of the I/O research has dealt with heterogeneous (global) predictors and criteria, obscuring interesting and useful relationships. Attending to both predictor constructs and job performance constructs as well as to the different relationships among them represents a paradigm shift.

The goal of most prediction situations is accurate prediction. In the world of work, because decisions typically are of the yes/no type (i.e., whether or not to hire or promote a person), this often has meant one predictor composite and one criterion composite. As organizations become less structured and more fluid, this will change. Personnel decisions in such settings are more likely to involve a series of placement decisions (e.g., staffing projects and teams rather than staffing jobs). In these circumstances, the goal is not likely to be prediction of overall job performance. Instead, it is more likely to be prediction of more specific criteria, such as, for example, a type of job performance competence required for overall team effectiveness for a particular project. In this scenario,

TABLE 2.9

Relationships (Uncorrected Mean Validities) Between Personality Constructs and Job Performance Constructs From Hough (1992)

| | CRITERION TYPE | | | JOB PERFORMANCE CONSTRUCT | | | | |
CONSTRUCT	JOB PROFICIENCY	EDUCATIONAL SUCCESS	IRRESPONSIBLE BEHAVIOR	SALES EFFECTIVENESS	CREATIVITY	TEAMWORK	EFFORT	COMBAT EFFECTIVENESS
Affiliation	.00	.01	.01	.19	−.25	—	.00	−.02
Potency	.10	.12	−.06	.25	.21	.08	.17	.08
Achievement	.15	.29	−.19	.27	.14	.14	.21	.13
Dependability	.08	.12	−.24	.06	−.07	.17	.14	.08
Adjustment	.09	.20	−.15	.18	−.05	.13	.16	.19
Agreeableness	.05	.01	−.08	—	−.29	.17	.15	−.04
Intellectance	.01	.13	−.15	.15	.07	.11	.11	−.07
Rugged individualism	.08	−.02	.00	—	.01	.08	−.03	.25

Note. Observed validities. From "The 'Big Five' Personality Variables—Construct Confusion: Description Versus Prediction," by L. M. Hough, 1992, *Human Performance, 5*, pp. 146, 152, 153. Copyright 1992 by Lawrence Erlbaum Associates, Inc. Adapted with permission of the author.

understanding the relationship between predictor and criterion constructs is critical. With this information, predictions can be targeted for a specific performance construct, resulting in more precise predictions for particular situations. In this scenario, the validation model of choice is synthetic (or component) validation, in which homogeneous constructs (predictors and criteria) and their nomological nets are researched and the results used to build predictor composites for particular prediction situations.

Expanded and Better-Defined Criterion Space

Significant research has increased I/O psychologists' knowledge of the criterion space, resulting in an expanded definition of job performance and its components. Organ (1988) referred to his "good citizenship" performance variable as extrarole behavior. Borman and Motowidlo's (1993) "contextual" performance, which incorporates much of Organ's good citizenship construct, is now considered a legitimate part of the criterion space. For example, it is incorporated into the performance appraisal systems of highly successful organizations (e.g., Hough, 1995, 2000). In these organizations, behavior that Borman and Motowidlo would label as contextual is expected, even required. Research to define more precisely the constructs that make up contextual performance is continuing (e.g., Motowidlo & Van Scotter, 1994; Organ, 1997; Van Dyne et al., 1995; Van Scotter & Motowidlo, 1996). This work represents expansion and better definition of the criterion space.

Other performance constructs have been subsumed within the global overall job performance variable. For example, performance constructs such as technical and functional proficiency, planning and organizing, decision making, problem solving, crisis handling, effort, administrative proficiency, and interpersonal competence have long been recognized as important in many jobs. Investigating and understanding these constructs is as important as understanding contextual performance constructs. In the current team-oriented information and service economy, other, less understood performance constructs are gaining importance. For example, working as a team; transferring knowledge; learning continuously; innovating; adapting to, accepting, and initiating change; and meeting customer needs are important performance constructs in this new world of work. Several researchers (Cannon-Bowers, Tannenbaum, Salas, & Volpe, 1995; Dickinson & McIntyre, 1997; Fisher, Hunter, & Macrosson, 1998; Jackson, May, & Whitney, 1995; Morgan, Salas, & Glickman, 1993; Stevens & Campion, 1994) have made significant progress in defining and understanding the components of teamwork and their importance for team effectiveness.

Of course, other types of criteria (other than performance constructs) should not be ignored. For example, education and training outcomes (e.g., training scores, grade point average, educational level achieved), financial outcomes (e.g., initial salary, current salary, salary growth), career-related outcomes (e.g., promotion, organizational level achieved, tenure, individual satisfaction), and organizational-level outcomes (e.g., return on equity, sales growth, stock price, customer satisfaction, stakeholder satisfaction, turnover) are important criteria. These are conceptually different from work/job performance constructs. Nonetheless, they need to be included in research to allow understanding of the multifaceted nature of the predictor space and criterion space and the many complex relationships among variables.

Expanded Definition of Competence

With an expanded view of the criterion space, I/O psychologists are more comfortable embracing the long tradition in psychology that defines human ability as multifaceted, a definition that includes social intelligence and emotional intelligence as facets of human ability. This tradition dates back to the 1920s, when E. L. Thorndike (1920) described three broad classes of abilities: (a) abstract, (b) mechanical, and (c) social. Others have defined human abilities as multifaceted as well. Gardner (1993); Ghiselli (1966); Goleman (1995); Guilford (1967); Legree (1995); Marlowe and Bedell (1982); Mayer, Caruso, and Salovey (1999); Mayer and Geher (1996); Mayer, Salovey, and Caruso (in press); O'Sullivan and Guilford (1975); Riemann and Abels (1994); Snow (1989); and R. L. Thorndike (1936) have all defined human ability as multifaceted and have incorporated social, interpersonal, or emotional intelligence into their definition. Many I/O psychologists have focused on cognitive ability as the primary competence required in the workplace. Accompanying the expanded definition of the criterion space is an expanded definition of the predictor space—that is, human ability—that includes emotional, social, and interpersonal ability.

Improved Job/Work Analysis

The two most common approaches to job/work analysis have been the task-oriented approach and the person-oriented approach (Ash, 1988). Task analysis is the identification of the tasks and activities involved in performing the job. Task analysis specifies the domain of job activities. A person-oriented analysis involves identifying the knowledge, skills, abilities, and other characteristics (KSAOs) that enable a person to perform the tasks associated with his or her job. Person-oriented analyses identify individual-difference variables likely to predict job performance. Job analysis procedures often involve judgment regarding the linkage between each KSAO and each task or task category. Unfortunately, in the past, even if emotional, social, or interpersonal abilities (personality variables) were on the KSAO list, they typically were eliminated from the final list of needed KSAOs because they rarely linked to tasks. With an expanded understanding and definition of job performance, personality variables have emerged as likely predictors of job performance.

An important research effort of the 1990s illustrates profound changes in how I/O psychologists approach job/work analysis. Dye and Silver (1999) chronicled the important changes in U.S. and world economies that have affected what work is, how work is organized, and how work gets done. They pointed out that job analysis and, in particular, the *Dictionary of Occupational Titles* (DOT; U.S. Department of Labor, 1991a, 1991b) reflected an industrial economy that emphasized products and tasks rather than information and services. Examination of the work description taxonomies of the new Occupational Information Network (O*NET), which is intended to replace the DOT, is revealing. The O*NET content model includes work context, work style, and organizational context. Work context consists of three groups of variables: (a) interpersonal relationships, (b) physical work conditions, and (c) structural job characteristics (Strong, Jeanneret, McPhail, Blakley, & D'Egidio, 1999). Work style consists of seven variables: (a) achievement orientation, (b) social influence, (c) interpersonal orientation, (d) adjustment, (e) conscientiousness, (f) independence, and (g) practical intelligence (Borman, Kubisiak, & Schneider, 1999). Organizational context consists of three variables: (a) type of industry, (b) structural characteristics, and (c) social processes (Arad, Hanson, & Schneider, 1999). When the multifaceted nature of work is recognized, the importance of personality variables is highlighted.

Increased Predictive Accuracy

An important consequence of adding personality variables to predictor equations has been greater variance accounted for in the criterion (i.e., improved predictive accuracy). Not only is overall job performance better predicted, but some criterion constructs are better predicted with personality variables than with cognitive variables. The research design and findings of the U.S. Army's Selection and Classification Project (Project A) allow this to be stated with considerable confidence. The overall goal of Project A, a multimillion-dollar, 7-year research effort conducted by the U.S. Army Research Institute and a consortium of three research organizations, was to generate criterion and predictor constructs, measures of those constructs, analytic methods, and validation data needed to develop an improved selection and classification system for all entry-level positions within the U.S. Army. The results clearly indicated that the Army could improve the prediction of overall job performance as well as components of job performance by adding personality predictors to its battery of cognitive tests (McHenry, Hough, Toquam, Hanson, & Ashworth, 1990).

When personality variables that correlate with a criterion are added to a predictor battery that includes cognitive ability, perceptual psychomotor, and interest measures, validity is increased because personality variables are essentially uncorrelated with these other predictor variables. Project A data are again informative. In samples ranging in size from 7,188 to 8,547, median correlations between personality variables and cognitive ability, perceptual psychomotor, and interest measures were .04, .03, and .10, respectively (Hough, Kamp, & Ashworth, 1993). Ackerman and Heggestad (1997) performed a meta-analysis of the correlations between general intelligence measures and personality variables of the Five-Factor Model and found that the average corrected correlations between the Big Five and general intelligence ranged from .01 to .33. The .33 correlation was between general intelligence and openness to experience (or *Intellectance*, as R. T. Hogan & J. Hogan, 1992, labeled it).[2] Ackerman and Heggestad's value of .33 was based on three studies with a total sample size of 555, perhaps not sufficient to provide a stable estimate. Nonetheless, it is apparent that most personality variables are essentially uncorrelated with cognitive variables, thereby providing for the possibility of increasing predictive accuracy.

Merit-Based Affirmative Action

The U.S. population is diverse, producing a heterogeneous customer base for many, if not most, organizations. In this market, many organizations find that having a diverse workforce makes good business sense. However, selection systems that consist solely or primarily of measures of cognitive abilities significantly adversely affect most protected groups, especially African Americans, Native Americans, and Hispanics. Evidence has indicated that the mean difference in general cognitive ability test scores between White Americans and African Americans is approximately 1 standard deviation (Herrnstein & Murray, 1994). White people are hired at a disproportionately high rate when typical cognitive ability tests are the primary selection tools. Organizations interested in increasing minority representation in their workforce are blocked from doing so with such a selection system because quota-based affirmative action programs and scoring tests based on within-group norms are illegal in the United States.

The data on personality variables indicate that they have much less, and often no, adverse impact on members of protected groups. Hough (1998) performed a meta-analysis of mean score differences between various protected groups and White Americans on personality variables. Table 2.10 shows the results. Mean score differences between African Americans and White Americans

---

[2]Openness to experience was not a personality variable included in Project A.

TABLE 2.10

Mean Score Differences Between White Americans and African Americans and Between White Americans and Hispanics From Hough (1998)

PERSONALITY CONSTRUCT	COMPARISON 1			COMPARISON 2		
	BLACK N	WHITE N	EFFECT SIZE[a]	HISPANIC N	WHITE N	EFFECT SIZE[a]
Affiliation	1,034	5,606	-.31	—	—	—
Potency	15,053	28,376	.15	1,911	22,770	.01
Achievement	14,019	22,770	.01	1,911	22,770	.04
Dependability	30,803	74,942	-.08	7,493	69,336	-.09
Adjustment	15,053	28,376	.04	911	22,770	-.01
Agreeableness	15,418	31,224	-.01	2,160	25,618	-.05
Openness to experience	1,034	5,606	-.28	—	—	—

Note. — = no data. From "Personality at Work: Issues and Evidence," by L. M. Hough, in M. Hakel (Ed.), *Beyond Multiple Choice: Evaluating Alternatives to Traditional Testing for Selection,* 1998, pp. 153, 154, Hillsdale, NJ: Erlbaum. Copyright 1998 by Erlbaum. Adapted with permission of the author. [a]Effect size is the standardized mean difference between the two groups' scores. A positive value indicates higher scores for African Americans or Hispanics; a negative value indicates lower scores for African Americans or Hispanics. Weighted by sample size.

ranged from .15 to −.31 standard deviations. African Americans scored .15 standard deviations higher than did White Americans on dominance or potency scales and .31 standard deviations lower than White Americans on affiliation scales. Sample sizes ranged from 5,606 to 74,942 for White Americans and 1,034 to 30,803 for African Americans. Mean score differences between Hispanics and White Americans ranged from .04 to −.09 standard deviations, indicating that there were virtually no differences between the two groups.

The adverse impact of a predictor battery consisting of cognitive variables with significant adverse impact and personality variables with little or no adverse impact is not simply the average of the adverse impact values. As studies by Sackett and Ellingson (1997); Schmitt, Rogers, Chan, Sheppard, and Jennings (1997); Hattrup, Rock, and Scalia (1997); and Bobko, Roth, and Potosky (1999) have illustrated, the actual amount of adverse impact is a function of several factors: intercorrelations between predictors, number of predictors in the composite, overall mean group differences on the predictors, selection ratio, weights given to each predictor, and weights given to each criterion. Unfortunately, when two uncorrelated predictors, one of which is a low or no adverse-impact predictor and the other is a high adverse-impact predictor, are combined to form an equally-weighted predictor composite, the reduction in adverse impact is less than might be expected.

Nonetheless, the inclusion of personality variables in a selection system often has the advantages of less adverse impact on protected groups and higher validity for predicting job performance. In short, an important strategy for affirmative action programs that address selection procedures is simply to predict job performance more accurately. Doing so is likely to reduce adverse impact against protected groups. The outcome is affirmative action based on merit.

Conclusion

The meta-analyses discussed in this chapter indicate that measurement method moderates validity. With the introduction of personality constructs it becomes equally clear that predictor constructs moderate validity. Greater understanding of the criterion space makes it clear that criterion constructs also moderate validity. The new world of work, with its changing prediction needs—from prediction of global job performance for hiring and promotion decisions to more precise placement decisions for project staffing—requires that I/O psychologists change their research approach. What is needed is a database that can be used with synthetic validation models to build prediction equations for specific situations. First, however, I/O psychologists need research data to provide information about the relationships among predictor constructs and criterion constructs and how best to operationalize measures. Table 2.11 illustrates one possible way to conceptualize this.

TABLE 2.11

Conceptualization: Mean Validities Summarized According to Predictor Construct, Measurement Method, and Criterion Construct

PREDICTOR × MEASUREMENT METHOD	CRITERION CONSTRUCT					
	TASK PROFICIENCY	INTERPERSONAL EFFECTIVENESS	TEAMWORK	CREATIVITY	COUNTERPRODUCTIVE BEHAVIOR	+ OTHERS . . .
Conscientiousness						
Interview (behavioral vs. situational; structured vs. unstructured)						
Biodata						
Accomplishment record						
T & E point method						
Self-report						
Others' ratings						
Simulation (live vs. virtual reality)						
Situational judgment						
Projective						
Genetic testing						
Paper and pencil vs. video vs. computer						
+ others						
Emotional stability						
Interview (behavioral vs. situational; structured vs. unstructured)						
Biodata						
Accomplishment record						
T & E point method						
Self-report						
Others' ratings						
Simulation (live vs. virtual reality)						

Situational judgment					
Projective					
Genetic testing					
Paper and pencil vs. video vs. computer					
+ others					
Agreeableness					
Interview (behavioral vs. situational; structured vs. unstructured)					
Biodata					
+ others					
Verbal ability					
Interview (behavioral vs. situational; structured vs. unstructured)					
Biodata					
+ others					
Math ability					
Interview (behavioral vs. situational; structured vs. unstructured)					
Biodata					
+ others					
Artistic ability					
Interview (behavioral vs. situational; structured vs. unstructured)					
Biodata					
+ others					
+ others					

Note. T & E = training and experience.

Already, greater awareness of the multifaceted nature of the predictor and criterion domains has resulted in improved job/work analysis methods and selection systems with greater validity and less adverse impact. Now, however, the cells of Table 2.11 need to be filled in. I/O psychologists then can use the accumulated knowledge to predict behavior in more fluid work situations and do so more quickly and with greater accuracy.

References

Ackerman, P. L., & Heggestad, E. D. (1997). Intelligence, personality, and interests: Evidence for overlapping traits. *Psychological Bulletin, 121*, 219–245.

Arad, S., Hanson, M. A., & Schneider, R. J. (1999). Organizational context. In N. G. Peterson, M. D. Mumford, W. C. Borman, P. R. Jeanneret, & E. A. Fleishman (Eds.), *An occupational information system for the 21st century: The development of O*NET* (pp. 147–174). Washington, DC: American Psychological Association.

Ash, R. A. (1988). Job analysis in the world of work. In S. Gael (Ed.), *The job analysis handbook for business, industry, and government* (Vol. 1, pp. 3–13). New York: Wiley.

Barrick, M. R., & Mount, M. K. (1991). The Big Five personality dimensions and job performance: A meta-analysis. *Personnel Psychology, 44*, 1–26.

Bobko, P., Roth, P. L., & Potosky, D. (1999). Derivation and implications of a meta-analytic matrix incorporating cognitive ability, alternative predictors, and job performance. *Personnel Psychology, 52*, 1–31.

Borman, W. C., Kubisiak, U. C., & Schneider, R. J. (1999). Work styles. In N. G. Peterson, M. D. Mumford, W. C. Borman, P. R. Jeanneret, & E. A. Fleishman (Eds.), *An occupational information system for the 21st century: The development of O*NET* (pp. 213–226). Washington, DC: American Psychological Association.

Borman, W. C., & Motowidlo, S. J. (1993). Expanding the criterion domain to include elements of contextual performance. In N. Schmitt & W. C. Borman (Eds.), *Personnel selection in organizations* (pp. 71–98). San Francisco: Jossey-Bass.

Borman, W. C., & Motowidlo, S. J. (1997). Task performance and contextual performance: The meaning for personnel selection research. *Human Performance, 10*, 99–109.

Campbell, J. P. (1990). Modeling the performance prediction problem in industrial and organizational psychology. In M. D. Dunnette & L. M. Hough (Eds.), *Handbook of industrial and organizational psychology* (Vol. 1, 2nd ed., pp. 687–732). Palo Alto, CA: Consulting Psychologists Press.

Campbell, J. P., Gasser, M. B., & Oswald, F. L. (1996). The substantive nature of job performance variability. In K. R. Murphy (Ed.), *Individual differences and behavior in organizations* (pp. 258–299). San Francisco: Jossey-Bass.

Campbell, J. P., McCloy, R. A., Oppler, S. H., & Sager, C. E. (1993). A theory of performance. In N. Schmitt & W. C. Borman (Eds.), *Personnel selection in organizations* (pp. 35–70). San Francisco: Jossey-Bass.

Cannon-Bowers, J. A., Tannenbaum, S. I., Salas, E., & Volpe, C. E. (1995). Defining team competencies and establishing team training requirements. In R. Guzzo & E. Salas (Eds.), *Team effectiveness and decision making in organizations* (pp. 333–380). San Francisco: Jossey-Bass.

Cronbach, L. J., & Meehl, P. E. (1955). Construct validity in psychological tests. *Psychological Bulletin, 52,* 281–302.

Dickinson, T. L., & McIntyre, R. M. (1997). A conceptual framework for teamwork measurement. In M. T. Brannick, E. Salas, & C. Prince (Eds.), *Team performance assessment and measurement: Theory, methods, and applications.* Mahwah, NJ: Erlbaum.

Dunnette, M. D. (1963). A note on *the* criterion. *Journal of Applied Psychology, 47,* 251–254.

Dye, D., & Silver, M. (1999). The origins of O*NET. In N. G. Peterson, M. D. Mumford, W. C. Borman, P. R. Jeanneret, & E. A. Fleishman (Eds.), *An occupational information system for the 21st century: The development of O*NET* (pp. 9–20). Washington, DC: American Psychological Association.

Fisher, S. G., Hunter, T. A., & Macrosson, W. D. K. (1998). The structure of Belbin's team roles. *Journal of Occupational and Organizational Psychology, 71,* 283–288.

Gardner, H. (1993). *Multiple intelligences: The theory in practice.* New York: Basic Books.

Ghiselli, E. E. (1966). *The validity of occupational aptitude tests.* New York: Wiley.

Goleman, D. (1995). *Emotional intelligence.* New York: Bantam Books.

Guilford, J. P. (1967). *The nature of human intelligence.* New York: McGraw-Hill.

Guion, R. M. (1961). Criterion measurement and personnel judgments. *Personnel Psychology, 14,* 141–149.

Guion, R. M., & Gottier, R. F. (1965). Validity of personality measures in personnel selection. *Personnel Psychology, 18,* 135–164.

Hattrup, K., Rock, J., & Scalia, C. (1997). The effects of varying conceptualizations of job performance on adverse impact, minority hiring, and predicted performance. *Journal of Applied Psychology, 82,* 656–664.

Herrnstein, R. J., & Murray, C. (1994). *The bell curve.* New York: Free Press.

Hogan, J., & Ones, D. S. (1997). Conscientiousness and integrity at work. In R. Hogan, J. Johnson, & S. Briggs (Eds.), *Handbook of personality psychology* (pp. 513–541). San Diego, CA: Academic Press.

Hogan, R. T., & Hogan, J. (1992). *Hogan Personality Inventory manual.* Tulsa, OK: Hogan Assessment Systems.

Hough, L. M. (1992). The "Big Five" personality variables—Construct confusion: Description versus prediction. *Human Performance, 5,* 139–155.

Hough, L. M. (1995). *Microsoft performance management, training and development, and career planning systems.* Redmond, WA: Microsoft Corp.

Hough, L. M. (1998). Personality at work: Issues and evidence. In M. Hakel (Ed.),

Beyond multiple choice: Evaluating alternatives to traditional testing for selection (pp. 131–159). Hillsdale, NJ: Erlbaum.

Hough, L. M. (2000). *Development of a content-valid competency model and HRM systems and tools for Sony managers* (Vols. 1–3; DG No. 17). St. Paul, MN: Dunnette Group.

Hough, L. M., Eaton, N. L., Dunnette, M. D., Kamp, J. D., & McCloy, R. A. (1990). Criterion-related validities of personality constructs and the effect of response distortion on those validities [Monograph]. *Journal of Applied Psychology, 75*, 581–595.

Hough, L. M., Kamp, J., Ashworth, S. D. (1993). *Development of Project A temperament inventory: Assessment of background and life experiences (ABLE)* (Institute Rep. No. 259). Minneapolis, MN: Personnel Decisions Research Institutes.

Hough, L. M., Ones, D. S., & Viswesvaran, C. (1998, April). Personality correlates of managerial performance constructs. In R. C. Page (Chair), *Personality determinants of managerial potential performance, progression and ascendancy*. Symposium conducted at 13th annual convention of the Society of Industrial and Organizational Psychology, Dallas, TX.

Huffcutt, A. I., & Arthur, W. Jr. (1994). Hunter and Hunter (1984) revisited: Interview validity for entry-level jobs. *Journal of Applied Psychology, 79*, 184–190.

Hunter, J. E. (1986). Cognitive ability, cognitive aptitudes, job knowledge, and job performance. *Journal of Vocational Behavior, 29*, 340–362.

Hunter, J. E., & Hunter, R. F. (1984). Validity and utility of alternative predictors of job performance. *Psychological Bulletin, 96*, 72–98.

Jackson, S. E., May, K. E., & Whitney, K. (1995). Understanding the dynamics of diversity in decision-making teams. In R. Guzzo & E. Salas (Eds.), *Team effectiveness and decision making in organizations* (pp. 204–261). San Francisco: Jossey-Bass.

Legree, P. J. (1995). Evidence for an oblique social intelligence factor established with a Likert-based testing procedure. *Intelligence, 21*, 247–266.

Marlowe, H. A. Jr., & Bedell, J. R. (1982). Social intelligence: Evidence for independence of the construct. *Psychological Reports, 51*, 461–462.

Mayer, J. D., Caruso, D. R., & Salovey, P. (1999). Emotional intelligence meets traditional standards for an intelligence. *Intelligence, 27*, 267–298.

Mayer, J. D., & Geher, G. (1996). Emotional intelligence and the identification of emotion. *Intelligence, 22*, 89–113.

Mayer, J. D., Salovey, P., & Caruso, D. (in press). Competing models of emotional intelligence. In R. J. Sternberg (Ed.), *Handbook of human intelligence* (2nd ed.). New York: Cambridge University Press.

McDaniel, M. A., Whetzel, D. L., Schmidt, F. L., & Maurer, S. D. (1994). The validity of employment interviews: A comprehensive review and meta-analysis. *Journal of Applied Psychology, 79*, 599–616.

McHenry, J. J., Hough, L. M., Toquam, J. L., Hanson, M. A., & Ashworth, S. (1990). Project A validity results: The relationship between predictor and criterion domains. *Personnel Psychology, 43*, 335–354.

Morgan, B. B. Jr., Salas, E., & Glickman, A. S. (1993). An analysis of team evolution and maturation. *Journal of General Psychology, 120,* 277–291.

Motowidlo, S. J., Borman, W. C., & Schmit, M. J. (1997). A theory of individual differences in task and contextual performance. *Human Performance, 10,* 71–83.

Motowidlo, S. J., & Van Scotter, J. R. (1994). Evidence that task performance should be distinguished from contextual performance. *Journal of Applied Psychology, 79,* 475–480.

Mount, M. K., & Barrick, M. R. (1995). The Big Five personality dimensions: Implications for research and practice in human resource management. *Research in Personnel and Human Resources Management, 13,* 153–200.

Ones, D. S., Viswesvaran, C., & Schmidt, F. L. (1993). Comprehensive meta-analysis of integrity test validities: Findings and implications for personnel selection and theories of job performance [Monograph]. *Journal of Applied Psychology, 78,* 679–703.

Organ, D. W. (1988). *Organizational citizenship behavior: The good soldier syndrome.* Lexington, MA: Lexington Books.

Organ, D. W. (1990). The motivational basis of organizational citizenship behavior. In B. M. Staw & L. L. Cummings (Eds.), *Research in organizational behavior: Vol. 12* (pp. 43–72). Greenwich, CT: JAI Press.

Organ, D. W. (1997). Organizational citizenship behavior: It's construct clean-up time. *Human Performance, 10,* 85–97.

Organ, D. W., & Ryan, K. (1995). A meta-analytic review of attitudinal and dispositional predictors of organizational citizenship behavior. *Personnel Psychology, 48,* 775–802.

O'Sullivan, M., & Guilford, J. P. (1975). Six factors of behavioral cognition: Understanding other people. *Journal of Educational Measurement, 12,* 255–271.

Reilly, R. R., & Chao, G. T. (1982). Validity and fairness of some alternative employee selection procedures. *Personnel Psychology, 35,* 1–62.

Riemann, R., & Abels, D. (1994). Personality abilities: Construct validation. *Personality Psychology in Europe. 5,* 201–215.

Robertson, I., & Callinan, M. (1998). Personality and work behaviour. *European Journal of Work and Organizational Psychology, 7,* 321–340.

Sackett, P. R., & Ellingson, J. E. (1997). The effects of forming multi-predictor composites on group differences and adverse impact. *Personnel Psychology, 50,* 707–721.

Salgado, J. F. (1997). The five factor model of personality and job performance in the European community. *Journal of Applied Psychology, 82,* 30–43.

Salgado, J. F. (1998). Big Five personality dimensions and job performance in army and civil occupations: A European perspective. *Human Performance, 11,* 271–288.

Schmidt, F. L., & Hunter, J. E. (1998). The validity and utility of selection methods in personnel psychology: Practical and theoretical implication of 85 years of research findings. *Psychological Bulletin, 124,* 262–274.

Schmitt, N., Gooding, R. Z., Noe, R. A., & Kirsch, M. (1984). Metaanalyses of validity studies published between 1964 and 1982 and the investigation of study characteristics. *Personnel Psychology, 37,* 407–422.

Schmitt, N., Rogers, W., Chan, D., Sheppard, L., & Jennings, D. (1997). Adverse impact and predictive efficiency of various predictor combinations. *Journal of Applied Psychology, 82,* 719–730.

Smith, P. C. (1976). Behaviors, results, and organizational effectiveness: The problem of criteria. In M. D. Dunnette (Ed.), *Handbook of industrial and organizational psychology* (pp. 745–775). Chicago: Rand McNally.

Snow, R. E. (1989). Cognitive–conative aptitude interactions in learning. In R. Kanfer, P. L. Ackerman, & R. Cudeck (Eds.). *Abilities, motivation and methodology* (pp. 435–474). Hillsdale, NJ: Erlbaum.

Stevens, M. J., & Campion, M. A. (1994). The knowledge, skill, and ability requirements for teamwork: Implications for human resource management. *Journal of Management, 20,* 503–530.

Strong, M. H., Jeanneret, P. R., McPhail, S. M., Blakley, B. R., & D'Egidio, E. L. (1999). Work context: Taxonomy and measurement of the work environment. In N. G. Peterson, M. D. Mumford, W. C. Borman, P. R Jeanneret, & E. A. Fleishman (Eds.), *An occupational information system for the 21st century: The development of O*NET* (pp. 127–146). Washington, DC: American Psychological Association.

Thorndike, E. L. (1920). Intelligence and its uses. *Harper's Monthly Magazine, 140,* 227–235.

Thorndike, R. L. (1936). Factor analysis of social and abstract intelligence. *Journal of Educational Psychology, 27,* 231–233.

U.S. Department of Labor. (1991a). *Dictionary of occupational titles* (4th ed., rev.). Washington, DC: U.S. Government Printing Office.

U.S. Department of Labor. (1991b). *The revised handbook for analyzing jobs.* Washington, DC: U.S. Government Printing Office.

Van Dyne, L., Cummings, L. L., & Parks, J. M. (1995). Extra role behaviors: In pursuit of construct and definitional clarity (a bridge over muddied waters). In L. L. Cummings & B. M. Staw (Eds.), *Research in organizational behavior: Vol. 17* (pp. 215–285). Greenwich, CT: JAI Press.

Van Scotter, J. R., & Motowidlo, S. J. (1996). Interpersonal facilitation and job dedication as separate facets of contextual performance. *Journal of Applied Psychology, 81,* 525–531.

CHAPTER 3

Citizenship Performance

Its Nature, Antecedents, and Motives

Walter C. Borman

Louis A. Penner

This chapter introduces the topic of contextual or citizenship performance and reviews research on this element of performance. In particular, it (a) describes an initial model of citizenship performance and how this performance domain is different from task performance; (b) discusses the origins of the construct (i.e., precursors to the citizenship performance concept); (c) reviews three research areas that represent attempts to learn more about citizenship performance; (d) describes research on motives for exhibiting citizenship; and, finally, (e) presents some conclusions about how this construct is likely to be even more important for organizations in the early 21st century.

The lay view of job performance typically is centered on task performance. Indeed, the most common job analysis method, task analysis, usually results in the identification of task dimensions or task categories. However, Borman and Motowidlo (1993, 1997) have focused on a separate job performance construct. Citizenship performance contributes to organizational effectiveness, but it is important primarily because it "shapes the organizational, social, and psychological context that serves as the critical catalyst for task activities and processes" (Borman & Motowidlo, 1993, p. 71). Citizenship performance includes such activities as helping others with their jobs, supporting the organization, and volunteering for additional work or responsibility. Borman and Motowidlo (1993) proposed a five-dimension model of citizenship performance: (a) persisting with enthusiasm and extra effort as necessary to complete one's own task activities successfully; (b) volunteering to carry out task activities that are not formally part of one's own job; (c) helping and cooperating with others; (d) following organizational rules and procedures; and (e) endorsing, supporting, and defending organizational objectives.

Origins of the Citizenship Performance Concept

We should make clear that the criterion construct of citizenship performance is significantly related to several earlier efforts. For example, as far back as 1938, Barnard discussed the "informal organization" and the need for organization members to be willing to cooperate for the good of the organization. Katz (1964) emphasized that cooperative and helpful behaviors that go beyond formal role prescriptions are important for organizational functioning.

More recently, Organ (e.g., Smith, Organ, & Near, 1983) introduced the notion of organizational citizenship behavior (OCB). They defined OCB as extrarole, discretionary behavior that helps other organization members perform their jobs or that shows support for and conscientiousness toward the organization. OCB has been studied primarily in relation to its links with job satisfaction and organizational justice (Organ, 1997). OCB clearly contains elements in common with Borman and Motowidlo's (1993) concept of citizenship performance.

Another closely related concept is prosocial organizational behavior (POB). Brief and Motowidlo (1986) defined POB as behavior that is directed toward an individual, group, or organization with the intention of promoting the welfare of that individual, group, or organization. Brief and Motowidlo identified nine functional dimensions (as opposed to damaging-to-the-organization behaviors such as helping a coworker with a personal problem but missing an important deadline as a result) that, again, cover constructs similar to those within the five-dimension citizenship performance taxonomy.

A third major source for the citizenship performance taxonomy was a model of soldier effectiveness developed for the U.S. Army by Borman, Motowidlo, and Hanser (1983). This model assumed that soldier effectiveness reflected more than just the successful performance of assigned tasks. In fact, the model contained only elements going beyond task performance or technical proficiency. Borman et al. argued that the concepts of organizational socialization, organizational commitment, and morale could be combined and integrated into a three-dimension performance model. Morale and commitment merge to form the performance dimension determination. The combination of morale and socialization yields the teamwork dimension, and socialization and commitment merge to form allegiance. Each of these three dimensions was in turn decomposed into five subdimensions (e.g., determination into perseverance, reaction to adversity, etc.).

These three concepts (i.e., OCB, POB, and the model of soldier effectiveness) were combined and integrated to form Borman and Motowidlo's (1993) five-dimension taxonomy. Borman and Motowidlo believed that this taxonomy reflected all of the elements of these concepts while at the same time providing a parsimonious representation of citizenship performance. Table 3.1 outlines the five-dimension taxonomy and identifies the source of each dimension.

Other researchers have explored alternative ways to configure citizenship performance. Coleman and Borman (2000) prepared a list of dimensions representing all of the concepts contained in the various dimension sets (i.e., OCB: Becker & Vance, 1993; Graham, 1986; Morrison, 1994; Organ, 1988; Smith et al., 1983; Van Dyne, Graham, & Dienesch, 1994; Williams & Anderson, 1991; POB: Brief & Motowidlo, 1986; model of soldier effectiveness: Borman et al., 1983). The resulting list of 27 dimensions and their definitions were then sent to 75 industrial/organizational (I/O) psychologists who were asked to sort the dimensions into categories according to their perceived content. Of the 75 who were asked to complete the sorting task, 44 did so, sorting the dimensions into 3 to 10 categories (M = 5.5). From these sorting solutions, a pooled 27 × 27 similarity matrix was developed, and then an indirect similarity correlation matrix was derived (see Borman & Brush, 1993, for a description of this method).

Coleman and Borman (2000) conducted factor analyses, multidimensional scaling analyses, and cluster analyses on this 27 × 27 correlation matrix, and a consensus three-category system emerged. This three-category system then formed the basis for a three-dimension model of citizenship performance. This new model appears in Table 3.2. The personal support dimension is virtually the same as the earlier helping and cooperating with others dimension. The organizational support dimension combines the conscientiousness and organizational support dimensions of the earlier model, and the conscientious initiative dimension reflects the extra effort and volunteering dimensions of the five-dimension model (Borman, Buck, Hanson, Motowidlo, Stark, & Drasgow, in press).

Citizenship Performance Distinguished From Task Performance

One important distinction between task performance and citizenship performance is that task activities vary across jobs, whereas citizenship activities are quite similar across jobs. In fact, task-based job analysis typically has as a purpose discovering the tasks and task dimensions that differentiate one job from others. However, activities such as volunteering and cooperating with others remain largely the same for different jobs. A second distinction is that task performance is likely to have as antecedents or predictors specific knowledge, skills, or abilities; predictors of citizenship performance are more likely to be volitional and predispositional in nature (e.g., personality).

A study supporting the distinction between task performance and citizenship performance was conducted by Conway (1996). Conway had a panel of

TABLE 3.1

Borman and Motowidlo's Five-Dimension Contextual Performance Taxonomy

TAXONOMY, DIMENSIONS, AND RELATED CONCEPTS	SOURCE
1. Persisting with enthusiasm and extra effort as necessary to complete one's own task activities successfully	
Demonstrating perseverance and conscientiousness	Borman, Motowidlo, & Hanser, 1983
Putting in extra effort on the job	Brief & Motowidlo, 1986; Katz & Kahn, 1978
2. Volunteering to carry out task activities that are not formally part of one's own job	
Suggesting organizational improvements	Brief & Motowidlo, 1986; Katz & Kahn, 1978
Demonstrating initiative and taking on extra responsibility	Borman et al., 1983; Brief & Motowidlo, 1986; Katz & Kahn, 1978
3. Helping and cooperating with others	
Assisting/helping coworkers	Borman et al., 1983; Brief & Motowidlo, 1986; Katz & Kahn, 1978
Assisting/helping customers	Brief & Motowidlo, 1986
Demonstrating organizational courtesy and not complaining	Organ, 1988
Displaying altruism	Smith, Organ, & Near, 1983

4. Following organizational rules and procedures

Following orders and regulations and showing respect for authority	Borman et al., 1983
Complying with organizational values and policies	Brief & Motowidlo, 1986
Demonstrating conscientiousness	Smith et al., 1983
Meeting deadlines	Katz & Kahn, 1978
Displaying civic virtue	Graham, 1986

5. Endorsing, supporting, and defending organizational objectives

Displaying organizational loyalty	Graham, 1986
Demonstrating concern for unit objectives	Borman et al., 1983
Staying with the organization during hard times and representing the organization favorably to outsiders	Brief & Motowidlo, 1986

TABLE 3.2
Revised Three-Dimension Model of Citizenship Performance

DIMENSION	ACTIVITIES
1. Personal support	Helping, cooperating, showing consideration
2. Organizational support	Representing the organization, supporting the organization's mission
3. Conscientious initiative	Persisting, showing initiative, engaging in self-development

I/O psychologists review the performance dimensions and their definitions from 14 studies appearing in the literature and sort each dimension into one of two categories: task performance or citizenship performance. Results showed that 55% of the dimensions were sorted very reliably into the task performance category and 30% of the dimensions were sorted very reliably into the citizenship performance category. There was some disagreement about the remaining 15% of the dimensions. These findings suggest that for most performance dimensions it is clear whether they are task performance or citizenship performance dimensions.

Four Streams of Citizenship Performance Research

We now briefly discuss research on (a) links between citizenship performance and organizational effectiveness; (b) the relative weight experienced supervisors assign to task performance and citizenship performance when making overall job performance judgments; and (c) whether personality predicts citizenship performance better than task performance. We then describe in more detail recent research in a fourth area, motives for exhibiting citizenship behavior in organizations (Penner, Midili, & Kegelemeyer, 1997).

Links With Organizational Effectiveness

It seems reasonable to assume that having organization members effective in task performance would be associated with organizational effectiveness. That is, a positive correlation between task performance on the part of organization members and organizational effectiveness would be expected. The analogous link between citizenship performance and organizational effectiveness is less obvious.

Recent research on the citizenship performance–organizational effectiveness relationship does, however, show a relatively high correlation. Podsakoff and MacKenzie (1997) first provided several theoretical and conceptual reasons why these links might exist. For example, citizenship behavior may help managers be more productive because when employees help each other managers have more time to work on productive tasks. Citizenship behavior also can improve the stability of organizational performance; for example, unit members picking up the slack for others can help reduce the variability of the work unit's performance.

Podsakoff and MacKenzie (1997) went on to review four empirical studies investigating the link between citizenship performance on the part of organization members and various indicators of organizational effectiveness. For example, Podsakoff, MacKenzie, and Bommer (1996) found that mean ratings of helping behavior and sportsmanship of paper mill crewmembers correlated significantly with the quantity of the paper produced by those crews. Overall, across 10 organizational effectiveness indicators used in the four studies, the median variance accounted for in organizational effectiveness by members' citizenship performance was 17.5%. There does appear to be a substantial link between citizenship performance on the part of organization members and the effectiveness of those organizations.

Factors Influencing Global Overall Performance Judgments

The second research stream addresses the question of what factors or cues supervisors use when making judgments regarding global overall performance, overall worth to the organization, and so forth. This is a very important question because we contend that these global effectiveness judgments often are rendered both formally (e.g., in performance appraisals) and informally (e.g., in daily assignments) and that such judgments made by supervisors have a substantial effect on subordinates' organizational lives. In this context, we are very interested in the relative weights supervisors assign to task performance and citizenship performance when making overall effectiveness judgments.

Several studies have examined this question. For example, Motowidlo and Van Scotter (1994) had each of more than 300 U.S. Air Force personnel rated by three supervisors: The first evaluated the ratee on overall performance, the second on task performance, and the third on citizenship performance. This design feature ensured that the ratings on the three constructs were made independently. The study found a task performance–overall performance correlation of .46 and a citizenship performance–overall performance correlation of .41. These findings suggest that task performance and citizenship performance are weighted roughly equally when supervisors make overall performance judgments. It is interesting to note, however, that when the judgment made was the likelihood of promoting an individual (rather than overall performance), the citizenship performance correlation was .34 and the task performance correlation was .14. Thus, when decisions affected promotability of organization members, citizenship performance was substantially more important to supervisors than task performance.

In another study, Borman, White, and Dorsey (1995) had more than 400 first-tour U.S. Army soldiers rated by supervisors and peers on several personal characteristics (e.g., dependability) and interpersonal relationship factors (e.g., likeability). As in the Motowidlo and Van Scotter (1994) study, different supervisors and different peers provided the ratings on the interpersonal and overall performance dimensions. Job knowledge and worksample test scores for the soldiers being rated were also available. The supervisory path model, with overall performance ratings as the exogenous variable, had almost exactly the same size path coefficient from one of the interpersonal factors, dependability (a citizenship performance variable), to overall performance as the path coefficient from worksample test scores (a task performance variable) to the overall performance rating. The peer rating path model also found these two path coefficients to be of about the same magnitude, with a third path coefficient from ratee obnoxiousness (a citizenship variable) to overall performance also significant (in the negative direction). Using different variables, this study also found that supervisors (and peers) weighted task and citizenship performance about the same when making overall performance judgments. Other studies have reported similar results (e.g., Dunn, Mount, Barrick, & Ones, 1995; Ferris, Judge, Rowland, & Fitzgibbons, 1994; Werner, 1994).

Antecedents of Citizenship Performance

A third research area relates to personality predictors of citizenship performance. Studies have shown that personality–citizenship performance correlations are for the most part higher than personality–task performance correlations. In one study conducted as part of Project A, the large-scale test validation effort undertaken by the U.S. Army Research Institute (e.g., Campbell, 1990), three summary personality factors were among several predictor measures developed for the study. In addition, five summary criterion constructs consistently emerged from the criterion research done on first-tour soldiers. One of the five, core technical proficiency, was seen as most unambiguously a task performance construct, and another, personal discipline, was clearly identified as a citizenship construct. Results of a concurrent validation study ($N = 4,039$) conducted as part of Project A showed, first, that general cognitive ability correlated substantially higher with the task performance dimension ($r = .33$) than it did with the citizenship performance dimension ($r = .08$). Second, all three personality factors correlated higher with the citizenship performance dimension than the task performance dimension, although only for dependability was the difference large (.30 vs. .11, respectively).

The Motowidlo and Van Scotter (1994) study discussed previously also produced data supporting the notion that personality constructs are good predictors of citizenship performance. Table 3.3 contains the correlations between

TABLE 3.3

Personality–Criterion Performance Correlations From Motowidlo and Van Scotter (1994)

PREDICTOR	TASK PERFORMANCE	CITIZENSHIP PERFORMANCE
Work orientation	.23	.36
Dominance	.04	.11
Dependability	.18	.31
Adjustment	.08	.14
Cooperativeness	.03	.22
Internal locus of control	.08	.26

Note. n = 252–256. From "Evidence That Task Performance Should be Distinguished From Contextual Performance," by S. J. Motowidlo and J. R. Van Scotter, 1994, *Journal of Applied Psychology, 79,* p. 479. Adapted with permission.

the personality predictors from that study and the task performance and citizenship performance ratings provided by supervisors. In general, correlations between these personality predictors and the citizenship performance ratings are higher than those for the task performance ratings. This pattern is clearest for work orientation, dependability, cooperativeness, and locus of control, where the personality–citizenship performance correlations are significantly different from the personality–task performance correlations ($p < .05$, one-tailed). Again, although the pattern is not evident for some personality predictors, the general finding is that personality correlates more highly with citizenship performance than with task performance.

A more direct approach to studying the links between personality and citizenship performance is to develop a personality inventory that directly targets these kinds of behaviors. Penner and his associates have done just that. Penner, Fritzsche, Craiger, and Freifeld (1995) created a 56-item self-report scale designed to measure prosocial personality orientation. Factor analyses of scale responses have consistently revealed two correlated dimensions (e.g., Midili & Penner, 1995; Penner et al., 1995; Penner & Finkelstein, 1998). The first is other-oriented empathy, or the tendency to experience empathy toward and feel responsibility for and concern about the well-being of others; in other words, prosocial thoughts and feelings. The second dimension is helpfulness, or a self-reported history of engaging in helpful actions and an absence of egocentric reactions to others' distress; in other words, prosocial behavior. There is a good deal of evidence to suggest that scores on this measure are related to a wide variety of prosocial behaviors, ranging from the speed with which people intervene in emergencies to the amount of time AIDS volunteers spend with people who are HIV positive or who have AIDS (see Dovidio & Penner, in press; Penner & Finkelstein, 1998; Penner et al., 1995, 1997).

Midili (1996; Midili & Penner, 1995) specifically examined the relationship between this personality orientation and OCB. Midili and others (e.g., Rioux, 1998; Tillman, 1998) have found significant positive correlations between the two dimensions of the prosocial personality and self-reports of OCB. Additionally, Midili (1996) found that both other-oriented empathy and helpfulness correlated significantly with peer ratings of OCB in a sample of retail store employees. These personality dimensions were entered, along with mood and organizational justice, into hierarchical regressions with peer ratings of the altruism and conscientiousness dimensions of OCB as the criterion variables. Other-oriented empathy and helpfulness were the only significant predictors of altruism, and they accounted for significant amounts of unique variance in the conscientiousness dimension as well. Negrao (1997) found that the same two personality dimensions predicted peer ratings of citizenship performance among mid-level managers in a food service organization.

More recently, Allen (1998, 1999) examined the relationship between the prosocial personality orientation and another type of citizenship performance behavior, the mentoring of new or junior employees by older or more experienced coworkers. In both a laboratory and a field study, Allen found significant positive relationships between the two dimensions of prosocial personality orientation and self-reports of mentoring behavior. These findings suggest that a prosocial personality orientation is positively associated with a propensity to engage in behaviors that are part of citizenship performance.

Motives for Citizenship Performance

A motivational approach to citizenship performance moves the focus of interest to why people might engage in such actions. To a certain extent, the motivational approach builds on the functional approach to explaining why people behave as they do (Snyder, 1994). The functional approach to behavior can trace its origins to the functionalists of the 19th century (e.g., J. Dewey, W. James). This approach argues that why a person acts as he or she does may be better understood if what function or purpose the behavior serves for that person is considered. Moreover, two people may engage in the same behavior for two quite different reasons. One early proponent of this point of view was F. H. Allport (1937), who believed that personality has a "functional significance" (p. 203) that determines each person's unique adjustments to his or her environment. Individuals may have distinctly different agendas or purposes for exhibiting the same trait. Thus, the same traits may serve quite different psychological functions for different people (Snyder, 1994).

The same functional theme proposed by Allport (1937) has been the focus of social psychological research regarding attitudes and persuasion (e.g., Katz, 1960; Smith, Bruner, & White, 1956). Functional attitude theories propose that people maintain certain attitudes because they serve particular functions for them; that is, these attitudes "help people meet needs, execute plans, and achieve ends" (Snyder, 1993, p. 254). Furthermore, it has been proposed that the same attitude may serve very different functions for different people. The implication of this theory is that to change a person's attitude, it is necessary to address the particular function that attitude serves for that person.

Several theorists have suggested multiple motives for citizenship performance (e.g., Bolino, 1999; Ferris et al., 1994). However, Penner and his associates (Penner et al., 1997; Rioux & Penner, 1999; Tillman, 1998) have explicitly addressed what these motives are and their contribution to citizenship performance. The basic premise of a functional approach to citizenship performance is that people engage in this behavior, at least in part, because it meets some need or serves some purpose for them. Again, different people may engage in the same behavior for different reasons. Consider, for example, two experienced supervisors at a large data processing company, each of whom volunteers to stay after work to teach a new subordinate how to use a particular piece of complex software. This seems to be a clear example of citizenship performance, but why has this behavior occurred? The functionalist would argue that this question cannot be completely answered without knowing the motives underlying the behavior. One supervisor may feel that he or she has a personal responsibility to help new workers succeed in their jobs. In this instance, the behavior has an altruistic motive; it serves to express the supervisor's values about helping others. The other supervisor might engage in the same behavior because of his or her positive feelings toward the organization and the belief that helping the new worker will benefit the organization. Note that, in this example, organizational commitment or perceived organizational justice would be associated with citizenship behavior more for the second supervisor than for the first. Thus, we argue that understanding the antecedents of citizenship performance may benefit from the identification and measurement of the motives that lead to it.

A good amount of empirical support for this position comes from studies of another largely discretionary behavior that occurs in an organizational context, that is, volunteerism. Volunteerism is the act of donating time and effort to promote the welfare of some cause or group of people (Omoto & Snyder, 1995; Penner et al., 1997). There are four studies of which we are aware that have measured motives and their relationships with various behaviors associated with volunteerism. In each of these studies, participants first rated the importance of each of several motives (e.g., altruism, personal development) as a cause of their behavior, and these ratings were then correlated with volunteer-related behaviors (e.g., tenure as a volunteer, intention to volunteer). Using a sample of crisis counseling volunteers, Clary and Orenstein (1991) found a positive association between altruistic motives and length of service.

Penner and Finkelstein (1998) first measured motives among volunteers at an AIDS service organization then, 10 months later, obtained self-reports of extent of volunteers' involvement with the organization and the amount of direct contact with people with HIV or AIDS. Among male (but not female) volunteers, there was a significant positive association between altruistic motives and both kinds of volunteer-related behaviors. Deaux and Stark (1996) studied volunteers working in a prison and found that both altruistic and self-serving motives predicted intention to volunteer. Finally, Omoto and Snyder (1995) studied the duration of service among AIDS volunteers and found that "personal, self-oriented, and perhaps even selfish functions served by volunteering was what kept volunteers involved" (p. 683). The inconsistency of the specific findings across these studies is, of course, cause for concern. However, in the context of this chapter, the critical point is that motives do indeed predict volunteerism.

Further evidence for a functional approach to volunteerism comes from a study by Clary et al. (1998). Clary et al. found that persuasive messages that specifically addressed a volunteer's motives for volunteering were more effective than those that addressed motives unrelated to the person's reasons for volunteering. In a second study, Clary et al. found that volunteers were most satisfied with their volunteer experience when the performance feedback they received addressed their motives for volunteering. These studies suggest that (a) motives do predict volunteer-related activities and (b) this is because volunteerism serves certain functions or meets certain needs for the volunteer.

Rioux (Rioux & Penner, 1999; Rioux & Penner, in press) has extended the functional approach to citizenship performance. Using the work of Clary et al. (1998) as a starting point, Rioux developed a scale measuring motives for engaging in citizenship performance. Factor analysis of scale items suggested three motives for citizenship performance: (a) prosocial values—a concern for others, a need to be helpful, and a desire to build relationships with others; (b) organizational commitment—a desire to be a well-informed employee and a feeling of pride in and commitment to the organization; and impression management —a desire to avoid presenting a poor appearance and to gain rewards. The scale was administered to a sample of municipal employees in a field study, and self-, peer, and supervisor ratings of OCB were obtained. The prosocial values motive was positively related to self-, peer, and supervisor ratings on the altruism dimension of OCB, whereas the organizational commitment motive was positively related to ratings associated with the conscientiousness dimension of OCB. Furthermore, these two motives also accounted for unique variance in OCB beyond that accounted for by organizational variables (e.g., job satisfaction, perceived organizational justice) and the two personality variables from the Prosocial Personality Battery (Penner et al., 1995). Tillman (1998) replicated these results for self-ratings of citizenship performance. In addition, he found that motives may moderate the effect of some organizational variables on citizenship performance. For example, Tillman found that perceived organizational justice was significantly and positively associated with citizenship performance only among respondents who also displayed a strong organizational commitment motive.

Thus, the motivational approach to citizenship performance considers the causes of this aspect of job performance. It suggests that three related motives —prosocial values, organizational commitment, and impression management —may underlie this behavior, and identifying the strength of such motives in an organization member may allow the prediction of the incidence and specific direction of his or her citizenship performance. Moreover, understanding the origins or causes of these motives may provide organizations with interventions for increasing or modifying citizenship performance among their members.

The Future of Citizenship Performance

We have tried to make the case that citizenship performance is important for contemporary organizations. There is evidence that citizenship performance on the part of organization members is linked to organizational effectiveness (e.g., Podsakoff & MacKenzie, 1997). Also, supervisors making important overall effectiveness judgments about subordinates weight citizenship performance about as highly as they do task performance. In our opinion, these findings argue for the salience of this performance domain. But what about the future? Is citizenship performance likely to be more (or less) important in the next several years? Four current trends suggest that it will be more important.

First, as global competition continues to raise the effort level required of employees, citizenship performance, especially organizational support and conscientious initiative, will be more important. Second, as team-based organizations become even more popular, citizenship performance, especially personal support, will be more important. Third, as downsizing continues to make employee adaptability and willingness to exhibit extra effort a necessity, citizenship performance, especially conscientious initiative, will be more important. And, finally, as customer service and client satisfaction are increasingly emphasized, all three dimensions of citizenship performance will be more important.

References

Allen, T. D. (1998, November). *Mentoring others: An investigation of linkages between personality, motives, willingness, and protégé evaluation.* Paper presented at the annual meeting of the Southern Management Association, New Orleans, LA.

Allen. T. D. (1999, April). *Mentoring others: Mentor dispositions and desired protégé characteristics.* Paper presented at the 14th annual meeting of the Society of Industrial and Organizational Psychology, Atlanta, GA.

Allport, F. H. (1937). Teleonomic description in the study of personality. *Character and Personality, 5,* 202–214.

Barnard, C. I. (1938). *The functions of the executive.* Cambridge, MA: Harvard University Press.

Becker, T. E., & Vance, R. J. (1993). Construct validity of three types of organizational citizenship behavior: An illustration of the direct products model with refinements. *Journal of Management, 19,* 663–682.

Bolino, M. C. (1999). Citizenship and impression management: Good soldiers or good actors? *Academy of Management Review, 24,* 82–98.

Borman, W. C., & Brush, D. H. (1993). Toward a taxonomy of managerial performance requirements. *Human Performance, 6,* 1–21.

Borman, W. C., Buck, D., Hanson, M. A., Motowidlo, S. J., Stark, S., & Drasgow, F. (in press). Comparing the relative reliability, validity, and accuracy of computerized adaptive rating scales. *Journal of Applied Psychology.*

Borman, W. C., & Motowidlo, S. J. (1993). Expanding the criterion domain to include elements of contextual performance. In N. Schmitt & W. C. Borman (Eds.), *Personnel selection in organizations* (pp. 71–98). San Francisco: Jossey-Bass.

Borman, W. C., & Motowidlo, S. J. (1997). Task performance and contextual performance: The meaning for personnel selection research. *Human Performance, 10,* 99–109.

Borman, W. C., Motowidlo, S. J., & Hanser, L. M. (1983, August). A model of individual performance effectiveness: Thoughts about expanding the criterion space. In *Integrated criterion measurement for large scale computerized selection and classification.* Symposium presented at the 91st Annual Convention of the American Psychological Association, Washington, DC.

Borman, W. C., White, L. A., & Dorsey, D. W. (1995). Effects of ratee task performance and interpersonal factors on supervisor and peer performance ratings. *Journal of Applied Psychology, 80,* 168–177.

Brief, A. P., & Motowidlo, S. J. (1986). Prosocial organizational behaviors. *Academy of Management Review, 11,* 710–725.

Campbell, J. P. (1990). An overview of the army selection and classification project (Project A). *Personnel Psychology, 43,* 231–239.

Clary, E. G., & Orenstein, L. (1991). The amount and effectiveness of help: The relationship of motives and abilities to helping behavior. *Personality and Social Psychology Bulletin, 17,* 58–64.

Clary, E. G., Snyder, M., Ridge, R., Copeland, J., Haugen, J., & Miene, P. (1998). Understanding and assessing the motivations of volunteers: A functional approach. *Journal of Personality and Social Psychology, 74,* 1516–1530.

Coleman, V. I., & Borman, W. C. (2000). Investigating the underlying structure of the citizenship performance domain. *Human Resource Management Review, 10*, 25–44.

Conway, J. M. (1996). Additional construct validity evidence for the task–contextual performance distinction. *Human Performance, 9*, 309–329.

Deaux, K., & Stark, B. E. (1996). *Identity and motive: An integrated theory of volunteerism.* Ann Arbor, MI: Society for the Psychological Study of Social Issues.

Dovidio, J. F., & Penner, L. A. (in press). Helping and altruism. In M. Brewer & M. Hewstone (Eds.), *International handbook of social psychology.* Cambridge, MA: Blackwell.

Dunn, W. S., Mount, M. K., Barrick, M. R., & Ones, D. S. (1995). Relative importance of personality and general mental ability in managers' judgments of applicant qualifications. *Journal of Applied Psychology, 80*, 500–509.

Ferris, G. R., Judge, T. A., Rowland, K. M., & Fitzgibbons, D. E. (1994). Subordinate influence and the performance evaluation process: Test of a model. *Organizational Behavior and Human Decision Processes, 58*, 101–135.

Graham, J. W. (1986, August). *Organizational citizenship informed by political theory.* Paper presented at the annual meeting of the Academy of Management, Chicago.

Katz, D. (1960). The functional approach to the study of attitudes. *Public Opinion Quarterly, 24*, 163–204.

Katz, D. (1964). The motivational basis of organizational behavior. *Behavioral Science, 9*, 131–146.

Katz, D., & Kahn, R. L. (1978). *The social psychology of organizations.* New York: Wiley.

Midili, A. R. (1996). *Predicting self, peer, and supervisor ratings of organizational citizenship behavior: An analysis of situational and personality influences.* Unpublished doctoral dissertation, University of South Florida, Tampa.

Midili, A. R., & Penner, L. A. (1995, August). Dispositional and environmental influences on organizational citizenship behavior. Paper presented at the 103rd Annual Convention of the American Psychological Association, New York.

Morrison, E. W. (1994). Role definitions and organizational citizenship behavior: The importance of the employee's perspective. *Academy of Management, 37*, 1543–1567.

Motowidlo, S. J., & Van Scotter, J. R. (1994). Evidence that task performance should be distinguished from contextual performance. *Journal of Applied Psychology, 79*, 475–480.

Negrao, M. (1997). *On Good Samaritans and villains: An investigation of the bright and dark side of altruism in organizations.* Unpublished manuscript, University of South Florida, Tampa.

Omoto, A., & Snyder, M. (1995). Sustained helping without obligation: Motivation, longevity of service, and perceived attitude change among AIDS volunteers. *Journal of Personality and Social Psychology, 68*, 671–687.

Organ, D. W. (1988). *Organizational citizenship behavior: The good soldier syndrome.* Lexington, MA: Lexington Books.

Organ, D. W. (1997). Organizational citizenship behavior: It's construct clean-up time. *Human Performance, 10,* 85–97.

Penner, L. A., & Finkelstein, M. A. (1998). Dispositional and structural determinants of volunteerism. *Journal of Personality and Social Psychology, 74,* 525–537.

Penner, L. A., Fritzsche, B. A., Craiger, J. P., & Freifeld, T. R. (1995). Measuring the prosocial personality. In J. Butcher & C. D. Spielberger (Eds.), *Advances in personality assessment* (Vol. 10). Hillsdale, NJ: Erlbaum.

Penner, L. A., Midili, A. R., & Kegelemeyer, J. (1997). Beyond job attitudes: A personality and social psychology perspective on the causes of organizational citizenship behavior. *Human Performance, 10,* 111–131.

Podsakoff, P. M., & MacKenzie, J. B. (1997). Impact of organizational citizenship behavior on organizational performance: A review and suggestions for future research. *Human Performance, 10,* 133–151.

Podsakoff, P. M., MacKenzie, J. B., & Bommer, W. (1996). Transformational leader behaviors and substitutes for leadership as determinants of employee satisfaction, commitment, trust, and organizational citizenship behaviors. *Journal of Management, 22,* 259–298.

Rioux, S. (1998). *Assessing personal motives for engaging in organizational citizenship behaviors: A functional approach.* Unpublished doctoral dissertation, University of South Florida, Tampa.

Rioux, S., & Penner, L. (1999, April). *Assessing personal motives for engaging in organizational citizenship behavior: A field study.* Paper presented at the 14th annual meeting of the Society of Industrial and Organizational Psychology, Atlanta, GA.

Rioux, S., & Penner, L. A. (in press). The causes of organizational citizenship behavior: A motivational analysis. *Journal of Applied Psychology.*

Smith, C. A., Organ, D. W., & Near, J. P. (1983). Organizational citizenship behavior: Its nature and antecedents. *Journal of Applied Psychology, 68,* 653–663.

Smith, M., Bruner, J., & White, R. (1956). *Opinions and personality.* New York: Wiley.

Snyder, M. (1993). Basic research and practice problems: The promise of a "functional" personality and social psychology. *Personality and Social Psychology Bulletin, 19,* 251–264.

Snyder, M. (1994). Traits and motives in the psychology of personality. *Psychological Inquiry, 5,* 162–166.

Tillman, P. (1998). *In search of moderators of the relationship between antecedents of organizational citizenship behavior and organizational citizenship behavior: The case of motives.* Unpublished master's thesis, University of South Florida, Tampa.

Van Dyne, L. V., Graham, J. M., & Dienesch, R. M. (1994). Organizational citizenship behavior: Construct redefinition, measurement, and validation. *Academy of Management Journal, 37,* 765–802.

Werner, J. M. (1994). Dimensions that make a difference: Examining the impact of in-role and extra-role behaviors on supervisory ratings. *Journal of Applied Psychology,* *79,* 98–107.

Williams, L. J., & Anderson, S. E. (1991). Job satisfaction and organizational commitment as predictors of organizational citizenship and in-role behaviors. *Journal of Management, 17,* 601–617.

CHAPTER 4

Personality at Work

Criterion-Focused Occupational Personality Scales Used in Personnel Selection

Deniz S. Ones

Chockalingam Viswesvaran

Employers have long been interested in finding out what personal characteristics job applicants possess. A large body of research has documented that there are significant differences among employees, even among individuals who hold the same job, in terms of productivity as well as a broad spectrum of other work-related behaviors (e.g., absenteeism, counterproductive behaviors, theft, and customer service; Hull, 1928; Hunter, Schmidt, & Judiesch, 1990; Schmidt & Hunter, 1983). For low-complexity jobs, employees who are one standard deviation above the mean level of productivity in a job produce 19% more than the average; the parallel value for employees in high-complexity jobs is 48%. How much do employees vary in their behaviors at work? The answer is a lot, even by the most conservative estimates (Cook, 1998). This is why employers have attempted to use a variety of means to screen and select workers. Much effort has been devoted to examining the roles of cognitive ability, job knowledge, and skills as predictors and determinants of job performance (Schmidt & Hunter, 1977, 1998). Research on personality determinants of work behaviors, however, was largely dormant from the 1960s until recently. The strong influence of situation-based views of personality (Mischel, 1968) and the low values assumed for the criterion-related validity of personality variables led to personality research and usage falling out of favor for over 2 decades.

The use of personality variables in personnel selection has recently expe-

---

The order of authorship is arbitrary; both authors contributed equally to this chapter. We thank Nathan Kuncel and Jeannette Shelton for their help with data management and manuscript preparation. We also thank them for their useful comments.

rienced a resurgence (Barrick & Mount, 1991; J. Hogan & Hogan, 1989; Hough, Eaton, Dunnette, Kamp, & McCloy, 1990; Hough & Oswald, 2000; Ones & Viswesvaran, 1999a,b; Ones, Viswesvaran, & Schmidt, 1993; Sackett, Burris, & Callahan, 1989). This has been paralleled by an increase in research attention directed at the role of personality in industrial–organizational (I/O) psychology (Costa & McCrae, 1995; Day & Silverman, 1989; Robertson & Kinder, 1993). This renaissance has been fueled in part by meta-analytic studies demonstrating substantial validities for personality variables across situations (Barrick & Mount, 1991; Hough & Oswald, 2000; Ones & Viswesvaran, 1998a; Ones et al., 1993) and in part by an emerging consensus among personality researchers that numerous personality measures can be expressed in terms of the Big Five framework (Costa & McCrae, 1992; Digman, 1990; Goldberg, 1993). Although disagreements still exist about the Big Five (e.g., Block, 1995; Eysenck, 1991), the considerable consensus that an individual's personality can be described in terms of the Big Five factors and their facets has provided a workable taxonomy, thereby facilitating meta-analytic cumulation.

In particular, meta-analyses in the personality domain have demonstrated that a construct-oriented approach can reveal meaningful relationships among personality variables and criteria (Barrick & Mount, 1991; Hough, 1992; Hough et al., 1990; Hough & Oswald, 2000; Ones et al., 1993; Salgado, 1997). As a result, human resources practitioners and researchers are now more optimistic about the potential of personality variables in personnel selection than ever before.

Background

Personality predictors used in personnel selection can be divided roughly into two categories. First, there are measures of normal adult personality. The initial purpose in the construction of these measures was the accurate description of individual differences in personality. That is, they were developed to provide broad descriptions of personality that could be used in a wide range of settings. Examples of this type of inventory are the NEO Personality Inventory, the Personality Research Form, and the 16 Personality Factor Questionnaire. The use of these inventories for personnel screening and selection is only one of their many applications.

The second category of personality measures used in personnel screening and selection can be referred to loosely as measures of personality at work. The initial purpose in construction of these measures was the accurate prediction of individual differences in work behaviors of interest. Examples of such measures are integrity tests, violence scales, drug and alcohol scales, sales potential scales, and managerial potential scales. Some of these measures of personality at work have been incorporated into normal adult personality inventories as separate scales (e.g., the California Personality Inventory, Gough & Bradley, 1996 and the Hogan Personality Inventory [HPI], R. Hogan & Hogan, 1992). However, most measures of personality at work are available in free standing form.

In this chapter, we refer to measures of personality at work as *occupational personality scales*. There are four defining characteristics of occupational personality scales:

1. They are paper-and-pencil instruments containing items similar to those found in traditional personality scales.

2. They were developed specifically to assess personality constructs of relevance for work environments.

3. They were designed for use with job applicants (this is reflected in their normative data).

4. Perhaps most important, they were designed to predict work behaviors.

In general, occupational personality scales have been developed for (a) particular job families (e.g., managers, sales personnel, clerical workers) or (b) predicting particular criteria of interest (e.g., violence at work, employee theft). The former can be referred to as *job-focused occupational personality scales* (JOPS), in that their objective is to predict job performance constructs for particular occupational categories. Examples of such scales include managerial potential scales and sales potential scales. The latter can be referred to as *criterion-focused occupational personality scales* (COPS) in that their goal is to predict particular criteria of interest in work environments. Examples include integrity tests (which aim to predict dishonest behaviors at work), violence scales (which aim to predict violent behaviors at work), drug and alcohol scales (which aim to predict substance abuse at work), stress tolerance scales (which aim to predict handling work pressures well), and customer service scales (which aim to predict serving customers well).

This chapter focuses on COPS. Specifically, we will review criterion-related validity, construct validity, and incremental validity data for three categories of COPS: (a) drug and alcohol scales, (b) stress tolerance scales, and (c) customer service scales. We attempt to answer the following questions regarding these scales:

- Do these scales predict work behaviors of interest?
- What do they measure?
- What are the implications for incremental validity?

Drug and Alcohol Scales

Drug and alcohol use at work has detrimental consequences (Cohen, 1984). The relationships among substance abuse, job performance, and other on-the-job behaviors have been studied (Normand, Lempert, & O'Brien, 1994). For example, Blum, Roman, and Martin (1993) found that heavy drinkers were poor on technical performance. Several studies have found that drug and alcohol abusers are significantly more likely to engage in a variety of counterproductive behaviors on the job. Such counterproductive behaviors include vandalism (Newcomb, 1988), withdrawal and antagonistic behaviors (Lehman & Simpson, 1992), absenteeism (Normand & Salyards, 1989; Sheridan & Winkler, 1989), accidents (Zwerling & Orav, 1990), and undesirable turnover (Kandel & Yamaguchi, 1987).

Employers have tried different strategies to ensure a drug-free workplace (Hanson, 1986; DeCresce, Mazura, Lifshitz, & Tilson, 1990). Employers' growing concern about drug abuse has resulted in increased drug testing of both current and prospective employees (Guthrie & Olian, 1989; Murphy & Thornton, 1992). Blood testing, breath analysis, and urinalysis are among the most common methods of drug testing. One technique that is increasingly being used in employment settings is the administration of paper-and-pencil preemployment tests to assess a job applicant's predisposition to drug and alcohol abuse (Jones, Joy, & Terris, 1991; Normand et al., 1994). These measures include integrity tests (Ones & Viswesvaran, 1998b, 1998c; Ones et al., 1993) as well as drug and alcohol scales (Jones et al., 1991).

Unlike blood testing and urinalysis, which indicate substance use, paper-and-pencil drug and alcohol scales are designed specifically to assess the drug and alcohol abuse *potential* of job applicants for the purpose of predicting drug and alcohol abuse. By using items regarding drugs and alcohol, drug and alcohol scales specifically attempt to tap into job applicants' attitudes, values, and perceptions toward drug and alcohol abuse. None of the scale items focus on other counterproductive behaviors, such as theft. There are several drug and alcohol scales currently available. These include the London House Personnel Selection Inventory (PSI) Drug Scale (London House, Inc., 1975), the Employee Reliability Inventory's Alcohol/Substance Use Scale (Borofsky, Friedman, & Maddocks, 1986), the Accutrac Substance Abuse Scale (Dubrow & Dubrow, 1982/1989), the Orion Survey Drug and Alcohol Attitudes Scale (Wilkerson, 1985), and the PEAK Procedure Substance Abuse Scale (Howard Arthur Company, Inc.). Similar to overt integrity tests (Ones et al., 1993), most drug and alcohol scales do not disguise the goal of the scale. That is, the purpose of the measure in assessing drug and alcohol use potential is transparent to test takers.

Stress Tolerance Scales

Work-related stress and its effects on organizational behavior have been extensively documented (Chen & Spector, 1992; Cooper & Cartwright, 1994). Myriad ways of combating the adverse consequences of stress in high-stress occupations have been suggested (Frankenhaeuser & Johansson, 1986). One potentially useful strategy for minimizing the undesirable consequences of work stress is careful personnel screening and selection. If individuals who are calm in crises and who can handle pressure well can be identified using standardized instruments, then job performance in high-stress occupations may be improved, and the adverse effects of a high-stress work environment may be mitigated.

There recently has emerged a category of potentially useful measures for predicting successful handling of stress on the job (i.e., stress tolerance scales). Stress tolerance scales are paper-and-pencil tests that have been developed for the purpose of identifying job applicants who can "handle pressure well" and who are "not tense and anxious" (R. Hogan & Hogan, 1992, p. 65). These scales are used primarily for personnel selection. Examples of stress tolerance scales include the HPI's Stress Tolerance Scale (R. Hogan & Hogan, 1992), the Employee Attitude Inventory Job Burnout Scale (London House, Inc., 1982/ 1984), the PEOPLE Survey Wellness Scale (Hartnett & Teagle, 1988), and the PEAK Procedure Stress Scale (Howard Arthur Company, Inc.). Some stress tolerance scales disguise the goal of the instrument, others do not. However, for most scales, items are similar to those found on personality measures. In fact, some have been adopted from content scales of some personality measures (e.g., HPI, R. Hogan & Hogan, 1992).

Customer Service Scales

Assessing the quality of customer service provided by employees has become increasingly common, especially in service organizations (Schneider, Chung, & Yusko, 1993). Although the primary requisite for an organization interested in delivering quality customer service is to employ individuals who provide exceptional service (Desatnick, 1987), from an organization's perspective there are potentially three strategies that can be used to ensure a workforce with customer service orientation. First, an organization can strive to alter the organizational climate to encourage the delivery of high-quality customer service (Schneider, Wheeler, & Cox, 1992). Second, an organization may train employees who are likely to come into contact with customers to achieve customer service orientation (Tompkins, 1992; Weaver, 1994; Zeithaml, Parasuraman, & Berry, 1990). Third, an organization can focus on selecting individuals who are naturally predisposed to providing good service (J. Hogan, Hogan, & Busch, 1984) so as to create a workforce that values and delivers high-quality customer service.

To the extent that customer service may be described as a dispositional individual-differences variable, the personnel selection approach is appropriate (Schneider & Schmitt, 1986). Several preemployment personnel selection inventories have been developed to assess applicants' customer service potential (e.g., J. Hogan et al., 1984; McLellan & Paajanen, 1994; Sanchez & Fraser, 1993; Saxe & Weitz, 1982). These are paper-and-pencil tests that have been developed specifically to predict customer service performance. There are at least six such preemployment selection measures available to U.S. organizations (McDaniel & Frei, 1994). These include the Personnel Decisions, International (PDI) Customer Service Inventory (Paajanen, Hansen, & McLellan, 1993), the HPI Service Orientation Scale (R. Hogan & Hogan, 1992), and the PSI Customer Relations Scale (London House, Inc., 1975). Most scales items are similar to those found on personality measures.

Criterion-Related Validity: Practical Value of Criterion-Focused Occupational Personality Scales

Do COPS predict the criteria they are intended to? Do drug and alcohol scales predict substance abuse–related problems at work? Do stress tolerance scales predict the ability to handle work pressures well? Do customer service scales predict the quality of customer service–related job performance? Criterion-related validity provides an index of the linear association between a predictor measure and performance on the criterion; it is expressed as a correlation coefficient (Nunnally, 1978). The criterion-related validity of a personnel selection instrument indicates the degree of its predictive usefulness (Schmidt & Hunter, 1998; Schmidt, Ones, & Hunter, 1992).

Our recent work has estimated the criterion-related validities of drug and alcohol scales (Ones & Viswesvaran, 2000a), stress tolerance scales (Ones & Viswesvaran, 2000b), and customer service scales (Ones & Viswesvaran, 1999a). These three studies report meta-analytically derived estimates of validity for multiple work-related criteria. In this chapter, we review the validities of COPS for three criteria: (a) avoiding counterproductive work behavior, (b) overall job performance, and (c) the criterion each COPS was designed to predict (i.e., substance abuse, stress tolerance, and customer service). Such a review allows the exploration of the potential differential validity of each COPS for predicting three criteria of differing bandwidths. That is, because the specificity of the criterion varies with specific behaviors, the COPS we reviewed were designed to predict broader and more inclusive criteria, such as overall job performance and questions of differential validity may be explored. It also facilitates comparison of validities among the three COPS examined in this chapter.

Table 4.1 reports the operational validities of the three sets of COPS. It presents the total sample size and number of validity estimates (K) associated with each analysis reviewed. The sample-size–weighted (uncorrected) mean observed validity (mean r) of each is reported as well. The parameters are the operational validity (operational r) and the lower 90% credibility value (CV). *Operational validity* refers to the mean observed validity corrected for unreliability in the criterion alone, but not corrected for unreliability in predictor or for range restriction. Note that because none of the operational validities presented were corrected for downward biasing effects of range restriction, all of the validities reported in Table 4.1 are likely to be underestimates. The lower 90% CV is used to determine whether COPS have positive validity across situations (i.e., validity generalization; Hunter & Schmidt, 1990; Ones et al., 1993).

Criterion-Related Validity of Drug and Alcohol Scales

The operational validity of drug and alcohol scales for predicting drug use was .33 (N = 931). This validity did not vary much for different criterion measurement methods (i.e., admissions vs. external detection). One study reported an observed correlation of .10 between drug and alcohol scale scores and urinalysis results in a sample of 357 applicants. That urinalysis results are dichotomous (i.e., positive or negative) may account for this lower observed validity. Three studies reported validities for predicting employees' admissions of alcohol use on the job; the operational validity was .41 (N = 128). This value is likely to be somewhat inflated as a result of the use of a self-report criterion (i.e., admissions) as well as the self-report predictor measure (see also Ones et al., 1993). Nonetheless, it appears that drug and alcohol scales can be useful in predicting substance abuse in personnel selection settings.

A number of studies have reported validities with composite indices of counterproductive behaviors on the job. These composites were derived by having job applicants or employees complete questionnaires indicating various counterproductive behaviors in which they had engaged. The operational validity was .54 (N = 437) for employee samples and .29 (N = 665) for job applicants.

Although drug and alcohol scales were designed to predict a very specific criterion, substance use, they appear to have some utility in predicting other types of counterproductive on-the-job behaviors as well. It is interesting to note that seven studies used drug and alcohol scale scores to predict supervisory ratings of overall job performance, a criterion that encompasses multiple aspects of work performance, not just counterproductive work behaviors. The operational validity for these studies was .19 (N = 1,436), suggesting that drug and alcohol scales can be useful in the prediction of this broader criterion. As for

TABLE 4.1

Criterion-Related Validities of Three Criterion-Focused Occupational Personality Scales

CRITERION	MEASUREMENT METHOD	N	K	MEAN r	OPERATIONAL r	LOWER 90% CV
Drug and alcohol scales[a]						
Drug use	Admissions and external detection	931	3	.31	.33	.12
Drug use[b]	Urinalysis[b]	357	1	.10	.10	—
Alcohol use on the job	Admissions	128	3	.38	.41	.41
Counterproductive behaviors on the job (composite)	Admissions (employees)	437	3	.45	.54	.50
Counterproductive behaviors on the job (composite)	Admissions (applicants)	665	3	.24	.29	.29
Overall job performance	Supervisory ratings	1,436	7	.14	.19	.19
Stress tolerance scales[c]						
Counterproductive behaviors on the job (composite)	Organizational records and supervisory ratings	594	5	.30	.42	.42
Overall job performance	Supervisory ratings	1,010	13	.34	.41	.22
Customer service scales[d]						
Customer service	Ratings	4,401	15	.23	.34	.34
Counterproductive behaviors on the job (composite)	Organizational records and non-self-report ratings	740	5	.30	.42	.24
Overall job performance	Supervisory ratings	6,944	33	.27	.39	.36

Note. K = number of validity estimates; mean r = sample-size-weighted (uncorrected) mean observed validity; operational validity, mean observed validity corrected for unreliability in criterion alone (not corrected for unreliability in predictor or for range restriction); CV = credibility value (one-tailed test). [a]From *Personality-Based Drug and Alcohol Scales Used in Personnel Screening: Predictive and Construct Validity Evidence*, by D. S. Ones and C. Viswesvaran, 2000. Manuscript submitted for publication. [b]No corrections for unreliability in the criterion were applied because of the unavailability of data in the studies. [c]From *Personality-Based Stress Tolerance Scales Used in Work Settings: Predictive and Construct Validity Evidence*, by D. S. Ones and C. Viswesvaran, 2000. Unpublished manuscript. [d]From *Personality-Based Customer Service Scales Used in Personnel Selection: Predictive and Construct Validity Evidence*, by D. S. Ones and C. Viswesvaran, 1999. Manuscript submitted for publication.

job performance, it also should be noted that there was no significant difference in operational validity between applicant and employee samples.

In general, these meta-analytic results offer some preliminary support for the usefulness of drug and alcohol scales in personnel selection. Although these scales appear to have some value in predicting substance abuse and other types of counterproductive work behaviors, they also may be useful as an addition to selection batteries when the goal is to predict overall job performance.

Criterion-Related Validity of Stress Tolerance Scales

Validities for two criteria are reported in Table 4.1: (a) composite indices of counterproductive behaviors on the job and (b) overall job performance. Noteworthy is the fact that we were unable to find a single criterion-related validity for tolerating stress on the job. The operational validity for predicting counterproductive behaviors on the job was .42 (N = 594). As for predicting job performance, the operational validity of stress tolerance scales was .41 (N = 1,010). These validities suggest that stress tolerance scales are likely to be useful in predicting both counterproductive work behaviors and overall job performance.

Criterion-Related Validity of Customer Service Scales

Customer service scales predict ratings of customer service ratings with an operational validity of .34 (N = 4,401). The operational validity for counterproductive behaviors on the job was .42 (N = 740). It was somewhat surprising to find higher validities for customer service scales for counterproductive behaviors than for customer service ratings. The credibility intervals for these operational validities did not overlap. They predicted supervisory ratings of overall job performance with an operational validity of .39 (N = 6,944). Again, the credibility intervals for customer service and overall job performance ratings did not overlap, suggesting small but potentially meaningful differences in the operational validity of customer service scales for these two criteria.

Taken together, these results suggest that COPS may be worth considering for inclusion in personnel selection systems. However, one important theoretical consideration is what constructs these measures tap into. The next section of our chapter attempts to address this question.

Construct Validity Evidence: Theoretical Underpinnings of Criterion-Focused Occupational Personality Scales

There has been very little research examining the construct validity of COPS. What do these scales measure? How do they relate to other widely used individual differences-based predictors used in personnel selection? There is a void in our knowledge about the individual-differences constructs measured by COPS.

An examination of the individual-differences constructs that COPS measure is important for two interrelated reasons. First, once relationships with other predictors are quantified, human resources managers can use this information in computing incremental validity and in combining COPS with other predictors in designing selection systems. If there is substantial construct overlap between COPS and other widely used predictors, then the value of the information that may be obtained from using COPS is diminished. However, if there is unique variance captured by COPS that is unavailable from other personnel selection measures, adding COPS to existing personnel selection systems can augment criterion-related validity. That is, to test if COPS add uniquely to existing predictors used in personnel selection, the relationships among COPS and other, well established predictors need to be investigated.

Second, investigating the construct validity of COPS can help explain why these scales are valid predictors of behavior on the job, thereby enhancing researchers' and employers' understanding of counterproductive behaviors on the job. Thus, embedding COPS in a nomological net is likely to provide a map in discerning what is measured by COPS among the predictors used in personnel selection. Developing such a nomological net also has the potential to explain the underlying process mechanisms by which such scales derive their predictive validity.

Our recent work (Ones & Viswesvaran, 1999a, 2000a, 2000b) has focused on investigating the construct validity of COPS used in the preemployment testing of job applicants. We have reported convergent and divergent validity evidence with cognitive ability, integrity, and personality measures. Next, we briefly review our rationale for investigating these three categories of measures.

First, cognitive ability has been established as the best predictor of overall job performance across jobs, organizations, and settings (Schmidt et al., 1992). As Hunter and Hunter (1984) indicated, the value of alternate predictors of on-the-job performance or its components (e.g., avoiding counterproductive behaviors) should be judged in terms of incremental validity. In creating personnel selection systems, the ideal is to combine uncorrelated (or virtually uncorrelated) predictors that are independently valid for the criteria of interest. By reporting on the relationships among cognitive ability and COPS, this review addresses whether COPS can successfully be combined with cognitive ability measures to enhance prediction.

Second, integrity tests are used widely in personnel selection (O'Bannon, Goldinger, & Appleby, 1989; Ones et al., 1993; Sackett et al., 1989; Sackett & Harris, 1984). Perhaps more relevant for this research, Ones et al. (1993) determined that integrity tests are valid predictors of counterproductive behaviors (including drug and alcohol abuse). In addition, in their review of 85 years of research on personnel selection, Schmidt and Hunter (1998) identified integrity tests as the single best supplement to tests of cognitive ability. Thus, it was considered crucial to examine the degree of overlap between the COPS discussed in this chapter and another COPS, integrity tests.

Third, given the resurgence of interest in using personality measures to predict on-the-job behaviors (Barrick & Mount, 1991; Hough, 1992; Hough et al., 1990; Salgado, 1997), it was considered important to investigate whether COPS assess personality constructs as well. The construct validity of the most widely used COPS, integrity tests, has been examined in a large-scale meta-analysis and in primary studies research (Ones, 1993; Ones, Schmidt, & Viswesvaran, 1994). This research indicated that integrity tests assess a linear combination of conscientiousness, agreeableness, and emotional stability. This same combination of personality dimensions was also found to underlie violence scales used to predict various forms of violent and aggressive behaviors at work (Ones, Viswesvaran, Schmidt, & Reiss, 1994). It is intriguing that previous research examining the construct validity of two different COPS (integrity tests and violence scales) used in personnel selection have identified the same three of the Big Five factors (i.e., Conscientiousness, Agreeableness, and Emotional Stability) as the constructs measured by these scales.

There are reasons each of these three dimensions of personality are likely to be measured to some extent by the three COPS examined in this chapter as well. Previous large-scale studies and meta-analyses of personality–job performance relationships (Barrick & Mount, 1991; Hough, 1992; Hough et al., 1990; Salgado, 1997) have shown conscientiousness to be a valid predictor of job performance. Conscientiousness is a dimension of personality with empirical evidence for predicting drug and alcohol abuse. For example, Ones and Viswesvaran (1996b) reported that the operational validity of conscientiousness for delinquency is .36 (K = 10), and for substance abuse is .37 (K = 25). *Neuroticism* (the negative pole of emotional stability) refers to the anxiety, anger–hostility, self-consciousness, impulsiveness, vulnerability, and depression experienced by an individual. McCrae, Costa, and Bosse (1978) reported that individuals low in emotional stability were more likely to have poor health habits (e.g., smoking). Agreeableness has been shown to be an important personality dimension to consider in behavioral medicine and health psychology, especially with conscientiousness and emotional stability, in explaining individuals' tendencies to engage in harmful and impulsive behaviors (Costa & McCrae, 1990). On the basis of these empirical results and theoretical rationale, COPS can be hypothesized as measuring conscientiousness, agreeableness, and emotional stability (Ones & Viswesvaran, 1999a, 2000a, 2000b). Table 4.2 summarizes the correlations between COPS (drug and alcohol scales, stress tolerance scales, and customer service scales) and cognitive ability, integrity, and

TABLE 4.2

Relationships Among Criterion-Focused Occupational Personality Scales and Dispositional Predictor Variables

VARIABLE	DRUG AND ALCOHOL SCALES[a]		STRESS TOLERANCE SCALES[b]		CUSTOMER SERVICE SCALES[c]	
	r	ρ	r	ρ	r	ρ
Cognitive ability	−.15	−.18	.13	.15	−.08	−.10
Integrity	.40	.51	.29	.35	.36	.47
Big Five personality measures						
Emotional stability	.32	.39	.55	.65	.46	.58
Extraversion	.00	−.02	.23	.28	.18	.23
Openness to experience	.09	.12	.20	.24	.14	.18
Agreeableness	.22	.28	.36	.44	.51	.70
Conscientiousness	.40	.48	.31	.38	.33	.43

Note. r = mean observed correlation; ρ = mean correlation corrected for unreliability in both measures. [a]From *Personality-Based Drug and Alcohol Scales Used in Personnel Screening: Predictive and Construct Validity Evidence,* by D. S. Ones and C. Viswesvaran, 2000. Manuscript submitted for publication. [b]From *Personality-Based Stress Tolerance Scales Used in Work Settings: Predictive and Construct Validity Evidence,* by D. S. Ones and C. Viswesvaran, 2000. Unpublished manuscript. [c]From *Personality-Based Customer Service Scales Used in Personnel Selection: Predictive and Construct Validity Evidence,* by D. S. Ones and C. Viswesvaran, 1999. Manuscript submitted for publication.

the Big Five measures of personality (i.e., emotional stability, extraversion, openness to experience, agreeableness, and conscientiousness).

The results reviewed in Table 4.2 are based on data from multiple samples. Furthermore, we used (Ones & Viswesvaran, 1999a, 2000a, 2000b) multiple measures to enhance the generalizability of the conclusions. Participants were administered various combinations of COPS, a cognitive ability test, Big Five personality measures, and integrity tests. A total of 300 to 500 participants completed any given instrument.

The Drug Avoidance scale of the PSI (London House, Inc., 1975) was used. The 20 items that make up the Drug Avoidance scale are scored such that high scores indicate less positive attitudes, beliefs, and values regarding drug and alcohol use. The Stress Tolerance Scale of the HPI (R. Hogan & Hogan, 1992), which consists of 25 items primarily taken from the HPI Adjustment and Ambition scales, also was used. "I keep calm in a crisis" is a typical item. Two customer service scales were used: the HPI Service Orientation Scale (R. Hogan & Hogan, 1992) and the PSI Customer Relations Scale (London House, Inc., 1975). Both of these measures are used in personnel selection for jobs that require customer contact.

The measure of cognitive ability used in all studies was the Wonderlic Personnel Test (Wonderlic & Associates, Inc., 1983). *The Wonderlic Personnel Test Manual* indicates that the objective of the Wonderlic Personnel Test is to provide "a highly accurate estimate of individual adult intelligence" (p. 5). In addition, it is described as a measure of "general *g*," that is, "the primary factor among the many factors comprising intellectual capacity" (Wonderlic & Associates, Inc., 1983).

Seven integrity tests were used: (a) the Reid Report (Reid Psychological Systems, 1951), (b) the Stanton Survey (Klump, 1964), (c) the PSI Honesty Scale (London House, Inc., 1975), (d) the Personnel Reaction Blank (Gough, 1954), (e) the PDI Employment Inventory (PDI-EI; Paajanen, 1985), (f) the HPI Reliability Scale (R. Hogan, 1981), and (g) the Inwald Personality Inventory Risk Scale (Inwald, 1992). The Reid Report, Stanton Survey, and PSI Honesty Scale have been identified as overt measures of integrity by all previous reviews of integrity tests (e.g., Goldberg, Grenier, Guion, Sechrest, & Wing, 1991; Ones et al., 1993; Sackett et al., 1989; Sackett & Harris, 1984). The Personnel Reaction Blank, PDI-EI, HPI Reliability Scale, and Inwald Personality Inventory Risk Scale have been identified as personality-based measures of integrity (e.g., Goldberg et al., 1991; Ones et al., 1993; Sackett et al., 1989; Sackett & Harris, 1984). Ones (1993) has shown that there is an underlying construct of integrity that spans all seven of these measures of integrity. Detailed descriptions of these measures can be found in *The Tenth Mental Measurements Yearbook* (Conoley & Kramer, 1989) and in various literature reviews (O'Bannon et al., 1989; Sackett et al., 1989; Sackett & Harris, 1984).

Three personality inventories were used. Participants were administered the Personal Characteristics Inventory (PCI; Mount & Barrick, 1994); 100 unipolar Five-Factor Markers (FFM; Goldberg, 1992), and the HPI (R. Hogan & Hogan, 1992). All three inventories are well established (both empirically and theoretically) in their measurement of the Big Five personality dimensions.

In assessing the relationships among the variables of interest, both the observed and the unreliability-corrected mean correlations were reviewed. The observed mean correlation between the measures indicates the degree of overlap in those measures. However, to examine the degree of overlap between the constructs assessed by the two measures, the mean correlations corrected for unreliability in both measures were reported (Hunter & Schmidt, 1990).

Construct Validity Evidence for Drug and Alcohol Scales

The observed correlation between the PSI Drug Avoidance Scale (London House, Inc., 1975) and the cognitive ability measure was $-.15$. The unreliability-corrected correlation between the two measures was $-.18$. Given these results, it appears that the Drug Avoidance Scale taps into a domain of constructs largely untapped by cognitive ability tests. High scores on the Drug Avoidance Scale indicated somewhat lower levels of cognitive ability.

The mean corrected correlation between the integrity tests and the PSI Drug Avoidance Scale (London House, Inc., 1975) was .51. To investigate the relationships among the Drug Avoidance Scale and personality variables, the correlations between the Drug Avoidance Scale and the three personality inventories (the PCI, the FFM, and the HPI) were computed. The mean corrected correlation across the three conscientiousness scales was .48. Notably, high zero-order correlations also were found for the agreeableness and emotional stability dimensions of personality. The mean corrected correlation was .39 for emotional stability and .28 for agreeableness. It appears that the Drug Avoidance Scale measures elements from three personality constructs, (a) conscientiousness, (b) emotional stability, and (c) agreeableness, with the strength of the relationships in that order. This result held across three widely used personality inventories, attesting to the robustness of these findings. The results also indicate that integrity tests correlate quite highly with the Drug Avoidance Scale. This is not surprising, as integrity tests measure conscientiousness, agreeableness, and emotional stability as well (Ones, 1993).

Construct Validity Evidence for Stress Tolerance Scales

The relationship of stress tolerance scales with cognitive ability was small (corrected $r = .15$). There was some overlap between the constructs measured by integrity tests and those measured by stress tolerance scales (corrected mean

$r = .35$). Stress tolerance scales appeared to measure primarily emotional stability. The mean corrected correlation between the variables was .65. However, the constructs measured by stress tolerance scales also correlated substantially with agreeableness and conscientiousness (.44 and .38, respectively). The relationships were lower for extraversion (.28) and openness to experience (.24).

Construct Validity Evidence for Customer Service Scales

The constructs measured by customer service scales and tests of cognitive ability appeared to be relatively independent. Customer service scales seem to tap into a domain of constructs untapped by cognitive ability tests. The mean corrected correlation between customer service scales and integrity tests was .47, suggesting substantial construct overlap.

Among the Big Five dimensions of personality, the strongest link of customer service orientation was with agreeableness. The corrected composite correlation between these two constructs was .70. The second strongest relationship was between customer service orientation and emotional stability (.58). The corrected composite correlation between customer service orientation and conscientiousness was .43. The construct of customer service orientation is strongly connected to three of the Big Five dimensions of personality: (a) agreeableness, (b) emotional stability, and (c) conscientiousness, in that order. The correlations between customer service scales and extraversion and openness to experience were lower, .23 and .18, respectively.

The construct validity investigations summarized reveal interesting findings. The three COPS discussed, despite having seemingly very different purposes, appear to tap the same personality dimensions: (a) conscientiousness, (b) agreeableness, and (c) emotional stability. In earlier work, Ones (1993) had found that these personality constructs tapped by integrity tests were also conscientiousness, agreeableness, and emotional stability. All COPS (including integrity tests) seem to share a substantive core from the personality domain. This substantive core consists of the three personality dimensions (conscientiousness, emotional stability,and agreeableness), however, it appears that the relative weights of the three personality constructs tapped by each COPS are different.

Implications for Incremental Validity of Criterion-Focused Occupational Personality

The studies reviewed examined (a) the usefulness of COPS for personnel selection and (b) the theoretical underpinnings of COPS from the personality and ability domains. Other meta-analytic cumulations of the criterion-related validities of general cognitive ability (Schmidt & Hunter, 1998), integrity tests (Ones et al., 1993), and the Big Five personality scales (Barrick & Mount, 1991; Salgado, 1997) have reached positive conclusions about the usefulness of these constructs. In addition we summarize a series of investigations that used these previous meta-analytic results in conjunction with the criterion-related validity and construct validity evidence for COPS to compute incremental validity (Ones & Viswesvaran, 1999a, 2000a, 2000b).

That the criterion-related validity of even I/O psychology's strongest predictor, cognitive ability, has been reported as only in the .50s suggests the possibility of improving a selection system by designing an optimal combination of different predictors. This has been an attractive research question for I/O psychologists (Schmidt & Hunter, 1992). That is, I/O psychologists have been advised to search for alternate predictors that supplement, but not replace, cognitive abilities (Hunter & Hunter, 1984) such that the chosen alternate predictors add incremental validity.

Computation of incremental validity requires knowledge of the relationship between each predictor and the criterion as well as the intercorrelations among the predictors. The criterion-related validities of COPS were taken from our meta-analytic investigations summarized above (Ones & Viswesvaran, 1999a, 2000a, 2000b). For the criterion-related validity of cognitive ability, we used the value used by Schmidt and Hunter (1998) in their investigation of incremental validity. For the criterion-related validity of integrity tests, we used the values reported by Ones et al. (1993). For the criterion-related validity of the Big Five for job performance, we used the values reported by Barrick and Mount (1991), whereas for counterproductive behaviors on the job, we used the validities reported by Hough (1992). If not already corrected, the criterion-related validities were corrected for unreliability in the criterion to ensure that all validities used were operational validities. The estimates of intercorrelations between the drug and alcohol scales and the other predictors were taken from the construct validity investigation reviewed above (Ones & Viswesvaran, 1999a, 2000a, 2000b).

For each predictor variable, we computed the multiple correlation (R) of using an optimally weighted combination of that predictor and each COPS. The gain in validity from adding the COPS also was computed. This was done for two criteria: (a) counterproductive behaviors on the job and (b) overall job performance.

The results of these investigations are summarized in Table 4.3. The first column of Table 4.3 presents the operational validity of each predictor for counterproductive behaviors on the job (top half of table) and for overall job performance (bottom half of table). Multiple correlation columns indicate the results of using each predictor in combination with a COPS. The gain in validity achieved by adding a COPS to each predictor is noted as well.

Incremental Validity Evidence for Drug and Alcohol Scales

Although drug and alcohol scales were designed for the purpose of predicting substance use, a form of counterproductive behavior, conscientiousness scales are much better than drug and alcohol scales in predicting a broad counterproductive behaviors criterion (operational validities of .47 and .29, respectively; Ones & Viswesvaran, in press). When the objective is to predict counterproductive behaviors on the job, adding a drug and alcohol scale to a conscientiousness scale results in negligible incremental validity (.01 correlational points; Table 4.3). Using an integrity test in conjunction with a drug and alcohol scale, however, results in a multiple correlation of .37 (incremental validity of 14% compared with integrity tests alone). It appears that organizations seeking to control counterproductivity would be better served by using drug and alcohol scales rather than measures of extraversion and agreeableness. As shown in Table 4.3, using drug and alcohol scales along with measures of emotional stability produces a multiple correlation of .43 (incremental validity of .04 over emotional stability alone). Similarly, using a drug and alcohol scale along with a measure of openness to experience produced a multiple correlation of .42 (incremental validity of .14 over openness to experience alone).

According to the data in Table 4.3, adding a drug and alcohol scale to a personnel selection system already containing a general cognitive ability test results in an incremental validity of 13%, or .07 correlational points. Adding drug and alcohol scales also maximizes the prediction of job performance ($R =$ .58). To the extent that organizations rely solely on drug and alcohol scales in the screening and selection of personnel, however, they will be sacrificing significant usefulness by overlooking an excellent predictor of job performance, that is, cognitive ability. A recommendation to organizations selecting personnel, particularly in industries in which drug and alcohol use on the job is prevalent, is to use cognitive ability tests and drug and alcohol scales in combination to maximize the usefulness of the screening and selection tools and enhance job performance. Although drug and alcohol scales can boost the predictive validity of four of the Big Five measures (emotional stability, extraversion, openness to experience, agreeableness), these combinations do not result in optimally valid employee selection systems compared with using a drug and alcohol scale alone. For example, adding a drug and alcohol scale to a selection system already containing an integrity test did not improve the prediction of overall job performance at all (incremental validity = .00; see Table 4.3). When organizations select for drug-related attitudes, they are likely to choose employees high in integrity as well. Similarly, as shown in Table 4.3, the incremental validity of

TABLE 4.3

Incremental Validity of Criterion-Focused Occupational Personality Scales

PREDICTOR MEASURE	OPERATIONAL VALIDITY	R (D&A + PREDICTOR)	GAIN IN VALIDITY FROM ADDING D&A SCALES TO PREDICTOR	R (ST + PREDICTOR)	GAIN IN VALIDITY FROM ADDING ST SCALES TO PREDICTOR	R (CS + PREDICTOR)	GAIN IN VALIDITY FROM ADDING CS SCALES TO PREDICTOR
		Criterion: Counterproductive behaviors on the job					
D&A scales[a]	.29	—	—	—	—	—	—
ST scales[b]	.42	—	—	—	—	—	—
CS scales[c]	.42	—	—	—	—	—	.14
Integrity tests	.32	.37	.05	.47	.15	.46	.14
Emotional stability scales	.39	.43	.04	.47	.08	.47	.08
Extraversion scales	.15	.33	.18	.42	.27	.43	.28
Openness to experience scales	−.28	.42	.14	.56	.28	.54	.26
Agreeableness scales	.09	.29	.20	.43	.34	.44	.35
Conscientiousness scales	.47	.48	.01	.55	.08	.55	.08

Criterion: Overall job performance

D&A scales[a]	.19	—	—	—	—	—	—
ST scales[b]	.41	—	—	—	—	—	—
CS scales[c]	.39	—	—	—	—	—	—
General cognitive ability tests	.51	.58	.07	.62	.11	.67	.16
Integrity tests	.41	.41	.00	.51	.10	.49	.08
Emotional stability scales	.12	.20	.08	.43	.31	.40	.28
Extraversion scales	.12	.22	.10	.41	.29	.39	.27
Openness to experience scales	.05	.19	.14	.41	.36	.39	.34
Agreeableness scales	.10	.20	.10	.41	.31	.41	.31
Conscientiousness scales	.23	.25	.02	.42	.19	.40	.17

Note. D&A = drug and alcohol; ST = stress tolerance; CS = customer service. [a]From *Personality-Based Drug and Alcohol Scales Used in Personnel Screening: Predictive and Construct Validity Evidence,* by D. S. Ones and C. Viswesvaran, 2000. Manuscript submitted for publication. [b]From *Personality-Based Stress Tolerance Scales Used in Work Settings: Predictive and Construct Validity Evidence,* by D. S. Ones and C. Viswesvaran, 2000. Unpublished manuscript. [c]From *Personality-Based Customer Service Scales Used in Personnel Selection: Predictive and Construct Validity Evidence,* by D. S. Ones and C. Viswesvaran, 1999. Manuscript submitted for publication.

adding a drug and alcohol scale over a conscientiousness scale alone was quite small (incremental validity = .02; see Table 4.3).

Incremental Validity Evidence for Stress Tolerance Scales

In predicting counterproductive behaviors on the job, stress tolerance scales have demonstrated criterion-related validity second only to conscientiousness scales (operational validities = .42 and .47, respectively). Interestingly, though, combining a conscientiousness scale with a stress tolerance scale produced a multiple correlation of .55, or an improvement of .08 (17%) over a conscientiousness scale alone. Unexpectedly, the best predictive validity was obtained for the combination of an openness to experience scale and a stress tolerance scale (R = .56). These findings support the addition of a stress tolerance scale to any selection system in which the goal is to predict counterproductive behaviors on the job.

Stress tolerance scales provide notable incremental validity with existing dispositional predictors in selection. As presented in Table 4.3, an employee selection system combining a general cognitive ability test and a stress tolerance scale produce a multiple correlation of .62 (incremental validity = .11). The combination of an integrity test and a stress tolerance scale results in a multiple correlation of .51 (incremental validity = .10). The incremental validity over a conscientiousness scale is .19, or 82% improvement in the prediction of overall job performance. Of course, when the criterion is overall job performance, the predictive validity of stress tolerance scales is superior to all the Big Five scales; stress tolerance scales therefore possess incremental validity over these scales as well.

Incremental Validity Evidence for Customer Service Scales

When the criterion of interest is counterproductive behaviors on the job, the largest multiple correlations were obtained by combining a customer service scale with either a conscientiousness scale (R = .55) or an openness to experience scale (.54). Given the slightly larger value of the first correlation, the best strategy may be to pair a customer service scale with a conscientiousness scale. It is interesting to note that, as shown in Table 4.3, there is some improvement in predictive validity (incremental validity = .14) of an integrity test when a customer service scale is added to the battery.

As demonstrated by the results presented in Table 4.3, the validity of a selection system for predicting overall job performance is maximized when a customer service scale is used in combination with a test of general cognitive ability (R = .67). Adding a customer service scale to a selection system that already contains a conscientiousness scale also improves predictive validity (incremental validity = .17, or 76% increase over validity of a conscientiousness scale alone).

General Conclusions and Discussion

Personality variables increasingly are being used in personnel selection systems. The particular type of personality scales, COPS, described in this chapter are paper-and-pencil scales that have been devised to (a) assess personality constructs that are relevant for work settings and (b) predict particular criteria of interest in work environments. These scales also have been specifically developed for use with job applicants. This chapter reviewed research on three COPS that are very different on the surface. We briefly summarized results of recent investigations on drug and alcohol scales, stress tolerance scales, and customer service scales (Ones & Viswesvaran, 1999a, 2000a, 2000b). For example, drug and alcohol scales aim to predict substance use and abuse at work. Stress tolerance scales aim to predict handling work pressures well. Customer service scales aim to predict serving customers well. Criterion-related validity, construct validity evidence, and incremental validity evidence for each of the three COPS were summarized.

Although they may seem very different, we found striking consistencies across these scales. For criterion-related validity, for example, we found that (a) highest predictive validities are not always obtained for criteria for which the scales were developed even though validities for these criteria were substantial (e.g., customer service scales did not produce the highest validities for customer service ratings); (b) validities for counterproductive behaviors on the job were high; and (c) validities for supervisory ratings of overall job performance were substantial. The operational validities of drug and alcohol scales were as follows: .33 for drug use, .29 for counterproductive behaviors on the job, and .19 for overall job performance. Stress tolerance scales predicted counterproductive behaviors on the job with an operational validity of .42 and overall job performance with a validity of .41 (no validities were reported for stress reactions). Customer service scales produced operational validities of .34 for customer service ratings, .42 for counterproductive behaviors on the job, and .39 for overall job performance. Also noteworthy is that these criterion-related validities for supervisory ratings of overall job performance are superior to those reported for the Big Five personality dimensions (Barrick & Mount, 1991; Mount & Barrick, 1995; Salgado, 1997) or more fine-grained personality dimensions (Hough, 1992). In fact, these criterion-related validities are on par with those reported for integrity tests (Ones et al., 1993), another COPS.

There also was striking consistency in the constructs tapped into by these COPS. None of them displayed significant correlations with general mental ability. All related substantially and substantively to integrity tests, however (ρ = .51 for drug and alcohol scales, ρ = .35 for stress tolerance scales, and ρ = .47 for customer service scales). In fact, we discovered that the COPS reviewed in this chapter all appeared to tap into the same three Big Five constructs as integrity tests: (a) conscientiousness, (b) agreeableness, and (c) emotional stability. However, the weights of the constructs differed according to scale. Each tapped into the following constructs in the order indicated: drug and alcohol scales, (a) conscientiousness, (b) emotional stability, and (c) agreeableness; stress tolerance scales, (a) emotional stability, (b) agreeableness, and (c) conscientiousness; customer service scales, (a) agreeableness, (b) emotional stability, and (c) conscientiousness. Previous work had revealed that integrity tests measure conscientiousness, agreeableness, and emotional stability, in that order (Ones, 1993). This overlap of constructs measured by COPS combined with the earlier finding that all of these scales predict counterproductive behaviors on the job and overall job performance, even though they were each designed to predict a much more specific criterion, suggests that all COPS may be deriving their validities for these broad criteria from their shared common core.

Each COPS taps into the same three of the Big Five dimensions of personality (i.e., conscientiousness, agreeableness, and emotional stability). However, the personality constructs measured by COPS have at best moderate criterion-related validity. That the predictive validities obtained from COPS are higher than those of the Big Five constructs or other all-purpose "normal" adult personality scales by themselves (e.g., Barrick & Mount, 1991; Hough, 1992) or in combination (Ones et al., 1994) suggests that these scales are particularly good at tapping into a construct that is at a higher level than those of the Big Five. That is, COPS measure a very broad construct, broader than any one of the Big Five.

Theoretical Implications

Is it coincidence that the higher order construct that occupies the intersection of conscientiousness, agreeableness, and emotional stability appears to be behind COPS that predict broad criteria such as counterproductive behaviors on the job and overall job performance? We think not. The evidence presented in this chapter suggests that the predictive validity of COPS for the criteria of counterproductive behaviors on the job and (b) overall job performance is due to a higher level factor and not, as one might assume, the variance associated with group factors at the Big Five level.

There is theoretical meaning to this superordinate grouping. Digman (1997) performed a series of factor analyses on 14 different databases to examine whether there was evidence of higher order factors other than the Big Five. The databases used both self- and others' ratings of personality. Data were collected for 4,269 individuals. Digman found evidence for two higher order factors to the Big Five. The first higher order construct was defined by the overlap among conscientiousness, agreeableness, and emotional stability. Digman labeled this *Super Factor Alpha*. The second higher order construct (*Super Factor Beta*) was defined by extraversion and openness to experience. COPS appear to tap into Factor Alpha.

There is theoretical meaning to the fact that all COPS appear to tap into Digman's (1997) higher order Factor Alpha construct. Digman (1997) indicated

> that Factor Alpha represents the socialization process itself. From Freud (1930) to Kohut (1977), from Watson (1929) to Skinner (1971), personality theorists of various persuasion have been concerned with the development of *impulse restraint* and *conscience*, and the reduction of *hostility, aggression,* and *neurotic defense*. From this point of view, Factor Alpha is what personality development is all about. Thus, if all proceeds according to society's blueprint, the child develops superego and learns to restrain or redirect id impulses and to discharge aggression in socially approved ways. Failure of socialization is indicated by neurosis, by deficient superego, or by excessive aggressiveness. (pp. 1249–1250)

From R. Hogan and Hogan's (1992) point of view, what COPS measure corresponds to a basic human aim toward peer popularity. COPS most often have come into existence when I/O psychologists have been faced with organizational personnel selection problems. In developing personality scales to predict specific criteria such as drug use or customer service behaviors, it appears that they have created personality scales that assess individuals who function well according to social rules. The fact that these scales also predict counterproductive behaviors on the job and overall job performance well is also evidence of the usefulness of functioning according to society's rules in organizational settings. Factor Alpha is perhaps the most important personality trait that should be systematically measured among job applicants. A high score on this higher order personality trait predicts a whole spectrum of work behaviors, from avoiding drug and alcohol use to engaging in appropriate customer service behaviors, from handling stress well to not stealing, from avoiding absenteeism to being an overall stellar performer on the job.

According to Cronbach and Gleser (1965), the usefulness of a test is a function of the number of decisions for which the test scores can be used. In other words, a test that predicts many criterion components contributes more utility than another predictor with higher validity that predicts only one criterion subcomponent. When the criterion to be predicted is broad, heterogeneous, and complex (such as job performance), it is relatively disadvantageous to use narrow, construct-limited predictors. This is why, in personnel selection, a broad personality construct such as Factor Alpha may be preferable to narrower constructs. The theoretical overlap between Factor Alpha and job performance and its dimensions seems to ensure that COPS are useful predictors in personnel selection.

Implications for Prediction in Personnel Selection and Practice

The results discussed in this chapter have significant practice implications. Given that COPS predict multiple criteria relevant for work, it clearly is advantageous to use them in personnel selection systems. In addition, there are some striking consistencies across COPS in terms of their incremental validity and comparative value with the Big Five. First, in predicting overall job performance, it appears most advantageous to pair COPS with a general cognitive ability test rather than with measures of the Big Five. This combination maximizes the overall predictive validity of the selection system. Second, the predictive validity advantage of adding COPS to a personnel selection system that already includes an integrity test is smaller. Third, in predicting counterproductive behaviors on the job, the criterion-related validity of conscientiousness scales is somewhat superior to those of COPS. Thus, organizations interested in predicting only the counterproductivity criterion may prefer to use conscientiousness scales instead. However, there was some incremental validity to combining a COPS with a conscientiousness scale.

Most COPS are instruments that have received little or no attention from the scientific community. Perhaps the publication of this research will spur collaboration from more test publishers in the form of sharing instruments with investigators so as to further research examining the construct and criterion-related validity of COPS. Such scales include violence scales and sales potential scales. Future research should continue to explore the interrelations between COPS and other personality scales. The construction of such a richer nomological net may help in the construction of personnel selection systems with greater predictive accuracy and lower costs, facilitating enhanced understanding of both the predictor and criterion domains. Constructing a nomological net across validated predictors used in organizations also may enable a more appropriate test of process mechanisms whereby predictors come to predict various criteria. Researchers then can examine why certain predictors work. Perhaps even long-standing debates in I/O psychology (e.g., the bandwidth–fidelity dilemma, Ones & Viswesvaran, 1996a) could be resolved.

References

Barrick, M. R., & Mount, M. K. (1991). The Big Five personality dimensions and job performance: A meta-analysis. *Personnel Psychology, 44,* 1–26.

Block, J. (1995). A contrarian view of the five-factor approach to personality description. *Psychological Bulletin, 117,* 187–215.

Blum, T. C., Roman, P. M., & Martin, J. K. (1993). Alcohol consumption and work performance. *Journal of Studies on Alcohol, 54*(1), 61–70.

Borofsky, G. L., Friedman, J., & Maddocks, A., Jr. (1986). *Employee reliability inventory (ERI).* Boston: Bay State Psychological Associates, Inc.

Chen, P. Y., & Spector, P. E. (1992). Relationships of work stressors with aggression, withdrawals, theft and substance use: An exploratory study. *Journal of Occupational and Organizational Psychology, 65,* 177–184.

Cohen, S. (1984). Drugs in the workplace. *Journal of Clinical Psychiatry, 12,* 4–8.

Conoley, J. C., & Kramer, J. J. (1989). *The tenth mental measurements yearbook.* Lincoln, NE: Buros Institute.

Cook, M. (1998). *Personnel selection: Adding value through people.* London: Wiley.

Cooper, C. L., & Cartwright, S. (1994). Healthy mind–Healthy organization: A proactive approach to occupational stress. *Human Relations, 47,* 455–471.

Costa, P. T. Jr., & McCrae, R. R. (1990). Personality disorders and the five-factor model of personality. *Journal of Personality Disorders, 4,* 362–371.

Costa, P. T., Jr., & McCrae, R. R. (1992). Four ways five factors are basic. *Personality and Individual Differences, 13,* 653–665.

Costa, P. T., Jr., & McCrae, R. R. (1995). Solid ground in the wetlands of personality: A reply to Block. *Psychological Bulletin, 117,* 216–220.

Cronbach, L. J., & Gleser, G. C. (1965). *Psychological tests and personnel decisions* (2nd ed.). Urbana: University of Illinois Press.

Day, D. V., & Silverman, S. B. (1989). Personality and job performance: Evidence of incremental validity. *Personnel Psychology, 42,* 25–36.

DeCresce, R., Mazura, A., Lifshitz, M., & Tilson, J. (1990). *Drug testing in the workplace.* Chicago: American Society of Clinical Psychologists Press.

Desatnick, R. L. (1987). Building the customer-oriented work force. *Training and Development Journal, 41*(3), 72–74.

Digman, J. M. (1990). Personality structure: Emergence of the five-factor model. *Annual Review of Psychology, 41,* 417–440.

Digman, J. M. (1997). Higher order factors of the Big Five. *Journal of Personality and Social Psychology, 73,* 1246–1256.

Dubrow, B. R., & Dubrow, B. H. (1989). *Accutrac Evaluation System.* Cincinnati, OH: Barbrisons Management Systems, Inc. [Original work published 1982]

Eysenck, H. J. (1991). Dimensions of personality: 16, 5, or 3 criteria for a taxonomic paradigm. *Personality and Individual Differences, 12,* 773–790.

Frankenhaeuser, M., & Johansson, G. (1986). Stress at work: Psychobiological and psychosocial aspects. *International Review of Applied Psychology, 35,* 289–299.

Freud, S. (1930). *Civilization and its discontents.* New York: Norton.

Goldberg, L. R. (1992). The development of markers for the Big-Five factor structure. *Psychological Assessment, 4,* 26–42.

Goldberg, L. R. (1993). The structure of phenotypic personality traits. *American Psychologist, 48,* 26–34.

Goldberg, L. R., Grenier, J. R., Guion, R. M., Sechrest, L. B., & Wing, H. (1991). *Questionnaires used in the prediction of trustworthiness in preemployment selection decisions.* Washington, DC: American Psychological Association.

Gough, H. G. (1954). *Personnel Reaction Blank.* Palo Alto, CA: Consulting Psychologists Press.

Gough, H. G., & Bradley, P. (1996). *CPI manual (3rd ed.).* Palo Alto, CA: Consulting Psychologists Press, Inc.

Guthrie, J. P., & Olian, J. D. (1989, April). *Drug and alcohol testing programs: The influence of organizational context and objectives.* Paper presented at the 4th annual meeting of the Society of Industrial and Organizational Psychology, Boston.

Hanson, D. J. (1986, June). Drug abuse testing programs gaining acceptance in work place. *Chemical and Engineering News,* 7–14.

Hartnett, J. J., & Teagle, M. A. (1988). *The P.E.O.P.L.E. Survey.* Abingdon, VA: Cross-Fire, Inc.

Hogan, J., & Hogan, R. (1989). How to measure employee reliability. *Journal of Applied Psychology, 74,* 273–279.

Hogan, J., Hogan, R., & Busch, C. (1984). How to measure service orientation. *Journal of Applied Psychology, 69,* 167–173.

Hogan, R. (1981). *Hogan Personality Inventory.* Minneapolis, MN: National Computer Systems.

Hogan, R., & Hogan, J. (1992). *Hogan Personality Inventory manual.* Tulsa, OK: Hogan Assessment Systems.

Hough, L. M. (1992). The "Big Five" personality variables—Construct confusion: Description versus prediction. *Human Performance, 5,* 139–156.

Hough, L. M., Eaton, N. K., Dunnette, M. D., Kamp, J. D., & McCloy, R. A. (1990). Criterion-related validities of personality constructs and the effect of response distortion on those validities. *Journal of Applied Psychology, 75,* 581–595.

Hough, L. M., & Oswald, F. (2000). Personnel selection: Looking toward the future— remembering the past. *Annual Review of Psychology, 51,* 631–664.

Howard Arthur Company, Inc. (undated). *PEAK Procedure.* Woodland Hills, CA: Author.

Hull, C. L. (1928). *Aptitude testing.* London: Harrap.

Hunter, J. E., & Hunter, R. F. (1984). Validity and utility of alternate predictors of job performance. *Psychological Bulletin, 96,* 72–98.

Hunter, J. E., & Schmidt, F. L. (1990). *Methods of meta-analysis: Correcting error and bias in research findings.* Newbury Park, CA: Sage.

Hunter, J. E., Schmidt, F. L., & Judiesch, M. K. (1990). Individual differences in output variability as a function of job complexity. *Journal of Applied Psychology, 75,* 28–42.

Inwald, R. (1992). *Inwald Personality Inventory.* Kew Gardens, NY: Hilson Research.

Jones, J. W., Joy, D. S., & Terris, W. (1991). Psychological correlates of illicit drug use among job applicants. In J. W. Jones (Ed.), *Preemployment honesty testing* (pp. 159–183). Westport, CT: Quorum Books.

Kandel, D. B., & Yamaguchi, K. (1987). Job mobility and drug use: An event history analysis. *American Journal of Sociology, 92,* 836–878.

Klump, C. S. (1964). *Stanton Survey.* Charlotte, NC: Stanton Corporation.

Kohut, H. (1977). *The restoration of the self.* New York: International Universities Press.

Lehman, W. E. K., & Simpson, D. D. (1992). Employee substance use and on the job behaviors. *Journal of Applied Psychology, 77,* 309–321.

London House, Inc. (1975). *Personnel Selection Inventory manual (12 versions).* Park Ridge, IL: Author.

London House, Inc. (1984). *Employee Attitude Inventory (EAI-6).* Park Ridge, IL: Author. [Original work published 1982]

McCrae, R. R., Costa, P. T. Jr., & Bosse, R. (1978). Anxiety, extroversion, and smoking. *British Journal of Social and Clinical Psychology, 17,* 269–273.

McDaniel, M. A., & Frei, R. L. (1994, April). *Validity of customer service measures in personnel selection: A meta-analysis.* Paper presented at the 9th annual convention of the Society of Industrial and Organizational Psychology, Nashville, TN.

McLellan, R. A., & Paajanen, G. (1994). *PDI Customer Service Inventory manual.* Minneapolis, MN: Personnel Decisions International.

Mischel, W. (1968). *Personality and assessment.* New York: Wiley.

Mount, M. K., & Barrick, M. R. (1994). *Personal Characteristics Inventory technical manual.* Iowa City: University of Iowa.

Mount, M. K., & Barrick, M. R. (1995). The Big Five personality dimensions: Implications for research and practice in human resources management. In G. R. Ferris (Ed.), *Research in personnel and human relations management* (Vol. 13, pp. 153–200). Greenwich, CT: JAI Press.

Murphy, K. R., & Thornton, G. C., III. (1992). Characteristics of employee drug testing policies. *Journal of Business and Psychology, 6,* 295–309.

Newcomb, M. D. (1988). *Drug use in the workplace: Risk factors for disruptive substance use among young adults.* Dover, MA: Auburn House.

Normand, J., Lempert, R. O., & O'Brien, C. P. (1994). *Under the influence? Drugs and the American work force.* Washington, DC: National Academy Press.

Normand, J., & Salyards, S. D. (1989). An empirical evaluation of preemployment drug testing in the United States Postal Service: Interim report of findings. In S. W. Gust & J. M. Walsh (Eds.), *Drugs in the workplace: Research and evaluation data* (pp. 111–138). Rockville, MD: National Institute on Drug Abuse.

Nunnally, J. C. (1978). *Psychometric theory*. New York: McGraw-Hill.

O'Bannon, R. M., Goldinger, L. A., & Appleby, G. S. (1989). *Honesty and integrity testing*. Atlanta, GA: Applied Information Resources.

Ones, D. S. (1993). *The construct validity of integrity tests*. Unpublished doctoral dissertation, University of Iowa, Iowa City.

Ones, D. S., Schmidt, F. L., & Viswesvaran, C. (1994, April). Do broader personality variables predict job performance with higher validity? In R. C. Page (Chair), *Personality and job performance: Big Five versus specific traits*. Symposium conducted at the 9th annual meeting of the Society of Industrial and Organizational Psychology, Nashville, TN.

Ones, D. S., & Viswesvaran, C. (1996a). Bandwidth–fidelity dilemma in personality measurement for personnel selection. *Journal of Organizational Behavior, 17*, 609–626.

Ones, D. S., & Viswesvaran, C. (1996b, April). A general theory of conscientiousness at work: Theoretical underpinnings and empirical findings. In J. Collins (Chair), *Personality predictors of job performance: Controversial issues*. Symposium conducted at the 11th annual meeting of the Society of Industrial and Organizational Psychology, San Diego, CA.

Ones, D. S., & Viswesvaran, C. (1998a). The effects of social desirability and faking on personality and integrity assessment for personnel selection. *Human Performance, 11*, 245–271.

Ones, D. S., & Viswesvaran, C. (1998b). Gender, age and race differences on overt integrity tests: Analyses across four large-scale applicant data sets. *Journal of Applied Psychology, 83*, 35–42.

Ones, D. S., & Viswesvaran, C. (1998c). Integrity testing in organizations. In R. W. Griffin, A. O'Leary-Kelly, & J. M. Collins (Eds.), *Dysfunctional behavior in organizations: Vol. 2. Nonviolent behaviors in organizations* (pp. 243–276). Greenwich, CT: JAI Press.

Ones, D. S., & Viswesvaran, C. (1999a). *Personality-based customer service scales used in personnel selection: Predictive and construct validity evidence*. Manuscript submitted for publication.

Ones, D. S., & Viswesvaran, C. (1999b). Relative importance of the Big Five dimensions of personality for expatriate selection. *Human Performance, 12*, 275–294.

Ones, D. S., & Viswesvaran, C. (2000a). *Personality-based drug and alcohol scales used in personnel screening: Predictive and construct validity evidence*. Manuscript submitted for publication.

Ones, D. S., & Viswesvaran, C. (2000b). *Personality-based stress tolerance scales used in work settings: Predictive and construct validity evidence*. Unpublished manuscript.

Ones, D. S., Viswesvaran, C., & Reiss, A. D. (1996). Role of social desirability in personality testing for personnel selection: The red herring. *Journal of Applied Psychology, 81*, 660–679.

Ones, D. S., & Viswesvaran, C. (in press). Integrity tests and other criterion-focused occupational personality scales (COPS) used in personnel selection. *International Journal of Selection and Assessment.*

Ones, D. S., Viswesvaran, C., & Schmidt, F. L. (1993). Comprehensive meta-analysis of integrity test validities: Findings and implications for personnel selection and theories of job performance [Monograph]. *Journal of Applied Psychology, 78,* 679–703.

Ones, D. S., Viswesvaran, C., Schmidt, F. L., & Reiss, A. D. (1994, August). The validity of honesty and violence scales of integrity tests in predicting violence at work. In S. Freedman (Chair), *Understanding violence at work.* Symposium conducted at the annual meeting of the Academy of Management, Dallas, TX.

Paajanen, G. (1985). *PDI Employment Inventory.* Minneapolis, MN: Personnel Decisions International.

Paajanen, G. E.. Hansen, T. L., & McLellan, R. A. (1993). *PDI employment inventory and PDI customer service inventory manual.* Minneapolis, MN: Personnel Decisions International.

Reid Psychological Systems. (1951). *Reid report.* Chicago: Author.

Robertson, I. T., & Kinder, A. (1993). Personality and job competencies: The criterion-related validity of some personality variables. *Journal of Occupational and Organizational Psychology, 66,* 225–244.

Sackett, P. R., Burris, L. R., & Callahan, C. (1989). Integrity testing for personnel selection: An update. *Personnel Psychology, 42,* 491–529.

Sackett, P. R., & Harris, M. M. (1984). Honesty testing for personnel selection: A review and critique. *Personnel Psychology, 37,* 221–246.

Salgado, J. F. (1997). The Five Factor Model of personality and job performance in the European community. *Journal of Applied Psychology, 82,* 30–43.

Sanchez, J. I., & Fraser, S. L. (1993). *Development and validation of the corporate social style inventory: A measure of customer service skills* (Tech. Rep. No. 93-108). Cambridge, MA: Marketing Science Institute.

Saxe, R., & Weitz, B. (1982). The SOCO scale measure of the customer orientation of salespeople. *Journal of Marketing Research, 19,* 343–351.

Schmidt, F. L., & Hunter, J. E. (1977). Development of a general solution to the problem of validity generalization. *Journal of Applied Psychology, 62,* 529–540.

Schmidt, F. L., & Hunter, J. E. (1983). Individual differences in productivity: An empirical test of estimates derived from studies of selection procedure utility. *Journal of Applied Psychology, 68,* 407–414.

Schmidt, F. L., & Hunter, J. E. (1992). Development of a causal model of processes determining job performance. *Current Directions in Psychological Science, 1,* 89–92.

Schmidt, F. L., & Hunter, J. E. (1998). The validity and utility of selection methods in personnel psychology: Practical and theoretical implications of 85 years of research findings. *Psychological Bulletin, 124,* 262–274.

Schmidt, F. L., Ones, D. S., & Hunter, J. E. (1992). Personnel selection. *Annual Review of Psychology, 43,* 627–670.

Schneider, B., Chung, B., & Yusko, K. P. (1993). Service climate for service quality. *Current Directions in Psychological Science, 2,* 197–200.

Schneider, B., & Schmitt, N. (1986). *Staffing organizations.* New York: Scott, Foresman.

Schneider, B., Wheeler, J. K., & Cox, J. F. (1992). A passion for service: Using content analysis to explicate service climate themes. *Journal of Applied Psychology, 77,* 705–716.

Sheridan, J. R., & Winkler, H. (1989). An evaluation of drug testing in the workplace. In S. W. Gust & J. M. Walsh (Eds.), *Drugs in the workplace: Research and evaluation data* (pp. 195–216; NIDA Research Monograph No. 91). Rockville, MD: National Institute on Drug Abuse.

Skinner, B. F. (1971). *Beyond freedom and dignity.* New York: Knopf.

Tompkins, N. C. (1992, November). Employee satisfaction leads to customer service. *HR Magazine, 37,* 93–95.

Watson, J. B. (1929). *Psychology from the standpoint of a behaviorist* (3rd ed.). Philadelphia: Lippincott.

Weaver, J. J. (1994, February). Want customer satisfaction? Satisfy your employees first. *HR Magazine, 39,* 110–112.

Wilkerson, M. (1985). *Orion survey.* Tulsa, OK: Loss Prevention Analysts, Ltd.

Wonderlic & Associates, Inc. (1983). *Wonderlic Personnel Test manual.* Northfield, IL: Author.

Zeithaml, V. A., Parasuraman, A., & Berry, L. L. (1990). *Delivering service quality.* New York: Free Press.

Zwerling, C. J., & Orav, E. J. (1990). The efficacy of pre-employment drug screening for marijuana and cocaine in predicting employment outcome. *Journal of the American Medical Association, 264,* 2639–2643.

CHAPTER 5

A Rose by Any Other Name

Are Self-Esteem, Generalized Self-Efficacy, Neuroticism, and Locus of Control Indicators of a Common Construct?

Timothy A. Judge
Joyce E. Bono

'Tis but thy name that is my enemy. . . .
What's in a name? That which we call a rose
By any other name would smell as sweet.
William Shakespeare, *Romeo and Juliet* (act 2, scene 2)

Self-esteem. Neuroticism. Locus of control. These are some of the most widely investigated traits in the history of personality psychology. In fact, a search of the PsycINFO database (1967–1999) identified (a) 17,665 articles referring to self-esteem, (b) 15,193 articles referencing neuroticism (or the alternate terms *emotional adjustment* or *emotional stability*), and (c) 12,030 articles citing locus of control. In comparing this level of interest to that for other frequently studied traits (e.g., need for achievement, self-monitoring, extraversion), we could find none that had been studied as extensively as these three. Because the individual-differences tradition of industrial/organizational (I/O) psychology draws heavily from personality psychology, these traits are among those most commonly investigated in I/O psychology as well. Thus, although there is much current interest in the Big Five structure of personality, given the number of past studies of these traits, self-esteem, neuroticism, and locus of control might well be labeled the "Big Three" of earlier personality and I/O psychology research.

Despite the prominence of and potential commonality among these three

We thank Amir Erez, Robert Hogan, Ed Locke, Brent Roberts, Frank Schmidt, and David Watson for their comments on an earlier version of this chapter.

traits, it is surprising that only recently have the relationships among them been considered. Although many investigations have included pairs of these traits in the same study, they almost always have considered them as distinct traits. Furthermore, very few studies have included self-esteem, neuroticism, and locus of control in the same study, and, outside of our own work, we are aware of no research that has explicitly considered the relationships among self-esteem, neuroticism, and locus of control.[1] Curiously, the quest of the past decade to identify broad personality constructs has ignored some of the most commonly studied traits. For example, although neuroticism has been considered a broad trait by even those researchers who do not endorse the five-factor model (FFM; Eysenck, 1990b), self-esteem, locus of control, and a closely related trait— generalized self-efficacy—continue to be studied as individual, isolated traits. However, as the quotation at the beginning of this chapter suggests, it is possible that these traits are merely different labels for the same thing.

The general purpose of this chapter is to describe a broad personality construct—core self-evaluations—that would explain empirical associations that may exist among self-esteem, generalized self-efficacy, neuroticism, and locus of control. We also consider similarities between core self-evaluations and neuroticism or emotional adjustment. Additionally, we address the question of whether the core self-evaluations trait matters. In answering this question, we review evidence relating core self-evaluations traits to outcomes, including the two perhaps most central to I/O psychology: job satisfaction and job performance. Finally, we present a research agenda that would further test the validity of the core self-evaluations construct and its implications for applied psychology.

Core Self-Evaluations Theory

In seeking to better understand the personological basis of job satisfaction, Judge, Locke, and Durham (1997) developed a theory of traits they termed core evaluations. According to this theory, *core evaluations* are basic conclusions, or bottom-line evaluations, held by individuals. Although Judge et al. argued that core evaluations could be directed toward others, their theory focused on core evaluations of the self. According to Judge et al., the core self-evaluations trait is a broad one that encompasses other, more specific, traits. To determine which

---

[1]According to our search of the literature, only 26 studies (0.09%) included *self-esteem, generalized self-efficacy, neuroticism,* or *locus of control* in their keyword listings. With the exception of our research (e.g., Judge, Erez, & Bono, 1998; Judge, Locke, & Durham, 1997; Judge, Locke, Durham, & Kluger, 1998), none of these 26 articles explicitly sought to determine whether these three traits measure distinct constructs or are manifested in a higher order construct.

traits would meet their definition of core self-evaluations, Judge et al. proposed three attributes of dispositional traits that would determine the degree to which they were indicative of core self-evaluations: (a) evaluation focus (i.e., the degree to which traits involve evaluations vs. descriptions); (b) fundamentality (Cattellian personality theory [Cattell, 1965] distinguishes between source traits and surface traits. Source traits are traits that are more basic than others and that underlie surface traits.); and (c) breadth or scope (Allport, 1961, considered the issue of scope in his distinction between cardinal and secondary traits. Cardinal traits are broader in scope than secondary traits, and they are more likely to relate to other traits, attitudes, and behaviors than are secondary or surface traits). In applying these criteria to the personality literature, Judge et al. initially identified three traits that met the definition for core self-evaluations: (a) self-esteem, (b) generalized self-efficacy, and (c) neuroticism.

Self-Esteem

Harter (1990) defined *self-esteem* as the overall value that one places on oneself as a person. If *self-concept* refers to the inferences individuals make about themselves (Baumeister, 1997), then self-esteem can be argued to be the single most global evaluation of self-concept. Although we will argue that self-esteem itself may be subsumed by an even broader construct, Greenwald, Bellezza, and Banaji (1988) considered self-esteem to be the single most important indicator of positive self-concept, an interchangeable term for positive core self-evaluations (Judge, Erez, & Bono, 1998). Of all possible traits, self-esteem appears to be the broadest and most fundamental core self-evaluation (Judge et al., 1997). Self-esteem is a somewhat curious trait in that it often is considered to be an outcome of situational influences, such as personal success (Rosenberg, Schooler, & Schoenbach, 1989). Self-esteem may be more susceptible than other traits to situational influences. From a measurement standpoint, it may be that self-esteem is more susceptible to transient error in that the measurement of trait self-esteem is more subject to temporal fluctuations. This is confirmed by evidence suggesting that although self-esteem is relatively stable, it is somewhat less stable than other traits.[2] Although self-esteem may be less stable than other traits, it has been demonstrated to be relatively stable over time (Costa & McCrae, 1994) and, like the Big Five personality traits, an ap-

---

[2]Conley (1984) reported on the relative stability of measures of personality and *self-opinion* (he classified measures of self-esteem as measures of self-opinion). We used Conley's data to predict the stability of self-esteem and neuroticism. Controlling for the time interval separating the measurements, and correcting the measures for unreliability (internal consistency), we predicted a test–retest reliability of .59 for self-esteem and .73 for neuroticism over a 10-year period.

preciable amount of the variance in self-esteem appears to be due to heritability (Roy, Neale, & Kendler, 1995). Thus, whereas there is considerable evidence attesting to the traitlike properties of self-esteem, it is somewhat more variable than neuroticism.

Generalized Self-Efficacy

Self-efficacy has been defined as a judgment of how well one can perform behaviors necessary to deal with prospective situations (Bandura, 1982, p. 122). It reflects self-confidence. Although Bandura (1982) considered self-efficacy to be a situation-specific phenomenon, other researchers have distinguished task-specific self-efficacy from generalized self-efficacy (Chen & Gully, 1997; Gist, 1987; Gist & Mitchell, 1992). *Generalized self-efficacy* represents a judgment of how well one can perform across a variety of situations. As noted by Locke, McClear, and Knight (1996), generalized self-efficacy is related to self-esteem because both are aspects of self-appraisal that relate to one's success or failure as a person. However, as Locke et al. noted, they are different in that self-efficacy does not have the self-worth component that self-esteem does. For example, an individual could have high generalized self-efficacy in that he or she may deem himself or herself capable in most situations yet have low self-esteem because he or she believes that what he or she has mastered has no fundamental value.

Neuroticism

Neuroticism, which is also known by terms that denote its converse (i.e., *emotional adjustment* or *emotional stability*), is one of the Big Five personality traits. Neuroticism is the most pervasive trait across personality measures; it is prominent in nearly every personality theory and inventory. Neuroticism manifests itself in at least two tendencies—one dealing with anxiety (e.g., emotional stability and proneness to stress) and the other addressing one's well-being (e.g., personal insecurity and depression). Thus, neuroticism refers generally to a lack of positive psychological adjustment and emotional stability. Individuals who score high in neuroticism are more likely to experience a variety of problems, including negative moods (e.g., anxiety, fear, depression, irritability) and physical symptoms than are individuals who score low in neuroticism. Evidence also has indicated that neurotic individuals are more likely to be adversely affected by negative life events and to have bad moods linger (Suls, Green, & Hillis, 1998).

Locus of Control

Although Judge et al. (1997) included only self-esteem, generalized self-efficacy, and neuroticism in their original theory, they did discuss other traits that subsequently have been studied in the context of core self-evaluations (e.g., locus of control). *Locus of control* refers to individuals' beliefs about the causes of events in their lives. When individuals believe that events in their lives are the result of luck or fate or are under the control of powerful others, they have an *external* locus of control (Rotter, 1966). Conversely, individuals who see events as being contingent on their own behavior have an *internal* locus of control. We believe locus of control is a core self-evaluations trait because it generally meets the criteria set forth by Judge et al. Although locus of control may be less clearly self-oriented than the other traits included in Judge et al.'s model, many items in Rotter's and other measures have a self-oriented focus (e.g., "My life is determined by my own actions"; Levenson, 1981). Furthermore, locus of control bears a strong resemblance to the other traits in Judge et al.'s model, most notably generalized self-efficacy. Individuals who believe themselves generally incapable (low generalized self-efficacy) are likely to believe they are not in control of their lives (external locus of control). Indeed, one popular measure of locus of control, Levenson's (1981) IPI scale, shares an identical item ("When I make plans, I am certain to make them work") with a common measure of generalized self-efficacy, Paulhus's (1983) personal efficacy scale.

Other Traits

In addition to locus of control, Judge et al. (1997) discussed several other traits that might be indicators of the core self-evaluations construct. First, dispositional optimism, or the tendency to expect events to turn out positively and the expectation that desired outcomes will occur, has been shown to affect (a) coping with adversity, (b) development of cognitive strategies to deal with goal-discrepant outcomes, (c) positive reinterpretation of negative events, and (d) the seeking of social support to deal with problems (Chang, 1998; Scheier, Weintraub, & Carver, 1986). Dispositional optimism may be an indicator of a core trait, for several reasons:

- It may not be distinct from other dispositional measures, such as negative affectivity (NA), that are indicators of core self-evaluations (T. W. Smith, Pope, Rhodewalt, & Poulton, 1989). Scheier, Carver, and Bridges (1994) sought to demonstrate that their measure of dispositional optimism was distinct from measures of self-esteem, neuroticism, and self-mastery (which seems closely related to generalized self-efficacy). However, the multiple correlation, corrected for unreliability, between measures of these three traits and Scheier et al.'s measure of dispositional optimism was .74. Furthermore, although Scheier et al. purported to demonstrate that dispositional optimism displays a differential pattern of correlations with 18 outcomes (e.g., coping, depression, drug use), the vector of correlations between dispositional optimism and the 18 outcomes correlates .93 with the vector of correlations involving self-mastery, .75 with the vector involving self-esteem, and −.76 with the vector involving neuroticism. These results suggest that dispositional optimism may not be distinct from the other core self-evaluations traits.

- Even if it is distinct from the other traits, dispositional optimism is likely a result of positive self-evaluations. It is hard to imagine someone who believes in himself or herself and his or her abilities (self-esteem and generalized self-efficacy) and who believes he or she is in control of his or her life (internal locus of control) being consistently pessimistic about the future.

Second, in the past 20 years, positive affectivity (PA) and negative affectivity (NA) have been widely studied in both personality psychology and applied psychology. *Positive affectivity* has been defined as the tendency to experience positive emotional states, whereas *negative affectivity* has been described as the tendency to experience negative ones. NA is close in meaning to neuroticism (Costa & McCrae, 1980); PA is related to extraversion (Watson, Clark, & Tellegen, 1988). The independence of PA and NA has been the subject of much debate in the personality psychology literature. Some researchers (e.g., Watson & Clark, 1984; Watson & Tellegen, 1985) have supported the independence view, whereas others (e.g., Diener, Larsen, Levine, & Emmons, 1985; Green, Goldman, & Salovey, 1993; Russell & Carroll, 1999a) have questioned it. The topic continues to be debated (Russell & Carroll, 1999b; Watson & Tellegen, 1999). We have meta-analytic evidence that suggests that measures of NA correlate as highly with neuroticism as do measures of neuroticism with each other. Thus, it might be argued that measures of NA are simply measures of neuroticism and therefore could be included in the concept of core self-evaluations. PA is somewhat harder to deal with. Watson and Clark (1997) argued that PA represents a central aspect of extraversion. However, other evidence has suggested that PA loads on the same concept as core self-evaluations (Judge, Thoresen, Pucik, & Welbourne, 1999). At this time, we are not certain how to deal with PA. It may be a measure of core self-evaluations, of extraversion, or of both.

Nature of the Core Self-Evaluations Construct

Higher order psychological constructs such as core self-evaluations can be considered to be either *latent* constructs, which are unobservable constructs that cause their dimensions (indicators) to be positively related, or *aggregate* constructs, which are formed from or composed of their dimensions. Latent constructs exist at a deeper level than their indicators and, in fact, causally influence their indicators or dimensions (Bollen & Lennox, 1991). Conversely, aggregate or composite constructs can be formed by an algebraic combination of their dimensions. An aggregate construct therefore is caused by its dimensions or facets (Bollen & Lennox, 1991).

Is core self-evaluations a latent or aggregate construct? Judge and his colleagues' conceptualization and treatment of the core self-evaluations construct has been inconsistent. Judge, Locke, Durham, and Kluger's (1998) writing on the subject appears to argue that core self-evaluations is a latent construct. For example, they stated, "A positive self-concept is not simply an accumulation of favorable self-regard in many spheres of life. Rather, favorable self-regard in these spheres is a result of a global self-concept" (p. 19). This suggests that, consistent with a latent model, the latent construct causes the individual core self-evaluations traits. However, in other writings, Judge and his colleagues have used language more in keeping with an aggregate model, that is, arguing that the core self-evaluation traits "comprise a common factor" (Judge, Erez, et al., 1998, p. 167). Data-analytic procedures also have been inconsistent. Judge, Locke, et al. (1998) used confirmatory factor analysis where the four core traits were indicators of a latent construct, which is the way data should be treated when one is analyzing a latent construct (Bollen & Lennox, 1991). Conversely, Judge, Erez, et al. (1998) used principal-components analysis to demonstrate the existence of a common factor. Because principal-components analysis seeks to identify a factor that is a linear combination of its components, this approach is more in line with an aggregate model.

Despite these inconsistencies, both the latent and aggregate models recognize a broad, multidimensional core self-evaluations construct. Furthermore, research has provided evidence supporting the broader construct (Judge, Erez, et al., 1998; Judge, Locke, et al., 1998). Judge, Erez, et al. (1998) argued,

> Core self-evaluations are fundamental premises that individuals hold about themselves and their functioning in the world. In contrast to some beliefs about self-concept, Judge et al. (1997) took a "top-down" focus in arguing that core evaluations are all encompassing and that situation-specific appraisals depend on these core evaluations. Thus, because they are fundamental, core evaluations are implicated in all lesser or more specific evaluations and influence the nature of those evaluations. Implicit in Judge et al.'s argument is that a positive self-concept is not simply an accumulation of favorable self-regard in many spheres of life. Rather, favorable self-regard in these spheres *is a result of* a global positive self-concept. Because this perspective holds that positive self-regard in specific situations is purely epiphenominal, as a trait it only makes sense to consider self-concept at a global level. (pp. 168–169)

Clearly, despite some inconsistencies in their treatment of the construct, the position Judge and his colleagues have taken is that core self-evaluations is a latent multidimensional construct. We agree with this viewpoint. The implications of this perspective are that self-esteem, generalized self-efficacy, neuroticism, and locus of control are measures (rather than components or causes) of the core self-evaluations construct, and it is the latent core construct that causes the individual traits to be intercorrelated.

However, although we believe that core self-evaluations is a latent construct, questions remain about the nature of the construct. In short, we are not certain of its exact nature. Is it a new higher order trait or part of a broader conceptualization of an existing trait?

Is Core Self-Evaluations Another Name for Neuroticism in the Five-Factor Model?

The Five-Factor Model of Personality

Although personality psychologists have studied hundreds of traits over the years, it has been in the past 15 years that there has been considerable agreement on the FFM as an appropriate taxonomy for describing the structure of personality. Although acceptance of the FFM is not universal (see Block, 1995, for a critique), researchers have, across diverse populations and measures, consistently replicated five broad factors. Current measures of the FFM emerged from two unique research traditions. In the lexical tradition, the five factors emerged from a list of descriptive adjectives found in common language (e.g., Goldberg's, 1992, markers). This is in contrast to the questionnaire tradition (Costa & McCrae, 1992a), in which three of the five factors (extraversion, neuroticism, and openness to experience) emerged from existing personality surveys designed to measure various aspects of personality theory (e.g., Jungian functions or Murray's needs), clinical questionnaires (e.g., the Minnesota Multiphasic Personality Inventory), and *Diagnostic and Statistical Manual of Mental Disorders* (3rd edition, revised; American Psychiatric Association, 1987) personality disorders. Thus, although there is considerable overlap in the content domains of each of the five factors, there are some differences. Specifically, because only descriptive adjectives were retained in the original factor analyses, five-factor measures from the lexical tradition do not contain an evaluative component. Five-factor measures based on the questionnaire tradition are unique in that they included "clinical" measures. Although the authors of the NEO Personality Inventory (Costa & McCrae, 1992a), the most commonly used measure of the Big Five in the questionnaire tradition, noted that neuroticism is not a measure of psychopathology, a high score on this trait does increase the likelihood of a clinical diagnosis (Zonderman, Herbst, Schmidt, Costa, & McCrae, 1993). Another noteworthy difference between these two traditions is the order in which the factors emerge. For example, in the questionnaire tradition, neuroticism emerges first (i.e., it is the largest factor), whereas in measures based on the lexical tradition, neuroticism is the fourth factor to emerge, and it represents a substantially smaller portion of the variation in personality captured by the FFM.

Neuroticism

Alternatively called *emotional stability*, *emotional adjustment*, or *negative affectivity*, neuroticism has been the most studied of all of the Big Five traits. According to Costa and McCrae (1992a), neuroticism includes the tendency to experience negative emotions such as fear, anger, guilt, and sadness. Individuals who are high in neuroticism also are less able to cope with life events and to control their impulses. In Costa and McCrae's model, six facets of neuroticism are defined: (a) anxiety, (b) angry hostility, (c) depression, (d) self-consciousness, (e) impulsiveness, and (f) vulnerability. At the opposite end of the neuroticism continuum are individuals who tend to be calm, even tempered, and relaxed. Considerable similarity can be seen between these descriptions of neuroticism and Goldberg's (1992) Factor IV. Adjective pairs used to describe neuroticism include nervous–at ease, angry–calm, tense–relaxed, moody–steady, emotional–unemotional, and insecure–secure. Similarly, although with a focus on the positive pole, Tupes and Christal (1961) defined the characteristics of emotional stability as (a) not neurotic, (b) placid, (c) poised, (d) not hypochondriacal, (e) calm, (f) emotionally stable, and (g) self-sufficient. Taking a slightly different approach, Watson and Clark (1984) labeled the factor NA, which they asserted primarily reflects variations among individuals in negative emotionality and self-esteem. Their model contrasts individuals who are distressed and upset and who hold a negative self-view (high NA) with those who are content, secure, and satisfied with themselves (low NA).

Regardless of the diverse labels applied to the factor, there is empirical evidence of strong relationships among the various conceptualizations. According to McCrae and Costa (1985), Norman's (1963) adjective markers for neuroticism correlated .63 with self-reports on the NEO Neuroticism subscales. Watson and Clark (1992) found an average correlation of .59 between their measure of NA (Negative Affect Schedule) and NEO Neuroticism. These correlations are stronger than the average correlation of .47 between various measures of conscientiousness found by Ones (1993). Clearly, there is considerable overlap among these traits. Descriptions of individuals high in neuroticism (or low in emotional stability) are consistent across the various labels: Individuals at the negative end of each of these traits tend to (a) be anxious, (b) experience a wide variety of negative emotions, (c) have a tendency to be depressed, and (d) have a poor self-concept. Despite some convergence between various conceptualizations, it is our contention that, used alone, each measure is a deficient or partial indicator of the broad underlying personality trait. Although it is likely that each measure contains specific factor variance not indicative of the broad factor of Neuroticism, we suggest that current conceptualizations of the underlying trait are too narrow, thus failing to capture the complete content domain of this one of the Big Five factors. That is, we posit that neuroticism, emotional stability, and NA each capture a slightly different piece of the personality space associated with the broader factor. As we will argue later in this chapter, it is imperative that this construct be measured broadly if the goal is to discover its true validity in influencing a wide array of outcomes in applied psychology.

Like the other factors of the FFM, Neuroticism has been demonstrated to be stable over time. For example, Costa and McCrae (1992b) found a stability coefficient for Emotional Stability of .70 over a 24-year period in an adult sample. In addition, Bouchard (1997) presented evidence of a genetic basis for this factor, with heritability coefficients ranging from .40 to .51 in a number of twin samples.

Outcomes of Neuroticism

Hundreds of studies have examined correlates of neuroticism. However, some of these studies are in the domains of pathology or psychopathology. Our focus is primarily on the nonclinical implications of neuroticism. Specifically, we are concerned with the relationships among neuroticism and subjective well-being (e.g., happiness, coping, and life satisfaction) and work-related outcomes (e.g., job satisfaction and job performance).

Subjective Well-Being

There is considerable evidence that there is a relationship between neuroticism and happiness, or subjective well-being. A negative relationship between neuroticism and life satisfaction also has been documented ($r = -.37$ when measures of neuroticism and life satisfaction were assessed at the same time; $r = -.29$ when measures were collected 2 years apart; McCrae & Costa, 1991). In a 1998 meta-analysis, DeNeve and Cooper identified neuroticism as one of the central traits associated with a "happy personality." Combining various measures of neuroticism, they found average weighted correlations of $-.24$ with life satisfaction and $-.25$ with happiness. (It should be noted, however, that because they have not been corrected for measurement error, as should be done in a meta-analysis, these correlations are downwardly biased.) DeNeve and Cooper concluded, "Being neurotic predisposes a person to experience less subjective well-being, regardless of whether you are examining reports of one's quality of life experiences, negative short-term emotions, or long-term positive emotions" (p. 220). There are several reasons why those high in neuroticism might be less satisfied with life than individuals who are low in neuroticism. Individuals high in neuroticism (a) are prone to negative appraisals of their environment (Watson

& Hubbard, 1996), (b) are predisposed to actually experiencing negative life events (Magnus, Diener, Fujita, & Pavot, 1993), and (c) use ineffective coping strategies when responding to problems and stress (McCrae & Costa, 1986; Watson & Hubbard, 1996).

Job Satisfaction and Job Performance

The findings regarding the relationship between neuroticism and job performance have been contradictory. In the past decade, several meta-analyses have examined this issue. The first two of these analyses were published nearly concurrently, but they reported substantially different results. Barrick and Mount (1991) found that the relationship between emotional stability and job performance was not significantly different from zero (ρ = .08) across criterion measures. Using different inclusion criteria (i.e., only confirmatory studies were included) but flawed analytical procedures, Tett, Jackson, and Rothstein (1991) found a corrected mean correlation of −.22 between neuroticism and job performance. A third meta-analysis, using a European Community sample, was conducted more recently. Salgado (1997) estimated a true validity of .19 for Emotional Stability. As a part of a larger study, Judge and Bono (1999) conducted yet another meta-analysis of neuroticism and job performance, using only direct measures of neuroticism (i.e., inventories specifically developed for that purpose). The results of this study are consistent with two of the three earlier analyses (ρ = .19). Although some explanation of the conflicting findings for the first two studies have been offered (Ones, Mount, Barrick, & Hunter, 1994), the nature of the relationship of neuroticism to job performance remains uncertain.

The relationship between neuroticism and job satisfaction has been examined as well, providing evidence that individuals high in neuroticism, who tend to view most events in their lives negatively, also tend to be less satisfied with their jobs. Several studies have shown that direct measures of neuroticism are negatively related to job satisfaction (Furnham & Zacherl, 1986; C. A. Smith, Organ, & Near, 1983; Tokar & Subich, 1997). Watson and Slack (1993) found inconsistent relationships between negative emotionality and job satisfaction. Although they identified only a weak relationship with overall job satisfaction (r = .09), they found moderate relationships at the facet level (e.g., r = −.32 with the work itself). Thoresen and Judge (1997) conducted a meta-analysis of 41 studies that investigated the relationship between negative affectivity and job satisfaction. They estimated the true-score relationship to be −.40. Judge, Locke, et al. (1998) performed a meta-analysis of results across three diverse samples and found a correlation of −.37 between direct measures of neuroticism and job satisfaction.

Core Self-Evaluations and Neuroticism— The Jangle Fallacy?

Because the two broad personality traits of core self-evaluations and neuroticism share common variance, it seems appropriate to explore more fully the relationship between them. In his critique of the FFM, Block (1995) cited the "jangle fallacy," referring to the tendency of psychologists to discover new traits without considering similar personality constructs already in existence. Thus, we will examine the construct validity of these two broad personality factors. According to Schwab (1980), construct validity involves both (a) conceptual issues such as definition and theoretical relationships with other constructs and (b) empirical issues such as convergent validity and location of the constructs of interest within their nomological networks (i.e., relationships with other variables). However, a caveat is in order regarding the following discussion. The FFM is a taxonomy of personality traits, not a theory of personality. For this reason, there is little theory to guide the processes of comparing and contrasting the various conceptualizations of neuroticism with other constructs (e.g., core self-evaluations). Therefore, we are limited to the use of definitions and implicit theories as the foundation for our discussion of the applicable conceptual issues.

As for the conceptual relationship between core self-evaluations and neuroticism, there are interesting similarities and differences. Judge et al. (1997) defined core self-evaluations primarily by its trait indicators, one of which is neuroticism. Thus, because neuroticism is subsumed within the core self-evaluations construct, it cannot be considered to be conceptually distinct. The question, then, is whether core self-evaluations is really broader than neuroticism. Does the core construct occupy personality space beyond that of neuroticism? In other words, are the other trait indicators of core self-evaluations (i.e., self-esteem, generalized self-efficacy, and locus of control) conceptually different from the various conceptualizations of neuroticism?

In the case of self-esteem, the answer to this question is not clear. Although Eysenck's (1990a) original conceptualization of neuroticism explicitly included low self-esteem as one of the nine primary traits of the neurotic type, not all FFM conceptualizations of neuroticism have included self-esteem (e.g., Costa & McRae, 1992a). As noted earlier, in the lexical approach to the FFM, evaluative adjectives were excluded from the adjective list submitted to factor analysis. Thus, any conceptualization of neuroticism emerging from this tradition would be narrower than the core self-evaluations construct in that one of the three defining criteria for the core traits, evaluation focus, was removed from neuroticism. The reason self-esteem is not in evidence in the questionnaire approach is less clear. Costa and McCrae (1992a) do not refer to self-esteem in describing their version of neuroticism, nor is self-esteem one of the facets of neuroticism they identify. In contrast, Watson and Clark's (1984) conceptualization of neuroticism explicitly references self-esteem. In fact, they suggest that low self-esteem, along with negative emotionality, defines NA. Thus, some conceptualizations of neuroticism are broad enough to include self-esteem.

The relationships of generalized self-efficacy and locus of control with neuroticism are even less clear. In the case of generalized self-efficacy, there has been only limited research, as self-efficacy traditionally has been considered to be task specific (Bandura, 1986). Furthermore, both generalized self-efficacy and locus of control involve beliefs about one's capabilities. In the case of generalized self-efficacy, the assessment is whether one is capable of carrying out the actions necessary to succeed, whereas in the case of locus of control, the assessment is whether an individual believes he or she is capable of influencing outcomes. Although the focal point of these traits is somewhat different (i.e., beliefs about oneself vs. beliefs about one's environment), the question is whether neuroticism is a sufficiently broad construct to be the common source of these beliefs. On the one hand, the conceptualization of neuroticism is quite broad and appears to be broad enough to explain the associations among these traits. On the other hand, typical measures of neuroticism do not explicitly assess beliefs about one's capabilities or control over one's environment. For example, there are no items in the NEO 12-item neuroticism scale (Costa & McRae, 1992a), Goldberg's 20-item neuroticism scale (Goldberg, 1999), or Eysenck's 12-item neuroticism scale (Eysenck & Eysenck, 1968) that reference control or capability. Therefore, we suggest that although the core self-evaluations construct is broader than neuroticism as it has been assessed, the processes that cause self-esteem, generalized self-efficacy, and locus of control may be the same as (or closely related to) those that are responsible for neuroticism. Furthermore, if, as we suggest, the neuroticism domain has not been measured as broadly as it should be, there may be considerable overlap between the domains of neuroticism and core self-evaluations.

Intercorrelations Among the Traits and Underlying Factors

There is evidence of a substantial relationship among the trait indicators of core self-evaluations, neuroticism, and the latent core construct. Judge and Bono (1999) performed a meta-analysis of data from 18 studies with multiple measures of the core constructs. They found an average intertrait correlation of .64. More specifically, the correlations of neuroticism with self-esteem, general self-efficacy, and locus of control were −.66, −.59, and −.51, respectively. These correlations are similar to those identified for the various measures of neuroticism noted earlier. When directly examining the correlation between core self-evaluations and neuroticism, one might argue that because the core self-evaluations construct includes a direct measure of neuroticism, any correlation between the two is inflated. For this reason, we used data collected by Judge and Bono to examine this issue. Rather than create a core self-evaluations composite with all four traits, we developed a composite using only self-esteem, generalized self-efficacy, and locus of control. The correlation between this composite and neuroticism was .68, as compared with .81 when the neuroticism measure was included in the core self-evaluations composite. Thus, even when direct overlap in measures is removed, there is a substantial correlation between the two constructs. Moreover, Schwab (1980) suggested that a more rigorous method of assessing convergent validity is to test a model in which the relationships between constructs have been specified a priori. Judge, Locke, et al. (1998) used confirmatory factor analysis to conduct such a test. They estimated a model with all four traits (self-esteem, generalized self-efficacy, neuroticism, and locus of control) loading on a single factor. Factor loadings were strong and significant, with an average factor loading of .72. More germane to this discussion, however, is model fit. If core self-evaluations and neuroticism are distinct constructs, forcing them to load on a single factor would be expected to yield poor model fit. Thus, the strong fit indices found by Judge, Locke, et al. provide additional evidence for the convergence of the core self-evaluations construct and neuroticism.

In determining whether two measures are distinct, it is important to examine their relationships with related constructs. Both core self-evaluations and neuroticism have been examined in relation to life satisfaction, job satisfaction, and job performance. To explore this issue, we compared the results of meta-analyses of these three criteria with (a) core self-evaluations and (b) neuroticism. However, no meta-analyses had been conducted regarding core self-evaluations and life satisfaction. Therefore, we used a weighted mean correlation based on three samples from Judge, Locke, et al. (1998). Table 5.1 presents these relationships and the sources of the data. Although there are differences in the relationships between each of the personality constructs and each of the outcomes, there is a clear pattern of similarities. In each case, the relationship between core self-evaluations and the outcome is stronger than the relationship between neuroticism and the outcome (although for life satisfaction, this difference is quite small). This finding is consistent with our hypothesis that core self-evaluations represents a broader measure of the underlying construct and, as such, better captures the relationship between the broad personality factor and theoretically related outcomes such as job satisfaction and job performance. Figure 5.1 presents a graphic comparison of these relationships.

In attempting to assess the degree to which core self-evaluations and neuroticism may represent the same construct, we have identified three key issues. First, there are conceptual reasons to believe that these two constructs may be alternative representations of the same higher order construct. Second, core self-evaluations and neuroticism have been proven empirically to be highly related (Judge, Erez, et al., 1998). We have presented considerable evidence for the

TABLE 5.1

Relationships of Neuroticism and Core Self-Evaluations With Life Satisfaction, Job Satisfaction, and Job Performance

| CONSTRUCT | CORE SELF-EVALUATIONS | | NEUROTICISM | |
	r	STUDY	r	STUDY
Life satisfaction	.25	Judge, Locke, Durham, & Kluger, 1998	.24	DeNeve & Cooper, 1998
Job satisfaction	.37	Judge & Bono, 1999	.24	Judge & Bono, 1999
Job performance	.27	Judge & Bono, 1999	.19	Judge & Bono, 1999

Note. To allow for comparison with the core self-evaluations measures, all neuroticism relationships represent the positive (i.e., emotional stability) pole of the factor. Results from the Judge and Bono (1999) meta-analysis (neuroticism and job performance) are presented here because it is the only meta-analysis that used solely direct measures of neuroticism. Correlations for life satisfaction are weighted means across studies. Correlations for job satisfaction and performance are estimated true-score correlations.

convergent validity of these two factors. Third, the two factors exhibit a similar pattern of relationships with theoretically relevant outcomes. Thus, there is strong evidence suggesting that core self-evaluations and neuroticism may represent the same higher order personality construct.

FIGURE 5.1

Relationship of core self-evaluations and neuroticism with life satisfaction, job satisfaction, and job performance. (To allow for comparison with the core self-evaluations measures, all neuroticism relationships represent the positive, that is, emotional stability, pole of the factor.)

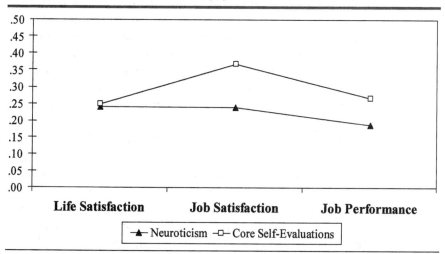

Also worth noting is a recently proposed construct that is closely related. Furr and Funder (1998) proposed a broad construct they termed *personal negativity* (PN). According to Furr and Funder, PN is a composite variable formed from measures of depression, happiness, life satisfaction, and self-esteem. They found that PN was associated with maladaptive social interactions, negative behavioral responses by others, negative social reputation, and poor self-image. Although we believe Furr and Funder's results are meaningful, we question the wisdom of distinguishing this construct from neuroticism in the same way we question the wisdom of distinguishing the construct of core self-evaluations from neuroticism. We do not believe that Furr and Funder have discovered a new personality construct. Rather, we believe they have shown—as we have —that when the construct of neuroticism is measured broadly, with broad, diverse measures, it predicts central outcomes in work and in life. Why do we question whether PN is distinct from neuroticism? Furr and Funder reported an average correlation of .44 between PN and Costa and McCrae's (1992a) six facets of neuroticism. This correlation is quite similar to the .46 average intercorrelation among the six NEO neuroticism facets identified in the *NEO User's Manual* (Costa & McCrae, 1992a). Thus, PN correlates with the facets of neuroticism about the same as those facets do among themselves. We prefer our construct of core self-evaluations to Furr and Funder's PN because, with the inclusion of measures of happiness and life satisfaction in their construct, it is more likely to be contaminated by situational elements and experiences.

Contributions and Implications

Because the construct of core self-evaluations is a new area of inquiry, much remains to be known about it. However, much has been learned, and many contributions have been made as a result of research regarding this construct.

A primary contribution of this research is that, for the first time, the relationships among the core traits of personality have been studied. Of the tens of thousands of studies that have investigated self-esteem, generalized self-efficacy, neuroticism, and locus of control, we are aware of only a relative few that have even questioned the discriminant validity of these traits (e.g., Hunter, Gerbing, & Boster, 1982). Furthermore, we are aware of no study that has directly investigated the possibility that the three most widely studied traits— self-esteem, neuroticism, and locus of control—represent a higher order construct. Given that our research suggests that these traits are indistinct measures of the same core trait, past research may have been mistaken in assuming that they are discrete traits. Future researchers should recognize that what we think of as separate measures of self-esteem, generalized self-efficacy, and locus of control may instead be alternative ways of measuring core self-evaluations. The main implication of this conclusion is that researchers should not measure these traits without acknowledging their common cause and considering the possibility that they are measures of core self-evaluations.

Another contribution of this line of research is that when emotional stability is measured broadly, it is predictive of the two central criterion variables of I/O psychology: job satisfaction and job performance. The search for dispositional correlates of job satisfaction is nearly as old as the study of job satisfaction itself. Studies by Weitz (1952) and P. C. Smith (1955) were landmarks, but the contributions of these studies remained dormant until the mid-1980s, when research by Brief, Staw, and their associates rekindled interest in the dispositional source of job attitudes (Brief, Burke, George, Robinson, & Webster, 1988; Brief, Butcher, & Roberson, 1995; Staw, Bell, & Clausen, 1986; Staw & Ross, 1985). Other research on the dispositional basis of job satisfaction has been published (e.g., Judge & Hulin, 1993), but consensus in the literature has been lacking regarding what dispositional traits best predict job satisfaction. Research on core self-evaluations has shown the construct to be the best dispositional predictor of job satisfaction.[3] Judge, Locke, et al. (1998) estimated that the average total effect of core self-evaluations on job satisfaction was .48 across three independent samples (.37 when the sources of data were independent), and Judge and Bono's (1999) meta-analysis estimated the true-score correlation to be .37. Why is core self-evaluations so important to job satisfaction? Research has shown that an important mechanism by which core self-evaluations influences job satisfaction is the intrinsic nature of the job (Judge, Locke, et al., 1998). In fact, we recently completed a study that showed that both objective and subjective measures of intrinsic job characteristics were related to core self-evaluations (Judge, Bono, & Locke, 2000). Thus, not only do individuals with a positive self-concept see more challenge in their jobs, but they also actually attain more complex jobs.

The other contribution of this line of research is that core self-evaluations is related to job performance. Our best estimate of the relationship between the broad trait of core self-evaluations and job performance is .27 (Judge & Bono, 1999). Indeed, emotional adjustment could be argued to be, along with conscientiousness, the primary dispositional predictor of job performance. The cor-

---

[3]Judge, Locke, et al.'s (1998) results from a usefulness analysis indicated that PA and NA explained somewhat more variance in job satisfaction than did core self-evaluations. However, placing these concepts in competition with each other would be inappropriate if PA and NA assess the same construct as core self-evaluations. Indeed, Judge, Locke, et al. found that PA and NA loaded on the same construct as the core traits. They noted, "Thus, our results suggest that rather than viewing affective disposition as a competing trait in predicting job and life satisfaction, it may actually be one of the facets of a broader aspect of the self-concept" (p. 31). This is an important area for future research.

relation of .27, which was based on 105 studies, is substantially higher than that found in past research regarding neuroticism. Why the difference? First, our estimates were corrected for construct validity, which Barrick and Mount (1991) did not do, although others have subsequently recommended this procedure (Mount & Barrick, 1995; Ones & Viswesvaran, 1996; Salgado, 1997).[4] Second, our study used only direct measures of the core traits, whereas most other research classified some measures post hoc as measures of neuroticism even if they were not intended as such. Obviously, such an approach introduces error into the measurement of the traits, which would reduce correlations between neuroticism and job performance. Finally, our meta-analysis showed that measures of neuroticism correlated less strongly with job performance (.19, exactly the same as Salgado's estimate) than did self-esteem (.26), generalized self-efficacy (.23), and locus of control (.22). Thus, if one used only measures of neuroticism to assess emotional adjustment, validity would be underestimated. (See the Future Research section for a discussion of why we believe measures of neuroticism underestimate the validity of the broad trait of emotional adjustment.) Clearly, it is preferable to use actual measures of constructs rather than correct for construct validity. However, because we have shown that typical measures of neuroticism are only one indicator of the broader core self-evaluations construct, our estimate of the validity of emotional adjustment is more accurate than previous estimates.

Future Research

Given the findings presented in this chapter, several research needs are apparent. First, research is needed on the validity of the core self-evaluations construct and whether it really is, as we have asserted, the same as the neuroticism component of the FFM. From discussions of this topic with colleagues who also are doing research in this area, we are aware that not everyone agrees with our assertion. It is an assertion that requires empirical confirmation. We have attempted to present both conceptual and empirical support for our assertion in this chapter, but this is a preliminary effort. Further work is needed. A second, related area of research that needs to be pursued is whether the core traits—self-esteem, generalized self-efficacy, neuroticism, and locus of control —are valid constructs worthy of further study in their own right or whether they merely measure core self-evaluations. We believe several pieces of evidence

---

[4]Consistent with procedures used by Mount and Barrick (1995) and Salgado (1997), we corrected the correlations for construct validity. For each of the traits, corrections were made to reflect the relationship between the individual trait and the underlying construct as reported in a factor analysis by Judge, Locke, et al. (1998).

support the view that these traits are simply indicators of neuroticism: The traits are highly correlated and, in fact, are manifested in a higher order factor. Furthermore, they correlate similarly with the most central criteria in I/O psychology: job satisfaction and job performance. In short, if there is discriminant validity among these traits in predicting broad criteria, we have not been able to identify it. Since 1967, there have been more than 1,200 studies published per year on these four traits, so obviously this is a critical issue.

In Judge et al.'s (1997) theoretical analysis, neuroticism was the only Big Five trait associated with the core self-evaluations construct. However, several of the core traits have been shown to be related to some of the Big Five traits. For example, Costa and McCrae (1992a) treat self-efficacy as a facet of conscientiousness. Other research has shown significant correlations between self-esteem and extraversion (Francis & James, 1996; Jackson & Gerard, 1996). Thus, it is important to investigate the relationships among core self-evaluations and the other traits of the FFM. As an initial effort, we estimated correlations between the other traits of the FFM and self-esteem and neuroticism (Judge & Bono, 2000). The uncorrected correlations are presented in Table 5.2. As the table shows, both self-esteem and neuroticism are moderately correlated with extraversion and conscientiousness. However, self-esteem does not correlate more strongly with the Big Five traits than does neuroticism. Furthermore, even though the correlations of self-esteem with extraversion and conscientiousness are moderate, they do not approach the correlation of self-esteem with neuroticism. If these results generalize, they suggest that the core self-evaluations construct is related to extraversion and conscientiousness, but these correlations are not strong in magnitude. Future research should investigate the relationship between core self-evaluations and the FFM.

Third, in light of the evidence that measures of neuroticism have the lowest correlations (of the four traits) with both job satisfaction and job performance,

TABLE 5.2

Relationship of Self-Esteem and Neuroticism to Five-Factor Model Traits

TRAIT	SELF-ESTEEM	NEUROTICISM	DIFFERENCE
Neuroticism	−.65**	—	—
Extraversion	.32**	−.25**	+.07
Openness to experience	.10	−.08	+.02
Agreeableness	.17*	−.23**	−.06
Conscientiousness	−.39**	−.39**	.00

Note. $N = 234$. Difference in correlations was computed after first reversing direction of neuroticism correlations (i.e., treating it as emotional stability). From data reported in "Five-Factor Model of Personality and Transformational Leadership," by T. A. Judge and J. E. Bono, 2000, Journal of Applied Psychology, 85, 237–249. *$p < .05$. **$p < .01$.

we also believe future research on the relationship of neuroticism to job performance is warranted. Neuroticism is a psychological concept with roots in psychopathology. Neuroticism and its more contemporary labels—emotional stability and emotional adjustment—recently have been used to describe "normal" individuals. However, we are not certain that the measures of neuroticism have completely shed their "abnormal" origins. For example, sample items from the NEO Personality Inventory (Costa & McCrae, 1992a), the most widely used measure of the FFM, appear in some cases to better reflect psychopathology than emotional adjustment (e.g., "Frightening thoughts sometimes come into my head," "I have sometimes experienced a deep sense of guilt or sinfulness," "At times I have been so ashamed I just wanted to hide," "I sometimes eat myself sick"). Furthermore, many items in neuroticism measures assess anxiety, proneness to stress, and nervousness. Although we are not arguing that such items have no place in measures of emotional adjustment, we believe that in many situations anxiety and proneness to stress are not relevant to job satisfaction and job performance. For example, individuals with a Type A personality pattern are more prone to stress than individuals with other personality patterns, yet Type A individuals perform better in some types of jobs (Taylor, Locke, Lee, & Gist, 1984). Conversely, it would be extremely difficult to identify any advantages, in any aspect of life, to having a negative self-concept. Thus, our view is that measures of neuroticism, emotional stability, and emotional adjustment must be examined for what they measure and whether, as we believe, items assessing anxiety or proneness to stress are less relevant to satisfaction and performance than items assessing a negative self-image.

Finally, given that there is a relationship between emotional adjustment and satisfaction and performance that generalizes across situations, causal models that address why and how the trait is related to these criteria are needed. Regarding job satisfaction, Judge et al. (1997) proposed several processes by which core self-evaluations could affect job satisfaction, including job choice, job perceptions, and job behaviors such as tenacity in the face of failure. With the exception of the perceptual mechanism and research on intrinsic job characteristics, very little is known about these processes. Even within the perceptual realm, there is room for further research. Numerous situational theories of job satisfaction have been proposed. However, for the most part, dispositional research has not been integrated with these situational theories. Thus, it is important that core self-evaluations theory be integrated with existing theories of job satisfaction. As for job performance, there is almost no understanding of how emotional adjustment is related to performance. Judge, Erez, et al. (1998) argued that positive self-concept was largely a motivational trait. If so, then emotional adjustment should be related to motivational process variables such as goal-setting behavior, expectancy perceptions, and self-regulatory processes.

However, to date, these processes have not been studied, and this remains an important area for future research.

Understanding the nature and structure of human personality has challenged psychologists for more than a century. Although our intent with this chapter was to examine and clarify the relationships among these four important personality traits and the underlying factor they represent, it appears that we have asked as many questions as we have answered. Therefore, it is our hope that the ideas and insights presented will stimulate both theoretical and empirical research in this vital area.

References

Allport, G. W. (1961). *Pattern and growth in personality*. New York: Holt, Rinehart & Winston.

American Psychiatric Association. (1987). *Diagnostic and statistical manual of mental disorders* (3rd ed., rev.). Washington, DC: Author.

Bandura, A. (1982). Self-efficacy mechanism in human agency. *American Psychologist, 37*, 122–147.

Bandura, A. (1986). *Social foundations of thought and action*. Englewood Cliffs, NJ: Prentice Hall.

Barrick, M. R., & Mount, M. K. (1991). The Big Five personality dimensions and job performance: A meta-analysis. *Personnel Psychology, 44*, 1–26.

Baumeister, R. F. (1997). Identity, self-concept, and self-esteem: The self lost and found. In R. Hogan, J. A. Johnson, & S. Briggs (Eds.), *Handbook of personality psychology* (pp. 681–710). San Diego, CA: Academic Press.

Block, J. (1995). A contrarian view of the five-factor approach to personality description. *Psychological Bulletin, 117*, 187–215.

Bollen, K., & Lennox, R. (1991). Conventional wisdom on measurement: A structural equation perspective. *Psychological Bulletin, 110*, 305–314.

Bouchard, T. J. Jr. (1997). The genetics of personality. In K. Blum & E. P. Noble (Eds.), *Handbook of psychiatric genetics* (pp. 273–296). Boca Raton, FL: CRC Press.

Brief, A. P., Burke, M. J., George, J. M., Robinson, B. S., & Webster, J. (1988). Should negative affectivity remain an unmeasured variable in the study of job stress? *Journal of Applied Psychology, 73*, 193–198.

Brief, A. P., Butcher, A., & Roberson, L. (1995). Cookies, disposition, and job attitudes: The effects of positive mood inducing events and negative affectivity on job satisfaction in a field experiment. *Organizational Behavior and Human Decision Processes, 62*, 55–62.

Cattell, R. B. (1965). *The scientific analysis of personality*. Baltimore: Penguin.

Chang, E. C. (1998). Dispositional optimism and primary and secondary appraisal of a stressor: Controlling for confounding influences and relations to coping and psychological and physical adjustment. *Journal of Personality and Social Psychology, 74,* 1109–1120.

Chen, G., & Gully, S. (1997, August). *Specific self-efficacy, general self-efficacy, and self-esteem: Are they distinguishable constructs?* Paper presented at the annual meeting of the Academy of Management, Boston.

Conley, J. J. (1984). The hierarchy of consistency: A review and model of longitudinal findings on adult individual differences in intelligence, personality and self-opinion. *Personality and Individual Differences, 5,* 11–25.

Costa, P. T. Jr., & McCrae, R. R. (1980). Influence of extraversion and neuroticism on subjective well-being: Happy and unhappy people. *Journal of Personality and Social Psychology, 38,* 668–678.

Costa, P. T. Jr., & McCrae, R. R. (1992a). *Revised NEO Personality Inventory and NEO Five-Factor Inventory.* Odessa, FL: Psychological Assessment Resources.

Costa, P. T. Jr., & McCrae, R. R. (1992b). Trait psychology comes of age. In T. B. Sonderegger (Ed.), *Nebraska Symposium on Motivation 1991: Vol. 39. Current theory and research in motivation* (pp. 169–204). Lincoln: University of Nebraska Press.

Costa, P. T. Jr., & McCrae, R. R. (1994). Set like plaster? Evidence for the stability of adult personality. In T. F. Heatherton & J. L. Weinberger (Eds.), *Can personality change?* (pp. 21–40). Washington, DC: American Psychological Association.

DeNeve, K. M., & Cooper, H. (1998). The happy personality: A meta-analysis of 137 personality traits and subjective well-being. *Psychological Bulletin, 124,* 197–229.

Diener, E., Larsen, R. J., Levine, S., & Emmons, R. A. (1985). Intensity and frequency: Dimensions underlying positive and negative affect. *Journal of Personality and Social Psychology, 48,* 1253–1265.

Eysenck, H. J. (1990a). Biological dimensions of personality. In E. Pervin (Ed.), *Handbook of personality* (pp. 244–276). New York: Guilford Press.

Eysenck, H. J. (1990b). Genetic and environmental contributions to individual differences: The three major dimensions of personality. *Journal of Personality, 58,* 245–261.

Eysenck, H. J., & Eysenck, S. B. G. (1968). *Manual for the Eysenck Personality Inventory.* San Diego, CA: Educational and Industrial Testing Service.

Francis, L. J., & James, D. J. (1996). The relationship between Rosenberg's construct of self-esteem and Eysenck's two-dimensional model of personality. *Personality and Individual Differences, 21,* 483–488.

Furnham, A., & Zacherl, M. (1986). Personality and job satisfaction. *Personality and Individual Differences, 7,* 453–459.

Furr, R. M., & Funder, D. C. (1998). A multimodel analysis of personal negativity. *Journal of Personality and Social Psychology, 74,* 1580–1591.

Gist, M. E. (1987). Self-efficacy: Implications for organizational behavior and human resource management. *Academy of Management Review, 12,* 472–485.

Gist, M. E., & Mitchell, T. R. (1992). Self-efficacy: A theoretical analysis of its determinants and malleability. *Academy of Management Review, 17*, 183–211.

Goldberg, L. R. (1992). The development of markers for the Big-Five factor structure. *Psychological Assessment, 4*, 26–42.

Goldberg, L. R. (1999). A broad-bandwidth, public-domain, personality inventory measuring the lower-level facets of several five-factor models. In I. Mervielde, I. J. Deary, F. De Fruyt, & F. Ostendorf (Eds.), *Personality psychology in Europe* (Vol. 7, pp. 7–28). Tilburg, The Netherlands: Tilburg University Press.

Green, D. P., Goldman, S. L., & Salovey, P. (1993). Measurement error masks bipolarity in affect ratings. *Journal of Personality and Social Psychology, 64*, 1029–1041.

Greenwald, A. G., Bellezza, F. S., & Banaji, M. R. (1988). Is self-esteem a central ingredient of the self-concept? *Personality and Social Psychology Bulletin, 14*, 34–45.

Harter, S. (1990). Causes, correlates, and the functional role of global self-worth: A life-span perspective. In R. J. Sternberg & J. Kolligan Jr. (Eds.), *Competence considered* (pp. 67–97). New Haven, CT: Yale University Press.

Hunter, J. E., Gerbing, D. W., & Boster, F. J. (1982). Machiavellian beliefs and personality: Construct validity of the Machiavellianism dimension. *Journal of Personality and Social Psychology, 43*, 1293–1305.

Jackson, L. A., & Gerard, D. A. (1996). Diurnal types, the "Big Five" personality factors, and other personal characteristics. *Journal of Social Behavior and Personality, 11*, 273–283.

Judge, T. A., & Bono, J. E. (1999, April). *Core self-evaluations and construct breadth: Effects on job satisfaction and job performance.* Paper presented at the 14th annual conference of the Society for Industrial and Organizational Psychology, Atlanta, GA.

Judge, T. A., & Bono, J. E. (2000). Five-factor model of personality and transformational leadership. *Journal of Applied Psychology, 85*, 751–765.

Judge, T. A., Bono, J. E., & Locke, E. A. (2000). Personality and job satisfaction: The mediating role of job characteristics. *Journal of Applied Psychology, 87*, 237–249.

Judge, T. A., Erez, A., & Bono, J. E. (1998). The power of being positive: The relationship between positive self-concept and job performance. *Human Performance, 11*, 167–187.

Judge, T. A., & Hulin, C. L. (1993). Job satisfaction as a reflection of disposition: A multiple-source causal analysis. *Organizational Behavior and Human Decision Processes, 56*, 388–421.

Judge, T. A., Locke, E. A., & Durham, C. C. (1997). The dispositional causes of job satisfaction: A core evaluations approach. *Research in Organizational Behavior, 19*, 151–188.

Judge, T. A., Locke, E. A., Durham, C. C., & Kluger, A. N. (1998). Dispositional effects on job and life satisfaction: The role of core evaluations. *Journal of Applied Psychology, 83*, 17–34.

Judge, T. A., Thoresen, C. J., Pucik, V., & Welbourne, T. M. (1999). Managerial coping with organizational change: A dispositional perspective. *Journal of Applied Psychology, 84,* 107–122.

Levenson, H. (1981). Differentiating among internality, powerful others, and chance. In H. M. Lefcourt (Ed.), *Research with the locus of control construct* (pp. 15–63). New York: Academic Press.

Locke, E. A., McClear, K., & Knight, D. (1996). Self-esteem and work. *International Review of Industrial/Organizational Psychology, 11,* 1–32.

Magnus, K., Diener, E., Fujita, F., & Pavot, W. (1993). Extraversion and neuroticism as predictors of objective life events: A longitudinal analysis. *Journal of Personality and Social Psychology, 65,* 1046–1053.

McCrae, R. R., & Costa, P. T. Jr. (1985). Updating Norman's "adequate taxonomy": Intelligence and personality dimensions in natural language and in questionnaires. *Journal of Personality and Social Psychology, 49,* 710–721.

McCrae, R. R., & Costa, P. T. Jr. (1986). Personality, coping, and coping effectiveness in an adult sample. *Journal of Personality, 54,* 385–405.

McCrae, R. R., & Costa, P. T. Jr. (1991). Adding *Liebe und Arbeit*: The full five-factor model and well-being. *Personality and Social Psychology Bulletin, 17,* 227–232.

Mount, M. K., & Barrick, M. R. (1995). The Big Five personality dimensions: Implications for research and practice in human resources management. *Research in Personnel and Human Resources Management, 13,* 153–200.

Norman, W. T. (1963). Toward an adequate taxonomy of personality attributes: Replicated factor structure in peer nomination personality ratings. *Journal of Abnormal and Social Psychology, 66,* 574–583.

Ones, D. S. (1993). *The construct validity of integrity tests.* Unpublished doctoral dissertation, University of Iowa.

Ones, D. S., Mount, M. K., Barrick, M. R., & Hunter, J. E. (1994). Personality and job performance: A critique of the Tett, Jackson, and Rothstein (1991) meta-analysis. *Personnel Psychology, 47,* 147–156.

Ones, D. S., & Viswesvaran, C. (1996). Bandwidth–fidelity dilemma in personality measurement for personnel selection. *Journal of Organizational Behavior, 17,* 609–626.

Paulhus, D. (1983). Sphere-specific measures of perceived control. *Journal of Personality and Social Psychology, 44,* 1253–1265.

Rosenberg, M. (1965). *Society and the adolescent self-image.* Princeton, NJ: Princeton University Press.

Rosenberg, M. J., Schooler, C., & Schoenbach, C. (1989). Self–esteem and adolescent problems: Modeling reciprocal effects. *American Sociological Review, 54,* 1004–1018.

Rotter, J. B. (1966). Generalized expectancies for internal versus external control of reinforcement. *Psychological Monographs, 80* (1, Whole No. 609).

Roy, M., Neale, M. C., & Kendler, K. S. (1995). The genetic epidemiology of self–esteem. *British Journal of Psychiatry, 166,* 813–820.

Russell, J. A., & Carroll, J. M. (1999a). On the bipolarity of positive and negative affect. *Psychological Bulletin, 125,* 3–30.

Russell, J. A., & Carroll, J. M. (1999b). The phoenix of bipolarity: Reply to Watson and Tellegen (1999). *Psychological Bulletin, 125,* 611–617.

Salgado, J. F. (1997). The five factor model of personality and job performance in the European Community. *Journal of Applied Psychology, 82,* 30–43.

Scheier, M. F., Carver, C. S., & Bridges, M. W. (1994). Distinguishing optimism from neuroticism (and trait anxiety, self-mastery, and self-esteem): A reevaluation of the Life Orientation Test. *Journal of Personality and Social Psychology, 67,* 1063–1078.

Scheier, M. F., Weintraub, J. K., & Carver, C. S. (1986). Coping with stress: Divergent strategies of optimists and pessimists. *Journal of Personality and Social Psychology, 51,* 1257–1264.

Schwab, D. P. (1980). Construct validity in organizational behavior. *Research in Organizational Behavior, 2,* 3–43.

Smith, C. A., Organ, D. W., & Near, J. P. (1983). Organizational citizenship behavior: Its nature and antecedents. *Journal of Applied Psychology, 68,* 653–663.

Smith, P. C. (1955). The prediction of individual differences in susceptibility to industrial monotony. *Journal of Applied Psychology, 39,* 322–329.

Smith, T. W., Pope, M. K., Rhodewalt, F., & Poulton, J. L. (1989). Optimism, neuroticism, coping, and symptom reports: An alternative interpretation of the Life Orientation Test. *Journal of Personality and Social Psychology, 56,* 640–648.

Staw, B. M., Bell, N. E., & Clausen, J. A. (1986). The dispositional approach to job attitudes: A lifetime longitudinal test. *Administrative Science Quarterly, 31,* 56–77.

Staw, B. M., & Ross, J. (1985). Stability in the midst of change: A dispositional approach to job attitudes. *Journal of Applied Psychology, 70,* 469–480.

Suls, J., Green, P., & Hillis, S. (1998). Emotional reactivity to everyday problems, affective inertia, and neuroticism. *Personality and Social Psychology Bulletin, 24,* 127–136.

Taylor, M. S., Locke, E. A., Lee, C., & Gist, M. E. (1984). Type A behavior and faculty research productivity: What are the mechanisms? *Organizational Behavior and Human Decision Processes, 34,* 402–418.

Tett, R. P., Jackson, D. N., & Rothstein, M. (1991). Personality measures as predictors of job performance: A meta-analytic review. *Personnel Psychology, 44,* 703–742.

Thoresen, C. J., & Judge, T. A. (August, 1997). *Trait affectivity and work-related attitudes and behaviors: A meta-analysis.* Paper presented at the annual convention of the American Psychological Association, Chicago, IL.

Tokar, D. M., & Subich, L. M. (1997). Relative contributions of congruence and personality dimensions to job satisfaction. *Journal of Vocational Behavior, 50,* 482–491.

Tupes, E. C., & Christal, R. E. (1961). *Recurrent personality factors based on trait ratings.* United States Air Force Aeronautical Systems Division Technical Report, No. 61-97.

Watson, D., & Clark, L. A. (1984). Negative affectivity: The disposition to experience aversive emotional states. *Psychological Bulletin, 96,* 465–490.

Watson, D., & Clark, L. A. (1992). On traits and temperament: General and specific factors of emotional experience and their relation to the five-factor model. *Journal of Personality, 60,* 441–476.

Watson, D., & Clark, L. A. (1997). Extraversion and its positive emotional core. In R. Hogan, J. Johnson, & S. Briggs (Eds.), *Handbook of Personality Psychology* (pp. 767–793). San Diego: Academic Press.

Watson, D., Clark, L. A., & Tellegen, A. (1988). Development and validation of brief measures of positive and negative affect: The PANAS scales. *Journal of Personality and Social Psychology, 54,* 1063–1070.

Watson, D., & Hubbard, B. (1996). Adaptational style and dispositional structure: Coping in the context of the five-factor model. *Journal of Personality, 64,* 737–774.

Watson, D., & Slack, A. K. (1993). General factors of affective temperament and their relation to job satisfaction over time. *Organizational Behavior and Human Decision Processes, 54,* 181–202.

Watson, D., & Tellegen, A. (1985). Toward a consensual structure of mood. *Psychological Bulletin, 98,* 219–235.

Watson, D., & Tellegen, A. (1999). Issues in the dimensional structure of affect—Effects of descriptors, measurement error, and response formats: Comment on Russell and Carroll (1999). *Psychological Bulletin, 125,* 601–610.

Weitz, J. (1952). A neglected concept in the study of job satisfaction. *Personnel Psychology, 5,* 201–205.

Zonderman, A. B., Herbst, J. H., Schmidt, C., Costa, P. T. Jr., & McCrae, R. R. (1993). Depressive symptoms as a nonspecific, graded risk for psychiatric diagnoses. *Journal of Abnormal Psychology, 102,* 544–552.

PART 2

Measurement and Assessment Issues in Applied Personality Psychology

CHAPTER 6

Accuracy in Personality Judgment

Research and Theory Concerning an Obvious Question

David C. Funder

What is psychology for? We psychologists do not ask ourselves this question very often. The day-to-day struggles for professional survival and advancement keep us busy enough without it. However, it might not do too much harm for us to consider, every once in a while, the reasons for the existence of an endeavor to which so many give so much time, energy, and commitment. Imagine a world in which psychology ceased to exist. I believe that psychology soon would be reinvented. Why? I propose three reasons.

Three Reasons Psychology Exists

First, there is the often-stated reason for climbing a mountain: Because it is there. Psychology is—or can be—a deeply involving intellectual pursuit. It delves into topics ranging from the schematic organization of long-term memory to the secretions of the hypothalamus to the best ways to weigh factor scores or account for latent variables in a multidimensional data array. Much like medieval monks memorizing texts and illuminating manuscripts, psychologists can and do—and should—pursue these issues for their intellectual sake.

Second, psychology is relevant to a wide range of immediate, pressing, and practical purposes. These include such diverse areas as treating mental illness; improving the quality of life; selecting personnel; selling commercial items such as soap and soda pop; and design of management structures, employee incentive schemes, and jet cockpit instrument arrays. In the eyes of society, the psychological monks earn their keep to a large extent when they deign to come out of the monastery to help with tasks such as these.

The third reason psychology exists is, I believe, the most important one. Psychology exists, psychology is the first or second most popular major on nearly every college campus, and the psychology section of most every book-store is almost as large as the real estate section, all for the same reason: People are curious about people. We want to know more about ourselves and each other, partly because such knowledge is useful, but mostly because we just want to know. Psychologists such as those likely to read this chapter probably have an extra measure of this curiosity, which may have determined their career choice. But nearly everyone has some degree of curiosity about what makes people "tick," and psychology developed to try to satisfy that curiosity. Psychology will thrive to the extent that it continues to have interesting things to say to the sincerely curious, and it will wither to the extent that it forgets that its first job is to find out things real people want to know (Block, 1993).

The Most Obvious Question About Personality Judgment

The study of *personality judgment*, which is also known as *social judgment, person perception*, and *social cognition*, concerns the judgments people make of the psychological attributes of themselves and each other. For example, we all have opinions concerning who, among the people we know, are and are not conscientious, honest, extraverted, energetic, shy, and so forth. We also could readily express opinions regarding whether we possess these characteristics ourselves.

What is the most obvious question one could ask about a personality judgment? That is, if you asked the proverbial "person on the street"—one who had never heard of attribution theory or weighted feature lists or schematic processing models of information processing—what he or she most wanted to know, what would that question be? I believe it would be this: Is the judgment accurate? If I say my acquaintance is honest, am I right? If I claim I am competent, am I correct? These are the types of questions that come immediately to mind for the ordinarily curious person.

The purpose of this chapter is to examine questions about accuracy and personality judgment from an applied perspective. I begin with a survey of the reasons why this issue was neglected for so long and why it is, nonetheless, crucially important. Next, I outline some research supporting the existence of personality traits and the ability of people to judge those traits accurately. I present four moderator variables that make accurate personality judgment more or less likely and I introduce a theoretical model of accurate judgment that can rationalize these moderators. I conclude with suggestions for new directions in research.

Ignoring the Obvious: The Accuracy of Personality Judgment

Psychology—to its peril, I believe—has had a history of often ignoring the obvious questions within its purview. The issue of the accuracy of personality

EXHIBIT 6.1
Reasons Why Accuracy in Personality Judgment Was Ignored

- Cronbach's complaint
- Process approach
- Person–situation debate
- Error paradigm
- Deconstructionism
- Criterion problem

judgment is a prime example. For the better part of 3 decades—roughly from 1955 to 1985—the accuracy of personality judgment was almost completely ignored by social and personality psychologists.[1] The topic even took on a slightly disreputable character: A major textbook of the period (Schneider, Hastorf, & Ellsworth, 1979) commented that the idea of studying accuracy had "lost a little of its intuitive charm" (p. 222) and therefore "there is almost no interest in accuracy" (p. 224).

Social and personality psychologists were not just being perverse. There were several fairly strong, if not good, reasons for avoiding the study of accuracy in personality judgment. For easy reference, these are listed in Exhibit 6.1.

First, there was what became known as "Cronbach's complaint," a powerful methodological critique of the then-lively field of accuracy research that was written by Lee J. Cronbach and published in 1955 (Cronbach, 1955; Gage & Cronbach, 1955). In a complex and difficult argument, Cronbach showed that the usual indicator of accuracy—self–other agreement in personality judgment —was a complex number determined by several factors, each with a different psychological interpretation. Cronbach did not deny the legitimacy of accuracy research, nor did he even raise some of the more difficult issues associated with it (e.g., the criterion problem, which is discussed later in this chapter), but he was widely interpreted—and sometimes still is cited—as having said that accuracy research is impossible. The stunning and almost immediate result was that social psychologists very rapidly abandoned the field of accuracy research. Accuracy research suddenly seemed to be very unfriendly terrain, whereas there were plenty of other topics that psychologists could investigate without having to master Cronbach's arguments, terminology, and statistical notation.

---

[1]Judgmental accuracy was not ignored by I/O psychologists, however. A large and lively literature on evaluating and improving the accuracy of interpersonal evaluation has steadily appeared over the years in the pages of *The Journal of Applied Psychology*, *Organizational Behavior and Human Performance* (the name of this journal was later changed to *Organizational Behavior and Human Decision Processes*), and other journals.

Thus, the second reason accuracy was ignored was that social psychologists interested in person perception simply found other things to do. Specifically, Solomon Asch (e.g., Asch, 1946) developed the process approach to studying person perception, which, as E. E. Jones noted years afterward, "solved the accuracy problem by bypassing it" (1985, p. 77). Asch and many who came later (e.g., Kunda, 1999) found that they could easily establish a laboratory paradigm in which (a) participants were presented with some artificial social stimulus (e.g., a paragraph about a person or a list of trait words said to characterize someone) and (b) the researcher examined how the participants interpreted the stimulus. The researcher then inferred the nature of the "judgment process" according to the transformations that occurred between the stimulus input and the judgmental output.

This paradigm can produce interesting results. For example, Asch (1946) used it to examine primacy effects, recency effects, and an important Gestalt view of impression formation. However, Jones (1985) was right when he noted that this paradigm—along with the later literatures of attribution theory and social cognition that grew out of Asch's approach (see Schneider et al., 1979; Kunda, 1999)—bypassed accuracy issues. The study of how people transform artificial social stimulus information is not relevant to accuracy because there is no "real" person to be judged, accurately or not. Moreover, so long as research remains within this paradigm there is no way of knowing how general the transformation processes identified in the laboratory are or whether they enhance or detract from accuracy in real environments (Funder, 1987).

The third reason accuracy was ignored was the effects of the "person–situation debate," which was triggered within personality psychology by Walter Mischel's 1968 book, *Personality and Assessment*. This debate had the effect—especially in related fields such as social psychology—of causing many psychologists to see personality as the unicorn of psychology. Although the existence of important individual differences in personality ultimately was confirmed (Kenrick & Funder, 1988), the damage to the field was done, and it has not yet been entirely repaired. For at least 2 decades, psychologists avoided studying the accuracy of personality judgment, in part because it seemed illogical to try to study the accuracy of something that did not exist.

The fourth reason accuracy was ignored was the importation from cognitive to social psychology of the error paradigm in the study of human judgment. This approach to human judgment emphasized the putative inferential errors said to fundamentally characterize it, and one particular error became especially well known: *Fundamental attribution error* was the label developed for the positive basic human tendency to perceive personality as important in cases in which behavior was merely determined by the situation (Ross, 1977). The widespread acceptance of this phenomenon and its label and the broader implication that human beings are inferentially inept hardly encouraged researchers who might otherwise have been interested in studying accuracy.

The fifth reason accuracy was ignored was the subtle but pervasive influence of postmodernist, deconstructionist intellectual viewpoints. In departments of English or Literature, where it usually is found, deconstructionism is the view that reality as a concrete entity does not exist. Instead, all that exist are alternative viewpoints or "constructions" of reality, and all have equal claim to validity. This viewpoint influenced modern social psychology in a way that many of its practitioners may not have even realized. One way its influence was felt was in the presumption often exhibited in social psychological writings that person perceptions are constructed out of little or nothing in the minds of social perceivers. Its influence also could be seen in the way social psychological research on person perception typically completely ignored the actual properties of the person perceived and seemed to assume implicitly that there really are not any actual properties.

The sixth and final reason for avoiding research on accuracy is perhaps the most important of all: the criterion problem. That is, any attempt to evaluate the accuracy of a personality judgment requires a criterion by which to determine the degree to which it is right or wrong. Some psychologists believed, in a deconstructionist way, that no such criterion can be found and that any attempt to evaluate accuracy amounts merely to setting one judgment against another. Deconstructionist leanings aside, it is easy to see that the criterion problem is difficult and, as I mentioned, there are plenty of other research topics on which to spend one's time.

Why Accuracy in Personality Judgment Is Important

Powerful as they may have been or even continue to be, none of these reasons for ignoring accuracy makes the topic any less important. There are three significant reasons why accuracy matters and why the topic will not go away even if psychologists do ignore it for long periods of time. These reasons are summarized in Exhibit 6.2.

First, the accuracy of personality judgments has an obvious, large amount of practical importance. Such judgments are an inescapable part of research processes in psychology. For example, if one result of child abuse is lower self-confidence later in life, how can we know this unless somebody, somehow, makes a personality judgment? And does it not obviously matter whether this judgment is accurate? If one could even imagine a psychology that did not include personality judgments, the result would be a much shrunken, less interesting, and less important field.

An additional practical consideration is that personality judgments inevi-

EXHIBIT 6.2

Reasons Why Accuracy in Personality Judgment Is Important

- Practical reasons
  Psychological methods
  Usefulness in daily life
- Theoretical reasons
  Inductive links from behavior to personality
  Deductive links from personality to behavior
- Philosophical reasons
  Perception and reality

tably affect most of the interpersonal transactions of daily life. These include such diverse activities as deciding whether to loan someone $5 until payday, choosing whom to ask for a date, and hiring employees. For example, employers make hiring decisions every day whether or not anyone provides them with useful techniques for doing so. Employers seeking guidance from industrial and organizational (I/O) psychologists helps to explain why the topic of accuracy did not disappear from I/O psychology when it did elsewhere. Everyone makes consequential personality judgments all the time, and making them more accurately would be as useful for ordinary people in their daily lives as it is for employers making hiring decisions.

Second, academically and theoretically, accuracy in personality judgment is important because it goes to the heart of the interaction between personality and social psychology. The *inductive* links from behavior to personality are the heart of the social psychological approach to person perception. When someone speaks in a loud voice, what do we infer about that individual's personality? The *deductive* links from personality to behavior are the heart of the enterprise of personality psychology. Given that we know something about an individual's personality, what can we predict he or she will do? (If he or she is extraverted, that individual can be expected to speak in a loud voice; Scherer, 1978.) Accuracy in personality judgment includes both inductive and deductive links. If we understand what we can correctly infer about a person on the basis of his or her behavior, we will understand what we can expect a person with a certain kind of personality to do. And when we know how to predict what a person will do, we will understand how to make correct inferences on one basis of the behaviors we observe.

The third reason accuracy is important is more philosophical. The oldest question in philosophy, and perhaps the most basic question underlying human curiosity, is, What is the connection between perception and reality? We think we see things; are they really there? We can never know the answer to this question for sure, but that does not make it any less interesting or important.

In the domain of personality judgment, this question becomes as follows: Are the judgments we make of the people around us, and of ourselves, accurate?

Agenda for Accuracy Research

Around 1980 or so, research on the accuracy of personality judgment began to revive (e.g., Funder, 1980), and by the early 1990s it was a thriving and even respectable field of research. As it progressed, the research moved through four stages. First, the person–situation debate had to be resolved in some way. Until it became plausible to assert that personality existed, it would be difficult, if not impossible, to persuade people to be interested in the accuracy of personality judgment. Second, the idea that personality judgments were basically always wrong (i.e., the fundamental attribution error) had to be countered with evidence that lay judgments of personality at least sometimes did manifest an important degree of validity. When these two preliminary issues had been addressed, then the real research on accuracy could begin. The third stage was the exploration of the moderators of accuracy (i.e., the factors that make accurate personality judgment more or less likely). The fourth stage, the point at which the research is now, is characterized by attempts to synthesize what has been learned into useful theories about how accurate personality judgment is possible.

Stage 1: The Existence of Personality

This is not the place for a lengthy exposition of the person–situation debate or how it ultimately was resolved (instead, see Funder, 2001, chap. 4; Funder, 1999, chap. 2; or Kenrick & Funder, 1988). However, it may be useful to make one relevant point that is sometimes overlooked.

Critiques of personality by Mischel (1968) and others (e.g., Ross & Nisbett, 1991) often have noted that the situation has powerful effects on behavior. The step then taken from this has been to infer that personality therefore has small, if any, effects. But this step is in fact not a logical one. The best way to show this is with data. For example, in some of my research (Funder & Colvin, 1991), pairs of undergraduate students of the opposite sex, who had never met before, were asked to sit before a videocamera and chat briefly (i.e., for 5 min). They returned a couple of weeks later and were paired with different partners whom they had not met before, but who also were there for their second visit. Independent teams of coders viewed the videotapes of these two conversations and rated the behaviors exhibited on 62 dimensions.

This is, of course, a repeated-measures experiment with 62 dependent variables. The differences between the two sessions were (a) the partners were changed and (b) at the time of the second encounter both partners had been

TABLE 6.1

Effect of Situation: Behavioral Differences Between Two Laboratory Situations

ITEM	1st SESSION	2nd SESSION	t FOR DIFFERENCE
1st SESSION HIGHER			
Talks at rather than with partner	3.98	3.51	4.96***
Exhibits awkward interpersonal style	4.19	3.60	4.50***
Shows physical signs of tension or anxiety	5.19	4.66	3.76**
Shows lack of interest in interaction	3.98	3.55	3.33**
Keeps partner at a distance	4.81	4.40	2.97**
Expresses insecurity or sensitivity	4.77	4.49	2.93**
Behaves in fearful or timid manner	3.98	3.64	2.85**
Exhibits high degree of intelligence	5.39	5.24	2.24*
Is physically animated	3.85	3.56	2.14*
Is irritable	3.76	3.60	1.95*
2nd SESSION HIGHER			
Exhibits social skills	5.94	6.46	−4.65***
Appears relaxed and comfortable	5.56	6.13	−3.98***
Says or does interesting things	5.78	6.08	−2.79**
Is expressive in face, voice, or gestures	5.11	5.42	−2.68**
Interviews partner (asks questions)	5.83	6.21	−2.56*
Speaks fluently	5.98	6.25	−2.38*
Is talkative	5.73	6.05	−2.33*
Engages in constant eye contact	6.08	6.37	−2.32*
Seems to genuinely enjoy interaction	5.90	6.14	−2.00*
Behaves in cheerful manner	5.89	6.11	−1.94*

Note. Item content is abbreviated. From "Explorations in Behavioral Consistency: Properties of Persons, Situations, and Behaviors," by D. C. Funder and C. R. Colvin, 1991, *Journal of Personality and Social Psychology, 52*, p. 783. Copyright 1991 by the American Psychological Association. Adapted with permission of the author.
*$p < .05$. **$p < .01$. ***$p < .001$.

there before. With this type of experimental design, it is possible to then perform a t test on each of the behavioral dependent variables and thereby see the power of the situation by applying the method routinely used by experimental social psychologists.[2] The results for this example are presented in Table 6.1.

---

[2]The only difference is that experimental social psychology studies rarely have more than one or two dependent variables.

The differences were many, strong, and interpretable. A total of 20 of the 62 behaviors coded were significantly changed ($p < .05$). In the first session, participants appeared relatively awkward, tense, disinterested, distant, insecure, and timid. However, in the second session, their behavior changed, and participants were relatively interesting, expressive, fluent, talkative, and cheerful. Participants clearly were much more relaxed at the second session, in which they were more experienced, compared with the first. This is a quick and easy demonstration of the power of the situation. The degree to which people exhibit awkward, tense, expressive, cheerful, and many other kinds of behavior is critically dependent on the situation.

The way the person–situation debate usually is framed, differences like these typically are used to imply that personality variables therefore are unimportant. Such an implication would be wrong, however. It turns out that the situational dependence of behavior has nothing to do with its cross-situational consistency; the correlation between behavior in the first and second situations is orthogonal to the differences both mathematically and empirically. See Table 6.2, which reflects the same data as Table 6.1, but is analyzed in terms of correlations rather than mean differences.

Even more behaviors were consistent, in a correlational sense, between the two sessions than behaviors that changed. Of the 62 behaviors coded, 37 yielded significant correlations ($p < .001$), and many of these correlations were large by any standard. Participants maintained their individual differences across sessions in the degree to which they appeared awkward ($r = .60$), laughed ($r = .63$), and were expressive ($r = .63$), among many others. Cross-situational consistency correlations were .60 or above for 8 behaviors; 26 correlations were .40 (i.e., the value touted as the ceiling for the personality coefficient by critics of the field; Nisbett, 1980) or above.

It is important to note that these consistency correlations are not across situations that could in any sense be considered to be the same. Table 6.1 illustrates that the differences between situations have strong and meaningful effects on behavior. The correlations presented in Table 6.2 show the consistency of individual differences across situations that have been shown to be consequentially different.

The conclusion that can be drawn from this demonstration is that, in an important way, the two sides of the person–situation debate talked past each other for many years. The undoubted evidence that situations affect behavior was taken to imply that the influence of personality was therefore weak when, in fact, no such implication followed. People change their behavior as the situation changes; however, they also, to a strong degree, maintain their differences between each other as they do so. The participants in the study described were less awkward in the second session than in the first, but those participants who

TABLE 6.2

Power of the Person: Behavioral Consistency Correlation Between Two Laboratory Situations

ITEM	r
Speaks in loud voice	.70
Behaves in fearful or timid manner	.65
Is expressive in face, voice, or gestures	.62
Laughs frequently	.63
Is reserved and unexpressive	.62
Exhibits awkward interpersonal style	.60
Smiles frequently	.60
Behaves in cheerful manner	.60
Shows high enthusiasm and energy level	.59
Speaks quickly	.59
Exhibits social skills	.58
Engages in constant eye contact	.57
Expresses insecurity or sensitivity	.56
Appears to regard self as physically attractive	.55
Shows lack of interest in interaction	.54
Appears relaxed and comfortable	.48
Exhibits condescending behavior	.47
Shows physical signs of tension or anxiety	.45
Is unusual or unconventional in appearance	.45
Exhibits high intelligence	.44
Is irritable	.43
Acts in sex-typed manner	.43
Seems to genuinely enjoy interaction	.42
Speaks fluently	.42
Initiates humor	.41
Expresses skepticism or cynicism	.40
Is physically animated	.39
Keeps partner at distance	.39
Tries to control interaction	.38
Talks at rather than with partner	.38
Expresses agreement frequently	.38
Is talkative	.38
Shows interest in intellectual matters	.36
Seems interested in what partner says	.34
Expresses hostility	.30
Offers advice to partner	.29
Expresses self-pity	.28

Note. Item content is abbreviated. All correlations are significant at $p < .001$ (two-tailed). From "Explorations in Behavioral Consistency: Properties of Persons, Situations, and Behaviors," by D. C. Funder and C. R. Colvin, 1991, *Journal of Personality and Social Psychology, 52,* p. 780. Copyright 1991 by the American Psychological Association. Adapted with permission of the author.

were the most awkward in the first session were also the most awkward in the second.

It is perhaps unfortunate that data like these were not readily available when the person–situation debate began in the late 1960s. But now that they are available, perhaps the debate can be set aside and personality psychology can move forward.

Stage 2: Defense of the Human Judge

Beginning with Mischel (1968), most critics of personality traits have realized the need to account for what is, in their view, a paradox: People still believe in traits. They use them constantly to characterize other people and themselves. To explain this paradox, trait critics have introduced a second idea, that all these people are wrong. Mischel's *Personality and Assessment* included a brief survey of research that indicated the existence of flaws in human judgment, but the potential of this argument was not fulfilled until 1977, when Lee Ross labeled the tendency to see personality where none exists as "the fundamental attribution error" (p. 184).

This phrase referred to the same phenomenon as E. E. Jones's "correspondence bias" (1985), but it had a greater impact on the thinking of psychologists at large. Together with the influential work of Daniel Kahneman and Amos Tversky (Kahneman & Tversky, 1973), it helped create a widespread view of the lay human judge as hopelessly incompetent (e.g., Shaklee, 1991). In addition, it served to further discourage, if further discouragement were needed, the study of accuracy in personality judgment.

But nothing lasts forever, not even popular research paradigms and widespread conventional wisdom. By the mid-1980s, research on error was receiving its share of criticism (Funder, 1987). Critics pointed out that errors—including the fundamental attribution error—are irrelevant to accuracy for several reasons, the most central being that normative models define accuracy given only certain assumptions that, although perhaps correct in experimental contexts, are of uncertain validity in the real world (Funder, 1987, 1999; McArthur & Baron, 1983; Swann, 1984). Indeed, the same processes that violate models that are normative in terms of narrowly defined stimuli and criteria have been found to lead to correct judgments in broader, more realistic contexts (Bernardin & Pence, 1980; Block & Funder, 1986; Borman, 1975, 1979). Although this may not describe the situation in every case, the possibility that errors reflect processes that are ordinarily adaptive parsimoniously explains why so many have been demonstrated and is consistent with analyses of errors in other domains of psychology, such as the study of illusions in visual perception.

Along with increasing criticism of the error paradigm itself, evidence rapidly accumulated showing that human judgment, even social judgment, is not wholly wrong. Personality judgments by acquaintances usually agree well with each other and with the self-judgments of the people they describe, and they also can predict behavior assessed independently (e.g., Funder & Colvin, 1991; Kolar, Funder, & Colvin, 1996).

Perhaps the most significant limitation of research that aims to document what people do wrong is that it can provide no information about what people do right.[3] The study of error wonders why people are not perfect. The study of accuracy, however, asks how people manage to ever be right. As will be discussed, this very different question yields very different kinds of answers.

Stage 3: Moderators of Accuracy

Even while debates about the very existence of personality and the fundamental erroneousness of human judgment were still going on, a small cadre of researchers began to address the issue of moderators of accuracy. Instead of continuing to ask *whether* personality judgments were accurate, they began to ask *when* they were accurate. That is, they asked the question, Under what circumstances are personality judgments more or less likely to be accurate? This question resulted in the search for moderator variables.

The Criterion Problem

The search for variables that affect judgment accuracy immediately runs up against the problem noted earlier: By what criterion can a personality judgment be identified as right or wrong? This is a complex issue that has been addressed elsewhere (e.g., Funder, 1987, 1999), but a few comments might be useful here.

There is no single criterion or gold standard for accuracy. All a researcher can do is gather multiple criteria and hope to find accuracy somewhere in their midst. This practice is useful for two reasons. First, no single criterion is infallible, so each serves as a check on the others. Second, the variation in accuracy as a function of criteria can itself be interesting and important (McCrae, 1994). For example, when a personality judgment can predict overt behavior but not emotional experience is itself an interesting difference with psychological implications (e.g., Spain, Eaton, & Funder, 2000).

The most common criterion in the accuracy literature is self-judgment. If an acquaintance's judgment of you matches your judgment of yourself, then it

---

[3]Actually, research on error could be informative about accuracy if it was assumed that errors demonstrated in the laboratory, like research on visual illusions, reflected processes that produce accurate perceptions in the real world. Researchers on error seldom do this. Instead, they assume that errors in the laboratory reflect processes that produce mistakes in the real world (Funder, 1987).

might be deemed accurate (e.g., Blackman & Funder, 1998). Similarly, an acquaintance's judgment of you might be compared to your scores on a well-validated self-report personality test (e.g., Paunonen & Jackson, 1987). I believe that it is unwise to stop there, however, because a personality judgment is itself a personality test of sorts, which needs its own validation with criteria that go beyond other personality tests or self-reports.

For this reason, other researchers and I have tried to use behavioral criteria as well. We have compared acquaintances' personality judgments (and self-judgments) with measurement of behavior taken in laboratory situations and also with reports of behavior in daily life and of emotional experiences reported through so-called "beeper" methods. These alternative criteria are both reassuring when they converge with the results using other criteria and interesting when they diverge (Kolar et al., 1996; Spain et al., 2000).

Four Moderators of Accuracy

I believe that the moderators of accuracy studied to date in my laboratory and elsewhere (see Funder, 1999, for a review) can be organized into four categories that I have labeled as follows: (a) *good judge*, (b) *good target*, (c) *good trait*, and (d) *good information*. The word *good* in each label, although perhaps redundant, serves as a reminder that what we are searching for are those factors that might make accurate personality judgment more likely.

The evidence regarding these moderators is reviewed elsewhere (Funder, 1995, 1999). However, it can be noted briefly that the good judge tends to be extraverted and well adjusted. The good target moderator is also associated with these traits (Colvin, 1993). *Good trait* (i.e., the kind of trait that is easiest to judge accurately) generally refers to overt and visible behavior and is not strongly loaded with social desirability considerations (Funder & Dobroth, 1987; John & Robins, 1994). Good information comes in two kinds, quantity and quality. On the quantity dimensions, more information (e.g., longer acquaintanceship) clearly is better (Blackman & Funder, 1998). The quality dimension is just beginning to receive its due attention, but already it seems clear that some kinds of acquaintanceship and contexts of observation are more informative than others.

It is possible to go further with this line of thinking. These four moderators yield six unique two-way interactions (see Table 6.3). In conjunction with work on the realistic accuracy model (RAM; see the next section), I have given each of these interactions a name and interpretation. For example, *expertise* is the interaction between judge and trait, and it identifies the possibility that some judges might be particularly good (i.e., expert) in judging certain traits but not others.

This list of moderators developed from a reading of the empirical literature.

TABLE 6.3

Interactions Among Moderators of Accuracy in Personality Judgment

MODERATOR	JUDGE	TARGET	TRAIT	INFORMATION
Judge	—	Relationship	Expertise	Sensitivity
Target	—	—	Palpability	Divulgence
Trait	—	—	—	Diagnosticity
Information	—	—	—	—

Note. Adapted from "On the Accuracy of Personality Judgment: A Realistic Approach," by David C. Funder, *Psychological Review, 102,* p. 659. Copyright 1995 by the American Psychological Association, p. 663.

It is not theoretically based, nor are the four moderators even listed in any particular order. Although this identification of moderators is useful, it is insufficient. To organize past research on accuracy into a system more meaningful than a mere list of relevant variables, to explain why these variables moderate accuracy, and to suggest new moderators that might be sought, some kind of theory was needed. For these reasons, the Realistic Accuracy Model (RAM) was developed (Funder, 1995).

Stage 4: Development of Theory

Assumptions of the Realistic Accuracy Model

The RAM begins with three assumptions:

1. *Personality exists.* The model begins with the idea that personality traits are things that people really have. It is interesting and sophisticated to think of traits as hypothetically "constructed" concepts with no actual basis in reality, but it is not very useful. Gordon Allport is said to have once pointed out that one could think of stars as mere hypothetical constructs in the minds of astronomers. This view might have merit, but it would halt the progress of astronomy. Similarly, an effort to understand and improve the accuracy of judgments of personality traits might profitably begin with the presumption that traits exist.

2. *People make judgments of personality traits, at least sometimes.* Some psychologists have claimed that people do not really judge traits; instead, they judge "affordances" or respond behaviorally without making judgments at all. However, the real difference between an affordance and a trait is not completely clear. More important, for the purposes of the RAM, it is not necessary to assume that people

constantly make personality trait judgments (although I suspect they do). Rather, it is only necessary to assume that anybody, even once, tried to make a judgment of the trait of another.

3. *These judgments are accurate, at least sometimes.* Again, concepts such as the fundamental attribution error have led some psychologists to argue that people are nearly always wrong in their judgments, whereas my own work has sometimes been read as claiming they are nearly always right. (I never said that, of course, but I may have thought it.) The RAM demands only the following: an acknowledgment that any judgment of any personality trait, ever and even once, was actually right. That is, one judgment at one time has correctly described a personality trait that really existed.

If this can be acknowledged to have ever happened, then a critical question immediately arises: How? That is, how was it ever possible for such an accurate judgment to be achieved? According to the RAM, for the personality trait of a target individual to be accurately reflected in someone's judgment, four things must happen. First, the target individual must do something *relevant*. For example, a courageous person must do something that shows courage. If he or she does not, then nobody will ever know of his or her courageousness.[4] Second, this behavior must be displayed in a manner and context in which it is *available* to a judge. If a courageous act is going on next door but you cannot see it, then it will not enter into your judgment. Third, this relevant and available behavior must be *detected*. If a judge is distracted or otherwise oblivious to what is going on in his or her presence, then the process of accurate judgment will end there, unsuccessfully. Finally, this relevant, available, and detected behavioral information must be correctly *utilized*. It must be interpreted correctly regarding the trait that it actually indicates.

This process is diagrammed in Figure 6.1. It is important to note that this is a different kind of process than traditionally examined in the study of social cognition. It is not the kind of cognitive process that is contained entirely within the head of the social perceiver. Rather, it is a social process that includes actions of the person who is perceived (*relevance*) and transactions between the perceiver and perceived (*availability* and *detection*) as well as information processing by the perceiver (*utilization*). The traditional study of social cognition includes only the final, utilization stage. Also noteworthy is the fact that this is a description of the process of not just any judgment, but of an *accurate* one. It

---

[4]"Act frequency" views of personality consider a trait like courage as something that exists only when and if it is displayed (Buss, 1983). I reject this interpretation in favor of the view that traits are latent entities waiting for the opportunity to be expressed under appropriate circumstances.

FIGURE 6.1

The realistic accuracy model: A model of the process of accurate personality judgment. Adapted from "On the Accuracy of Personality Judgment: A Realistic Approach," by David C. Funder, Psychological Review, 102, p. 659. Copyright 1995 by the American Psychological Association.

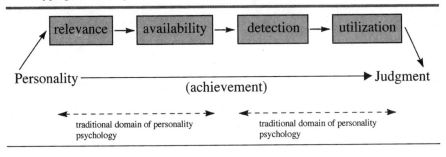

does not describe what happens all the time, only what must happen for accurate judgment to be achieved.

Implications of the Realistic Accuracy Model

RAM is a simple model as models go, but it yields several implications. The first implication is that accurate judgment is difficult. Unless all of the four stages are successfully traversed, accurate judgment will fail to be achieved. To view this in a slightly quantitative light, imagine that each of the four stages was about half as good as it potentially could be, receiving a value of .50. The resulting accuracy—multiplying the terms together—would have a value of only .06. This illustrates how rather than being concerned that accuracy fails to be perfect, researchers perhaps should more often marvel about how it is not always 0.

A second implication is that the moderators of accuracy identified in previous research must all be the result of things that happen at one or more of the stages of the model. For example, the good judge is someone who can detect and utilize information. Therefore, the good judge is likely to be someone who is perceptive, has wide knowledge and experience relevant to personality, and is free of judgment-distorting biases or defensive tendencies. The good target will be someone who emits a good deal of relevant information that is made available in a wide range of situations. Thus, the good target will be someone who has a high activity level (i.e., emitting many behaviors) and who is nondeceptive and consistent in his or her behaviors across contexts. The good trait will be one that refers to overt and visible behaviors that are available in many different contexts. And, as the literature suggests, good information will have two facets. More information—the quantity aspect—will tend to make more behavioral information available, and its detection more likely, on purely probabilistic grounds. Acquaintance in different contexts—the quality variable—will make different behaviors, relevant to different traits, differentially available.

Emerging Issues

As the study of accuracy in personality judgment becomes a more mature field that can move beyond justifying its existence and identifying basic issues, new issues will emerge. Such issues include increasing self-knowledge and improving the accuracy of personality judgment, both of which may benefit from application of the RAM.

Increasing Self-Knowledge

RAM was devised to account for the moderators of accuracy in interpersonal judgment, that is, judgments made of other people. But it may be helpful in illuminating the process of self-knowledge as well.

The relevance stage of RAM implies that people who "test themselves" by pursuing such endeavors as mountain climbing, traveling, or otherwise entering new contexts will then emit behaviors that they might not otherwise have performed, thereby learning things about themselves that they might otherwise never have known. Relevance also implies that people who grow up in cultural or family contexts that inhibit the free expression of wide ranges of behaviors (e.g., collectivist cultural environments) might therefore never emit many relevant behaviors, never learn much about themselves, or perhaps even fail to develop much of a sense of self. The detection stage of RAM implies that people who are prone to perceptual defense (e.g., failing to notice unpleasant facts about themselves) will be deficient in self-knowledge. The utilization stage implies that the same factors that promote or inhibit judgment in general will tend to promote and inhibit accurate self-knowledge.

Improving Accuracy in Personality Judgment

Over the years, I/O psychology has steadily tried to devise techniques for improving judgmental accuracy. RAM might contribute to this effort by identifying four possible places at which to intervene. Many traditional approaches to both error and the improvement of accuracy identify—in practice, not by name—the utilization stage as the focus of effort. That is, the judge's brain is seen as the source of the problem and the place that needs improvement. Think well, and judge better.

This is good advice, but the RAM implies that it is only 25% of the picture. To judge someone better, it is important to watch them closely (detection). It is important to view them in a wide rather than narrow range of contexts (availability). Perhaps most important, it implies that what should be observed are behaviors that are relevant to the judgments to be made. Not just any observations will do. Moreover, one who would accurately judge personality should take care not to inhibit the behaviors that might be most informative (i.e., as might a boss who is unwilling to hear anything but praise and good news or a parent who makes clear what he or she is and is not willing to know). Doing so will reduce the likelihood of accurate judgment by preventing relevant behaviors from emerging (i.e., becoming available).

Accuracy and the Real World

Research on accuracy and RAM has been aimed at judgments of general traits of personality, not job performance or other attributes of direct relevance to the concerns of I/O psychology. But broad traits of personality, such as conscientiousness, have been shown in recent research (e.g., Ones, Viswesvaran, & Schmidt, 1993) to be important for a wide range of occupational outcomes. Perhaps even more important, the basic process of interpersonal judgment described by the RAM is completely general. In the real world, people often need to know things about, for example, the people they would employ, who would supervise them, or who would be their customers. In all such situations, it is possible to accurately learn these things only if (a) the person in question does something that is relevant (b) in a context in which this behavior is available and it (c) is detected and then (d) utilized. The path between attributes of people and our judgments is a rocky and steep one, but the Realistic Accuracy Model may provide the beginnings of a map.

References

Asch, S. E. (1946). Forming impressions of personality. *Journal of Abnormal and Social Psychology, 9,* 258–290.

Bernardin, H. J., & Pence, E. C. (1980). Effects of rater training: Creating new response sets and decreasing accuracy. *Journal of Applied Psychology, 65,* 60–66.

Blackman, M. C., & Funder, D. C. (1998). The effect of information on consensus and accuracy in personality judgment. *Journal of Experimental Social Psychology, 34,* 164–181.

Block, J. (1993). Studying personality the long way. In D. C. Funder, R. D. Parke, C. Tomlinson-Keasey, & K. Widaman (Eds.), *Studying lives through time: Personality and development* (pp. 9–41). Washington, DC: American Psychological Association.

Block, J., & Funder, D. C. (1986). Social roles and social perception: Individual differences in attribution and error. *Journal of Personality and Social Psychology, 51,* 1200–1207.

Borman, W. C. (1975). Effect of instructions to avoid halo error on reliability and validity of performance ratings. *Journal of Applied Psychology, 62,* 64–69.

Borman, W. C. (1979). Format and training effects on rating accuracy and rater errors. *Journal of Applied Psychology, 64,* 410–421.

Buss, D. M. (1983). The act frequently approach to personality. *Psychological Review, 90,* 105–126.

Colvin, C. R. (1993). Judgable people: Personality, behavior, and competing explanations. *Journal of Personality and Social Psychology, 64,* 861–873.

Cronbach, L. J. (1955). Processes affecting scores on "understanding others" and "assumed similarity." *Psychological Bulletin, 52,* 81–302.

Funder, D. C. (1980). On seeing ourselves as others see us: Self–other agreement and discrepancy in personality ratings. *Journal of Personality, 48,* 473–493.

Funder, D. C. (1987). Errors and mistakes: Evaluating the accuracy of social judgment. *Psychological Bulletin, 101,* 75–90.

Funder, D. C. (1995). On the accuracy of personality judgment: A realistic approach. *Psychological Review, 102,* 652–670.

Funder, D. C. (1999). *Personality judgment: A realistic approach to person perception.* San Diego, CA: Academic Press.

Funder, D. C. (2001). *The personality puzzle* (2nd ed.). New York: Norton.

Funder, D. C., & Colvin, C. R. (1991). Explorations in behavioral consistency: Properties of persons, situations, and behaviors. *Journal of Personality and Social Psychology, 60,* 773–794.

Funder, D. C., & Dobroth, K. M. (1987). Differences between traits: Properties associated with interjudge agreement. *Journal of Personality and Social Psychology, 52,* 409–418.

Gage, N. L., & Cronbach, L. J. (1955). Conceptual and methodological problems in interpersonal perception. *Psychological Review, 62,* 411–422.

John, O. P., & Robins, R. W. (1994). Determinants of interjudge agreement on personality traits: The Big Five domains, observability, evaluativeness, and the unique perspective of the self. *Journal of Personality, 61,* 521–551.

Jones, E. E. (1985). Major developments in social psychology during the past five decades. In G. Lindzey & E. Aronson (Eds.), *The handbook of social psychology* (3rd ed., Vol. 1, pp. 47–101). New York: Random House.

Kahneman, D. T., & Tversky, A. (1973). On the psychology of prediction. *Psychological Review, 80,* 237–251.

Kenrick, D. T., & Funder, D. C. (1988). Profiting from controversy: Lessons from the person–situation debate. *American Psychologist, 43,* 23–34.

Kolar, D. W., Funder, D. C., & Colvin, C. R. (1996). Comparing the accuracy of personality judgments by the self and knowledgeable others. *Journal of Personality, 64,* 311–337.

Kunda, Z. (1999). *Social cognition: Making sense of people.* Cambridge, MA: MIT Press.

McArthur, L. Z., & Baron, R. M. (1983). Toward an ecological theory of social perception. *Psychological Review, 90,* 215–238.

McCrae, R. R. (1994). The counterpoint of personality assessment: Self-reports and observer ratings. *Assessment, 1,* 159–172.

Mischel, W. (1968). *Personality and assessment.* New York: Wiley.

Nisbett, R. (1980). The trait construct in lay and professional psychology. In L. Festinger (Ed.), *Retrospections on social psychology* (pp. 109–130). New York: Oxford University Press.

Ones, D., Viswesvaran, C., & Schmidt, F. L. (1993). Comprehensive meta-analysis of integrity test validities: Findings and implications for personnel selection and theories of job performance. *Journal of Applied Psychology, 78,* 679–703.

Paunonen, S. V., & Jackson, D. N. (1987). Accuracy of interviewers and students in identifying the personality characteristics of personnel managers and computer programmers. *Journal of Vocational Behavior, 31,* 26–36.

Ross, L. (1977). The intuitive psychologist and his shortcomings. In L. Berkowitz (Ed.), *Advances in experimental social psychology* (Vol. 10, pp. 174–214). New York: Academic Press.

Ross, L., & Nisbett, R. E. (1991). *The person and the situation: Perspectives of social psychology.* New York: McGraw-Hill.

Scherer, K. R. (1978). Personality inference from voice quality: The loud voice of extraversion. *European Journal of Social Psychology, 8,* 467–487.

Schneider, D. J., Hastorf, A. H., & Ellsworth, P. C. (1979). *Person perception* (2nd ed.). Reading, MA: Addison-Wesley.

Shaklee, H. (1991). An inviting invitation [Review of *An invitation to cognitive science: Vol. 3. Thinking*]. *Contemporary Psychology, 36,* 940–941.

Spain, J., Eaton, L., & Funder, D. C. (2000). Predicting behavior and emotion from self and acquaintance ratings. *Journal of Personality, 68,* 837–867.

Swann, W. B. Jr. (1984). Quest for accuracy in person perception: A matter of pragmatics. *Psychological Review, 91,* 457–477.

Conquering the Next Frontier

Modeling Personality Data With Item Response Theory

Michael J. Zickar

ndustrial and organizational (I/O) psychologists' rediscovery of personality theory and personality measurement has resulted in improved prediction and understanding of job-related behaviors. This focus also has revitalized personality psychology by providing an applied context within which to demonstrate the usefulness of I/O psychologists' theories and measures. The goal of this chapter is to introduce practitioners from both fields (I/O psychology and personality psychology) to some relatively new technical developments in measurement theory that can help resolve applied and theoretical issues. Specifically, this chapter provides a nontechnical introduction to item response theory (IRT), discusses issues related to using IRT in personality research, and presents examples of how IRT can be used to examine two complex issues involved in personality measurement: (a) faking and (b) aberrant respondents.

IRT has had a profound influence on the measurement of cognitive abilities and educational achievement, but its effect on the measurement of personality traits has been relatively small. This is unfortunate, because the potential benefits of IRT are vast. These benefits include microscopic level of item analysis, development of adaptive tests, detailed item-bias analysis, analysis of item and response option wording, scale equating, and analysis of individuals' response behaviors. To better understand the possibilities of IRT, an explanation of some of the basic concepts of IRT is necessary.

Item Response Theory

Classical test theory (CTT) has served as the foundation for most commonly used scale development techniques, such as internal consistency estimates and the Spearman–Brown prophecy formula (Gulliksen, 1950; Lord & Novick,

1968). CTT is a weak test theory, which means that it has assumptions that are easily met in most data sets. However, like most weak theories, CTT is limited in the precision of its predictions. With CTT, it can be difficult to predict how an individual will respond to a particular item even given information about his or her responses to other items. This is because CTT is focused at the scale level. Complex psychometric applications, such as adaptive testing, require an understanding of the interaction among items and individuals.

IRT, which was made prominent by Lord and Novick (1968), relates properties of items and characteristics of individuals to the probability of affirming individual items. The cornerstone of IRT is the item response function (IRF). The IRF is a nonlinear regression of the probability of affirming item i on a latent trait commonly denoted θ (theta).

An example of an IRF for the item "bright" from Goldberg's (1992) Adjective Checklist's (ACL) Intellect scale (Goldberg, 1992) is presented in Figure 7.1. Respondents were asked the following question: "Is this an accurate description of you or not?" It is possible to determine the probability that someone will

FIGURE 7.1

Item Response Functions for the Item "Bright." Note that the response format was modified to be dichotomous.

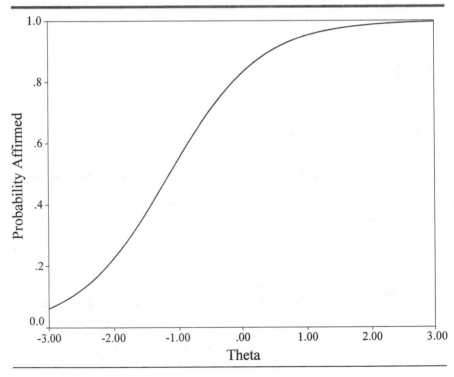

respond that the item is accurate given his or her level of intellect, referred to in IRT terms as a *latent trait* or *theta* (θ). Theta is distributed standard normal, similar to a z-score distribution, so that someone with a theta equal to zero would be at the mean level of agreeableness; similarly, someone with a theta equal to -2.0 would have a level of agreeableness equal to two standard deviations below the sample mean. Given the IRF for "bright," it is possible to compute the likelihood that a respondent with a particular theta would answer the item in the positive direction. For example, individuals with thetas equal to -2.0 (a low amount of agreeableness) would be expected to have a 20% probability of answering that "bright" is an accurate descriptor. As can be seen in the IRF, this probability increases as an individual's theta increases, so that an individual with a theta equal to $+2.0$ (a high amount of agreeableness) would be expected to answer positively with near 100% probability. The shapes of the IRF are determined by the choice of a particular IRT model (this IRF was based on the two-parameter logistic, or 2PL, model) and a set of parameters estimated from a sample of item responses.

Table 7.1 lists several IRT models that have been used to model personality data. Programs commonly used to estimate IRT models are identified in the table. In addition, heuristic sample-size requirements[1] based on previous research are given for each of these models. Note, however, that these guidelines should be treated as estimates rather than strict rules. Many factors besides sample size (e.g., scale length, quality of items, distribution of ability, estimation method) influence estimation accuracy and should be considered. As can be seen in the table, more complex models (i.e., models with more parameters to be estimated) require larger sample sizes for accurate estimation. The sections that follow describe some of these models in more detail.

Dichotomous Models

For dichotomously scored personality items (e.g., *right/wrong, describes me/does not describe me*), the 2PL and three-parameter logistic (3PL) models are the models most appropriate for personality data. The formula for the 3PL model is as follows:

$$P(u_i = 1 | \theta) = c_i + (1 - c_i) \frac{1}{1 + e^{-1.7a_i(\theta - b_i)}} \tag{1}$$

where the probability that a person with a latent trait, θ, affirms an item i (i.e., $u_i = 1$) is a function of three parameters: a_i, a discrimination parameter; b_i, a

---

[1]The power and precision of IRT analyses come at the price of the larger sample sizes needed to estimate item-level statistics accurately.

TABLE 7.1
Models and Their Characteristics

MODEL	REFERENCE	ASSUMPTIONS	N	SOFTWARE	EXAMPLES OF PERSONALITY APPLICATIONS
		Dichotomous models			
Rasch	Rasch (1960)	Assumes equal discrimination across items No guessing Monotonicity, logistic shape, unidimensionality	150	Bilog Multilog	de Jong-Gierveld & Kamphuis (1985) Lange, R., & Houran (1999)
Two-parameter logistic	Birnbaum (1968)	No guessing Monotonicity, logistic shape, unidimensionality	300	Bilog Multilog Parscale	Reise & Waller (1993) Zickar & Drasgow (1996) Zumbo, Pope, Watson, & Hubley (1997)
Three-parameter logistic	Birnbaum (1968)	Monotonicity, logistic shape, unidimensionality	300	Bilog Multilog Parscale	Harvey & Murry (1994) Zumbo, Pope, Watson, & Hubley (1997)
Multilinear formula scoring	Levine (1984)	No significant assumptions	3,000	Fourscore	Zickar (1997a)
		Polytomous models			
Graded response model	Samejima (1969)	Equal discrimination across options Ordinal patterning of options Smooth option response functions	500	Multilog Parscale	Flannery, Reise, & Widaman (1995) Zickar & Drasgow (1996)
Nominal model	Bock (1972)	Smooth option response functions	1,000	Multilog	Zickar & Drasgow (1996)
Multilinear formula scoring	Levine (1984)	No significant assumptions	3,000	Fourscore	No personality applications

threshold parameter[2]; and c_i, a pseudoguessing parameter. Because these parameters are essential to many different IRT models, it is important to consider them in some detail.

The a parameter is related to how well the item measures the construct being assessed by the scale. This parameter is similar to CTT's measure of discrimination, the item–total correlation. The a parameter determines the steepness of the IRF. The probability of affirming items with large a parameters varies sharply as a function of theta, whereas the probability of affirming items with low a parameters varies weakly as a function of theta. Low a parameters usually are associated with items that measure other unintended traits instead of (or in addition to) the intended construct. Low a parameters (e.g., <0.80) can be used as justification for discarding items.

The b parameter is related to the theta level needed for a high probability of item affirmation. Items with high b parameters will be endorsed only by respondents with large, positive thetas, whereas items with low b parameters will be endorsed by everyone except individuals with the most extreme negative thetas. With cognitive ability items, the b parameter relates to the difficulty of the item. The interpretation of the b parameter for personality items is less well understood, although it probably is related to social desirability and the ease of enacting the behavior implied in personality items. The CTT statistic most related to the b parameter is the percentage of respondents in a sample who endorse the item.

The c parameter introduces a nonzero lower asymptote to the IRF so that respondents with large, negative thetas will have a nonzero probability of affirming the item. The c parameter is necessary with multiple-choice cognitive ability items because even the lowest ability respondents should have a nonzero probability of answering correctly as a result of guessing. For personality items, the c parameter may be warranted when faking or socially desirable responding is expected. There is no analogous CTT statistic.

The 2PL formula is a submodel of the 3PL model and can be obtained by fixing the c parameter to zero. This model contains the implicit assumption that respondents with the lowest theta values will have a zero probability of affirming the item. This assumption seems warranted when respondents are motivated to respond accurately and express no need to respond in socially desirable ways. An even simpler model, the Rasch (1960) model, can be formed by setting the c parameter to zero and making the discrimination parameter equal across all items. This assumption of equal discrimination across all items

---

[2]As another example of IRT's indebtedness to ability measurement, the b parameter is called the *difficulty parameter* by most IRT theorists, even though the concept of difficulty makes little sense in nonability contexts such as personality and attitude measurement.

generally is unwarranted, however. Therefore, the Rasch model should be used only when sample sizes are too low to estimate the 2PL and 3PL models.

These IRT models assume that the latent trait, theta, is the only individual characteristic that can be used to predict item response choice. Therefore, only unidimensional scales can be analyzed by these models. This can be a problem, because strict unidimensionality is rarely achieved in personality data sets. Luckily, Drasgow and Parsons (1983) demonstrated that deviations from unidimensionality would not destroy the usefulness of these models so long as the deviations were modest (i.e., the first factor has a much larger eigenvalue than secondary factors). Unfortunately, many personality constructs may have higher levels of multidimensionality than the levels identified as acceptable by Drasgow and Parsons.

Nonparametric Models

A more appropriate model for data with suspect unidimensionality may be a nonparametric model that has the flexibility to represent multidimensional data. Levine's (1984) multilinear formula scoring (MFS), which characterizes items as linear combinations of a fixed number of complex orthogonal functions, is one such model. IRFs estimated by MFS can be nonmonotonic; this freedom may help in fitting sets of items that are not strictly unidimensional. The 2PL and 3PL models assume smooth, monotonically increasing IRFs. By relaxing these IRF shape constraints, the MFS estimation program may be able to recover a unidimensional continuum for a multidimensional theta (Levine & Tsien, 1997). The disadvantages of using MFS are that it is more data intensive than the simpler models and that, by giving up monotonicity constraints, psychological interpretation of the theta dimension may be more difficult than for the parametric 2PL and 3PL models.

Polytomous Models

Most personality items have response scales that have more than two response options. For example, the original format[3] of Goldberg's (1992) ACL has a nine-point response scale that ranges from *extremely inaccurate* to *extremely accurate*. To address this, polytomous IRT models that allow modeling of option response functions (ORFs) exist. ORFs are similar to IRFs except that theta is related to the probability of choosing a particular option. Therefore, an item with nine response options will have nine ORFs, one corresponding to each option.

There are two different types of polytomous models that are important to

---

[3]The response format of the ACL item "bright" depicted in Figure 7.1 was modified to be dichotomous.

personality researchers. *Graded* models assume that there is an ordering between response options, as in Goldberg's (1992) ACL. These models assume that someone who chooses the first option probably has a smaller theta than someone who chooses the second option and so forth. *Nominal* models assume no a priori ordering of response options. For example, with situational judgment tests, a scenario is presented (e.g., a cranky customer complains in the presence of other customers) and the respondent has to choose between several possible responses. It may be difficult to determine the ordering of response options in terms of how they relate to the focal construct. Nominal models provide more flexibility than graded models, but that flexibility comes at the cost of the greater sample sizes needed to estimate the model accurately.

Multidimensional Models

Models that specify multiple thetas have been developed (Carlson, 1987; McDonald, 1985; McKinley & Reckase, 1983). These models may provide more psychologically interpretable models than the nonparametric unidimensional models such as MFS. With multidimensional IRT (MIRT) models, an item response surface replaces the IRF. To date, MIRT models have yet to be applied to personality data. Additional work needs to be done on estimation procedures; large sample-size requirements may make these types of models impractical for most data sets.

However, I believe that MIRT modeling eventually will be an important contribution to personality measurement. This modeling may allow estimation of substantive traits to be separated from estimation of response tendencies (e.g., social desirability), thereby allowing decision makers access to uncontaminated trait information. In addition, MIRT may be better able to model the often complex data structures of personality tests.

An example of this complexity can be seen with the Hogan Personality Inventory (HPI; Hogan & Hogan, 1992) substantive scales, which are composed of items that belong to a homogenous item composite (HIC). There are approximately five items per HIC and five HICs per scale. For example, the Intellectance scale has items that belong to six HICs: science ability, curiosity, thrill seeking, intellectual games, generates ideas, and culture. Although all items on the Intellectance scale are hypothesized to relate to the general trait of Intellectance, items within the same HIC should have a higher level of interdependence than items that do not share the same HIC. This hierarchical factor structure might produce data that are multidimensional and thus inappropriate for strictly unidimensional IRT models. In previous research (Zickar, 1997a), the 2PL and 3PL models were found to misfit HPI data, whereas the MFS model provided good fit. However, the MFS IRFs were jagged. It is difficult to determine the cause of these sharp deviations of monotonicity in the IRFs.

MIRT models might be able to produce fit comparable to the MFS models while retaining psychological interpretability.

The complexity of MFS and MIRT models often is not needed for ability tests that were designed to be unidimensional. For example, a nominal polytomous model fit the Verbal portion of the Armed Services Vocational Aptitude Battery (Department of Defense, 1992) as well as the more complex MFS model (Drasgow, Levine, Tsien, Williams, & Mead, 1995); the nominal model fit only slightly worse for the quantitative portion of the same test. In contrast, I found (Zickar, 1997a) that the 2PL and 3PL models fit much worse for five of the HPI scales and five of the Army's Assessment of Background and Life Events (ABLE) scales (White, Nord, Mael, & Young, 1993). This suggests that there are some fundamental differences between personality and ability measurement that should be considered when choosing a model.

Differences Between Personality and Cognitive Ability Measurement

There are several fundamental differences between the assessment of cognitive abilities and the assessment of personality traits that need to be considered when evaluating the usefulness of transferring measurement techniques between domains. These differences include (a) transparency, self-insight, (c) item interpretation, (d) factor complexity, and (e) aberrant respondents. It is important to recognize these differences because they may influence choice of models, sample sizes needed for estimation, and use of IRT-based tools.

Transparency

Personality items typically are transparent. That is, a respondent often can determine the relation between a particular option and the level of the trait that corresponds to that option. This generally is not the case in ability testing, however, in which the respondent knows the correct answer only if he or she possesses the requisite knowledge demanded by the item. The transparency of personality items can introduce several competing motivations as potential influences on item responses. In a selection context, for example, the motivation to respond accurately may be displaced by the motivation to respond in a way that would appear favorable to those making hiring decisions. If there are differences in motivations among applicants (i.e., some applicants fake responses whereas some do not), multidimensionality could be introduced into the data set.

In addition, differences in motivation to respond accurately among applicants and incumbents may make it difficult to generalize item-level statistics generated on incumbents to applicants. Robie, Zickar, and Schmit (1999) tested the measurement equivalence of a Personnel Decisions, Inc., (1997) personality inventory across applicants and incumbents. They found that ORFs were similar for most items for both applicant and incumbent samples. However, there were a fair number of items that had different ORFs across the two samples. Unfortunately, they were not able to explain why some items had different ORFs and others did not.

Self-Insight

Research has shown that individuals differ in the clarity and accuracy of their self-knowledge (Mabe & West, 1982; see also Horney, 1942; Ludwig, 1997). Item responses may be influenced not only by an individual's possession of the personality trait and his or her motivation to respond accurately, but also by the individual's ability to accurately judge subjective experiences and feelings. Some individuals may have relatively accurate insight into their personality, whereas others may be relatively ignorant of important internal states (e.g., unconscious thoughts and motivations). In an extreme example, some researchers claim that individuals with multiple personality disorders (MPD) who are present in one personality state often cannot recall relevant personal information about their other personalities (Putnam, Guroff, Silberman, Barban, & Post, 1986; however, see Spanos, 1996 for a different perspective on MPD). Paulhus (1984) proposed that some individuals from nonclinical populations would be higher in denial or benign self-deception than others. These differences in self-insight may be partially responsible for the seemingly inherent multidimensionality in personality data.

Item Interpretation

Cognitive ability items generally are written within the context of a formal system (e.g., Euclidean geometry or English grammar) that is accepted by both the test developer and the test-taker (albeit perhaps misunderstood by the test-taker). Items on personality tests often contain a number of words with ambiguous meaning. For example, for the item, "Are you often sad?", test developers and respondents may have different interpretations of what it means to be sad and what level of frequency is associated with the word *often*. For example, Hakel (1968) found differences in interpretations of words associated with numerical frequency. Undergraduate students were asked to estimate how many times out of 100 acts were likely to occur when signified by particular frequency words. For example, numerical frequency estimates of acts associated with the word *sometimes* ranged from 21% to 45%. These differences in item interpretation could further reduce the quality of personality data.

Factor Complexity

Personality scales typically have more complexity in their factor structures than cognitive ability tests. It is common to obtain internal consistency estimates above .90 for ability tests, whereas in a 1994 meta-analysis, Peterson found that the mean alpha value for personality measures was .75. The addition of self-insight and item interpretation may be partially responsible for this complexity. In addition, many personality measures have behaviorally focused items (e.g., "Do you attend parties often?"). As noted by many personality theorists (e.g., Funder, 1997), behavior usually is determined by a multitude of factors, of which the personality trait being assessed by the scale is only one. This additional complexity might require more complex models, such as nonparametric or multidimensional models, for personality measurement than are needed for ability measurement.

Aberrant Respondents

Personality psychologists have been concerned that there may be a small percentage of individuals who do not respond to personality items in an expected manner (e.g., Berg, 1957; Sechrest & Jackson, 1963). The response patterns for these aberrant individuals appear to be either random or paradoxical. For example, an individual may answer some conscientiousness items as if he or she was extremely conscientious yet respond to other items as if he or she were unconscientious. Tellegen (1988) had proposed the concept of *traitedness* to explain this phenomenon.

Tellegen posited that there are some individuals for whom certain nomothetic (i.e., general to all individuals) personality traits are not relevant. For example, a person for whom the trait of extraversion is not relevant may perform inconsistently on behaviors that trait researchers hypothesize are related to the construct of extraversion. For example, this individual may enjoy talking to strangers and attending parties, but he or she may not enjoy variety and may not like to be the center of attention at social gatherings. This individual would be labeled *untraited* on the construct of extraversion because he or she does not conform to the expected pattern of behaviors related to extraversion.

The plausibility of untraited individuals for ability tests seems to be lower than for personality tests. A small number of ability test response patterns may appear to be random because of misreading directions, unmotivated responding, language problems, and misgridding answer sheets. However, the prevalence of these behaviors should be fairly low in most ability-testing situations. Therefore, the possibility of aberrant response patterns is likely to be higher for personality tests. If untraited people exist for personality inventories, this suggests that models that fit the majority of people may misfit untraited individuals. Therefore, IRT-based techniques, such as adaptive testing, may provide misleading results for untraited individuals. Techniques to address this topic are discussed in the next section.

Applications of Item Response Theory to Modeling in the Personality Domain

The primary contribution of IRT to ability testing has not been in better test development, but rather in the introduction of psychometric tools that are either impossible or extremely awkward without IRT. These tools include adaptive testing, testing for item-level measurement equivalence, and identification of mismeasured individuals. The applications of IRT to personality measurement have been fewer in number, but I will discuss two different personality applications to demonstrate the wide range of benefits that can accrue from using IRT in an applied personality context.

Traitedness Research

Appropriateness measurement, a technique developed using IRT, has been used by several researchers to identify aberrant responses (e.g., Reise & Waller, 1993; Zickar & Drasgow, 1996). In appropriateness measurement, an item response model is estimated for normal respondents. Consistent deviations from this normative model can be thought of as indications of some form of deviancy. Appropriateness measurement is similar to outlier detection in regression analyses.

In a study to determine the prevalence of untraited cases on a personality test, Reise and Waller (1993) used an appropriateness index, Z_L, that is the standardized value of the likelihood of a response pattern given a specific theta (Drasgow, Levine, & Williams, 1985). Individuals with extremely low Z_L index scores could be considered untraited because their response patterns do not conform to the model used to characterize normal respondents. In addition, using a data set of personality item responses, Reise and Waller found that the reliability of Z_L was too low for practical use.

Levine and Drasgow (1988) introduced another form of appropriateness measurement, called optimal appropriateness measurement (OAM). In OAM, aberrance classification decisions are based on a hypothesis-testing statistic that is based on the Neyman–Pearson lemma. Unlike the Z_L approach, in which a model is formulated only for the normal data, models in OAM are formulated for both normal and aberrant (e.g., untraited) respondents. The OAM model for normal respondents typically is a 2PL or 3PL model estimated from real data. The OAM model for aberrant respondents can be formulated on the basis of the user's theoretical question or need. A likelihood ratio statistic comparing the likelihood of the data under the normal model with the likelihood of the data under the aberrant model provides the highest possible detection of aberrant responses. The explicit modeling of aberrance in OAM may increase the reliability of the statistic compared to Z_L.

Zickar (1997a) developed three aberrance models to describe how untraited respondents would respond to items on a personality test. The first model, *random responding*, claimed that untraited respondents answered personality tests as if their item responses were produced by a random number generator. This model is based on Berg's (1959) idea that deviant respondents answer items seemingly independent of item content. This essentially is a baseline model to which to compare more realistic models of aberrance. The second model, the *Gaussian model*, operationalized untraitedness as responding to items with a theta from a personal normal distribution. Instead of a fixed value for theta that other models assume, in the Gaussian model, an individual's theta varies across items and can be characterized by a normal distribution with mean, θ_0, and standard deviation, σ. Traited respondents would have small sigmas (σ), whereas untraited respondents would have relatively large sigmas. The third model, *random facets*, relies on the notion that, within a construct, theoretically distinct but correlated facets[4] exist. In this untraited model, facets were independent for untraited respondents, whereas the same facets were correlated for traited respondents. This last model corresponds to Sechrest and Jackson's (1963) definition of deviation as a unique structuring of traits.

Using these models, Zickar (1997a) estimated the prevalence of untraited respondents in normal samples. As expected, prevalence estimates differed according to the particular model used to operationalize untraited responding. Prevalence estimates based on the random responding model suggested that approximately 2% to 5% (depending on the particular scale) of the respondents were untraited. These prevalence rates probably are similar to the prevalence of random responding that would be found with ability tests. Individuals classified as responding randomly may have had language difficulties, misinterpreted instructions, or had poor motivation, all factors that could be present in respondents taking ability tests. These prevalence estimates are small enough to be of little concern to most researchers and practitioners.

The other operationalizations of untraitedness, however, resulted in prevalence estimates that might be of concern to personality researchers. The Gaussian model produced estimates that, depending on the scale, ranged from approximately 10% to as high as 40%. Finally, the random facets model produced estimates of approximately 10% for most scales. Unlike the random responding model, untraited responding consistent with either the Gaussian or random facets models retained some psychometric information about the individual.

---

[4]The HPI HICs can be considered facets.

Therefore, using an IRT model based on traited respondents will result in some inaccuracy for these untraited individuals, but the theta estimates that result from those incorrect models should be somewhat predictive of the thetas of untraited persons that would be computed using the correct (e.g., Gaussian or random facets) model.

The differences in prevalence estimates suggest that more theoretical work is needed to determine how untraited respondents respond to items. If personality traits typically used to make hiring decisions and assess theoretical relationships are irrelevant for a significant proportion of respondents, true relations between constructs would be misestimated, and personnel decisions could be based on partial misinformation. This analysis of untraited respondents suggests that the precision and rigor of IRT methods can be used as an impetus for developing more precise personality theories.

As a side note, the use of MFS was necessary to produce stable and reasonable prevalence estimates of the various operationalizations of untraitedness. The 2PL model often produced prevalence estimates near 100%; these results were deemed to be inflated due to the lack of the 2PLs fit to the normal data. This is further evidence that complex models may be needed for personality data.

Simulating the Effects of Faking

Several questions regarding fakability have surrounded the use of personality scales in organizational settings since the first structured personality tests. These questions are related to whether personality scales can be faked and the consequences of faking on test validity. The first question has been answered conclusively by a long series of studies, culminating in a meta-analysis by Viswesvaran and Ones (1999) that showed that people instructed to fake personality tests received higher scores than those not instructed to fake. The second question about consequences of faking has been more difficult to answer.

There are two primary paradigms for determining the effects of faking; unfortunately, both paradigms have inherent flaws. The first paradigm involves experimental methodology in which participants are randomly assigned to faking and honest conditions. Participants are instructed to complete a personality inventory under a variety of possible motivations (e.g., honest, fake like you want a job, fake like you do not want to be drafted by the military). Differences between the experimental conditions are adduced to faking. The limitation of this paradigm is that the type of faking that is done in a laboratory is different from actual settings (Kroger & Turnbull, 1975)

The other paradigm involves a comparison of applicant samples to incumbent samples; again differences between the two groups are adduced to faking. There are two inherent limitations to this approach. First, because there was no random assignment to conditions, there may be other important differences between applicants and incumbents besides faking. For example, incumbents may be more conscientious than applicants because unconscientious incumbents would have been fired. Second, it is impossible to determine the extent and prevalence of faking within applicant samples. Applicants are generally not willing to admit that they faked their responses to a personality inventory used for hiring.

I have used a third paradigm, IRT-based computational modeling, which resolves many of the previously mentioned problems (although it has its own inherent limitations). Using computational modeling, it is possible to specify and manipulate the nature of faking, the extent of faking, and test characteristics. In a series of simulations, I have demonstrated that test validity, as operationalized by the correlation coefficient, is relatively insensitive to faking (Zickar, 2000; Zickar, Rosse, & Levin, 1996).

These simulations use IRT as a foundation for generating data. The 2PL IRT model was fit to a sample of incumbents (in which there should be no motivated faking) who completed the ABLE. The resulting IRFs were used to generate data for a sample of honest responders. Next, a statistical model was developed to mimic the process used when fakers respond to personality items. We used a simple model, called the theta-shift, which assumed that when individuals are faking, their true theta is temporarily increased by a certain amount. The amount of the shift would presumably be related to their motivation and ability to fake. See Figure 7.2 for a graphical presentation of the theta-shift model. The arrow in the figure connotes how an item becomes "easier" for respondents who are faking.

Given the regular 2PL model and the theta-shift model, which is just a modification of the 2PL model, it is possible to generate simulation data sets by using a random number generator. First, a simulee's theta is generated by sampling randomly a number from a prespecified distribution, usually the standard normal distribution. This randomly sampled theta is then used along with Equation 1 (see page 143) to compute the likelihood of the simulee affirming the item. Finally, another random number is drawn from a uniform distribution that ranges from 0 to 1. If this number is less than or equal to the computed probability of affirming the item, then the simulee is recorded as affirming the item; otherwise, the response is recorded as not-affirm. Using a Pentium processor with 166MHz and a custom-written Turbo Pascal program, I can generate 10,000 simulees in about 30 seconds!

In the simulation studies, I have varied the following factors: percentage of sample who is faking, magnitude of faking (amount of shift), validity of the test, correlation of the amount of the theta shift with a simulated criterion, and the correlation between the amount of theta shift and theta (Zickar, 1997b;

FIGURE 7.2
Theta-Shift Model.

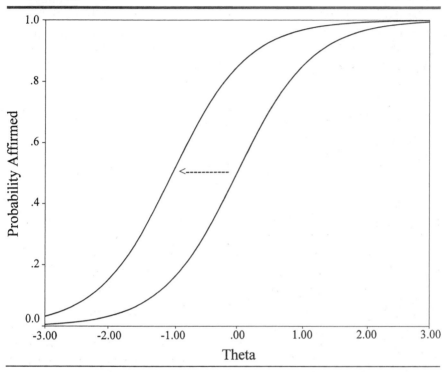

Zickar, Rosse, & Levin, 1996). A computer simulation might be the only way to manipulate some of these variables, such as test validity.

In this research, there were two important dependent variables, the percent decrease in validity that results in faking when compared to the validity with no faking and the mean theta of individuals receiving top scores on the scale. As expected, increased magnitudes of faking caused large decreases in test validity. Increased magnitudes of faking also led to lower mean thetas of individuals who received top scores on the test. Top scores are attained either by having a large true theta or faking a large amount. Therefore, when there is a large magnitude of faking, the fakers tend to rise to the top of the score distribution.

Test validity was not related to the percentage decrease in validity due to faking but was related positively to the mean theta of simulees with the top score. The percentage of validity decrease was negatively related to the correlation between the amount of faking and the criterion as well as the correlation between the amount of faking and theta. Therefore, if people who fake are more likely to be successful on their jobs or have higher personality scores, the decrease in validity due to faking is likely to be slight.

Finally, the decrease in validity was most pronounced when there were roughly equal numbers of fakers and honest respondents in a particular sample. If all of the sample was faking, the validity decrement was less than if only half were faking.

These results are important in that they provide information that can be used to help practitioners ask hypothetical questions, such as "what would happen to the validity of my test if 75% of the sample were faking?" Another interesting finding was that the amount of the validity decrement was generally slight in the presence of faking (e.g., a test with a true validity of .30 may be decreased to .20 with large amounts of faking), even though the rank ordering of simulees could be changed drastically by the presence of faking. When fakers rise to the top of the distribution, top-down hiring procedures could result in some poor quality decisions.

As alluded to before, the simulation paradigm has its own inherent limitation. The model used to simulate item response behavior is only an approximation of the real process used by respondents. Therefore, questions about the fidelity of the simulation are germane. With this faking research, a series of IRT studies have been conducted to help develop a more realistic model of faking than the theta-shift model. An IRT analysis has been conducted using experimental fakers and honest respondents, which examines the nature of ORF differences between the two samples (Zickar & Robie, 1999). Another study examines ORF differences between a sample of incumbents and a sample of applicants (Robie, Zickar, & Schmit, 1999). Both of these studies will be used to generate more refined models of faking.

As with the traitedness research, the framework of IRT was used to develop statistical models in an area without much precise theory. With the use of methods that rely on IRT, it may be possible to better understand the role of faking in the response process of job applicants. Future research may develop methods to better identify respondents who are faking (although see Zickar & Drasgow, 1996, for an early failure at IRT-based faking detection).

Conclusion

Personality researchers are starting to become enthusiastic about the potential for IRT to help them develop scales and answer theoretical questions. This enthusiasm for IRT bodes well for the future of personality measurement. However, two caveats need to be stated. First, as discussed throughout much of this chapter, most of the considerable literature on IRT is based on ability measurement; concepts and methods that work for ability measurement need to be scrutinized and refined before being applied to the personality domain. Second, IRT is a powerful tool but, like many powerful tools, is not always necessary.

Just as there is little need for a Concorde jet when flying from Toledo to Detroit, simple scale development activities, such as identifying items with poor discrimination, can be completed satisfactorily using traditional methods (with less hassle!).

There always has been a sizable gap between research in basic psychometrics and personality research. Thirty years ago, Ralph Heine lamented, "I would like to echo a wish of the author [Donald Fiske] that a much larger area of collaboration be established between measurement specialists and personality theorists" (1971, p. vi). Because of the applied nature of I/O psychology and its keen interest in prediction, it is doubly crucial that the gulf between personality and psychometrics be reduced. I am optimistic about the potential of IRT to affect the practice of personality measurement and look forward to a closer collaboration between personality theorists, the I/O psychologists who use personality scales to predict job performance, and measurement specialists.

References

Berg, I. A. (1957). Deviant responses and deviant people: The formulation of the deviation hypothesis. *Journal of Counseling Psychology, 4*, 154–161.

Berg, I. A. (1959). The unimportance of item content. In B. M. Bass & I. A. Berg (Eds.), *Objective approaches to personality assessment* (pp. 83–99). New York: Van Nostrand.

Birnbaum, A. (1968). Some latent trait models and their use in inferring an examinee's ability. In F. M. Lord & M. R. Novick (Eds.), *Statistical theories of mental test scores* (pp. 395–479). Reading, MA: Addison-Wesley.

Bock, R. D. (1972). Estimating item parameters and latent ability when responses are scored in two or more nominal categories. *Psychometrika, 37*, 29–51.

Carlson, J. E. (1987). *Multidimensional item response theory estimation: A computer program* (ACT Research Rep. No. 87-19). Iowa City, IA: American College Testing Program.

de Jong-Gierveld, J., & Kamphuis, F. (1985). The development of a Rasch-type loneliness scale. *Applied Psychological Measurement, 9*, 289–299.

Department of Defense. (1992). *ASVAB 18/19 counselor manual*. North Chicago, IL: U.S. Military Entrance Processing Command.

Drasgow, F., Levine, M. V., Tsien, S., Williams, B., & Mead, A. D. (1995). Fitting polytomous item response theory models to multiple-choice tests. *Applied Psychological Measurement, 19*, 143–165.

Drasgow, F., Levine, M. V., & Williams, E. A. (1985). Appropriateness measurement with polychotomous item response models and standardized indices. *British Journal of Mathematical and Statistical Psychology, 38*, 67–86.

Drasgow, F., & Parsons, C. K. (1983). Application of unidimensional item response theory models to multidimensional data. *Applied Psychological Measurement, 7*, 189–199.

Flannery, W. P., Reise, S. P., & Widaman, K. F. (1995). An item response theory analysis of the general and academic scales of the Self-Description Questionnaire II. *Journal of Research in Personality, 29*, 168–188.

Funder, D. C. (1997). *The personality puzzle.* New York: Norton.

Goldberg, L. R. (1992). The development of markers for the Big-Five factor structure. *Psychological Assessment, 4*, 26–42.

Gulliksen, H. (1950). *Theory of mental tests.* New York: Wiley.

Hakel, M. D. (1968). How often is often? *American Psychologist, 23*, 533–534.

Harvey, R. J., & Murry, W. D. (1994). Scoring the Myers–Briggs Type Indicator: Empirical comparison of preference score versus latent-trait methods. *Journal of Personality Assessment, 62*, 116–129.

Heine, R. W. (1971). Preface. In D. W. Fiske (Ed.), *Measuring the concepts of personality* (pp. v–vii). Chicago: Aldine.

Hogan, R., & Hogan, J. (1992). *Hogan Personality Inventory manual.* Tulsa, OK: Hogan Assessment Systems.

Horney, K. (1942). *Self-analysis.* New York: Norton.

Kroger, R. O., & Turnbull, W. (1975). Invalidity of validity scales: The case of the MMPI. *Journal of Consulting and Clinical Psychology, 43*, 48–55.

Levine, M. V. (1984). *An introduction to multilinear formula score theory* (Measurement Series 84-4). Champaign: University of Illinois, Department of Educational Psychology.

Levine, M. V., & Drasgow, F. (1988). Optimal appropriateness measurement. *Psychometrika, 53*, 161–176.

Levine, M. V., & Tsien, S. (1997). A geometric approach to two dimensional measurement. In A. J. Marley (Ed.), *Choice, decision, and measurement* (pp. 207–223). Hillsdale, NJ: Erlbaum.

Lord, F. M., & Novick, M. (1968). *Statistical theories of mental test scores.* Reading, MA: Addison-Wesley.

Ludwig, A. M. (1997). *How do we know who we are? A biography of the self.* Oxford, England: Oxford University Press.

Mabe, P. A., & West, S. G. (1982). Validity of self-evaluation of ability: A review and meta-analysis. *Journal of Applied Psychology, 67*, 280–296.

McDonald, R. P. (1985). Unidimensional and multidimensional models for item response theory. In D. J. Weiss (Ed.), *Proceedings of the 1982 Computerized Adaptive Testing Conference* (pp. 127–148). Minneapolis: University of Minnesota, Department of Psychology, Psychometrics Methods Program.

McKinley, R. L., & Reckase, M. D. (1983). MAXLOG: A computer program for the estimation of the parameters of a multidimensional logistic model. *Behavioral Research Methods and Instrumentation, 15*, 389–390.

Paulhus, D. L. (1984). Two-component models of socially desirable responding. *Journal of Personality and Social Psychology, 46*, 598–609.

Personnel Decisions, Inc. (1997). *Selection systems test scale manual.* Minneapolis, MN: Author.

Peterson, R. A. (1994). A meta-analysis of Cronbach's coefficient alpha. *Journal of Consumer Research, 21*, 381–391.

Putnam, F. W., Guroff, J. J., Silberman, E. K., Barban, L., & Post, R. M. (1986). The clinical phenomenology of multiple personality disorder: 100 recent cases. *Journal of Clinical Psychiatry, 47*, 285–293.

Rasch, G. (1960). *Probabilistic models for some intelligence and attainment tests.* Copenhagen: Danish Institute for Educational Research.

Reise, S. P., & Waller, N. G. (1993). Traitedness and the assessment of response pattern scalability. *Journal of Personality and Social Psychology, 54*, 143–151.

Robie, C., Zickar, M. J., & Schmit, M. J. (1999, May). *Measurement equivalence between applicant and incumbent groups: An IRT analysis of personality factors.* Paper presented at the Applied Personality Conference, Tulsa, OK.

Samejima, F. (1969). Estimation of latent ability using a response pattern of graded scores. *Psychometrika Monographs, 34*(Suppl. 17).

Sechrest, L., & Jackson, D. N. (1963). Deviant response tendencies: Their measurement and interpretation. *Educational and Psychological Measurement, 23*, 33–53.

Spanos, N. P. (1996). *Multiple identities and false memories.* Washington, DC: American Psychological Association.

Tellegen, A. (1988). The analysis of consistency in personality assessment. *Journal of Personality, 56*, 621–663.

Viswesvaran, C., & Ones, D. S. (1999). Meta-analyses of fakability estimates: Implications for personality measurement. *Educational and Psychological Measurement, 59*, 197–210.

White, L. A., Nord, R. D., Mael, F. A., & Young, M. C. (1993). The Assessment of Background and Life Experiences (ABLE). In T. Trent & J. H. Laurence (Eds.), *Adaptability screening for the armed forces* (pp. 101–162). Washington, DC: Office of the Assistant Secretary of Defense.

Zickar, M. J. (1997a). *Detecting untraitedness using model-based measurement.* Unpublished doctoral dissertation, University of Illinois at Urbana–Champaign.

Zickar, M. J. (1997b, April). *Developing models for faking on personality scales.* Presented at the annual meeting of the Society of Industrial and Organizational Psychology, St. Louis, MO.

Zickar, M. J. (2000). Modeling faking on personality tests. In D. R. Ilgen & C. L. Hulin (Eds.), *Computational modeling of behavior in organizations: The third scientific discipline* (pp. 95–108). Washington, DC: American Psychological Association.

Zickar, M. J., & Drasgow, F. (1996). Detecting faking on a personality instrument using appropriateness measurement. *Applied Psychological Measurement, 20*, 71–87.

Zickar, M. J., & Robie, C. (1999). Modeling faking good on personality items: An item-level analysis. *Journal of Applied Psychology, 84,* 551–563.

Zickar, M. J., Rosse, J., & Levin, R. (1996, May). Modeling the effects of faking on a personality test. In C. L. Hulin (Chair), *The third discipline: Computational modeling in organizational research.* Symposium conducted at the annual meeting of the Society of Industrial and Organizational Psychology, San Diego, CA.

Zumbo, B. D., Pope, G. A., Watson, J. E., & Hubley, A. M. (1997). An empirical test of Roskam's conjecture about the interpretation of an ICC parameter in personality inventories. *Educational and Psychological Measurement, 57,* 963–969.

CHAPTER 8

The Personality Hierarchy and the Prediction of Work Behaviors

Sampo V. Paunonen

Adelheid A. A. M. Nicol

I ndustrial and organizational (I/O) psychologists have, it seems, been carefully studying the personality psychology literature. Their interest has focused primarily on the discovery of new and useful predictors of job performance. Such predictors are needed to make accurate decisions regarding the selection, classification, and promotion of employees. That I/O psychologists have turned their attention to personality is implicit recognition of personality factors as important determinants of work behaviors and, consequently, of employee productivity (cf. Guion & Gottier, 1965).

In this chapter, we first briefly examine the area of research in personality psychology that I/O psychologists are finding so interesting. We then present a conclusion that some of these psychologists have reached regarding the prediction of work behaviors using personality information. Finally, we take issue with that conclusion and proffer a contrary view. We provide support for our view with empirical data from a study in which a number of personality measures were used to predict a variety of work-relevant criteria.

The Personality Hierarchy

An area of personality psychology that currently is the subject of vigorous research and theoretical activity is personality structure. Psychologists have been interested in personality structure for decades. However, it has been only relatively recently that researchers have begun to express a convergence of ideas regarding the organization presumed to underlie human behavior.

This research was supported by Social Sciences and Humanities Research Council of Canada Research Grant No. 410-98-1555.

As early as 1947, personality was conceptualized as having a formal hierarchical structure (Eysenck, 1947). This hierarchy was proposed to be organized by the breadth of behaviors involved, as shown in Figure 8.1, which illustrates the suggested organization of one personality factor, Conscientiousness (see Paunonen, 1998). Various specific behaviors or acts determine an individual's habitual response patterns. Several related habitual response patterns create what is commonly called a personality trait. Some of these relatively narrow personality traits (e.g., responsibility, orderliness, ambition, endurance, and methodicalness), it is believed, combine to form a broad factor of personality (e.g., Conscientiousness).

Although a hierarchical organization of personality and behavior has long had theoretical appeal, it has been only relatively recently that researchers have begun to identify empirically and with some consensus the components of that hierarchy. Some of these components are included in what is known as the Five-Factor Model of personality structure (FFM) (see McCrae & John, 1992). The FFM posits that there are five personality factors, often referred to as the Big Five, that account for the majority of variations in human behavior. These factors have been labeled Extraversion, Agreeableness, Conscientiousness, Neuroticism, and Openness to Experience (or Intellect).

The Big Five personality factors are thought by some to be universal and to have a biological origin (McCrae, Costa, del Pilar, Rolland, & Parker, 1998). They also are believed to represent the topmost level of the personality hierarchy (see Figure 8.1), with each broad factor being uniquely defined by several distinct, narrow traits (see Digman, 1990; John, 1990; McCrae & John, 1992).

The Personality Hierarchy and Prediction

That personality may be organized hierarchically with the Big Five factors at the top, as shown in Figure 8.1 for the example of the Conscientiousness factor, has not been lost on I/O psychologists. The FFM also has attracted the attention of clinical psychologists, social psychologists, and developmental psychologists, as well as others. Why are researchers from other areas of psychology interested in theoretical developments in personality? The answer is this: If five factors account for the majority of variation in human behavior, and if one is interested in using personality variables as predictors of some criterion of interest, why not simply use measures of a few personality factors as predictors rather than potentially many more measures of those factors' constituent personality traits?

The recommendation to use higher level factor measures of personality for prediction rather than lower level trait measures is based not only on the fact that the former are fewer in number, but also on the fact that the factor measures are broader in that they account for more varied behaviors than do typical

FIGURE 8.1

Hierarchical model of personality structure. From "Hierarchical Organization of Personality and Prediction of Behavior," by S. V. Paunonen, 1998, Journal of Personality and Social Psychology, 74, p. 539. Copyright 1998 by the American Psychological Association.

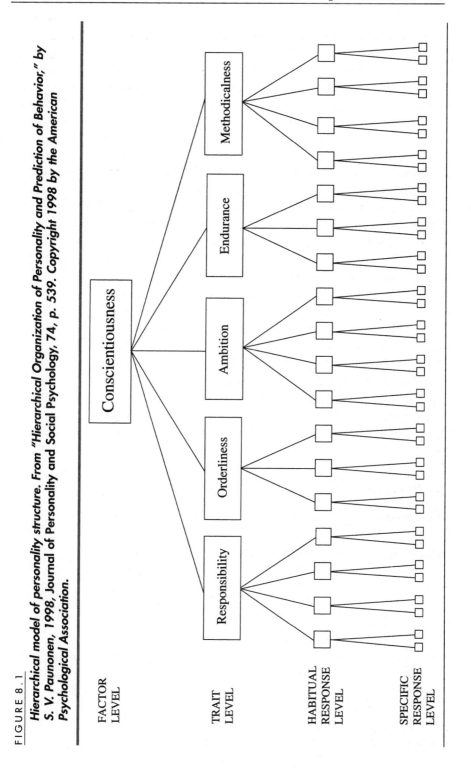

trait measures. It has been argued (e.g., J. Hogan & Roberts, 1996; Ones & Viswesvaran, 1996) that such broad-bandwidth measures should predict certain criteria more accurately than narrow-bandwidth measures. For example, the thinking in I/O psychology is that most criteria related to job performance are complex and multidimensional. As such, the relatively broad Big Five measures of personality should be able to capture the diverse aspects of criterion variance better than any of the more narrow traits that make up the factors.

Paunonen, Rothstein, and Jackson (1999) have taken the opposite view. They have proposed that use of the broad five-factor measures of personality for prediction can result in certain costs. In an I/O context these costs include both attenuated empirical accuracies in predicting job performance and a poorer understanding of the network of personality–work behaviors associations. We reiterate that position in this chapter.

The first problem with using a Big Five personality measure for prediction is that it represents an unweighted aggregate of several distinct underlying facets. That is, it represents the common part of several constituent traits. What it does not represent, however, is the specific variances of those traits that distinguish them from one another. In some contexts, that trait-specific variance may be what is predictive of the criterion of interest. Validity coefficients therefore may be lower when broad rather than narrow traits are used.

The second problem with using Big Five personality measures for prediction is one of interpretation. If it is found, for example, that a Conscientiousness measure predicts employee productivity, is it because more productive employees are more orderly, more responsible, or higher in achievement motivation? These three variables are all thought to be components of Conscientiousness and are summed together in the typical Big Five Conscientiousness measure. Without the individual facet–criterion correlations, however, it is difficult to explain the prediction results and to understand the antecedents and consequences of work behaviors.

A Prescription for Prediction

One need not sacrifice criterion prediction or behavior explanation when using narrow trait measures to predict broad work criteria. How is this possible? The esteemed psychometrician Jum C. Nunnally gave his recommendation regarding this matter in 1978:

> As some will argue, the criterion usually is factorially complex and consequently can be predicted best by a factorially complex predictor test. Instead of building the factorial complexity into a particular test, it is far better to meet the factorial complexity by combining tests in a battery by multiple regression, in which case tests would be selected to measure the different factors that are thought to be important. (p. 268)

As recognized by Nunnally, several narrow, unidimensional variables of personality can be entered into a regression equation to predict a complex criterion such as job performance (see also Mershon & Gorsuch, 1988). The specific variance of each variable can then add to (or not) the empirical accuracy of overall prediction. Furthermore, that overall prediction always will be greater than (or equal to) the prediction of an unweighted composite of the predictor variables, as might be derived for a Big Five factor measure. Note that this regression approach allows disparate, even orthogonal, variables to be used in the same regression equation, even if those variables have nothing more in common than their ability to predict the separate facets of a multidimensional criterion (see also Schneider, Hough, & Dunnette, 1996).

The advantage of using several unidimensional predictors of work behaviors for behavior explanation is that those predictors are not combined into a multidimensional composite measure except when it is necessary to generate predicted criterion scores. Instead, it is possible to interpret employees' scores on distinct, psychologically meaningful personality traits. By determining which of the individual facets of a Big Five factor are predictive of job performance, for example, one can develop a general theory about the nomological network of personality trait–work behaviors associations.

Paunonen (1998) empirically evaluated the differential predictiveness of broad Big Five measures and narrow personality trait measures (see also Ashton, Jackson, Paunonen, Helmes, & Rothstein, 1995; Paunonen, 1993). Study participants were undergraduate university students; criteria were several complex behaviors thought to have, at least in part, some basis in personality. These criteria included such behaviors and characteristics as cigarette consumption, grade point average (GPA), and fraternity membership. The Big Five predictors were measured by NEO Five-Factor Inventory scales (Costa & McCrae, 1992). The lower level trait predictors were measured by Personality Research Form (PRF) scales (Jackson, 1984).

In general, the data from that study (Paunonen, 1998) showed that both the Big Five factor scales and the personality trait scales predicted most of the criteria to some extent. In addition, when multiple regression analysis was used, the Big Five factor scales were able to increment the predictiveness of the lower level trait scales. However, the lower level trait scales were able to increment the predictiveness of the Big Five factor scales as well. Most interesting, however, was the fact that the incremental validity of the personality trait predictors generally was much higher than that of the personality factor predictors. A separate data set with different participants and using Jackson Personality Inventory (JPI) scales (Jackson, 1976, 1994) as measures of the lower level traits yielded essentially the same results.

The conclusion reached by Paunonen (1998) bears directly on the increasingly common practice in contemporary research of using the Big Five factor measures as the only measures of personality; that is, that combining narrow personality traits into their underlying broad factors can entail predictive losses, losses that are due to the ensuing elimination of trait-specific but criterion-valid variance. We add here that the practice of using only Big Five measures also can entail interpretive losses (see also Paunonen, 1993; Paunonen et al., 1999). In using only Big Five measures one forgoes the information that, for example, it might be only one facet of the Big Five that is entirely responsible for the criterion prediction or that the Big Five facets are differentially aligned with the various facets of a multidimensional criterion.

Other researchers have reached this same conclusion concerning the differential operation of individual Big Five facet scales in their associations with other variables. It is important to note that among those are the creators of two well-regarded instruments designed to measure the Big Five factors. In developing the Hogan Personality Inventory (HPI), R. Hogan and Hogan (1992) explicitly acknowledged (p. 13) that the lower level measures in the HPI, called homogeneous item composites (HICs), may not all be equal in their ability to predict a criterion, even if those HICs represent the same Big Five factor (see also J. Hogan & Hogan, 1986, 1989). Costa and McCrae (1992), developers of the Revised NEO Personality Inventory (NEO–PI–R), expressed exactly the same view regarding the predictive merits of their Big Five facet scales (p. 46).

Study Purpose

The purpose of the study discussed in this chapter was to replicate, in part, Paunonen's (1998) earlier study using better measures of the Big Five factor variables and a more varied array of behavior criteria. Again, both broad Big Five factor measures and narrower lower level trait measures were used to determine which type of variable is better able to account for variance in a set of personality-relevant criterion variables.

Although this study focused on I/O concerns, it was not conducted in an actual work setting predicting the job performance of real employees. Instead, participants were undergraduate university students. Many of the behavior criteria used, however, can be argued to have links to performance for some jobs.

Method

Overview

Study participants completed several self-report measures of both lower level personality traits and higher level personality factors (i.e., the Big Five). They also were measured on 12 separate behavior criteria, criteria that did not rely only on subjective self-ratings. The personality trait variables and the personality factor variables were then evaluated in terms of their relative ability to predict the criterion variables.

The specific behavior criteria chosen for this study were selected to be complex, multidimensional variables potentially having multiple personality determinants. Such criteria, therefore, should be predicted by some personality traits or factors in an omnibus assessment. We also sought criterion behaviors that are arguably relevant to performance at some job tasks so that the results achieved with university students would have some relevance to the work behaviors of actual employees.

Participants and Procedure

A total of 141 undergraduate students (46 men and 95 women) enrolled in an introductory psychology course volunteered to participate in the study in return for course credit. Participants completed several published and unpublished questionnaire measures of personality, ability, and other characteristics in two assessment sessions 1 week apart. They also completed a Behavior Report Form that contained some of the criterion measures (see also Paunonen, 1998). Modal group size for each assessment session was 12 participants.

Personality Predictors

Two sets of lower level trait measures, representing facets of the Big Five personality factors, and two sets of higher level factor measures, representing the Big Five factors themselves, were used as criterion predictors. These measures are described below.

Trait Measures

All participants completed two separate batteries of lower level personality trait measures. The first of these included the 30 facet scales of the NEO–PI–R (Costa & McCrae, 1992). The second battery included scales from the PRF (Jackson, 1984) and the JPI (Jackson, 1976, 1994). In the evaluations that follow, the 21 scales of the PRF (20 trait scales and Desirability) plus 15 scales of the JPI were considered together as one set of lower level trait measures to parallel the 30 NEO–PI–R measures.

To compare the NEO–PI–R and PRF/JPI trait measures fairly, the numbers of variables in the two sets (i.e., 30 and 36, respectively) had to be equated. We did this by omitting 6 JPI scales from the analysis. Two of these scales, Breadth of Interest and Social Participation, were deleted because of their strong overlap with the PRF scales of Understanding and Affiliation, respectively. The other 4 JPI scales, Energy Level, Risk Taking, Social Adroitness, and Value Orthodoxy, were deleted because they have shown particularly poor fit in the factor space of the Big Five in past analyses (see Ashton, Jackson, Helmes, & Paunonen, 1998; Paunonen & Jackson, 1996).

Factor Measures

The two sets of lower level personality trait scales described above were each combined to create two sets of higher level personality factor measures. This was relatively straightforward for the NEO–PI–R set: The 30 facet scales were each arranged onto their corresponding Big Five factor or domain scale. The term domain scale is used by the authors of the NEO–PI–R to refer to the aggregated facet scales. Each NEO–PI–R facet is designed to measure an aspect of one of the Big Five factors, with 6 facets representing each personality factor. Thus, total scores for each of the 6 facets are simply added together to get an (unweighted) domain total score for each Big Five factor.

The second set of personality trait scales used, the 30 PRF/JPI scales, were also aggregated into a set of Big Five composite measures. The 30 trait scales were factored with a principal components analysis and rotated five dimensions with varimax. The resulting factors, which accounted for 57.7% of the scales' total variance, closely resembled typical Big Five personality factors. They also largely replicated the results of other factor analyses of these same trait scales (e.g., Ashton, Jackson, Helmes, & Paunonen, 1998; Jackson, Paunonen, Fraboni, & Goffin, 1996; Paunonen & Jackson, 1996). Factor scores were then calculated for each participant to derive the second set of (weighted) measures of the Big Five dimensions.

Correlations between participants' NEO–PI–R domain scores and their corresponding PRF/JPI factor scores were computed. These were, in descending order, Conscientiousness = .79, Extraversion = .71, Agreeableness = .68, Openness to Experience = .60, and Neuroticism = .40. Overall, these correlations are quite high. However, they are not so high that they necessarily preclude the independent operation of the two sets of Big Five scores in predicting the criteria of this study (particularly in the case of Neuroticism).

Behavior Criteria

The criteria for this study were chosen so that they did not simply represent variants of the personality predictors used. Instead, we selected behavior variables that might reasonably be thought to be (a) causally linked to personality, (b) complex and multidetermined, and (c) relevant to work behaviors. The 12 criteria measured for each participant are described below and summarized in Table 8.1.

TABLE 8.1

The 12 Criterion Variables

CRITERION	DESCRIPTION
1. Questionnaire neatness	Mean of 3 evaluators' ratings of neatness of computerized answer sheet
2. Task completion time	Mean order of completion of 2 assessment sessions
3. Tardiness to experiment	Mean order of arrival to 2 experimental sessions
4. Absenteeism from experiments	Number of unfulfilled experimental credits
5. Grade point average	Freshman-year grade point average
6. General knowledge	Multidimensional Aptitude Battery Information subscale score
7. Numerical ability	Multidimensional Aptitude Battery Arithmetic subscale score
8. Blood donations	Self-report of frequency of blood donations
9. Willingness to share money	Score on money-allocation task of altruism
10. Willingness to gamble	Score on money-wagering task of risk taking
11. Traffic violations	Mean number of traffic violations per year of driving
12. Admissions of dishonesty	Honesty questionnaire Admissions subscale score

The 12 criteria were as follows:

1. Three evaluators rated each participant's completed PRF computerized answer sheet for neatness. The average rating was used as a measure of questionnaire neatness.

2. Participants generally finished an assessment session at different times. The mean order in which each participant completed all experimental forms, averaged across the two assessment sessions, was taken as a measure of task completion time.

3. Participants generally arrived to an experimental session at different times. The mean order of each participant's arrival, averaged across the two experimental sessions, was a measure of tardiness to experiment.

4. A requirement of the introductory psychology course is 5 hr as an experiment participant. The number of missed experimental hours out of 5 was counted for each participant as part of an absenteeism from experiments criterion.

5. Freshman-year grades were obtained for each participant from the university registrar's office. These grades formed a GPA criterion.

6. Participants were administered two subscales from the Multidimensional Aptitude Battery (MAB; Jackson, 1990). Participants' scores on the MAB Information subscale were used as a general knowledge criterion.

7. Participants' scores on the MAB Arithmetic subscale were used as a numerical ability criterion.

8. The Behavior Report Form asked participants to estimate the frequency with which they had donated blood in the past. Participants' self-reports of frequency of blood donations were used as a criterion.

9. Participants completed an experimental 5-item money-allocation task of altruism, in which each participant had to decide, in five hypothetical scenarios, whether or not to share a certain amount of money with another person at the expense of keeping a larger amount of money for himself or herself. Scores on this task formed a willingness to share money criterion.

10. Participants completed an experimental 8-item money-wagering task of risk taking, in which each participant had to decide, in eight hypothetical scenarios, on the amount of money he or she was willing to gamble for a given monetary prize at a given probability of success. This scale yielded a willingness to gamble criterion.

11. One of the items on the Behavior Report Form asked participants to estimate the number of speeding, parking, and other traffic violations received in the past. The mean number of traffic violations received per year of driving experience was computed for each participant.

12. An experimental honesty questionnaire we have been developing contains an Admissions scale that asks respondents to admit to past dishonest behaviors. This scale, which predicted actual incidents of theft and cheating by an independent group of 109 students in a controlled laboratory context ($r = .34$ and $.16$, respectively; Nicol, 1999), formed an admissions of dishonesty criterion measure.

Results

Reliability of Measures

Coefficient alpha reliabilities were computed for all of the PRF/JPI and NEO–PI–R variables. Reliabilities were computed separately for both sets of lower level personality trait measures and both sets of higher level personality factor measures.

Personality Research Form/Jackson Personality Inventory

The PRF/JPI factor measures were derived as the factor scores from a varimax rotation of five factors underlying the 30 lower level trait scales. The reliabilities of these weighted composites (see Nunnally, 1978, p. 250) were very high, all exceeding .92. For comparison with the unweighted NEO–PI–R domain scales, reliabilities also were computed for the PRF/JPI factors in the following way. First, the 30 PRF/JPI personality trait scales were each temporarily assigned to only one factor. Coefficient alpha reliabilities were then computed on the 5 resulting unweighted composite scales. The trait–factor assignments and reliabilities are shown in Table 8.2. These assignments were based on each variable's highest factor loading in the varimax analysis. The reliabilities for the 5 (unweighted) composite scales ranged from .86 (Agreeableness) to .93 (Extraversion), with a mean of .90. The reliabilities of the 30 lower level PRF/JPI trait scales ranged from .56 (Desirability) to .88 (Order), with a mean of .73.

Revised NEO Personality Inventory Measures

Reliabilities were computed for the 5 NEO–PI–R domain scales and their 30 constituent facet scales. The assignment of the facet scales to the domain scales is shown in Table 8.3, which represents the standard scoring of that instrument (Costa & McCrae, 1992). Table 8.3 also presents the computed reliabilities of the higher level domain scales and the lower level trait scales. Reliabilities for the domain scales ranged from .88 (Openness) to .90 (Neuroticism) with a mean of .89. Reliabilities for the facet scales ranged from .54 (Dutifulness) to .83 (Depression), with a mean of .70.

Overall, the reliabilities for both the PRF/JPI trait scales and the NEO–PI–R domain and facet scales are consistent with those published in the scales' respective manuals (Jackson et al., 1996; Costa & McCrae, 1992). Furthermore, we judged the PRF/JPI and NEO–PI–R factor measures to have equivalent mean levels of reliability in these data, as have the PRF/JPI and NEO–PI–R trait measures. The much longer factor measures, however, are substantially more reliable than the trait measures.

TABLE 8.2

Trait–Factor Assignments and Reliabilities for Personality Research Form/ Jackson Personality Inventory Factor Scales and 30 Constituent Trait Scales

FACTOR SCALE	RELIABILITY	TRAIT SCALE	RELIABILITY
Neuroticism	.92	Succorance	.78
		Autonomy	.69
		Conformity	.82
		Interpersonal affect	.77
		Social recognition	.74
		Harmavoidance	.87
		Anxiety	.77
Extraversion	.93	Affiliation	.73
		Self-esteem	.85
		Exhibition	.87
		Dominance	.85
Openness	.90	Complexity	.71
		Understanding	.67
		Sentience	.69
		Nurturance	.73
		Innovation	.86
		Tolerance	.60
		Change	.66
Agreeableness	.86	Aggression	.79
		Defendence	.74
		Abasement	.68
		Responsibility	.66
Conscientiousness	.91	Organization	.75
		Order	.88
		Impulsivity	.74
		Cognitive structure	.60
		Desirability	.56
		Achievement	.72
		Play	.63
		Endurance	.71

Predictor–Criterion Correlations

Correlations between each of the personality predictor variables and each of the behavior criteria were computed. The focus of this evaluation was the relative predictive validities of the lower level trait measures versus the higher level factor measures. Note, however, that the former variables are much greater in number than the latter. That is, for each criterion, 30 trait scale correlations are computed and compared to only 5 factor scale correlations. The chance of the trait scales yielding spuriously significant coefficients of correlation is, therefore,

TABLE 8.3

Facet–Domain Scale Assignments and Reliabilities for Revised NEO Personality Inventory Domain Scales and 30 Constituent Facet Scales

DOMAIN SCALE	RELIABILITY	FACET SCALE	RELIABILITY
Neuroticism	.90	Anxiety	.72
		Angry hostility	.78
		Depression	.83
		Self-consciousness	.66
		Impulsiveness	.61
		Vulnerability	.71
Extraversion	.88	Warmth	.73
		Gregariousness	.74
		Assertiveness	.78
		Activity	.59
		Excitement seeking	.56
		Positive emotions	.67
Openness	.88	Fantasy	.73
		Aesthetics	.82
		Feelings	.73
		Actions	.61
		Ideas	.76
		Values	.60
Agreeableness	.90	Trust	.82
		Straightforwardness	.71
		Altruism	.74
		Compliance	.77
		Modesty	.76
		Tender mindedness	.57
Conscientiousness	.88	Competence	.64
		Order	.70
		Dutifulness	.54
		Achievement striving	.74
		Self-discipline	.68
		Deliberation	.70

six times that of the factor scales. The solution to this problem was to evaluate the correlations for the lower level traits using a level of alpha, which sets the Type I error rate for each correlation, at one-sixth the level used for the higher level scales (see also Paunonen, 1998). Thus, whereas the criterion correlations for the factor-based measures were assessed in terms of the usual level of significance of $p = .05$, the trait-based predictors were evaluated in terms of a level of significance of $p = .008$. Moreover, all of the correlations reported are shrunken values; that is, adjusted for the number of participants and number of predictors in each analysis.

Personality Research Form/Jackson Personality Inventory Measures

First computed were the multiple correlations of the 5 PRF/JPI factor-based personality scales in predicting each of the 12 separate criteria. A stepwise procedure was used to select predictors only if they exceeded the predetermined level of statistical significance (i.e., $p < .05$). Included as the first predictor in these analyses was the variable of participant sex. Sex differences in both predictor and criterion variables could, of course, contribute to a correlation between the two variables when no such correlation actually existed in either single-sex sample. Therefore, it was thought important to control for sex.

Table 8.4 shows the results of using the PRF/JPI factor-based personality scales in predicting the various criterion measures. The second column of the table lists any factor measures that significantly ($p < .05$) incremented the level of criterion prediction achieved by participant sex alone. For each criterion that was significantly predicted by one or more factor measures, the next two columns present that criterion's multiple correlation with the listed factor predictor

TABLE 8.4

Validity in Predicting Criteria: Personality Research Form/Jackson Personality Inventory (PRF/JPI) Factor Scales

CRITERION	PRF/JPI PREDICTORS ($p = <.05$)	$R_{SEX+PRF}$	R_{SEX}	%
1. Questionnaire neatness	Conscientiousness	.27	.11	6.1
2. Task completion time	Agreeableness	.16	.00	2.5
3. Tardiness to experiment	Openness–	.17	.00	2.9
4. Absenteeism from experiments				
5. Grade point average	Conscientiousness, openness	.27	.00	7.5
6. General knowledge	Openness	.37	.29	5.5
7. Numerical ability				
8. Blood donations	Openness	.14	.00	2.0
9. Willingness to share money	Agreeableness, openness, extraversion–	.47	.18	18.8
10. Willingness to gamble	Neuroticism	.26	.04	6.7
11. Traffic violations				
12. Admissions of dishonesty	Agreeableness–	.35	.29	3.9
M		.27	.10	6.2

Note. Blank row = no PRF/JPI factor scale significantly increased criterion prediction at $p < .05$; $R_{SEX+PRF}$ = multiple correlation of sex plus listed PRF/JPI factor scale(s) with criterion; R_{SEX} = multiple correlation of sex alone with criterion; % = percentage change in criterion variance accounted for by the addition of PRF/JPI factor scale(s). A minus (–) sign beside a predictor indicates a negative regression coefficient.

or predictors plus sex (column 3) and that criterion's multiple correlation with sex alone (column 4). The last column indicates the proportional difference in the two multiple correlations (i.e., the percentage increase in criterion variance accounted for by using sex plus the significant factor scale or scales as a predictor or predictors vs. using sex alone).

The results shown in Table 8.4 indicate that the PRF/JPI personality factor scales significantly predicted 9 of the 12 criteria. Moreover, the factor scales accounted for 6.2% more variance in the criterion measures, on average, than that accounted for by participant sex alone. In short, the PRF/JPI factor-based personality scales were able to predict to some extent most of the behavior criteria under study.

PRF/JPI lower level personality trait scales were used as criterion predictors in the next set of analyses. Table 8.5 lists the results of using those trait scales as predictors compared with using sex alone as a predictor. Note that the PRF/JPI trait scales incremented the prediction of 8 of the 12 criteria ($p < .008$) compared with using participant sex as a predictor. Moreover, the amount of extra criterion variance accounted for by these lower level personality traits was

TABLE 8.5

Validity in Predicting Criteria: Personality Research Form/Jackson Personality Inventory (PRF/JPI) Trait Scales

CRITERION	PRF/JPI PREDICTORS ($p = <.008$)	$R_{SEX+PRF}$	R_{SEX}	%
1. Questionnaire neatness	Order	.24	.11	4.5
2. Task completion time				
3. Tardiness to experiment				
4. Absenteeism from experiments	Organization−, order	.40	.00	16.0
5. Grade point average	Desirability	.29	.00	8.6
6. General knowledge	Understanding, aggression	.46	.29	13.4
7. Numerical ability	Play	.26	.13	5.0
8. Blood donations	Harmavoidance−	.26	.00	6.8
9. Willingness to share money	Responsibility, abasement	.57	.18	29.1
10. Willingness to gamble				
11. Traffic violations				
12. Admissions of dishonesty	Responsibility−	.44	.29	10.9
M		.37	.13	11.8

Note. Blank row = no PRF/JPI trait scale significantly increased criterion prediction at $p < .008$; $R_{SEX+PRF}$ = multiple correlation of sex plus listed PRF/JPI trait scale(s) with criterion; R_{SEX} = multiple correlation of sex alone with criterion; % = percentage change in criterion variance accounted for by addition of PRF/JPI trait scale(s). A minus (−) sign beside a predictor indicates a negative regression coefficient.

11.8%, an amount almost twice that accounted for by the higher level personality factors (6.2%; Table 8.4).

Revised NEO Personality Inventory Measures

Table 8.6 lists the results of the NEO–PI–R domain scales in predicting the 12 criteria. These factor-based personality scales were able to predict 10 of the criteria significantly ($p < .05$) beyond the level of prediction achieved by participant sex. In addition, these domain scales accounted for, on average, an additional 6.8% of criterion variance compared with sex alone.

The separate NEO–PI–R facet scales were next used as predictors of the 12 criteria. As seen in Table 8.7, 10 of the 12 criteria were significantly ($p < .008$) predicted by one or more of the lower level personality facet scales beyond the level of prediction achieved by participant sex. The average increment in criterion prediction over that due to sex was 11.5% for these scales. The NEO–PI–R lower level personality scales, therefore, were substantially better at pre-

TABLE 8.6

Validity in Predicting Criteria: Revised NEO Personality Inventory (NEO–PI–R) Domain Scales

CRITERION	NEO–PI–R PREDICTORS ($p = <.05$)	$R_{SEX+NEO}$	R_{SEX}	%
1. Questionnaire neatness	Conscientiousness	.31	.11	8.1
2. Task completion time	Agreeableness	.15	.00	2.2
3. Tardiness to experiment	Agreeableness–	.16	.00	2.5
4. Absenteeism from experiments				
5. Grade point average	Conscientiousness	.34	.00	11.9
6. General knowledge	Openness	.38	.29	6.4
7. Numerical ability				
8. Blood donations		.17	.00	2.8
9. Willingness to share money	Agreeableness	.38	.18	11.6
10. Willingness to gamble	Neuroticism–	.23	.04	5.0
11. Traffic violations	Neuroticism	.14	.00	2.0
12. Admissions of dishonesty	Agreeableness–	.49	.29	15.4
M		.28	.10	6.8

Note. Blank row = no NEO–PI–R domain scale significantly increased criterion prediction at $p < .05$; $R_{SEX+NEO}$ = multiple correlation of sex plus listed NEO–PI–R domain scale(s) with criterion; R_{SEX} = multiple correlation of sex alone with criterion; % = percentage change in criterion variance accounted for by addition of NEO–PI–R domain scale(s). A minus (–) sign beside a predictor indicates a negative regression coefficient.

TABLE 8.7

Validity in Predicting Criteria: Revised NEO Personality Inventory (NEO–PI–R) Facet Scales

CRITERION	NEO–PI–R PREDICTORS (p = <.008)	$R_{SEX+NEO}$	R_{SEX}	%
1. Questionnaire neatness	Self-discipline	.29	.11	7.0
2. Task completion time				
3. Tardiness to experiment	Actions–	.25	.00	6.5
4. Absenteeism from experiments	Compliance–	.27	.00	7.5
5. Grade point average	Self-discipline	.40	.00	15.9
6. General knowledge	Fantasy	.39	.29	6.8
7. Numerical ability	Values, competence–	.35	.13	10.6
8. Blood donations	Activity	.30	.00	9.0
9. Willingness to share money	Modesty, deliberation	.54	.18	25.8
10. Willingness to gamble	Vulnerability–	.28	.04	7.7
11. Traffic violations				
12. Admissions of dishonesty	Straightforwardness–, ideas–	.52	.29	18.6
M		.36	.10	11.5

Note. Blank row = no NEO–PI–R facet scale significantly increased criterion prediction at p < .008; $R_{SEX+NEO}$ = multiple correlation of sex plus listed NEO–PI–R facet scale(s) with criterion; R_{SEX} = multiple correlation of sex alone with criterion; % = percentage change in criterion variance accounted for by addition of NEO–PI–R facet scale(s). A minus (–) sign beside a predictor indicates a negative regression coefficient.

diction compared with their higher level counterparts (i.e., 11.5% vs. 6.8%: Table 8.6), replicating the general findings with the PRF/JPI scales.

Predictors and Incremental Validity

Rather than comparing the lower level and higher level personality measures for simple validity in predicting a criterion, one can compare them in terms of incremental validity. That is, it is possible to determine whether one type of predictor accounts for variance in a criterion beyond that accounted for by the other type. For example, one can assess whether the Big Five personality factor scales increment the criterion prediction achieved by lower level personality trait scales. Conversely, it is also possible to determine whether the lower level trait scales increment the criterion prediction achieved by the Big Five factor scales. What is of interest here, of course, is whether the common variance underlying the broad factor scales optimally predicts the criterion of interest or whether the specific variance underlying the narrow trait scales adds something unique to criterion prediction.

In the analyses reported below, lower level trait scales were first searched for significant criterion predictors in a stepwise multiple regression. The set of higher level factor measures was then searched, again using stepwise regression, for scales that increased the degree of criterion prediction already achieved with the lower level predictors. The reverse also was evaluated (i.e., the personality factor scales were entered into the prediction equation first, followed by the personality trait scales).

Three aspects of these incremental validity analyses should be noted. First, participant sex was again used as the initial criterion predictor in each analysis. All incremental validities were then compared after any effects of participant sex were removed. Second, the PRF/JPI factor scales were not compared with the PRF/JPI trait scales, nor were the NEO–PI–R domain scales compared with the NEO–PI–R facet scales. This was because the higher level measures in both cases are simply arithmetic linear combinations of the lower level measures. Instead, the PRF/JPI factor scales were compared with the NEO–PI–R facet scales and the NEO–PI–R domain scales were compared with the PRF/JPI trait scales to determine incremental prediction. Third, the size of alpha used to decide whether a predictor was statistically significant differed according to the set of predictors being assessed. As in the previous analyses, the higher level personality predictors were evaluated for significance at $p < .05$, whereas the larger number of lower level personality predictors were evaluated at $p < .008$. Furthermore, all multiple correlations reported were corrected for shrinkage.

Personality Research Form/Jackson Personality Inventory Factor Scales Versus Revised NEO Personality Inventory Facet Scales

In our initial evaluation of incremental validity, we first searched the NEO–PI–R facet scales for significant ($p < .008$) predictors of each criterion (after participant sex was partialed out). We then searched the PRF/JPI factor scales for additional significant ($p < .05$) predictors. The results of these analyses are shown in Table 8.8. As shown in the table, the PRF/JPI factor-based scales significantly incremented the predictive accuracy of the NEO–PI–R facet scales for 3 of the 12 criteria. The mean increment in criterion variance accounted for by those three factor scales over the facet scales, however, was only 2.9%.

In the next analysis, we reversed the order of entry of the predictors into the regression equations described in the previous analysis. We first entered the PRF/JPI factor scales into a stepwise regression equation (after participant sex), followed by the NEO–PI–R facet scales. As illustrated in Table 8.9, the NEO–PI–R facet scales incremented significantly the predictive ability of the PRF/JPI factor scales for 8 of the 12 criteria. Furthermore, the increment in criterion variance accounted for by the facet scales was 8.4%, almost three times the corresponding value achieved by the factor scales (2.9%; Table 8.8).

TABLE 8.8

Incremental Validity in Predicting Criteria: Personality Research Form/ Jackson Personality Inventory (PRF/JPI) Factor Scales Versus Revised NEO Personality Inventory (NEO–PI–R) Facet Scales

CRITERION	PRF/JPI PREDICTORS (p = <.05)	$R_{NEO+PRF}$	R_{NEO}	%
1. Questionnaire neatness				
2. Task completion time	Agreeableness	.16	.00	2.5
3. Tardiness to experiment				
4. Absenteeism from experiments				
5. Grade point average				
6. General knowledge	Openness	.43	.39	3.2
7. Numerical ability				
8. Blood donations				
9. Willingness to share money	Openness	.56	.54	2.9
10. Willingness to gamble				
11. Traffic violations				
12. Admissions of dishonesty				
M		.38	.31	2.9

Note. Blank row = no PRF/JPI factor scale significantly increased criterion prediction at p < .05; $R_{NEO+PRF}$ = multiple correlation of NEO–PI–R facet scales plus listed PRF/JPI factor scale(s) with criterion; R_{NEO} = multiple correlation of NEO–PI–R facet scales with criterion; % = percentage change in criterion variance accounted for by addition of PRF/JPI factor predictor(s) to NEO–PI–R facet predictor(s).

Revised NEO Personality Inventory Domain Scales Versus Personality Research Form/Jackson Personality Inventory Trait Scales

We then used stepwise multiple regression to identify the best lower level criterion predictors from the PRF/JPI trait measures. This was followed by the inclusion of the NEO–PI–R domain scales as a separate predictor set. The relevant results are presented in Table 8.10. As shown in the table, the NEO–PI–R domain scales incremented criterion prediction significantly beyond that achieved by the PRF/JPI trait scales for 8 of the 12 criteria. The amount of extra criterion variance accounted for by the domain scales, however, averaged only 3.6%.

We reversed the order of variable entry into the regression analyses by using the NEO–PI–R domain scales as the first set of predictors. The PRF/JPI trait scales were then added to the analysis as a separate predictor set. As can be seen in Table 8.11, the PRF/JPI lower level trait measures incremented criterion prediction significantly over the factor-based domain scales for 4 of the 12

TABLE 8.9

Incremental Validity in Predicting Criteria: Revised NEO Personality Inventory (NEO–PI–R) Facet Scales Versus Personality Research Form/ Jackson Personality Inventory (PRF/JPI) Factor Scales

CRITERION	NEO–PI–R PREDICTORS (p = <.008)	$R_{PRF+NEO}$	R_{PRF}	%
1. Questionnaire neatness	Values	.34	.27	4.5
2. Task completion time				
3. Tardiness to experiment				
4. Absenteeism from experiments	Compliance–	.27	.00	7.5
5. Grade point average	Self-discipline	.39	.27	7.7
6. General knowledge	Fantasy	.43	.37	4.5
7. Numerical ability	Values, competence–	.35	.13	10.6
8. Blood donations	Activity	.31	.14	7.4
9. Willingness to share money	Modesty, deliberation	.57	.47	10.6
10. Willingness to gamble				
11. Traffic violations				
12. Admissions of dishonesty	Straightforwardness–, ideas–	.52	35	14.1
M		.40	.25	8.4

Note. Blank row = no NEO–PI–R facet scale significantly increased criterion prediction at p < .008; $R_{PRF+NEO}$ = multiple correlation of PRF/JPI factor scales plus listed NEO–PI–R facet scale(s) with criterion; R_{PRF} = multiple correlation of PRF/JPI factor scales with criterion; % = percentage change in criterion variance accounted for by addition of NEO–PI–R facet predictor(s) to PRF/JPI factor predictor(s). A minus (–) sign beside a predictor indicates a negative regression coefficient.

criteria. Moreover, the increase in predictive accuracy amounted to 10.9% more criterion variance accounted for. This increment for the trait scales was again about three times the corresponding value for the factor scales (3.6%; Table 8.10).

Best Factor Scale Versus Best Trait Within Factor Scale

In this last set of analyses we wanted to determine more directly how much is gained or lost in criterion prediction by combining narrow facet scales into broad factor scales. To do this, we simply correlated a factor scale and its corresponding facet scales with each criterion (uncorrected for shrinkage or for sex differences). We then calculated the amount of gain or loss in criterion correlation resulting from the aggregation.

TABLE 8.10

Incremental Validity in Predicting Criteria: Revised NEO Personality Inventory (NEO–PI–R) Domain Scales Versus Personality Research Form/ Jackson Personality Inventory (PRF/JPI) Trait Scales

CRITERION	NEO–PI–R PREDICTORS ($p = <.05$)	$R_{PRF+NEO}$	R_{PRF}	%
1. Questionnaire neatness	Conscientiousness	.30	.24	3.5
2. Task completion time	Agreeableness	.15	.00	2.2
3. Tardiness to experiment	Agreeableness–	.16	.00	2.5
4. Absenteeism from experiments				
5. Grade point average	Conscientiousness	.36	.29	4.5
6. General knowledge				
7. Numerical ability				
8. Blood donations				
9. Willingness to share money	Neuroticism	.58	.57	1.7
10. Willingness to gamble	Neuroticism–	.23	.04	5.0
11. Traffic violations	Neuroticism	.14	.00	2.0
12. Admissions of dishonesty	Agreeableness–	.52	.44	7.5
M		.31	.20	3.6

Note. Blank row = no NEO–PI–R domain scale significantly increased criterion prediction at $p < .05$; $R_{PRF+NEO}$ = multiple correlation of PRF/JPI trait scales plus listed NEO–PI–R domain scale(s) with criterion; R_{PRF} = multiple correlation of PRF/JPI trait scales with criterion; % = percentage change in criterion variance accounted for by addition of NEO–PI–R domain predictor(s) to PRF/JPI trait predictor(s). A minus (–) sign beside a predictor indicates a negative regression coefficient.

Personality Research Form/Jackson Personality Inventory Measures

Table 8.12 presents the correlations between the 12 criterion measures and their "best" PRF/JPI personality predictors. The second and third columns list, for each criterion, the single best factor-based predictor (column 2) and its coefficient of correlation (column 3). The next two columns identify the single best trait-based predictor included within the best factor (column 4) and its coefficient of correlation (column 5). The last column indicates whether each comparison of criterion predictability favors the factor-based personality measure (+) or the narrower trait-based personality measure (–).

An examination of the last column of Table 8.12 reveals that the factor-based personality measures were able to predict 4 of the 12 criteria better than any of the individual trait scales within those factor scales. However, in the other 8 cases, the opposite was true—a single, narrow trait measure was a better predictor of the criterion than a broader weighted aggregate of all the traits. Furthermore, some of the differences favoring the lower level trait mea-

TABLE 8.11

Incremental Validity in Predicting Criteria: Personality Research Form/ Jackson Personality Inventory (PRF/JPI) Trait Scales Versus Revised NEO Personality Inventory (NEO–PI–R) Domain Scales

CRITERION	PRF/JPI PREDICTORS (p = <.008)	$R_{NEO+PRF}$	R_{NEO}	%
1. Questionnaire neatness				
2. Task completion time				
3. Tardiness to experiment				
4. Absenteeism from experiments	Organization–, order	.40	.00	16.0
5. Grade point average				
6. General knowledge	Abasement–	.43	.38	4.2
7. Numerical ability				
8. Blood donations	Harmavoidance–	.29	.17	5.6
9. Willingness to share money	Responsibility, abasement	.57	.38	17.6
10. Willingness to gamble				
11. Traffic violations				
12. Admissions of dishonesty				
M		.42	.23	10.9

Note. Blank row = no PRF/JPI trait scale significantly increased criterion prediction at $p < .008$; $R_{NEO+PRF}$ = multiple correlation of NEO–PI–R domain scales plus listed PRF/JPI trait scales with criterion; R_{NEO} = multiple correlation of NEO–PI–R domain scales with criterion; % = percentage change in criterion variance accounted for by addition of PRF/JPI trait predictor(s) to NEO–PI–R domain predictor(s). A minus (–) sign beside a predictor indicates a negative regression coefficient.

sures were substantial in size. In the prediction of admissions of dishonesty, for example, the Agreeableness factor correlated –.25, whereas a single facet of Agreeableness, Responsibility, correlated –.42.

Revised NEO Personality Inventory Measures

Table 8.13 lists the correlations of each of the 12 criterion measures with its best-predicting NEO–PI–R domain scale and the best-predicting facet within the domain. An examination of the differences between these two sets of correlations (summarized in the last column of the table) indicates that the NEO–PI–R domain scale scores were able to outpredict those domains' best constituent facet scales for only two criteria. In contrast, 10 of the 12 criteria were best predicted by a single facet scale. In those 10 cases, aggregating six facet scales into a broader domain score resulted in losses in predictive accuracy. In some cases, the losses were substantial. For example, the Modesty facet scale

TABLE 8.12

Criterion Correlations: Best Personality Research Form/Jackson Personality Inventory (PRF/JPI) Factor Scale Versus Best Trait Within the Factor Scale

CRITERION	BEST FACTOR	r	BEST TRAIT	r	DIFFERENCE
1. Questionnaire neatness	Conscientiousness	.27	Order	.25	+
2. Task completion time	Agreeableness	.17	Defendence	−.16	+
3. Tardiness to experiment	Openness	−.20	Change	−.19	+
4. Absenteeism from experiments	Conscientiousness	−.21	Organization	−.32	−
5. Grade point average	Conscientiousness	.25	Desirability	.31	−
6. General knowledge	Openness	.19	Understanding	.31	−
7. Numerical ability	Conscientiousness	−.10	Play	.26	−
8. Blood donations	Openness	.18	Understanding	.24	−
9. Willingness to share money	Agreeableness	.38	Responsibility	.50	−
10. Willingness to gamble	Neuroticism	−.30	Harmavoidance	−.24	+
11. Traffic violations	Conscientiousness	−.14	Impulsivity	.19	−
12. Admissions of dishonesty	Agreeableness	−.25	Responsibility	−.42	−

Note. + = PRF/JPI factor scale's correlation exceeds its trait scale's correlation; − = PRF/JPI trait scale exceeds its factor scale's correlation.

TABLE 8.13

Criterion Correlations: Best Revised NEO Personality Inventory (NEO–PI–R) Domain Scale Versus Best Facet Within the Domain Scale

CRITERION	BEST DOMAIN	r	BEST FACET	r	DIFFERENCE
1. Questionnaire neatness	Conscientiousness	.31	Self-discipline	.28	+
2. Task completion time	Agreeableness	.14	Compliance	.16	–
3. Tardiness to experiment	Agreeableness	–.20	Altruism	–.28	–
4. Absenteeism from experiments	Neuroticism	.15	Impulsiveness	.22	–
5. Grade point average	Conscientiousness	.35	Self-discipline	.41	–
6. General knowledge	Openness	.26	Ideas	.27	–
7. Numerical ability	Conscientiousness	–.16	Deliberation	–.21	–
8. Blood donations	Extraversion	.20	Activity	.30	–
9. Willingness to share money	Agreeableness	.39	Modesty	.48	–
10. Willingness to gamble	Neuroticism	–.26	Vulnerability	–.31	–
11. Traffic violations	Conscientiousness	–.17	Deliberation	–.22	–
12. Admissions of dishonesty	Agreeableness	–.48	Straightforwardness	–.47	+

Note. + = NEO–PI–R domain scale's correlation exceeds its facet scale's correlation; – = NEO–PI–R facet scale's correlation exceeds its domain scale's correlation.

of the NEO–PI–R was able to predict the criterion of willingness to share money with a correlation of .48. But when the Modesty scale was combined with five other scales into an Agreeableness composite, the accuracy of prediction dropped to .39.

Discussion

I/O psychologists have argued that measures of job performance usually are complex and multidimensional. It has also been argued that, for this reason, the predictors of job performance should be equally complex and multidimensional. The purpose of that recommendation is to provide each facet of the multidimensional predictor with the opportunity to statistically align itself with a facet of the multidimensional criterion (J. Hogan & Roberts, 1996). The result should be maximal predictive accuracy overall. In the case of personality-based predictors, the use of broadband measures such as those representing the Big Five personality factors has been recommended (Ones & Viswesvaran, 1996).

We agree in general with the recommendation to evaluate carefully the various components of job performance and then to choose a set of criterion-relevant predictors (Schneider et al., 1996). However, we do not believe that it is advisable to combine those predictors into a single multidimensional aggregate such as a measure of the Big Five personality factors. Instead, separate, homogeneous, high-fidelity personality assessments can be used in a multiple regression, as recommended by Nunnally (1978). Such a multivariate prediction strategy has at least two advantages: (a) a predictive advantage and (b) an explanatory advantage.

Predictive Advantage

The first advantage of using lower level personality trait measures in a multivariate paradigm is that it is not necessary to limit the predictor set to correlated trait scales that load on a common personality factor. Instead, correlated traits, uncorrelated traits, and even negatively correlated traits can be included in the same prediction equation. Any reduction in predictor redundancy can result in nontrivial increases in the accuracy of criterion prediction, as demonstrated in some of the multiple regression results of the study discussed in this chapter.

There are some good examples in the literature of the use of empirical methods to combine diverse personality scales into multidimensional composites that are maximally predictive of complex criteria. Noteworthy is the construction of the occupational scales of the HPI (R. Hogan & Hogan, 1992), a questionnaire based on the FFM. The HPI Reliability occupational scale, for example, was initially developed by evaluating the empirical associations between 43 quite narrow HIC scales and a very broad criterion of juvenile delinquency (operationalized as a binary variable representing incarcerated delinquents vs. nondelinquent controls). The result of that analysis (J. Hogan & Hogan, 1989) was the selection of 9 HICs to be keyed (with unit weights) on the new occupational scale, but HICs that represented five different HPI domain scales (i.e., Intellectance, Adjustment, Prudence, Sociability, and Likability).

As a multidimensional composite, the HPI Reliability scale has excellent predictive properties for diverse criteria manifestly related to employee dependability (see R. Hogan & Hogan, 1992, p. 67). As Hogan and Hogan recognize, however, most of those criteria are clearly multifaceted (delinquency, for example, consists of behaviors related to hostility, impulsiveness, insensitivity, alienation, etc.), and different Reliability scale components, from different Big Five factors, could be accounting for different parts of those criteria. Accordingly, they (J. Hogan & Hogan, 1986; R. Hogan & Hogan, 1992) have urged careful analyses at the lower facet or HIC level to identify important reasons for predictive successes or failures at higher levels of assessment.

Explanatory Advantage

The second advantage of the strategy for prediction based on using lower level personality traits concerns behavior explanation. It is easier to understand the antecedents and consequences of work behaviors when information about the specific relations between the individual predictor facets and the criterion is available. One might find, for example, that some predictor facets have linear relations with components of the criterion, others have curvilinear relations, whereas others have indirect effects through mediating, moderating, or suppressing properties. Simply using, for example, a Big Five composite measure for prediction would preclude acquiring this type of information for the personality factor's constituent trait variables.

Regarding the differences in explanatory value when using Big Five facets versus factors, let us reconsider some of the specific results of the study described in this chapter. In Table 8.12, for example, it is evident that the PRF/JPI Conscientiousness factor was the single best predictor of the Questionnaire neatness criterion ($r = .27$). That correlation might make some theoretical sense, but it hides the fact that it is the Order component of the Conscientiousness factor that was most responsible for the prediction ($r = .25$). It was not the participants' level of Achievement that best predicted the neatness with which they filled out their questionnaires ($r = .17$), nor was it their level of Cognitive Structure ($r = .14$), nor even their degree of Organization ($r = .15$). It is clear from this example that these separate facet–criterion correlations are theoretically more informative than the single factor–criterion correlation.

Consider the effectiveness of the NEO–PI–R scales in predicting the admissions of dishonesty criterion (Table 8.13). The Agreeableness domain scale was the best predictor of that criterion, and a very good one ($r = -.48$). That association may seem theoretically puzzling at first, until one examines the separate facet-criterion correlations. One then sees that the Straightforwardness facet scale of the Agreeableness domain accounted for most of that factor's predictive accuracy ($r = -.47$). Agreeableness also includes Altruism, Compliance, Modesty, Tender-Mindedness, and Trust. However, those facets, although given equal weight within the factor, were not nearly as important as Straightforwardness in predicting admissions of dishonesty. Hidden within the Agreeableness factor's correlation of $-.48$ was the fact that, for example, Tender-Mindedness correlated only $-.13$ with dishonesty.

Other examples like those described abound in the results of the study discussed in this chapter, which, in our view, demonstrate that consideration of the individual Big Five facet scales leads to a better understanding of the personality–criterion relations than does a consideration of the Big Five factor scales. Furthermore, in many cases, the facet scale data are strongly predictive of the criterion measures even when the factor scale data are partialed out, indicating important contributions of trait-specific variance to criterion prediction.

Provisos

The extent to which our comparative results for the facet versus factor scales can be replicated is now of concern, and cross-validation studies are in order. We note, however, that these results might be considered conservative by some. Conspicuously relevant is the fact that the comparative analyses discussed were conducted using factor measures that were much more reliable than the constituent trait-based measures, as indicated in Tables 8.2 and 8.3. If all the variables were to be equated for measurement error, either statistically through disattenuation formulas or experimentally by using scales of equal length, the differences in predictive accuracy favoring the lower level trait measures would be even more pronounced.

One possible criticism of these results and conclusions is that the criteria used in this empirical study were, perhaps, narrower than typical job performance criteria. Therefore, the study's prediction situation may not necessarily have favored broad factor predictors. Recall that the idea is that broad predictors are to be preferred when dealing with equally broad criteria (Ones & Viswesvaran, 1996). To evaluate this possibility with our data, we combined 10 of the 12 predictors into a very broad (unweighted) criterion labeled overall student performance. To derive such a composite, we simply added together the positive indicators of performance (e.g., GPA) and subtracted the negative indicators of performance (e.g., admissions of dishonesty). All 10 variables were standardized before being aggregated, and the absenteeism from experiments and willingness to gamble criteria were omitted because of a certain amount of pairwise missing data.

The new overall student performance criterion was significantly ($p < .05$) predicted by two PRF/JPI factors (Openness to Experience and Conscientiousness), with a multiple correlation of .37. However, two individual trait scales of those factors (Tolerance and Achievement) did substantially better, showing a significant ($p < .008$) multiple correlation of .44. As for the NEO–PI–R domain scales, the same two personality factors significantly ($p < .05$) predicted the overall performance criterion, with a multiple correlation of .41. In contrast, two facet scales taken from those domain scales (Values and Self-Discipline) produced a much more significant ($p < .008$) multiple correlation of .52. Once again, the narrower personality trait predictors did better at criterion prediction than the broader personality factor predictors of which they were a part, despite the fact that the criterion used in this case was inarguably very broad. (The 12 criterion variables used in this study are, in fact, quite multidimensional as a set, defining at least five independent dimensions in an orthogonal factor analysis.)

A Final Note

In the context of personality and prediction, the so-called bandwidth–fidelity dilemma has sometimes been raised. That is, with a fixed assessment time, one can be faced with the choice of broadly sampling many personality predictors but measuring each with minimal fidelity or narrowly sampling few personality predictors but measuring each with greater fidelity. Ones and Viswesvaran (1996) have maintained that this dilemma should not exist in most work contexts in which the criterion to be predicted is some broad indicator of overall job performance, stating that "the nature of the construct of job performance dictates that we use broad personality traits for prediction" (p. 616). They argued that the better ability of a broadband predictor to account for variance in a multidimensional criterion would generally outweigh any loss in measurement fidelity resulting from the increase in predictor heterogeneity. (However, see Paunonen et al., 1999, pp. 396–397, regarding some contradictions in Ones and Viswesvaran's, 1996, interpretation and empirical evaluation of the bandwidth–fidelity dilemma.)

Although we certainly agree with those who propose that for optimal prediction the bandwidth of the predictors should generally match the bandwidth of the criteria, we are reminded once again of Nunnally's (1978, p. 268) comments regarding factorial complexity. As Nunnally emphatically stated, it is indeed important for the predictor battery to represent all aspects of a complex, multidimensional criterion. Researchers therefore, must sample broadly. (Whether or not this actually entails a material dilemma regarding measurement fidelity is debatable in most realistic assessment contexts, as J. Hogan and Roberts, 1996, and Paunonen et al., 1999 have observed.) However, sampling predictors broadly in no way obliges one to combine them into a single broad aggregate score. Instead, by keeping the multiple, narrow predictors separate, it is possible to use modern multivariate techniques to provide maximum accuracy in predicting the criterion. Scores on the narrow predictor measures, assuming they have construct validity, are then individually interpretable in terms of a psychological construct, a fact that can be invaluable in the identification of the personality antecedents of work behaviors.

Conclusion

Although some researchers have argued for relatively broad personality measures in the prediction of complex criteria such as job performance, we advocate the opposite view. Our contrary position is that multiple, construct-valid measures of unidimensional personality traits are preferred in the prediction of work and other criteria. The advantages of this approach include more accuracy in criterion prediction and a better understanding of the concomitants of work behaviors.

References

Ashton, M. C., Jackson, D. N., Helmes, E., & Paunonen, S. V. (1998). Joint factor analysis of the Personality Research Form and the Jackson Personality Inventory? *Journal of Research in Personality, 32,* 243–250.

Ashton, M. C., Jackson, D. N., Paunonen, S. V., Helmes, E., & Rothstein, M. G. (1995). The criterion validity of broad factor scales versus specific trait scales. *Journal of Research in Personality, 29,* 432–442.

Costa, P. T. Jr., & McCrae, R. R. (1992). *Revised NEO Personality Inventory (NEO–PI–R) and NEO Five-Factor Inventory (NEO–FFI) professional manual.* Odessa, FL: Psychological Assessment Resources.

Digman, J. M. (1990). Personality structure: Emergence of the Five-Factor Model. *Annual Review of Psychology, 41,* 417–440.

Eysenck, H. J. (1947). *Dimensions of personality.* London: Routledge.

Guion, R. M., & Gottier, R. F. (1965). Validity of personality measures in personnel selection. *Personnel Psychology, 18,* 135–164.

Hogan, J., & Hogan, R. (1986). *Hogan Personnel Selection Series manual.* Minneapolis, MN: National Computer Systems.

Hogan, J., & Hogan, R. (1989). How to measure employee reliability. *Journal of Applied Psychology, 74,* 273–279.

Hogan, J., & Roberts, B. W. (1996). Issues and non-issues in the fidelity-bandwidth trade-off. *Journal of Organizational Behavior, 17*, 627–637.

Hogan, R., & Hogan, J. (1992). *Hogan Personality Inventory manual.* Tulsa, OK: Hogan Assessment Systems.

Jackson, D. N. (1976). *Jackson Personality Inventory manual.* Port Huron, MI: Research Psychologists Press.

Jackson, D. N. (1984). *Personality Research Form manual.* Port Huron, MI: Research Psychologists Press.

Jackson, D. N. (1990). *Multidimensional Aptitude Battery manual.* Port Huron, MI: Sigma Assessment Systems.

Jackson, D. N. (1994). *Jackson Personality Inventory—Revised manual.* Port Huron, MI: Sigma Assessment Systems.

Jackson, D. N., Paunonen, S. V., Fraboni, M., & Goffin, R. G. (1996). A five-factor versus a six-factor model of personality structure. *Personality and Individual Differences, 20*, 33–45.

John, O. P. (1990). The "Big Five" factor taxonomy: Dimensions of personality in the natural language and in questionnaires. In L. A. Pervin (Ed.), *Handbook of personality: Theory and research* (pp. 66–100). New York: Springer-Verlag.

McCrae, R. R., Costa, P. T. Jr., del Pilar, G. H., Rolland, J.-P., & Parker, W. D. (1998). Cross-cultural assessment of the Five-Factor Model: The revised NEO Personality Inventory. *Journal of Cross-Cultural Psychology, 29*, 171–188.

McCrae, R. R., & John, O. P. (1992). An introduction to the five-factor model and its applications. *Journal of Personality, 60*, 175–215.

Mershon, B., & Gorsuch, R. L. (1988). Number of factors in the personality sphere: Does increase in factors increase the predictability of real-life criteria? *Journal of Personality and Social Psychology, 55*, 675–680.

Nicol, A. A. M. (1999). *A measure of workplace honesty.* Unpublished doctoral dissertation, University of Western Ontario, London, Canada.

Nunnally, J. C. (1978). *Psychometric theory.* New York: McGraw-Hill.

Ones, D. S., & Viswesvaran, C. (1996). Bandwidth-fidelity dilemma in personality measurement for personnel selection. *Journal of Organizational Behavior, 17*, 609–626.

Paunonen, S. V. (1993, August). *Sense, nonsense, and the Big Five factors of personality.* Paper presented at the 101st Annual Convention of the American Psychological Association, Toronto, Ontario, Canada.

Paunonen, S. V. (1998). Hierarchical organization of personality and prediction of behavior. *Journal of Personality and Social Psychology, 74*, 538–556.

Paunonen, S. V., & Jackson, D. N. (1996). The Jackson Personality Inventory and the Five-Factor Model of personality. *Journal of Research in Personality, 30*, 42–59.

Paunonen, S. V., Rothstein, M. G., & Jackson, D. N. (1999). Narrow reasoning about the use of broad personality measures in personnel selection. *Journal of Organizational Behavior, 20*, 389–405.

Schneider, R. J., Hough, L. M., & Dunnette, M. D. (1996). Broadsided by broad traits: How to sink science in five dimensions or less. *Journal of Organizational Behavior, 17*, 639–655.

CHAPTER 9

The Character of Self-Enhancers

Implications for Organizations

Richard W. Robins

Delroy L. Paulhus

J.S. is an employee at a large accounting firm. He was hired on the basis of a college degree and an impressive interview. Relative to initial expectations, however, J.S. has turned out to be a controversial employee. Supervisor reports have been mixed, and J.S. has been the source of complaints from some, although not all, of his coworkers. The promotion committee trying to evaluate J.S. has access to multiple sources of information from a 360-degree performance appraisal, but the inconsistent evaluations are puzzling to committee members. All concerned agree that his cardinal trait is an exceptionally high level of self-confidence.

Positive thinking has been touted as the way to success at least as far back as Norman Vincent Peale (1952). With his series of best-selling books, Peale convinced millions of the benefits of a positive attitude toward oneself. Bookstores—their business sections in particular—continue to offer large numbers of similar books encouraging people to promote their virtues and ignore their self-doubts. The core message of these books—to err on the positive side in evaluating oneself—has become a canon of contemporary American life. Promised benefits range from financial triumphs to personal bliss to successful personal relationships.

But what does the empirical literature have to say about self-enhancement? How widespread are such tendencies? Is self-enhancement as uniformly beneficial as the authors of self-help books would have people believe? Of particular concern in this chapter is the question of whether organizations should be hiring and promoting self-enhancing individuals such as J.S.

A body of research has accumulated to the point that this chapter can offer some answers to these questions. On the whole, it appears that people do tend to hold overly positive views of themselves. This self-enhancing tendency has been empirically established for people's perceptions of their task performance, their explanations for success and failure, and their general beliefs about their abilities. As this chapter shows, self-enhancement can have benefits, but it also can lead to a variety of negative consequences.

Issues surrounding self-enhancement clearly are relevant to organizations, where skills and abilities are routinely scrutinized and performance has important implications for advancement and compensation. The literature on self-enhancement in organizations covers a wide variety of complex issues, many of which have been reviewed elsewhere (Podsakoff & Organ, 1986; Rosenfeld, Giacalone, & Riordan, 1995; Zerbe & Paulhus, 1987). However, little attention has been paid to individual differences in self-enhancement (Atwater & Yammarino, 1997). We attempt to remedy this deficit by investigating the underlying character of the self-enhancing individual. We combine recent research from the social–personality literature with the small existing body of research in the organization literature (for a review, see Atwater & Yammarino, 1997). J.S., the hypothetical self-enhancer introduced earlier, appears as an example throughout the chapter.

The chapter is structured around three basic issues concerning self-enhancement bias and its relevance to organizational issues.[1] First, we discuss the nature of the self-enhancement process. We describe several psychological mechanisms presumed to underlie the process and argue that self-enhancement is not a universal phenomenon, as some psychologists have claimed (Taylor, 1989). Second, we review the literature on individual differences in self-enhancement and identify several variants, including impression management and self-deceptive enhancement and denial. We argue that the underlying personality of the self-enhancer (and self-deceptive enhancement in particular) is equivalent to so-called "normal narcissism"—a character syndrome that includes grandiosity, entitlement, defensiveness, and a willingness to manipulate others. Third, we discuss whether it is adaptive to self-enhance, that is, whether self-enhancers make good employees. We argue that self-enhancement is best viewed as a trait with mixed blessings, entailing both costs and benefits to the individual and to the organization.

What Is Self-Enhancement?

Taylor and Brown (1988) organized the self-enhancement literature into three categories: (a) unrealistically positive views of the self, (b) illusions of control, and (c) unrealistic optimism. Related effects include false consensus and biased attributions. In this chapter, we focus on the first category, which has received

---

[1]For more general reviews of research on the self, see Baumeister (1998), Brown (1998), and Robins, Norem, and Cheek (1999).

the greatest attention. We use the term *self-enhancement* to refer to the tendency to describe oneself in overly positive terms.

One source of evidence for self-enhancement is a set of studies that showed that individuals evaluate themselves more positively than they evaluate others. For example, 89% of respondents in a large survey rated themselves more positively than they rated others (Brown, 1998, p. 62). The same pattern appeared in research comparing self-ratings on other evaluative dimensions (e.g., personality, intelligence, ethics, driving ability). A second source of evidence for self-enhancement bias is a set of studies that showed that self-ratings are more positive than a credible criterion (Kenny, 1994; Robins & John, 1997b). Such criteria include objective tests (e.g., IQ tests) and knowledgeable informants (e.g., peers, spouses, expert raters). Regardless of the criterion, people's evaluations of themselves tend to be biased in the positive direction.

In work settings, as in other areas of everyday life, there is ample support for the proposition that people's self-impressions are inflated by a general tendency to self-enhance (Ashford, 1989; Hoffman, 1923; Podsakoff & Organ, 1986; Taylor & Brown, 1988). Not surprisingly, most employees tend to think they are superior to the average employee in their organization and tend to see themselves more positively than appraisals of them from other sources (for reviews, see Mabe & West, 1982; Podsakoff & Organ, 1986). Thus, for our hypothetical example, we would expect J.S.'s ratings of his own performance to be more positive than his ratings of others or ratings of his performance by his subordinates, peers, and supervisors.

Mechanisms for Self-Enhancement

Two classes of explanations have been advanced in the social and personality psychology literatures to explain these self-enhancement biases: (a) cognitive explanations, which focus on the information available to the self, prior beliefs and expectancies, and processes of attention, encoding, and retrieval of self-relevant information, and (2) motivational or affective explanations, which focus on the motive to maintain and enhance self-esteem, the desire to reduce negative affect and increase positive affect, and self-presentational concerns such as the need for social approval.

Purely cognitive explanations for self-serving biases have been offered since the cognitive revolution began. One notion is that positive self-relevant information tends to be more available than negative self-relevant information (Miller & Ross, 1975). Another explanation is that self-serving biases are one of a set of mechanisms that act to preserve cognitive structures (Greenwald, 1980). More recently, Paulhus and Levitt (1986) proposed the concept of "automatic egotism." They suggested that self-enhancement is automatized through repetition of positive self-descriptions and accentuated under high cognitive load (Paulhus, 1993).

A variety of motivational theories also have been advanced. These theories typically assume that self-enhancement stems from a general motive to gain and maintain high self-esteem (e.g., Brown, 1998; Tesser, 1988). That is, perceiving oneself positively is one way to increase self-esteem. From this perspective, self-enhancement may be viewed simply as a side effect of the self-esteem maintenance.

Self-presentational theories suggest that self-enhancement involves conscious strategies to impress others, primarily for instrumental purposes (e.g., Jones & Pittman, 1982; Schlenker, 1980; Snyder, 1987). According to these theories, a valued goal such as sex, affection, or financial gain is achieved by tailoring one's behavior to suit the specific situation and audience.

Evolutionary psychologists have argued that, whatever the operative mechanisms, self-enhancement is likely to have been adaptive during some key period of selective advantage (Lockard & Paulhus, 1988). From a traditional evolutionary perspective, to the extent that a mechanism is of central importance to human adaptation (e.g., the capacity to love, to feel fear, and to affiliate with others), it should be a ubiquitous part of human nature. More recent thinking among evolutionary psychologists, however, has suggested that individual differences in personality can be explained in terms of dimorphisms or frequency-dependent selection (e.g., Buss & Schmitt, 1993). This notion of multiple adaptive niches could be used to explain individual differences in self-enhancement (Robins, Norem, & Cheek, 1999).

Is Self-Enhancement Universal?

Self-enhancement undoubtedly is more common than self-effacement. In a meta-analysis of the industrial and organizational (I/O) psychology literature, 15 of 22 studies showed a significant tendency toward self-enhancement (Mabe & West, 1982). However, 3 of those studies showed a significant self-effacement effect, suggesting that self-enhancement is far from universal. The mean self-enhancement effect typically is small to moderate in magnitude (John & Robins, 1994; Mabe & West, 1982). One possible explanation is that extremely distorted self-perceptions are rare and that most people show only mild levels of self-enhancement bias (e.g., Taylor & Armor, 1996). Another possibility is the existence of substantial individual differences in both the magnitude and direction of the effect. That is, some people have self-views that are dramatically exaggerated, some have only mild illusions, and others have accurate or even overly negative self-views. This possibility is difficult to evaluate, however, because most studies report only aggregate statistics about the general tendency within the sample.

Contrary to the assumption of universality, the few studies that have reported the percentages of self-enhancing individuals have suggested that self-enhancers are in the minority. For example, John and Robins (1994) found that only 32% of participants clearly overestimated their performance in a 6-person group-interaction task, whereas 53% were relatively accurate and 15% actually underestimated their performance. Many individuals do not maintain positive illusions about themselves, and a not insignificant number actually see themselves more negatively than others see them. Similar percentages were reported by Paulhus (1998a). In organizational studies, the proportions of self-enhancers have been reported to be even smaller, and self-enhancers may not exceed self-effacers (Atwater & Yammarino, 1992), presumably because employees expect that their self-evaluations will be compared with supervisors' ratings (Mabe & West, 1982). Other factors minimizing the observed degree of self-enhancement include (a) the rater's previous experience with self-evaluation, (b) instructions guaranteeing anonymity of the self-evaluation, and (c) self-evaluation instructions emphasizing comparison with others (Mabe & West, 1982).

Thus, the research literature suggests that some people self-enhance, some people are accurate, and some people self-efface. However, a number of questions remain to be considered: Are these differences systematic and psychologically meaningful? That is, should individual differences in self-enhancement be thought of as traitlike? If so, what is the psychological nature of the trait? That is, how should individual differences in self-enhancement be conceptualized and measured?

Individual Differences in Self-Enhancement

> There is consensus among supervisors and coworkers that J.S. is a chronic self-promoter. Although this behavior is consistent across situations, it is difficult to tell whether J.S. actually believes his own inflated self-presentations. One distinct possibility is that his behavior is purposeful, that J.S. strategically exaggerates his accomplishments to make a positive impression on his supervisors. Another possibility is that J.S. actually believes his self-aggrandizing statements—that is, he lacks insight into his actual abilities and achievements.

To the extent that self-enhancing tendencies are internalized and chronic, deeper personality structures are implicated. There are a number of personality traits that may underlie observed individual differences in self-enhancement.

Personality Measures of Self-Enhancement

The two possible interpretations of J.S.'s character are referred to in the assessment literature as *impression management* and *self-deception* (e.g., Paulhus, 1984).

Impression management refers to conscious strategies tailored to make a positive impression on others, whereas *self-deception* refers to unconscious, narcissistic self-promotion. In the latter case, an individual really believes his or her own exaggerations. Note that both tendencies can be construed as personality traits (Crowne & Marlowe, 1964; Paulhus, 1986). Research has shown that trait self-enhancement can take both forms and that observed differences derive, in part, from personality differences.

Impression Management

The conceptualization of impression management as a personality variable has varied from a need for approval (Crowne & Marlowe, 1964) to an ability to monitor demands from the social environment (Snyder, 1974). In either case, the result is habitual self-promotion whenever a situation indicates some advantage to positive self-presentation.

Most research on impression management has used one of two self-report measures of this construct. The Self-Monitoring Scale (Snyder, 1974) has been used in numerous studies (see Snyder, 1987, for a review). Scale items involve self-reported tendencies to be aware of and engage in impression management (e.g., "At parties and social gatherings, I attempt to do or say things that others will like."). Although popular, this measure has been seriously criticized (Briggs & Cheek, 1988; John, Cheek, & Klohnen, 1996). The most up-to-date review (Gangestad & Snyder, 2000) retains some aspects of the original construct and discards others. Another measure, the Impression Management (IM) scale, is a subscale of the Balanced Inventory of Desirable Responding (BIDR; Paulhus, 1991, 1998b). Its rationale is that the items are so overt and clear-cut that exaggeratedly high scores must be due to conscious self-presentation (e.g., "I don't gossip about other people's business."). Its reliability and validity have been well documented (Paulhus, 1984, 1991, 1998b). Of particular interest is the evidence for its usefulness in organizational contexts (e.g., Booth-Kewley, Edwards, & Rosenfeld, 1992; Rosse, Stecher, Miller, & Levin, 1998).

The two measures appear to serve different purposes: The Self-Monitoring Scale (Snyder, 1974) is useful for identifying in advance those individuals who are likely to engage in impression management behaviors (e.g., Rowatt, Cunningham, & Druen, 1998). In contrast, the Impression Management scale (Paulhus, 1984, 1991, 1998b) identifies which individuals are engaging in impression management while they are completing a set of self-report questionnaires (Paulhus, Bruce, & Trapnell, 1995).

Assessments of the value of impression management scales in organizational settings clearly depend on the commentator. Encouraging perspectives have been presented by Rosenfeld, Giacalone, and Riordan (1995); Holden and Hibbs

(1995); and Hough (1998). More critical commentaries may be found in Nicholson and Hogan (1990) and Ones, Viswesvaran, and Reiss (1996).

Self-Deception and Narcissism

Given the availability of reviews of the impression management literature, the focus of this chapter is the relatively neglected concept of self-deception (Paulhus, 1984). The concept of self-enhancement bias reflects at least some degree of narcissistic self-deception or lack of self-insight.

Much of the research on self-deception has relied on the Self-Deceptive Enhancement (SDE) scale, which is included (along with the IM scale) in the BIDR (Paulhus, 1991, 1998b). A representative SDE scale item is "My first impressions about people are always right." Studies of the underlying personality syndrome suggest a dogmatic overconfidence. High scores on the SDE scale are predictive of overclaiming, hindsight bias, and overly positive self-perceptions (e.g., Hoorens, 1995; Paulhus, 1991, 1998a, 1998b; Robinson & Ryff, 1999). Of particular interest for this chapter is research showing that high SDE scores are indicative of high expectations but disappointing performance (Johnson, 1995).

A complementary construct, self-deceptive denial, derives from work by Sackeim and Gur (1978). This construct concerns the tendency to exaggerate moral and interpersonal aspects of one's character by denying any socially deviant behavior. Its measure, the Self-Deceptive Denial (SDD) scale, was developed more recently and, therefore, has not been as well–researched as the SDE scale (Paulhus & Reid, 1991). Scale items include "I rarely have sexual fantasies" and "I have never felt like I wanted to kill someone." Extreme scores suggest a sanctimonious character that may have interesting consequences for workplace behaviors.

The enhancement and denial forms of individual differences in self-deception have been compared at length by Paulhus and John (1998). They applied the terms *egoistic bias* and *moralistic bias* and showed that each bias is linked to a corresponding set of values and traits. Thus, the emergence of these particular self-deceptive biases is linked to the fact that human social interactions can be simplified into two fundamental forms of social interaction referred to as *agency* and *communion* (Wiggins, 1991) or "getting ahead" and "getting along" (Hogan, 1983). In short, agentic self-enhancers exaggerate how competent and successful they are, whereas communal self-enhancers exaggerate how dutiful and proper they are (Paulhus & John, 1998).

As a personality construct, self-deceptive enhancement is reminiscent of the construct of narcissism. The history of narcissism as a clinical syndrome stretches back to psychoanalysis (Freud, 1914/1953). Among other things, narcissistic individuals are assumed to hold unrealistically positive beliefs about their abilities and achievements (e.g., Millon, 1990; Westen, 1990).[2] This collection of attributes is now placed in the category of personality disorders and is described in the standard psychiatric manual, the *Diagnostic and Statistical Manual of Mental Disorders* (*DSM–IV*; American Psychiatric Association, 1994). Specified diagnostic criteria include a grandiose sense of self-importance; a tendency to exaggerate achievements and talents and an expectation to be recognized as superior without commensurate achievements; and fantasies of unlimited success, power, brilliance, and beauty.

More recently, narcissism has been studied as a normal personality dimension. Rather than an all-or-none clinical syndrome, narcissism is now considered to vary in degree among ordinary people. This perspective was first advanced by Leary (1957), but it entered the research literature with work by Raskin and his colleagues (Raskin & Hall, 1979; Raskin & Terry, 1998). The character of normal narcissism has been described as similar although not identical to the clinical version (e.g., Emmons, 1987). Some clarification of its meaning has been obtained by mapping it onto standard measures of personality. Normal narcissism has been found to fall into the high-dominance/low-nurturance quadrant of the interpersonal circumplex (Wiggins & Pincus, 1994). In terms of the Five-Factor Model of personality (John & Srivastava, 1999), narcissism correlates positively with Extraversion and negatively with Agreeableness (Wiggins & Pincus, 1994). As for life goals, narcissistic individuals tend to have long-term aspirations related to being successful and getting ahead in life rather than helping the community and getting along with others (Roberts & Robins, 2000). However, these standard dimensions do not seem to capture the concept completely.

Narcissism has been assessed with a number of instruments. For example, John and Robins (1994) showed convergence across four different measures of narcissism: (a) the Narcissistic Personality Inventory (NPI; Raskin & Hall, 1979, 1981); (b) the California Psychological Inventory Narcissism Scale (Wink & Gough, 1990); (c) observer ratings based on the *DSM–IV* (American Psychiatric Association, 1994) diagnostic criteria; and (d) a narcissistic profile scored from consensual observer assessments using the California Adult Q-Set (Wink, 1992). Another set of measures, however, fall on an independent factor of narcissism, possibly one linked more closely to clinical narcissism. These other measures include the Minnesota Multiphasic Personality Inventory Narcissism scale (Wink & Gough, 1990), the Hypersensitive Narcissism Scale (Hendin & Cheek, 1997), and the Morey Narcissism Scale (Morey & Glutting, 1994). However, the bulk of the empirical work on narcissism has been conducted with the NPI.

---

[2]In contrast to individuals with high self-esteem, narcissistic individuals feel entitled to manipulate others in a self-serving manner, and they describe themselves as special, extraordinary people who are particularly deserving of attention and rewards.

Over the past 10 years, there has been a surge of interest in narcissistic tendencies, and active research has clarified the nature of normal narcissism. Much of this research has focused on understanding the personality processes associated with narcissistic tendencies and, in particular, the way narcissistic individuals respond to threats to their self-worth. This research has shown that, when threatened, relatively narcissistic individuals perceive themselves more positively than is justified (Gabriel, Critelli, & Ee, 1994; John & Robins, 1994; Paulhus, 1998a), denigrate others (Morf & Rhodewalt, 1993), engage in arrogant social behaviors (Paulhus, 1998a), assign self-serving attributions for their behavior (Farwell & Wohlwend-Lloyd, 1998), and react with hostility toward others (Bushman & Baumeister, 1998; Rhodewalt & Morf, 1998). Amazingly, their inflated self-perceptions cannot be altered even when these individuals are confronted with videotaped recordings of their actual performance on a task (Robins & John, 1997a).

Thus, both self-deceptive enhancement and narcissism help provide a psychological portrait of the self-enhancing individual. It is important to note that the primary measure of narcissism—the NPI—and the primary measure of self-deceptive enhancement—the SDE—converge empirically as well as conceptually. When disattenuated for measurement error, correlations between the two measures approach unity (McHoskey, Worzel, & Szyarto, 1998; Paulhus, 1998a). Moreover, they show very similar correlations with relevant external criteria (Paulhus, 1998a). In Paulhus and John's (1998) terminology, *egoistic bias* subsumes the common elements of self-deceptive enhancement, normal narcissism, and agentic bias (Paulhus & John, 1998; Raskin, Novacek, & Hogan, 1991a, 1991b; Robins & John, 1997a).

Criterion-Based Discrepancy Measures of Self-Enhancement

Measures of self-deception enhancement and narcissism tap into personality constructs that are assumed to reflect distorted self-views, but they are not direct operationalizations of those distortions. An alternative approach compares self-evaluations to some external criterion and thus more directly gauges accuracy. One difficulty with this approach, however, is the question of how to operationalize reality. Unfortunately, there are no absolute, perfectly objective measures of an individual's traits, capabilities, needs, and so on. This "criterion problem," as it is called, is well known in social–personality, and I/O psychology.

Some studies of self-enhancement have attempted to circumvent the criterion problem by inferring bias from apparent intrapsychic inconsistencies in individuals' judgments. For example, several studies have shown that individuals' self-ratings are, on average, more positive than their ratings of a hypothetical "average other" (e.g., Brown, 1986). This finding has been widely interpreted as evidence of self-enhancement bias because, according to researchers, it is logically impossible for the majority of people to be better than average. However, this approach has been criticized on the grounds that no indicator of external reality is involved (Colvin, Block, & Funder, 1995; John & Robins, 1994). The same criticism applies to Krueger's (1998) measure of self-enhancement bias, which is based on the correlation between an individual's self-ascribed traits and his or her ratings of the desirability of those traits, controlling for the group average desirability of those traits. A more convincing index of self-enhancement should involve an explicit standard for gauging bias.

For the most part, researchers interested in self-enhancement bias have used two types of external criteria: (a) operational criteria and (b) social consensus criteria. In some contexts, clear-cut *operational criteria* are available. For example, the number of words spoken in a conversation provides an unambiguous criterion for self-ratings of talkativeness. Another example is when there is a direct measure of task performance (e.g., Beyer & Bowden, 1997; Gosling, John, Craik, & Robins, 1998; Robins & John, 1997b) or intelligence (e.g., Paulhus & Lysy, 1995; Gabriel et al., 1994). In organizational settings, operational criteria may include the number of units sold as a criterion for sales performance and the numbers of customer complaints and compliments as a criterion for customer service ability. The advantage of operational criteria is that they are objectively measured; the disadvantages are that they may not capture the entire construct of interest and they are not available for many rating dimensions.

For situations in which there are no operational criteria available, *social consensus ratings* may serve as a useful means to gauge the accuracy of self-evaluations. Judgments by informed observers (e.g., friends, spouses, coworkers, psychologists) are widely used to evaluate the validity of self-reports in social–personality, I/O, developmental, and clinical psychology (Funder, 1995; Kenny, 1994; McCrae & Costa, 1989).

Note that any single accuracy criterion can be criticized. For example, observer ratings suffer from the criticism that different types of observers differ in perspective (Campbell & Fehr, 1990). There also is evidence that observers are biased against self-enhancing individuals and therefore give them inappropriately negative ratings (Bass & Yammarino, 1991). This "observer harshness" effect may be partially responsible for the observed self–other discrepancy (John & Robins, 1994). If possible, therefore, we recommend the use of multiple criteria to examine self-enhancement bias in evaluations of performance in a group-discussion task.

An example is the study by Robins and John (1997a). They used a leaderless group-discussion task that often is used in managerial assessment programs (e.g., Chatman, Caldwell, & O'Reilly, 1999). Participants were assigned to a decision-making group in which they presented, debated, and then reached consensus about the relative strengths and weaknesses of six employees nominated for a merit bonus. In this simulated compensation committee meeting, participants competed for a fixed amount of money to be distributed by group consensus. After the group discussion, participants evaluated their performance relative to other group members. Three criteria were used to examine self-enhancement bias: two social consensus criteria (performance ratings by the other task participants and by psychologists who observed the interaction) and an operational criterion (how much money each participant received for the employee he or she was representing at the compensation committee meeting). The convergence of findings across all three criteria provided more powerful evidence about accuracy and bias than any single criterion.

Two other studies are worth noting because they also demonstrated consistency across discrepancy measures. Paulhus (1998a) found convergence between (a) self–acquaintance discrepancy measures collected on a pretest and (b) self–other discrepancy measures collected after seven meetings with strangers. Colvin et al. (1995) collected discrepancy measures on the same participants before and after a 7-year interval and found substantial stability in scores. In summary, discrepancy scores themselves behave in a traitlike fashion by showing consistency across time and situations.

Once a relevant criterion has been identified and measured, an additional thorny methodological issue remains—how to index the discrepancy between the self-evaluation and the criterion. The most common procedure is to compute a simple difference score; that is, to subtract the criterion measure from the self-evaluation (this procedure, of course, requires that both measures be on the same metric). A second procedure involves computing a residualized difference score (Colvin et al., 1995; John & Robins, 1994; Paulhus, 1998a). Specifically, the self-evaluation is regressed onto the criterion measure (i.e., the criterion measure is used to predict the self-evaluation) and the residual scores are retained. These residuals represent the magnitude and direction of bias in the self-evaluation relative to the criterion. Finally, if the data were collected using a round-robin design (i.e., everyone rates everyone else), Kenny's (1994) Social Relations Model provides a third approach. Specifically, it is possible to identify the unique variance in the self-evaluation that is not related to others' ratings of the self (*target variance* in Kenny's terminology) or to the self's general tendency to see others positively versus negatively (*perceiver variance* in Kenny's terminology; Kwan, Bond, Kenny, John, & Robins, 2001). This "uniqueness" component of self-ratings can be interpreted as a measure of self-enhancement bias that is independent of reality (as defined by others' ratings) and unaffected by an individual's general rating style (e.g., to see everyone, including the self, positively).

Which of these methods is best? Despite decades of debate, no clear consensus has emerged regarding which is the best way to assess discrepancies. Much of the debate has revolved around statistical theory and the results of Monte Carlo simulations. In our view, research that systematically compares the various methods using real data sets is needed. It may turn out that each method is optimal for a different set of conditions. In fact, in the most comprehensive analysis to date, Zumbo (1999) reached this conclusion. He also provided a useful flowchart for determining, based on a set of sample parameters (e.g., the variances, reliabilities, and intercorrelations of the self and criterion measures), whether a difference score or a residual score is preferable in a particular situation.

Convergence Between Personality and Criterion-Based Discrepancy Approaches

The conclusion that self-enhancement is traitlike requires evidence of convergence across independent measures of self-enhancement, in particular between the two personality scales (i.e., the SDE and NPI) and direct criterion-based measures of bias. However, only a handful of relevant studies have been conducted.

We reviewed the social–personality and I/O psychology literatures and identified relevant studies using the following criteria: (a) the study compared self-evaluations with an explicit external criterion; (b) self-enhancement bias was operationalized by the discrepancy between an individual's self-evaluation and the criterion; (c) self-enhancement bias was correlated with a measure of narcissism; and (d) the study was published in a peer-reviewed journal. Only seven studies met all of these criteria. A summary of these studies is presented in Table 9.1.

In every study (except Colvin et al., 1995), the basic self-enhancement effect was observed at the mean level. More important for the arguments in this chapter, however, the relation between narcissism and self-enhancement bias held across a wide range of observational contexts and for a wide range of dimensions (see the last column of Table 9.1). The highly replicable link with narcissism demonstrates that individual variability in self-enhancement tendencies is not simply due to random fluctuations, but rather is related to a theoretically relevant personality characteristic. The magnitude of the narcissism effect varied somewhat across studies (range = $-.13$–$.54$), but it tended to be moderate in size (median $r = .27$). Perhaps the most striking finding from this review is the wide range of criteria that have been used to establish self-enhancement and its relation to narcissism, including ratings by other participants in the same interaction as the target, ratings by close friends, ratings by psychologists, codings of videotaped behaviors, objective task outcomes, academic outcomes, and standardized tests. Although each criterion is imperfect and poses its own set of interpretational problems, collectively these studies bolster the contention that narcissistic individuals have inflated views of themselves relative to some standard of what they are really like. This review also demonstrated that this effect holds in a variety of observational contexts, both in the laboratory and the real world. Finally, the review revealed the wide range of dimensions on which a self-enhancement bias exists: Narcissistic individuals have inflated views of themselves regardless of whether they are evaluating their task performance, personality traits, expected academic performance, behavioral acts, intelligence, or physical attractiveness. The link with narcissism provides clues about the psychological factors underlying self-enhancement bias. Specifically, it adds to the growing evidence that self-enhancement bias provides a mechanism for regulating self-esteem in response to the threat of failure.

The narcissistic interpretation of self-enhancing individuals also suggests that positive illusions about the self may rest on a foundation of fragile self-esteem (e.g., Farwell & Wohlwend-Lloyd, 1998; John & Robins, 1994; Raskin, Novacek, & Hogan, 1991b; Robins & John, 1997b). Self-enhancing individuals may be likely to regularly seek affirmation of their positive self-views (e.g., Sedikides & Strube, 1997). Self-worth may become contingent on each performance, thus making self-enhancers likely to experience greater threats to their self-worth, even with minor tasks (Morf & Rhodewalt, 1993). Consistent with this view, self-enhancers tend to show higher levels of ego involvement, that is, they care more about performing well than non-self-enhancers (Robins & Beer, 2001). This suggests that narcissistic self-aggrandizement is particularly likely to occur in organizational contexts, in which performance goals are emphasized and threats to self-worth are likely.

Summary

We have reviewed the literature on the trait aspects of self-enhancement and distinguished its two primary variants: (a) impression management and (b) self-deceptive enhancement. The character underlying self-deceptive enhancement appears equivalent to so-called "normal narcissism." Although not pathological, the character syndrome includes grandiosity, entitlement, defensiveness, and willingness to manipulate others. A review of the research revealed that personality measures of self-enhancement converge with measures of discrepancy between self-ratings and criterion measures (e.g., observer ratings or test scores). On the basis of this research, we conclude that self-enhancement bias is best conceptualized as a stable disposition reflecting the operation of narcissistic personality processes.

To say that self-enhancement is traitlike does not imply that it manifests itself independently of the situational context.[3] In fact, self-enhancement bias can be assumed to be particularly pronounced in some contexts and virtually

---

[3]We differ in this respect from Taylor and Armor (1996), who argue that self-enhancement cannot be a trait because it is influenced by situational factors.

TABLE 9.1

Studies of Self-Enhancement Bias

STUDY	PARTICIPANTS	OBSERVATIONAL CONTEXT	JUDGMENT DIMENSION	CRITERION	SELF-ENHANCEMENT EFFECT (d)	CORRELATION WITH NARCISSISM (MEASURE)
John & Robins (1994)	102 MBA students	40-min group interaction	Task performance	11 psychologists	.18	.44 (composite)
			Task performance	5 task participants	.22	.48 (composite)
Gabriel, Critelli, & Ee (1994)	146 college students	Naturalistic	Intelligence	Intelligence test	$.85^a$	$.29^a$ (NPI)
			Physical attractiveness	2 people rated photographs of targets	$.33^a$	$.30^a$ (NPI)
Colvin, Block, & Funder (1995)						
Study 1	101 community members	Interviews and other assessment interactions	Personality dimensions	4 psychologists	−.51	.54 (CAQ)
Study 2	101 community members	Interviews and other assessment interactions	Personality dimensions	6 psychologists	.42	.53 (CAQ)
Study 3	140 college students	Naturalistic (peer group)	Personality dimensions	2 close friends	−.06	—
Robins & John (1997a)	124 MBA and college students	40-min group interaction	Task performance	11 psychologists	.30	$.24^b$ (NPI)
				3–5 task participants	.33	$.27^b$ (NPI)
				Objective outcome	.23	$.29^b$ (NPI)
Gosling, John, Craik, & Robins (1998)	88 MBA students	40-min group interaction	Task-specific behaviors	4 coders of videotaped interaction	.43	.27 (NPI)

Study						
Farwell & Wohlwend-Lloyd (1998)						
Study 1	97 college students	Naturalistic (academic)	Predicted grades	Actual grades	.90	.22 (NPI)
Study 2	97 college students	Naturalistic (academic)	Predicted grades	Actual grades	.08	.32 (8-item NPI)
Paulhus (1998a)						
Study 1	124 college students	20-min group interaction (weekly over 7 weeks)	Task performance	3–4 task participants	.55	−.13 Week 1 (NPI) .33 Week 7 (NPI)
Study 2	89 college students	20-min group interaction (weekly over 7 weeks)	Task performance	4–6 task participants	39	.00 Week 1 (NPI) .30 Week 7 (NPI)
Robins & Beer (in press)						
Study 1	360 college students	20-min group interaction	Task performance	4 task participants	.33	.13 (NPI)
Study 2	498 college students	Naturalistic (academic)	Academic ability	Standardized tests and academic achievement	—	.30 (NPI)

Note. Self-enhancement effect = discrepancy (in standard score units) between self-ratings on dimension and criterion (Positive values indicate self-enhancement; negative values indicate self-effacement. In some cases, information needed to compute standardized self-enhancement effect was not provided in original article, and authors were contacted to obtain relevant values.); MBA = master of business administration; NPI = Narcissistic Personality Inventory (Raskin & Hall, 1979); composite = composite of 4 self- and observer measures of narcissism; CAQ = Narcissism prototype score from California Adult Q-Set (Wink, 1992). [a]Sample weighted average of effect sizes for men and women. [b]Average effect size across 2 experimental conditions (normal; reversed perspective); — = no data.

absent in others. The question at issue is not whether the general tendency to self-enhance varies across contexts, but whether individual differences in the tendency are systematic and linked to psychologically meaningful constructs and outcomes. Self-enhancers may respond to an evaluative context by engaging in further self-promotion or by expressing hostility toward the evaluator. Those without the trait might respond with anxiety and disengagement or by working harder to maximize their chances of success. It is clear that these different ways of responding to the same situation are likely to have important implications for behavior in organizational contexts.

In summary, individual differences in self-enhancement reflect a deep-seated, albeit complex, facet of personality, not some sort of conditioned response to contextual factors. Nonetheless, we do not consider self-enhancement itself to be the trait, but rather a concrete manifestation of the trait. The source trait is a narcissistic self-evaluation with self-deceptive overtones. This point is particularly important because the underlying trait has other public manifestations (e.g., hostility, manipulation) that shape the choice of self-enhancing behaviors as well as observers' reactions to the self-enhancement.

Is Self-Enhancement Adaptive? Individual and Organizational Perspectives

The promotion committee evaluating J.S. had access to reports from two supervisors after J.S.'s 6-month probation period.

> *Supervisor 1:* So far, J.S. has been a very successful employee. He possesses unwavering self-confidence and undaunted optimism and has unusually ambitious plans for future accomplishments. He showed no sign of the hesitation and dependence on others that typify most new employees. He seems to be at ease with prestigious new clients and engages them as equals. J.S. is highly likely to rise quickly up the corporate ladder.

> *Supervisor 2:* So far, J.S. is a problematic employee,. He presents himself as important and successful. Objective data (i.e., productivity figures) do not support these exaggerated claims. Furthermore, J.S. has alienated many of his coworkers, who complain about his unjustified arrogance, grandiosity, and sense of entitlement. Those working with him on a regular basis eventually recognized his manipulative tactics and lack of respect for their opinions. J.S. should be terminated.

Can this be the same J.S. the two supervisors are describing? Which is the real J.S.? According to the research described above, these apparently conflicting perspectives can, in fact, be reconciled within the character of the narcissistic self-enhancer.

The basic premise of this chapter is that individuals vary dramatically in how accurately they evaluate their abilities: Some have highly inflated views of themselves, others are reasonably accurate, and others self-effacing. Who is likely to be the more successful and productive employee—the individual with overly positive self-perceptions or the one with an accurate self-view? Norman Vincent Peale clearly would say the former. In his book, *The Amazing Results of Positive Thinking,* Peale (1959) posed the following question: "Does positive thinking always work?" His answer was short but clear: "Of course it does." (p. 28).

It has been only in the past 20 years or so that researchers have presented evidence supporting the value of positive thinking (e.g., Alloy & Abramson, 1979; Lewinsohn, Mischel, Chaplin, & Barton, 1980; Paulhus, 1986; Sackeim & Gur, 1978). This research has indicated that accurate self-appraisals might contribute to depression. In an integration of this literature, Taylor and Brown (1988) argued that positive illusions promote psychological adjustment as well as "higher motivation, greater persistence, more effective performance and ultimately, greater success" (p. 199). So influential was this work that a National Institute of Mental Health report (1995) on the state of behavioral science stated that there was considerable evidence for the psychological benefits of positive illusions.

However, others have warned about the dark side of self-enhancement (Bushman & Baumeister, 1998; Hogan, Raskin, & Fazzini, 1990). There is a substantial body of evidence supporting this side of the argument as well. In particular, the studies reviewed above have suggested that the personality substrate for trait self-enhancement is normal narcissism, an attribute usually conceptualized as more maladaptive than not (John & Robins, 1994). An extension of that work by Colvin et al. (1995) showed that a discrepancy index of self-enhancement predicted an array of negative traits over a 6-year interval. Paulhus (1998a) found that self-enhancers were rated negatively after a 7-week acquaintance period.

On the basis of the evidence available from the personality literature, we argue that a simple, global characterization of self-enhancers is not justified. Trait self-enhancement can be adaptive, maladaptive, or both, as implied in Paulhus's (1998a) characterization of the outcome pattern as a mixed blessing. The positivity of the outcome depends on (a) the nature of the position, (b) the outcome measure, (c) the time frame of the outcome measure, and (d) whether the outcome is for the individual or the organization.

Nature of Position

Person—organization fit plays an important role in the success of a hiring decision (Chatman, 1989; Schneider, 1987; Furnham, chapter 10, this volume). Self-enhancers can be placed in a beneficial niche within many organizations. Recall from Paulhus's (1998a) study that self-enhancers came across rather well in their first meeting with total strangers. They were considered to be interesting and confident and, because they spoke up and joked around, were valued for "breaking the ice." J.S., our hypothetical employee, was valued by Supervisor 1 for his ability to connect with new contacts—even those who might intimidate a nonnarcissist. Many organizations have positions that require such characteristics and behaviors and might benefit from hiring a self-enhancer. Another possible organizational niche for the self-enhancer is one in which a certain degree of self-absorption and a belief in the importance of one's own ideas is adaptive. For example, Feist (1994) found that highly eminent scientists were characterized as arrogant, hostile, and exploitative—all characteristics of the narcissistic personality.

In contrast, a position that requires building sustained relationships with subordinates and coworkers, especially relationships that depend on interpersonal trust, might not be appropriate for a self-enhancer. The self-enhancer's manipulation, intimidation, and entitlement tendencies can cause resentment and lead to breakdowns in cooperation (Morf & Rhodewalt, 1993).

Nature of Outcome

An employee can be successful in one sense but unsuccessful in another. If success is defined in terms of subjective well being, then there is reason to believe that self-enhancement is beneficial (Taylor & Armor, 1996). Self-enhancers appear to be self-confident and happy. However, it seems reasonable to question the validity of happiness that is based on lack of insight and redefine this outcome as negative (Bass & Yammarino, 1991; Block & Thomas, 1955). However, it can be argued that a positive outlook sets the stage for positive attitudes and future ambitions (Robinson & Ryff, 1999). If defined in terms of interpersonal relations with coworkers, then self-enhancement is likely to be maladaptive (Atwater & Yammarino, 1997; Colvin et al., 1995; Paulhus, 1998a). More than other workers, self-enhancers are likely to show a divergence between getting ahead and getting along (Hogan, 1983).

Time Frame

Another significant factor is whether the outcome is assessed in the short term or long term. As described earlier, Paulhus (1998a) found that self-enhancers made positive first impressions but were actively disliked after 7 weeks of interactions. Together with other studies, this research suggests that employee evaluations restricted to a single time frame might be misleading. In a longer term study, Robins and Beer (2001) found that self-enhancing individuals experienced a boost in positive affect following a group-interaction task, but over the course of college, they declined in well-being and increasingly disengaged from the academic context. The explanation may lie in other research that has shown that self-enhancers are unlikely to seek feedback, thus minimizing the possibility of self-improvement (Ashford, 1989; Fedor, Rensvold, & Adams, 1992). Even when clear feedback is provided, self-enhancers may not be capable of benefiting from it (Robins & John, 1997a).[4] Finally, career derailment may be the ultimate fate of self-enhancers (McCall & Lombardo, 1983). For these reasons, self-enhancers may be successful in the short run but fail in the end.

Mixed Blessings for Organizations

Although they usually dovetail, there may be situations in which individual and organizational outcomes diverge. On the positive side, Paulhus (1998a) found that self-enhancers were appreciated in initial meetings because they initiated conversation and entertained others. In our example, one of J.S.'s supervisors agreed that such qualities were of great benefit to the organization.

Divergences are most likely when the self-enhancer succeeds to the detriment of coworkers and, possibly, to the organization as a whole. For example, in pushing for their self-interests regarding recognition and promotion, self-enhancers may handicap the productivity of other team members through derogation, hostility, and condescension (Morf & Rhodewalt, 1993; Paulhus, 1998a). Supervisors also eventually may become frustrated at the failure of self-enhancers to seek or accept feedback, thus minimizing the possibility of self-improvement (Ashford, 1989). The egoistic concern of self-enhancers will benefit organizations only to the extent that their goals coincide with those of the organization. However, divergence is likely to occur at some point.

The case of Steve Jobs, the founder of Apple computers, is illustrative. During the early stages of the company's development, Jobs's self-promoting, self-aggrandizing style was conducive to launching breakthrough technology that had the potential to revolutionize an entire industry. Jobs's belief in his own genius may have helped to overcome skepticism about the whole enterprise. Despite these advantages, when the organization was up and running, Jobs's personality style created interpersonal problems and became a serious handicap to the organization. Apple employees reported that Jobs was a manipulative, hostile, and condescending manager. Ultimately, Jobs was relieved from his position (Deutschman, 2000). Thus, in the context of an organization, the costs and benefits of having a narcissistic CEO may depend on the stage of development of the organization.

In summary, the research literature on individual differences in self-

---

[4]Note that self-enhancers are not entirely disconnected from reality. Paulhus (2000) found that self-enhancers respond to accountability demands.

enhancement does not uniformly support either its construal by Taylor (1989) as a "positive illusion" or the traditional clinical construal of it as a maladaptive disorder. Rather, the studies to date suggest that positive illusions have both adaptive and maladaptive consequences: In other words, self-enhancement is best viewed as a mixed blessing (Paulhus, 1998a; Robins & Beer, in press).

Concluding Point

How bad is the prognosis for our hypothetical self-enhancer, J.S.? It is important to note that such individuals are not doomed to failure. In fact, a number of famous, successful narcissists readily come to mind. Pablo Picasso, the icono-clastic painter, has been described as a classic narcissist—arrogant, critical, interpersonally insensitive, defensive in response to criticism—in short, a meg-alomaniac with an overly grandiose view of himself. And, undoubtedly, a gen-ius. The famous industrialist Armand Hammer is another example. He clearly thought quite highly of himself: "The brilliance of my mind can only be de-scribed as dazzling. Even I am impressed by it." (Blumay & Edwards, 1992, p. 94). But narcissism is hardly limited to the intellectual domain. Supermodel Naomi Campbell became infamous for her arrogant statement, "I don't get out of bed for less than $10,000." And sports icons such as Muhammad Ali seem to be so inspired by their own arrogance ("I am the greatest") that it facilitates their success.

It is not clear, however, whether others can learn from these exceptionally successful narcissists. For these individuals, narcissism did not preclude success in their respective pursuits, and it may well have contributed to it. Just as compelling is the alternative view that these individuals possessed exceptional talents and that their narcissism developed as a consequence of unremitting praise from an admiring public.

Either way, the costs of narcissism in such prominent cases are not entirely clear. Successful narcissists often are in the spotlight and easily brought to mind, whereas the unsuccessful are not. For every successful narcissist, there likely are numerous "failed" narcissists, wallowing in obscurity and complaining about how their exceptional talents remain unrecognized by their supervisors and coworkers. Given the research cited above, the "rapid-rise-and-fall" trajectory is particularly likely. In fact, in their book on career derailment, McCall and Lom-bardo (1983) specifically cited excessive self-promotion as a key factor in the downfall of many initially successful executives.

Regardless of whether the self-enhancer proves to be an asset or a liability in the workplace, we believe that it is important that organizations identify and take such individuals into account. For better or for worse, organizations cannot afford to overlook them.

References

Alloy, L. B., & Abramson, L. Y. (1979). Judgments of contingency in depressed and nondepressed patients: Sadder but wiser? *Journal of Experimental Psychology: General, 108,* 441–485.

American Psychiatric Association. (1994). *Diagnostic and statistical manual of mental disorders* (4th ed.). Washington, DC: Author.

Ashford, S. (1989). Self-assessments in organizations: A literature review and integrative model. In L. L. Cummings & B. M. Staw (Eds.), *Research in organizational behavior: An annual review of analytical essays and critical reviews, 1989* (Vol. 11, pp. 133–174). Greenwich, CT: JAI Press.

Atwater, L. E., & Yammarino, F. J. (1992). Does self–other agreement on leadership perceptions moderate the validity of leadership and performance predictions? *Personnel Psychology, 45,* 141–164.

Atwater, L. E., & Yammarino, F. J. (1997). Self–other rating agreement: A review and model. In G. R. Ferris & K. M. Rowland (Eds.), *Research in personnel and human resources management* (Vol. 15, pp. 121–174). Greenwich, CT: JAI Press.

Bass, B., & Yammarino, F. J. (1991). Congruence of self and others' leadership ratings of naval officers for understanding successful performance. *Applied Psychology: An International Review, 40,* 437–454.

Baumeister, R. F. (1998). The self. In D. T. Gilbert, S. T. Fiske, & G. Lindzey (Eds.), *The handbook of social psychology Vol.* (4th ed.) (pp. 680–740). Boston, MA: McGraw-Hill.

Beyer, S., & Bowden, E. M. (1997). Gender differences in self-perceptions: Convergent evidence from three measures of accuracy and bias. *Personality and Social Psychology Bulletin, 23,* 157–172.

Block, J., & Thomas, H. (1955). Is satisfaction with self a measure of adjustment? *Journal of Abnormal and Social Psychology, 51,* 254–259.

Blumay, C., & Edwards, H. (1992). *The dark side of power: The real Armand Hammer.* New York: Simon & Schuster.

Booth-Kewley, S., Edwards, J. E., & Rosenfeld, P. (1992). Impression management, social desirability, and computer administration of attitude questionnaires: Does the computer make a difference? *Journal of Applied Psychology, 77,* 562–566.

Briggs, S. R., & Cheek, J. M. (1988). On the nature of self-monitoring: Problems with assessment, problems with validity. *Journal of Personality and Social Psychology, 54,* 663–678.

Brown, J. D. (1986). Evaluations of self and others: Self-enhancing biases in social judgments. *Social Cognition, 4,* 353–376.

Brown, J. D. (1998). *The self.* Boston: McGraw-Hill.

Bushman, B. J., & Baumeister, R. F. (1998). Threatened egotism, narcissism, self-esteem, and direct and displaced aggression: Does self-love or self-hate lead to violence? *Journal of Personality and Social Psychology, 75*, 219–229.

Buss, D. M., & Schmitt, D. P. (1993). Sexual strategies theory: A contextual evolutionary analysis of human mating. *Psychological Review, 100*, 204–232.

Campbell, J. D., & Fehr, B. (1990). Self-esteem and perceptions of conveyed impressions: Is negative affectivity associated with greater realism? *Journal of Personality and Social Psychology, 58*, 122–133.

Chatman, J. A. (1989). Improving interactional organizational research: A model of person–organization fit. *Academy of Management Review, 14*, 333–349.

Chatman, J. A., Caldwell, D. F., & O'Reilly, C. A. (1999). Managerial personality and performance: A semi-idiographic approach. *Journal of Research in Personality, 33*, 514–545.

Colvin, C. R., Block, J., & Funder, D. C. (1995). Overly-positive self-evaluations and personality: Negative implications for mental health. *Journal of Personality and Social Psychology, 68*, 1152–1162.

Crowne, D. P., & Marlowe, D. (1964). *The approval motive.* New York: Wiley.

Deutschman, A. (2000). *The second coming of Steve Jobs.* New York: Broadway Books.

Emmons, R. A. (1987). Narcissism: Theory and measurement. *Journal of Personality and Social Psychology, 52*, 11–17.

Farwell, L., & Wohlwend-Lloyd, R. (1998). Narcissistic processes: Optimistic expectations, favorable self-evaluations, and self-enhancing attributions. *Journal of Personality, 66*, 65–83.

Fedor, D., Rensvold, R., & Adams, S. (1992). An investigation of factors expected to affect feedback seeking: A longitudinal field study. *Personnel Psychology, 45*, 779–805.

Feist, G. J. (1994). Personality and working style predictors of integrative complexity: A study of scientists' thinking about research and teaching. *Journal of Personality and Social Psychology, 67*, 474–484.

Freud, S. (1953). On narcissism: An introduction. In J. Strachey (Ed. and Trans.), *The standard edition of the complete psychological works of Sigmund Freud* (Vol. 14, pp. 69–102). London: Hogarth Press. (Original work published 1914)

Funder, D. C. (1995). On the accuracy of interpersonal judgments: A realistic approach. *Psychological Review, 102*, 652–670.

Gabriel, M. T., Critelli, J. W., & Ee, J. S. (1994). Narcissistic illusions in self-evaluations of intelligence and attractiveness. *Journal of Personality, 62*, 143–155.

Gangestad, S. W., & Snyder, M. (2000). Self monitoring: Appraisal and reappraisal. *Psychological Bulletin, 126*, 530–555.

Gosling, S., John, O. P., Craik, K. H., & Robins, R. W. (1998). Do people know how they behave? Self-reported act frequencies compared with on-line codings by observers. *Journal of Personality and Social Psychology, 74*, 1337–1349.

Greenwald, A. G. (1980). The totalitarian ego: Fabrication and revision of personal history. *American Psychologist, 33*, 603–618.

Hendin, H. M., & Cheek, J. M. (1997). Assessing hypersensitive narcissism: A reexamination of Murray's Narcissism Scale. *Journal of Research in Personality, 31*, 588–599.

Hoffman, G. J. (1923). An experiment in self-estimation. *Journal of Abnormal and Social Psychology, 18*, 43–49.

Hogan, R. (1983). A socioanalytic theory of personality. In M. M. Page (Ed.), *Nebraska Symposium on Motivation* (pp. 336–355). Lincoln: University of Nebraska Press.

Hogan, R., Raskin, R., & Fazzini, D. (1990). The dark side of charisma. In K. E. Clark and M. B. Clark (Eds.), *Measures of leadership* (pp. 343–354). West Orange, NJ: Leadership Library of America.

Holden, R. R., & Hibbs, N. (1995). Incremental validity of response latencies for detecting fakers on a personality test. *Journal of Research in Personality, 29*, 362–372.

Hoorens, V. (1995). Self-favoring biases, self-presentation, and the self–other asymmetry in social comparison. *Journal of Personality, 63*, 793–818.

Hough, L. M. (1998). Effects of intentional distortion in personality measurement and evaluation of suggested palliatives. *Human Performance, 11*, 209–244.

John, O. P., Cheek, J. M., & Klohnen, E. C. (1996). On the nature of self-monitoring: Construct explication with Q-sort ratings. *Journal of Personality and Social Psychology, 71*, 763–776.

John, O. P., & Robins, R. (1994). Accuracy and bias in self-perception: Individual differences in self-enhancement and the role of narcissism. *Journal of Personality and Social Psychology, 66*, 206–219.

John, O. P., & Srivastava, S. (1999). The big five trait taxonomy: History, measurement, and theoretical perspectives. In L. A. Pervin & O. P. John (Eds.), *Handbook of personality: Theory and research, 2nd ed.* (pp. 102–138). New York: Guilford.

Johnson, E. A. (1995). Self-deceptive coping: Adaptive only in ambiguous contexts. *Journal of Personality, 63*, 759–792.

Jones, E. E., & Pittman, T. S. (1982). Toward a general theory of strategic self-presentation. In J. Suls (Ed.), *Psychological perspectives on the self* (Vol. 1, pp. 49–67). Hillsdale, NJ: Erlbaum.

Kenny, D. A. (1994). *Interpersonal perception: A social relations analysis.* New York: Guilford Press.

Krueger, J. (1998). Enhancement bias in descriptions of self and others. *Personality and Social Psychology Bulletin, 24*, 505–516.

Kwan, V., Bond, M., Kenny, D. A., John, O. P., & Robins, R. (2001). *Self-enhancement from a social relations perspective.* Unpublished manuscript, University of California, Berkeley.

Leary, T. (1957). *Interpersonal diagnosis of personality.* New York: Ronald Press.

Lewinsohn, P. M, Mischel, W., Chaplin, W., & Barton, R. (1980). Social competence and depression: The role of illusory self-perceptions. *Journal of Abnormal Psychology, 89*, 203–212.

Lockard, J. S., & Paulhus, D. L. (1988). *Self-deception: An adaptive mechanism?* New York: Prentice Hall.

Mabe, P. A., & West, S. G. (1982). Validity of self-evaluation of ability: A review and meta-analysis. *Journal of Applied Psychology, 67*, 280–296.

McCall, M., & Lombardo, M. (1983). *Off the track: Why and how successful executives get derailed* (Technical Rep. No. 21). Greensboro, NC: Center for Creative Leadership.

McCrae, R. R., & Costa, P. T. Jr. (1989). Different points of view: Self-reports and ratings in the assessment of personality. In J. P. Forgas & J. M. Innes (Eds.), *Recent advances in social psychology: An interactional perspective* (pp. 429–439). Amsterdam: Elsevier.

McHoskey, J. W., Worzel, W., & Szyarto, C. (1998). Machiavellianism and psychopathy. *Journal of Personality and Social Psychology, 74*, 192–210.

Miller, D., & Ross, M. (1975). Self-serving biases in the attribution of causality. *Journal of Personality and Social Psychology, 82*, 901–906.

Millon, T. (1990). The disorders of personality. In L. A. Pervin (Ed.), *Handbook of personality: Theory and research.* New York: Guilford Press.

Morey, L. C., & Glutting, J. H. (1994). The Personality Assessment Inventory: Correlates with normal and abnormal personality. In S. Strack & M. Lorr (Eds.), *Differentiating normal and abnormal personality* (pp. 402–420). New York: Springer.

Morf, C. C., & Rhodewalt, F. (1993). Narcissism and self-evaluation maintenance: Explorations in object relations. *Personality and Social Psychology Bulletin, 19*, 668–676.

National Institute of Mental Health. (1995). *Basic behavioral science research for mental health* (NIH publication no. 95-3682). Washington, DC: U.S. Government Printing Office.

Nicholson, R. A., & Hogan, R. (1990). The construct validity of social desirability. *American Psychologist, 45*, 290–292.

Ones, D. S., Viswesvaran, C., & Reiss, A. D. (1996). Role of social desirability in personality testing for personnel selection: The red herring. *Journal of Applied Psychology, 81*, 660–679.

Paulhus, D. L. (1984). Two-component models of socially desirable responding. *Journal of Personality and Social Psychology, 46*, 598–609.

Paulhus, D. L. (1986). Self-deception and impression management in test responses. In A. Angleitner & J. S. Wiggins (Eds.), *Personality assessment via questionnaire* (pp. 143–165). New York: Springer-Verlag.

Paulhus, D. L. (1991). Measurement and control of response bias. In J. P. Robinson, P. R. Shaver, & L. S. Wrightsman (Eds.), *Measures of personality and social psychological attitudes* (pp. 17–59). San Diego, CA: Academic Press.

Paulhus, D. L. (1993). Bypassing the will: The automatization of affirmations. In D. M.

Wegner & J. W. Pennebaker (Eds.), *Handbook of mental control* (pp. 573–587). Hillsdale, NJ: Erlbaum.

Paulhus, D. L. (1998a). Interpersonal and intrapsychic adaptiveness of trait self-enhancement: A mixed blessing? *Journal of Personality and Social Psychology, 74,* 1197–1208.

Paulhus, D. L. (1998b). *Manual for the Balanced Inventory of Desirable Responding (BIDR-7).* Toronto, Ontario, Canada: Multi-Health Systems.

Paulhus, D. L. (2000, February). *Individual differences in self-enhancement: Departures from reality.* Paper presented at the 1st meeting of the Society for Personality and Social Psychology, Nashville, TN.

Paulhus, D. L. (in press). Socially desirable responding: Evolution of a construct. In H. Braun, D. Wiley, & D. N. Jackson (Eds.), *The psychology of constructs in personality and intellect.* New York: Erlbaum.

Paulhus, D. L., Bruce, M. N., & Trapnell, P. D. (1995). Effects of self-presentation strategies on personality profiles and their structure. *Personality and Social Psychology Bulletin, 21,* 100–108.

Paulhus, D. L., & John, O. P. (1998). Egoistic and moralistic bias in self-perception: The interplay of self-deceptive styles with basic traits and motives. *Journal of Personality, 66,* 1025–1060.

Paulhus, D. L., & Levitt, K. (1986). Desirable responding triggered by affect: Automatic egotism? *Journal of Personality and Social Psychology, 52,* 245–259.

Paulhus, D. L., & Lysy, D. (1995). *Correlates of self-enhancement on intelligence.* Unpublished manuscript, University of British Columbia, Vancouver, Canada.

Paulhus, D. L., & Reid, D. B. (1991). Enhancement and denial in socially desirable responding. *Journal of Personality and Social Psychology, 60,* 307–317.

Peale, N. V. (1952). *The power of positive thinking.* New York: Prentice Hall.

Peale, N. V. (1959). *The amazing results of positive thinking.* Englewood Cliffs, NJ: Prentice Hall.

Podsakoff, P., & Organ, D. (1986). Self-reports in organizational research: Problems and prospects. *Journal of Management, 12,* 531–544.

Raskin, R. N., & Hall, C. S. (1979). A Narcissistic Personality Inventory. *Psychological Reports, 45,* 590.

Raskin, R. N., & Hall, C. S. (1981). The Narcissistic Personality Inventory: Alternative form reliability and further evidence of construct validity. *Journal of Personality Assessment, 45,* 159–162.

Raskin, R. N., Novacek, J., & Hogan, R. T. (1991a). Narcissism, self-esteem and defensive self-enhancement. *Journal of Personality, 59,* 19–38.

Raskin, R. N., Novacek, J., & Hogan, R. T. (1991b). Narcissistic self-esteem management. *Journal of Personality and Social Psychology, 60,* 911–918.

Rhodewalt, F., & Morf, C. C. (1998). On self-aggrandizement and anger: A temporal analysis of narcissism and affective reactions to success and failure. *Journal of Personality and Social Psychology, 74,* 672–685.

Roberts, B. W., & Robins, R. W. (2000). Broad dispositions, broad aspirations: The intersection of personality and major life goals. *Personality and Social Psychology Bulletin, 26,* 1284–1296.

Robins, R. W., & Beer, J. (2001). Positive illusions about the self: Their correlates and consequences. *Journal of Personality and Social Psychology, 80,* 340–352.

Robins, R. W., & John, O. P. (1997a). Effects of visual perspective and narcissism on self-perception: Is seeing believing? *Psychological Science, 8,* 37–42.

Robins, R. W., & John, O. P. (1997b). The quest for self-insight: Theory and research on the accuracy of self-perceptions. In R. Hogan, J. Johnson, & S. R. Briggs (Eds.), *Handbook of personality psychology* (pp. 649–679). San Diego, CA: Academic Press.

Robins, R. W., Norem, J. K., & Cheek, J. M. (1999). Naturalizing the self. In L. A. Pervin & O. P. John (Eds.), *Handbook of personality: Theory and research* (2nd ed., pp. 443–477). New York: Guilford Press.

Robinson, M. D., & Ryff, C. D. (1999). The role of self-deception in perceptions of past, present, and future happiness. *Personality and Social Psychology Bulletin, 25,* 595–606.

Rosenfeld, P., Giacalone, R. A., & Riordan, C. A. (1995). *Impression management in organizations.* New York: Routledge.

Rosse, J. G., Stecher, M. D., Miller, J. L., & Levin, R. A. (1998). The impact of response distortion on preemployment personality testing and hiring decisions. *Journal of Applied Psychology, 83,* 634–664.

Rowatt, W. C., Cunningham, M. R., & Druen, P. B. (1998). Deception to get a date. *Personality and Social Psychology Bulletin, 24,* 1228–1242.

Sackeim, H. A., & Gur, R. C. (1978). Self-deception, other-deception, and consciousness. In G. E. Schwartz & D. Shapiro (Eds.), *Consciousness and self-regulation: Advances in research* (Vol. 2, pp. 139–197). New York: Plenum.

Schlenker, B. R. (1980). *Impression management: The self-concept, social identity, and interpersonal relations.* Monterey, CA: Brooks/Cole.

Schneider, B. (1987). E = f(P,B): The road to a radical approach to person–environment fit. *Journal of Vocational Behavior, 31,* 353–361.

Sedikides, C., & Strube, M. J. (1997). Self-evaluation: To thine own self be good; to thine own self be sure, to thine own self be true, and to thine own self be better. In *Advances in experimental social psychology* (Vol. 29, pp. 209–269). San Diego, CA: Academic Press.

Snyder, M. (1974). Self-monitoring of expressive behavior. *Journal of Personality and Social Psychology, 30,* 526–537.

Snyder, M. (1987). *Public appearances; private realities: The psychology of self-monitoring.* New York: Freeman.

Taylor, S. E. (1989). *Positive illusions: Creative self-deception and the healthy mind*. New York: Basic Books.

Taylor, S. E., & Armor, D. A. (1996). Positive illusions and coping with adversity. *Journal of Personality, 64*, 873–898.

Taylor, S. E., & Brown, J. D. (1988). Illusion and well-being: A social psychological perspective on mental health. *Psychological Bulletin, 103*, 193–210.

Tesser, A. (1988). Toward a self-evaluation maintenance model of social behavior. In L. Berkowitz (Ed.), *Advances in experimental social psychology* (Vol. 21, pp. 181–227). New York: Academic Press.

Westen, D. (1990). Psychoanalytic approaches to personality. In L. A. Pervin (Ed.), *Handbook of personality: Theory and research* (pp. 21–65). New York: Guilford Press.

Wiggins, J. S. (1991). Agency and communion as conceptual coordinates for the understanding and measurement of interpersonal behavior. In W. Grove & D. Cicchetti (Eds.), *Thinking clearly about psychology: Essays in honor of Paul Meehl* (Vol. 2, pp. 89–113). Minneapolis: University of Minnesota Press.

Wiggins, J. S., & Pincus, A. L. (1994). Personality structure and the structure of personality disorders. In P. T. Costa Jr. & T. A. Widiger (Eds.), *Personality disorders and the Five-Factor Model of personality* (pp. 73–93). Washington, DC: American Psychological Association.

Wink, P. (1992). Three Narcissism scales for the California Q-Set. *Journal of Personality Assessment, 58*, 51–66.

Wink, P., & Gough, H. G. (1990). New Narcissism scales for the California Psychological Inventory and MMPI. *Journal of Personality Assessment, 54*, 446–462.

Zerbe, W., & Paulhus, D. L. (1987). Socially desirable responding in organizations. *American Academy of Management Review, 12*, 250–264.

Zumbo, B. D. (1999). The simple difference score as an inherently poor measure of change: Some reality, much mythology. *Advances in Social Science Methodology, 5*, 269–304.

PART 3

Emerging Themes in Applied Personality Psychology

CHAPTER 10

Personality and Individual Differences in the Workplace

Person–Organization–Outcome Fit

Adrian Furnham

The relationship between personality psychology and industrial and organizational (I/O) psychology has never been close (R. Hogan, Hogan, & Roberts, 1996). Whereas some personality psychologists have allied themselves with clinical and social psychologists (more so in the United Kingdom than in the United States), applied and I/O psychologists have tended to focus on situational explanations of work-related behaviors. Additionally, although both personality and I/O psychologists have favored correlational rather than experimental methodologies, for most of the 20th century, I/O psychologists stressed external or interpersonal, rather than intrapersonal, determinants of the most often studied work-related behaviors (i.e., motivation, productivity, and satisfaction).

Applied psychologists interested in personality and individual differences have frequently been stimulated by crises—most significantly war and unemployment, when large numbers of people require screening and assessment. Psychologists have been called on to devise assessment measures to best determine the skill/ability–job fit for military personnel. Military psychologists often are requested to measure specific and general abilities as well as personality traits, particularly those that may render military personnel vulnerable to specific problems (Furnham, 1992, 1997). Military data are particularly useful because of the large, representative samples available for study.

In times of high unemployment, the numbers of unemployed individuals and applicants for vacant positions increase dramatically. As a result, personality psychologists frequently are requested to help develop biodata instruments that offer more efficient (and valid) means than the selection interview to distinguish among appropriate and inappropriate candidates (Gunter, Furnham, & Drakeley, 1993). In the 1980s, there were simultaneous increases in unemploy-

223

ment in developed Western countries and greater commercial interest in the use of personality and ability measures (Salgado, 1998).

However, the interest of I/O psychologists and practitioners in personality and individual-differences correlates of work-related behaviors is also to some extent a function of fashion and the number of test developers and publishers aggressively marketing their tests at a given time. The laws of supply and demand inevitably dictate the number of organizations both selling and using individual-differences measures and data for recruitment, selection, development, and training. However, the use of particular personality measures can change abruptly as a result of academic reports of shortcomings (Blinkhorn & Johnson, 1990).

In fact, it is possible to plot timelines depicting interest in personality research (as an academic discipline) and I/O psychology applications in organizational settings. Personality research showed steady growth from the 1930s until the end of the 1970s but was badly shaken by the person–situation debate (Funder & Ozer, 1983; Furnham, 1981) that lasted until the mid-1980s. General acceptance of the big five personality dimensions (Barrick & Mount, 1991) has, however, considerably revived the area, which is now more vigorous than it has ever been. Personality testing was fairly steady until the 1980s, when unemployment and the growth of the test publishers made it very widespread in industry, particularly in Europe (Funder, 1997). Nevertheless, there is a considerable increase in interest among I/O researchers, human resources specialists, and others in personality and individual-differences prediction of work-related behaviors (J. Hogan, Rybicki, Motowidlo, & Borman, 1998; R. Hogan, 1991; R. Hogan & Shelton, 1998).

This chapter first reviews different approaches to personality at work. It then considers the topic of individual–job fit, which is the area in which I/O psychologists have traditionally shown the greatest interest in personality theory and measurement. The issue of motivation at work and its relationship to personality is discussed briefly as well. The evidence from one area, personality and sales, is then presented. Various reasons for low correlations and disappointing validity data are discussed, and then the problems of neglected organizations and cultural and situational variables are addressed.

Six Approaches to the Study of Personality at Work

Furnham (1992, 1997) suggested that an examination of the literature reveals that there are six distinct approaches to considering how personality and individual differences affect work behaviors and outcomes. These approaches have been characterized as follows: (a) classic personality theory, (b) classic I/O theory, (c) work-specific individual-differences measures, (d) fit measures, (e) longitudinal studies, and (f) biographical and case-history studies.

Classic Personality Theory

Although personality theorists generally are not particularly, or even very frequently, interested in validating their theories and measures in work settings, opportunities sometimes present themselves (Eysenck, 1967). Personality and individual-differences measures may be cognitively or biologically based tests measuring so-called "normal" or "abnormal" traits and using either single- or multiple-trait measures. The personality trait measure used usually is soundly theoretically conceived and carefully psychometrically constructed. However, the selection of the work-related measure frequently is opportunistic and pragmatic, partly because of the need to use the measures available. Inevitably, the more complex the job, the more difficult it is to obtain robust and sensitive output measures aggregated over time. It is always best to have multiple dependent measures with different kinds of data (e.g., observational, self-report, test), but this very rarely is available. Sales has been popular as a research area partly because sales figures are easy to measure. Many personality theorists view studies in this area simply as opportunities to validate their theories in a different applied setting.

Classic I/O Theory

I/O psychologists nearly always are interested in understanding a work-related process such as environmental determinants of stress, the relationship between productivity and satisfaction, or techniques to improve group creativity or innovation. They frequently strive to collect work-related data using self-reports or through behavioral measures. Ideally, these data are aggregated to ensure better reliability and are collected among, rather than simply within, organizations to ensure better generalizability. However, many researchers have become aware that there are considerable individual differences in work performance. When examining the ratio of output of the best and worst performers in a variety of occupations, Hull (1928) noted that "the best is twice as good as the worst." However, the lack of up-to-date knowledge regarding personality theory and measurement techniques means that many I/O psychology researchers frequently choose outdated, poorly validated tests that have been commercially exploited through face validity and presentation packaging. Furthermore, the statistical analysis of relationships often is simple and naïve and fails to reflect developments in causal modeling. Finally, such correlational studies often are exploratory and piecemeal rather than based on hypothesis testing, and the results often disappoint the researchers, confirming their belief that personality traits are not important.

Work-Specific Individual-Differences Measures

For both academic and commercial reasons, attempts have been made to develop work process or product measures to be used in applied settings. One example is Spector's (1982) Work Locus of Control Scale, which is a sphere-specific measure of the well-known locus of control variable (Furnham & Steele, 1994). These measures differ with regard to various criteria: Some focus on single traits, whereas others measure multiple traits. Many are self-reports, whereas some attempt to apply cognitive or behavioral measures of personality. Some focus on attitudes and others on attributions. With some of these measures, there is the danger that they are tautological. That is, the independent (personality) variables are self-reported measures of a particular work outcome, yet the dependent variable is an (objective) measure of that precise variable. Both variables often are conceived of very narrowly, and the results appear to be of limited interest to the wider academic audience. Furthermore, these measures often have little incremental validity, which is precisely the reason they are constructed.

Fit Measures

One of the oldest themes in I/O psychology is the concept of the best fit between the ability, motivation, and traits of the individual and the skills and traits required to do the job. At their core, selection and training are about maximizing the fit between employee and job (Furnham, in press).

There are various differences among the fit measures available. Some concepts of fit are more impressionistic than geometric or statistical. Others base the fit concept more clearly on similarity than complementarity, and there is significant debate as to the different types and distinctions to be made regarding fit or congruity. The simple idea underlying all of this research is that the better and closer the fit between an individual's interests, values, traits, and skills and the demands and requirements of the job, the happier and more productive he or she will be and the more satisfied the organization will be with his or her performance (Furnham, 1997).

Longitudinal Studies

Studies examining change and stability in behaviors over time are particularly valuable for exploring patterns of causation. Unfortunately, because longitudinal work is so difficult and expensive it is comparatively rarely done. However, it is most important to examine how, for instance, ability and traits measured at selection can predict various aspects of an individual's organizational career. Studies have differed as to the length of time over which they have occurred, from relatively short periods of 1 or 2 years to much longer studies lasting up to 20 years. Most studies examine individuals within a particular organization even though it is preferable to do between-organization longitudinal studies so that the effect of organizational culture and structure can be examined systematically. Finally, because of problems associated with accurate data gathering, the best longitudinal studies are prospective rather retrospective in design.

Biographical and Case-History Studies

Biographical, autobiographical, clinical, and case studies of the working lives of individuals occasionally are the most illuminating of the role of personality at work. Studies have been undertaken of both individuals and groups, but most have examined a very narrow range of often highly successful entrepreneurs. Many are impressionistic and tend to present the central character in either the best or worst possible light. Nevertheless, they often can provide some insight on the complex intrapsychic processes involved in both management success and derailment.

Caveat

These rather different approaches inevitably yield different types and quality of data, which tend to be published for very different audiences. It is therefore particularly difficult for researchers to perform critical and comprehensive reviews of findings in the area they wish to study.

Fitting the Person to the Job

Most I/O psychologists have some interest in personality research when they consider the issue of employee selection. Whereas I/O psychologists have seen their role to be that of fitting the individual to the job through selection and development, ergonomists have concentrated on fitting the job to the individual through better equipment design (Furnham, 1997). Both techniques involve thorough analysis of both the individual and the job to establish levels of compatibility.

However, this approach is rather static and often ignores dynamic forces that operate with individuals at work. At least four issues can be identified:

> **1.** People *choose* their job and working environment (Furnham, 1981). This inevitably reduces the variability of individuals in particular jobs. Occupational choice reflects a number of features, such as pay, location, job security, training, and so on. It also is a

function of personality traits, attitudes, and values (Furnham, 1997). This choice is a matter of balancing various factors that may be implicit or explicit. An organization also makes a choice in the selection process and may well have a number of quite specific criteria, such as size (e.g., minimum height), fitness (e.g., not needing vision correction), skills (e.g., literacy, numeracy), or demography (e.g., sex, age, education). Again, this may considerably reduce the variance on a number of specific variables, and this should be taken into consideration when doing research.

2. Individuals *adapt* to their job. Partly out of necessity, individuals adapt aspects of their working style to their requirements of the job, often quite soon after they start a job. Most organizations attempt, through primary socialization (i.e., induction, mentoring, training), to adjust individual employee behaviors to the pattern of work behaviors acceptable within the organization. That is, they try to adapt employees to the jobs to which they are assigned. This might involve, for example, adaptation to the time of day an employee is required to work, the pace of work, and responsiveness to colleagues and customers. Some adaptations may be relatively easy, whereas others may prove to be very difficult because they represent a style of work or behavior that may be somewhat incompatible with an individual's personality traits. For example, if extraverts trade accuracy for speed to increase arousal and introverts do the opposite, it may prove very difficult for an extravert to adapt to the requirements of a proofreader, whereas an introvert may have great difficulty being an auctioneer.

3. Individuals *change* various aspects of the job they perform. They change their physical and social environments and personalize many aspects of their working lives. This can be observed, for example, in the very different ways employees with identical office spaces and equipment arrange their personal working spaces. These changes may be made to facilitate productivity or reflect different working styles, or they may be little more than exercises in impression management. The less technical, team based, or computerized the work, the more scope individuals have to change their job to suit their needs, traits, and values. Employees may negotiate (with management or unions), earn (through job performance), or unilaterally change the ways in which they do their job, which may or may not affect their output.

4. Jobs themselves *evolve* with new technology, markets, and global requirements. Many aspects of a job may change while an individ-

ual remains in it. For example, automation, client needs, or market changes may necessitate a change or changes in the way an individual performs his or her job. Thus, an individual carefully selected and trained for a job at Time A may or may not be suited to do that job at Time B.

Experimental paradigms for investigating personality at work often involve designing a situation in which individuals with different traits work under different conditions. Therefore, a classic 2 × 2 design might involve introverts and extraverts working on either a people-oriented or nonpeople-oriented task. Although these experimental conditions can usefully test theoretically derived hypotheses, they do not always take the factors outlined above into sufficient consideration. Introverts may (a) try to avoid people-oriented jobs, (b) attempt to be more sociable in them, (c) change the job to reduce the people contact, or (d) work for promotion so that they manage customer-facing employees (through e-mail and other more indirect methods) rather than interact with customers directly.

Personality and Work Motivation

A second issue that often stimulates I/O psychologists to consider personality and individual differences is that of motivation in the workplace. Surprisingly, few studies have looked at personality correlates of work motivation, although some studies have considered personality and job satisfaction (Bass & Barrett, 1981; Spector, 1982) as well as more general relationships among personality and work (Cooper & Payne, 1967). Furnham and Zacherl (1986) looked at the relationships among personality and job satisfaction in a group of computer specialists. They found that extraversion was modestly positively correlated with job satisfaction, whereas psychoticism and neuroticism were negatively correlated with all seven specific and overall combined job satisfaction scores. The measure of job satisfaction concentrated most clearly on what would be classified according to Hertzberg, Mauser, and Snyderman (1959) as *hygiene factors*.

There are other reasons to believe that personality is important in job motivation and satisfaction. Staw and Ross (1985) argued that employee attitudes (i.e., motivation and satisfaction) are as much a function of stable personality traits as organizational conditions: "Job attitudes may reflect a biologically based trait that predisposes individuals to see positive or negative content in their lives" (p. 471). Arvey, Bouchard, Segal, and Abraham (1989) demonstrated that there is a genetic component in terms of the jobs that are sought and held by individuals. They showed that job satisfaction is heritable and that genetic factors (which, in part, determine personality and ability) account for about 30% of the variance in job satisfaction.

More recently, Furnham, Forde, and Ferrari (1999) looked at the relationships among the three Eysenckian superfactors (Extraversion, Neuroticism, and Lie) and 21 primary factors and various work motivations grouped under Herzberg et al.'s (1959) two-factor model. According to Herzberg et al.'s theory, individuals have two major needs: (a) *hygiene needs*, which are influenced by the physical and psychological conditions in which they work, and (b) *motivator needs*, which Herzberg described as being very similar to the higher order needs in Maslow's (1954) hierarchy factors (or dissatisfiers). These include supervision, interpersonal relations, physical working conditions, salary, company policies and administrative practices, benefits, and job security. When these factors are unfavorable, job dissatisfaction results. Conversely, when these factors are positive, such as when employees perceive that their pay is fair and their working conditions are good, then barriers to job satisfaction are removed. However, the fulfillment of hygiene needs cannot in itself result in job satisfaction; it can result only in the reduction or elimination of dissatisfaction.

Motivator needs are fulfilled by what Hertzberg et al. (1959) labeled *motivator factors* or *satisfiers*: achievement, recognition, the work itself, responsibility, and advancement. Motivator factors are concerned with the nature of the work itself, the consequences of work, and those facets of the job that satisfy an individual's need for self-actualization (i.e., self-fulfillment) in his or her work, and it is only from the performance of the task that individuals can enjoy the rewards that will reinforce their aspirations.

Furnham, Forde, et al. (1999) demonstrated that nearly one third of the variance in hygiene factors could be accounted for by neuroticism, whereas one fifth of the variance in motivator factors could be accounted for by extraversion. These results are interpreted partly in terms of Gray's (1975) theory, which proposed that extraverts are particularly sensitive to reward and introverts to punishment:

> If there are systematic differences in the work-related factors different people seek out and value, it would be well for managers to pay attention to trait variables in selection to ensure a better P–E fit. Equally, if extraverts seek out recognition, reward, and responsibility more than introverts, it may be useful for managers to introduce different performance management schemes for different groups of workers. If it is true that extraverts value—and are presumably motivated and satisfied by—Herzbergian motivator factors, it would benefit organisations and managers to attempt to provide these facets. Thus job rotation and empowerment should be motivating for the extraverts as well as the practice of instituting performance appraisal and public reward schemes. On the other hand, neurotics are likely to become demotivated and job dissatisfied. (p. 1042)

The topic of personality and job motivation requires further research even though the latter is particularly difficult to measure.

Research Into Personality as a Predictor of Sales Success

General Sales Performance

To illustrate the application of personality to the workplace, one area of research —the trait correlates of sales performance—is discussed. Reasons for the particular interest in this field are that the dependent variable (i.e., sales revenues and costs) is easy to measure and organizations typically maintain extensive data on individual sales representatives. However, classic studies that investigated personality as a predictor of sales performance generally produced inconsistent and inconclusive results. For example, Ghiselli and Barthol (1953) evaluated the validity of personality tests involving salespeople. Although this study revealed substantial validity coefficients (r = .36), it illustrates a common limitation of the early personality-performance studies. Personality dimensions were combined into broad categories. This approach often led to the conclusion that personality variables were less valid predictors of sales performance than other measures such as cognitive ability tests. This, in turn, led to neglect of research into personality as a predictor of sales performance, until interest was renewed in the 1980s (Hogan, 1991).

Churchill, Ford, Hartley, and Walker (1985) performed meta-analyses that examined a range of predictors of different types of salespeople's performance. It was found that, on the basis of self-report, manager and peer ratings, and objective organizational data, aptitude and personal characteristics (i.e., personality) accounted for only 2% of the variance in work outcome measures. No single predictor could account for more than 10% of the variance. Churchill et al. postulated that the strength of the relationship between the major determinants and salespeople's performance is affected by the type of products sold, the specific tasks to be performed, and the type of customer. One limitation of this study is that the classification scheme for predictors collapses across very meaningful categories, which obscures potentially important information (e.g., "aptitude" includes cognitive ability, personality dimensions, and many other nondemographic individual-differences variables).

Additional meta-analyses performed by Schmidt, Gooding, Noe, and Kirsch (1984) analyzed sales validity coefficients and found an uncorrected correlation of .17 for all types of predictors and criteria for sales jobs. Personality factors were found to have the lowest validity coefficient of any predictor group. Robertson and Kinder (1993) suggested that this low validity may have been the result of the meta-analysis procedure. Before the rest of the meta-analysis was performed, validity coefficients within a single predictor category (e.g., personality) were averaged to produce a summary validity coefficient. This procedure could have limited the validity observed for personality measures by including in the averaging process scales that would not be expected to predict the relevant criterion, as well as those that would be expected to show validity on a priori grounds.

Barrick and Mount (1991) improved the meta-analytic procedure by grouping their predictor information according to the Big Five personality scales (Digman, 1990). They also generated specific hypotheses about which personality criteria should predict which performance criteria. Barrick and Mount were able to show the differential relations between the personality dimensions and occupational performance across five different occupational groups. Performance measures within these groups were classified into three broad criteria: (a) job proficiency, (b) training proficiency, and (c) personnel data. Relationships for salespersons were found with Conscientiousness ($r = .23$) and Extraversion ($r = .15$); the correlations for the other dimensions of the Big Five were considerably lower. The low correlations could have been a result of the general performance criteria and the focus on the prediction of specific performance measures; this focus may reduce the "noise" in the correlation as coefficients. Furnham and Coveney (1996) found Extraversion and Conscientiousness to be important correlates of measures of customer service ability. In addition, as Furnham and Coveney predicted, Neuroticism was a clear predictor of poor customer relations.

In a follow-up study, Mount and Barrick (1995) found that the overall Conscientiousness score and both of its dimensions (Dependability and Achievement) predicted specific performance criteria better than did global criteria (e.g., overall rating of job performance). The subdimensions of Conscientiousness (dependability and achievement) outpredicted the broad dimension of Conscientiousness only when there were theoretically relevant links between the subdimensions criteria. This supports the suggestion by Robertson and Kinder (1993) that correlation coefficients of personality and work performance may increase if researchers make a priori theoretical links between the personality dimensions and the performance criteria. This highlights the importance of breaking down both the performance criteria and the personality dimensions into components and making theoretical links between specific dimensions and criteria rather than computing massive correlation matrixes and finding less-than-chance significant relationships.

Hough (1992) investigated the relationships of a different set of personality factors and a range of performance criteria. Four of the Big Five were retained: Adjustment (Emotional Stability), Agreeableness, Intellectance (Openness to Experience), and Extraversion. Extraversion was divided into two subdimensions: Affiliation (sociability) and Potency (impact, assertiveness, and energy). Conscientiousness was divided into Achievement and Dependability. Two other dimensions that do not correspond to the Big Five were Rugged Individualism (decisiveness, action oriented) and Locus of Control (one's belief in the amount of control one has over rewards and punishments). The results showed that each of the nine personality constructs correlated with important job and life criteria and that each of the nine constructs had a different pattern of relationships with the criteria.

In the light of Hough's (1992) data, it appears that Barrick and Mount (1991; Mount & Barrick, 1995) overemphasized the broad dimensions of Conscientiousness at the expense of other useful personality traits. They pointed out that Conscientiousness had been shown to be valid across occupational groups and criteria and that the other Big Five constructs with comparable validities were only predictive for a subset of occupational types or criterion categories. However, that other personality variables are not correlated with all occupational categories or criterion types does not necessarily mean they are unimportant. Different jobs make different demands on employees and may contribute to a pattern of validity coefficients that are different from those of other jobs. Although the Hough model appears to do a good job of predicting work performance, its findings were limited to a military setting.

Vinchur, Schippmann, Switzer, and Roth (1998) used meta-analysis to evaluate personality as a predictor of objective and subjective sales performance measures. A number of personality measures were investigated, including the original Big Five and Hough's (1992) nine-factor model. Extraversion and Conscientiousness were found to predict both subjective and objective sales performance with validity coefficients of .21 and .31, respectively. These results support the findings of Barrick and Mount (1991). The subdimensions suggested by Hough were particularly strong predictors of sales success. Potency (.28) and Achievement (.41) were most predictive of sales performance, whereas Rugged Individualism predicted subjective performance ratings (.20). Potency applied to the assertiveness and intensity of interpersonal interactions. Vinchur et al. (1998) suggested that it may be this aspect of Extraversion that is particularly associated with high sales performance. This study indicated that specific personality subdimensions were able to more accurately predict specific sales performance criteria than broad personality dimensions.

Matteson, Ivancevich, and Smith (1984) found no significant relationship between Type A behavior and three measures of sales performance (i.e., policy amount, premium income, and total policies sold) in a sample of insurance salespeople. Similarly, Lee and Gillen (1989) investigated the relationships among Type A behavior and global quantitative and qualitative measures of sales performance but found no significant associations in a sample of 83 sales representatives. These findings may be due to the use of restricted sales performance measures, in terms of both objective sales criteria and global measures. However, Bluen, Barling, and Burns (1990) found that the achievement striving dimension of Type A behavior was predictive of the number of policies sold, but that the impatience−irritability dimension behavior was unrelated to sales performance and negatively associated with job satisfaction. One limitation of this study was that it used only one measure of sales ability (i.e., number of insurance policies sold). It could be that Type A behavior is predictive of other types of sales performance criteria.

A lack of understanding of the nature of the sales job itself may have contributed substantially to this underestimation of the predictive validity of personality in sales performance. However, previous research often used unreliable performance criteria. These often were based on self-report measures, subjective ratings of performance, and global measures. J. P. Campbell (1990) outlined a model of the multidimensional nature of performance criteria based on objective sales measures that focused on outcome-based effectiveness and subjective ratings that reflect more of the controllable parts of the employee's job, such as "organizational citizenship" behaviors (see chapter 3, this volume). Robertson and Kinder (1993) showed that validity coefficients rose from .20 to .30 when specific performance criteria were correlated with specific personality constructs. Although there may be a relationship between personality traits and some aspects of performance, personality dimensions may not necessarily be important in the prediction of all types of criteria.

One major reason that much of the previously published research into personality as a predictor of sales performance has failed to find predictive validity is because researchers tried to predict performance across different types of salespeople, in different types of sales jobs, and in different industries using the same performance criteria and the same set of predictor variables and measures. The previous research into personality and sales performance indicated that personality may be a more useful predictor when performance is broken down into components and specific work-related personality dimensions are targeted. There is sufficient evidence that personality traits predict occupational behavior only if the forms are sensitively measured, the performance criteria are reliably and validly measured, and there is good theoretical reason to expect the two to be empirically related.

Telemarketing

The significant increase in telesales has meant that this job has now become the focus of research (Furnham, Jackson, & Miller, 1999). A study by Hakstian, Scratchley, Macleod, Tweed, and Siddarth (1997) highlighted the importance of effective hiring practices in achieving optimal sales performance in telemarketing specifically. A predictive validity study in which telemarketing employees were administered a battery of cognitive ability self-report trait measures before being hired was performed. Employees were assessed 3 months later on their job performance across a range of objective and subjective job-specific performance criteria. Two cognitive ability tests and three personality scales from the California Psychological Inventory (Self-Acceptance, Socialization, and Achievement via Conformance) showed significant validities for at least one of the aggregated performance measures.

These factors were incorporated into an assessment instrument. Utility analysis demonstrated a significant gain in sales following the use of a valid selection procedure. The actual figure was found to be 632 more sales over a 3-month period per employee selected by a valid procedure. In a large company, 50 to 100 telemarketing employees might be hired in a year; the resulting gains could be very substantial. This research was performed on a relatively small American sample ($N = 85$), and the instrument's usefulness for selection across a range of telemarketing organizations may be limited. However, the results highlight the importance of effective selection procedures within an industry in which performance is closely linked to number of units sold and, therefore, real monetary value to the company.

Singh, Goolsby, and Rhoads (1994) have demonstrated the characteristic high burnout rate of customer service representatives in telemarketing positions. Burnout can have consistent, significant, and dysfunctional consequences and can lead to increased employee turnover. Effective recruitment may lead to improved job performance and satisfaction and reduce the high turnover rate that is characteristic of this industry. In addition, the results of these studies illustrate the importance of effective recruitment to reduce organizational costs as well as increase overall income.

There is little published research clarifying the key variables that are important for successful performance in telemarketing. Nancy Lamberton (cited in Stone, 1994) outlined five relevant characteristics for telemarketing personnel: (a) communication skills, (b) persistence, (c) organizational skills, (d) telephone personality, and (e) flexibility. Domanski (1991) identified four additional traits: (a) integrity, (b) hearing and listening skills, (c) team orientation, and (d) stress tolerance. However, the extent that these characteristics can be effectively applied to the selection process is limited because they are purely descriptive and based on intuition rather than empirically based or logically related to primary personality traits.

McGraw-Hill/London House (1989) developed a special instrument for telemarketer selection. The Telemarketing Applicant Inventory (TMAI) includes 11 scales that measure characteristics that are assumed to be related to work performance. In a series of in-house validity studies (summarized in Halverson, Behrens, & Nerad, 1990) the TMAI scales were shown to possess varying levels of validity for a number of performance criteria that were mostly based on subjective supervisor ratings.

The few published empirical studies focusing on telemarketing have not provided a coherent and consistent group of job performance predictors, and no published research using a well-known, widely available selection instrument appears to exist. Variables that have previously been investigated in telemarketing include locus of control, self-monitoring, communication skills, extraversion, and neuroticism, but each of these variables has not been examined in more than one study.

Kalechstein and Nowicki (1994) found that those telemarketers with high internal locus of control and a high need for recognition and status achieved a significantly higher value of objective sales than did other telemarketers. Achievement was defined as the dollar amount of the items sold by telemarketers over a designated 6-month period. After locus of control and need for recognition had been controlled for, length of employment (tenure) predicted significant difference in objective sales. Neither age nor gender was related to significant differences in achievement. Therefore, it would appear that locus of control as a personality variable had higher predictive validity than demographic variables.

This finding is consistent with the evidence regarding locus of control from Phares (1976). Phares demonstrated that when the appropriate valued reward contingency is in place, it can be expected that those individuals with a higher internal locus of control are more likely to make a response than those with an external locus of control. The telemarketing environment usually incorporates pay bonuses that are directly contingent on levels of sales made in a certain time period. Therefore, it would be expected that those employees with an internal locus of control would work harder to reach the targets than those with an external locus of control.

Furnham and Miller (1997) predicted that because of the nature of telemarketing Extraversion would be positively correlated with subjective ratings of overall sales performance and Neuroticism with absenteeism. Performance was measured by subjective appraisal ratings of performance and potential performance rather than objective sales figures. Absenteeism was measured by the periods of leave taken and the total numbers of sick days taken. Contrary to the predictions, moderate positive correlations were found with periods of absence (rather than actual recorded sick days) and young extraverted sales representatives. It was postulated that these short periods of absence might be the result of boredom. Young extraverts would be likely to take the odd day off to relieve the monotony of the job rather than being particularly prone to illness. Therefore, this could indicate that they may be an unreliable group to work in the telemarketing environment.

However, as predicted, extraverts were also rated as being higher performers and as having more potential than introverts. This finding is in line with the idea that extraverts are more sociable and responsive, are more comfortable dealing with strangers, and enjoy the variety of telemarketing. Although it was not found to be significant, a negative trend with Neuroticism and supervisor ratings was observed. However, these findings reflected only subjective ratings of performance, and further investigation is necessary to determine whether they generalize to a range of performance criteria. Demographic variables alone did not predict performance or absenteeism. These results therefore indicate the contribution of personality to the prediction of telemarketing performance.

It was suggested by Weitz (1981) that successful salespeople examine situational cues and adapt the sales interaction so as to present the product in a way that matches customer needs. The ability to adapt to different customers in different situations was viewed as the most effective form of sales ability. It was suggested that salespeople who are adaptive also would be high self-monitoring individuals. A study by Predmore (1992) used a process method to examine the effect of personality factors on the sales interactions of telemarketers. These findings supported Weitz's work. It was found that high self-monitoring individuals have significantly more sales success than low self-monitoring individuals do. It also was found that low self-monitoring salespeople complete sales calls more quickly than high self-monitoring salespeople do. In the sales situation, it would seem that the more self-monitoring a salesperson does, the greater the searching for cues should be, requiring additional conversation to elicit those cues and therefore slower progression through the different phases of a sales interaction. Although this takes more time, high self-monitoring salespeople are more successful at achieving more customer compliance than low self-monitoring salespeople, and they therefore close more sales.

A study by Squires, Torkel, Smither, and Ingate (1991) investigated the skills necessary for success in a telemarketing job. A role-play was conducted as a telephone interview to assess sales ability, communication skills, influence style, and social sensitivity, which is similar to self-monitoring. A trained rater evaluated employees' overall performance on these dimensions. It was found that these evaluations were significantly correlated with the objective and subjective performance criteria of the telemarketers. This finding has implications for training programs that seek to develop employees' communication and influence style skills.

Summary

These studies on sales illustrate three points. First, it is important to understand which personality traits, measured at which level, are likely to be predictive of the outcome measures. This involves careful scrutiny of the personality literature. Second, it remains important to obtain reliable measures of sales success that reflect all aspects of the job (e.g., cost, sales volume, customer contact, and absenteeism data). Third, it is important to replicate studies across organizations to take into account the effect of organizational cultural variables. There are three salient variables that interact: (a) personality, (b) work-outcome, and (c) corporate cultural variables.

The Person, the Task, and the Situation

There are three factors that interact in the workplace: (a) the personality (and ability and motivation) of the employee, (b) the task the employee is performing, and (c) the environment in which he or she is performing it. Focusing on personality and task outcome yet ignoring structural, cultural, or situational differences can lead to serious misinterpretations of the data, as can ignoring individual differences in traits or abilities. This point will be illustrated by examining research on background (e.g., music, television) distraction in the workplace.

Music

Since the beginning of the 20th century, researchers have been interested in the possible benefits of music at work. During the 1940s and 1950s there was a flurry of interest in whether music affected either morale (satisfaction) or productivity at work (Newman, Hunt, & Rhodes, 1956) or both. More recently, Oldham, Cummings, Mischel, Schmidthe, and Zhan (1995) found that for those who preferred to work with music, its relaxing qualities had significant effects on performance, organizational satisfaction, and ratings of fatigue. In an imaginative study, North, Hargreaves, and McKendrick (1999) argued and demonstrated that music with strong national associations activated related knowledge and led to purchasing products from that particular country.

The scattered literature on this topic can be grouped according to whether the primary interest was the style or type of music, the task being done, or personality effects. Investigations into the effects of music on performance have focused mainly on different musical styles (Sogin, 1988); or characteristics of the music, such as volume (Wolfe, 1983); or complexity (Furnham & Allass, 1999) and have produced mixed results. Fogelson (1973) saw that popular instrumental music significantly reduced scores on a reading comprehension test. This effect was also seen in a study by Williams (1961). Williams also found that classical music had no effect on performance, unlike Rauscher, Shaw, and Ky (1993), who found that listening to Mozart resulted in a significant improvement in spatial IQ scores. Some researchers, such as Sogin (1988), have failed to show any significant effect of music (in this case, jazz, pop, and classical) on task performance, whereas Furnham and Bradley (1997) demonstrated that pop music can significantly impair performance.

Daoussis and McKelvie (1986) provided participants with their preferred music and measured the extent of distraction from the results of a reading comprehension test. By comparing distracted performances with those undertaken in silence, they found that although there was no difference in the performance of either condition for extraverts, the performance of introverts was significantly impaired by the presence of low-volume music.

Mayfield and Moss (1989) examined the effect of music tempo on task performance in two studies. The task was collecting and choosing stock prices and calculating the percentage of change in price from week to week. One group performed the task in silence, one listened to fast-paced music, and one listened to slow-paced music. Mayfield and Moss found no difference in the quality or quantity of the work produced by the groups. A second replicative study, however, did yield significant differences: The (student) participants' performances were higher in the fast-paced (rock music) condition than with the slow music, although the subjective level of distraction was higher. They could not fully explain the inconsistent findings but argued that complex managerial tasks are probably best performed in silence. These results suggest that various features associated with music—pace, familiarity, volume, and presence of vocals—can all affect the performance of tasks of various types.

The conflicting results seen in these studies could have been the result of, at least in part, the types of tasks used to assess performance. The most frequently used tasks have been reading comprehension tests (Freeburne & Fleischer, 1952; Kiger, 1989) and tests of short-term memory (Furnham & Allass, 1999; Salamé & Baddeley, 1989; Vitulli & McNeill, 1990). Others have used the Stroop color-word test (Houston & Jones, 1967) and motor tasks (Kjellberg & Skoldstrom, 1991). Strong evidence for the type of task influencing the ability of music to distract comes from a study by Konz (1962), who noted that letter-matching task scores were significantly negatively affected by the presence of music, whereas scores on a manual assembly task were not significantly affected by the same music. Similarly, Furnham and Bradley (1997) found that reading comprehension scores were significantly affected by the presence of pop music yet this music had no significant effect on scores on immediate and delayed free-recall memory tests. This implies that the characteristics of the particular task may play an important role in the effect of music on performance.

Other studies have focused very specifically on individual differences, particularly extraversion. Vermolayeva-Yomina (1964) found that individuals with a strong nervous system tended to learn more in distracting situations than those with a weak nervous system. Furnham and Allass (1999) hypothesized that introverts would be more negatively, and extraverts more positively, affected by the introduction of extra stimulation (e.g., music) into their work environment. However, it could be argued that, because of the complexity of the music or the task, the musical stimulation might be too great even for extraverts, hence leading to an overall negative effect on performance. Konecni (1982) argued that all music processing inevitably takes up cognitive capacity and, therefore, potentially any music may be detrimental to all performance. Indeed, the existing literature does suggest that background music is more likely to lower performance in particular individuals than raise it above baseline levels in silence.

It has been demonstrated that when studying in a library, introverts were significantly more likely to choose a place to work away from the bustle of certain areas, whereas extraverts were more attracted to the latter (J. B. Campbell & Hawley, 1982). This provides further evidence of the regulation of arousal differences between introverts and extraverts. Careful experimental work measuring critical arousal electrodermally and manipulating arousal by caffeine dosages also has shown that playing simple tunes can significantly alter the cognitive task performance of extraverts and introverts (Smith, Wilson, & Davidson, 1984). The results showed very clearly that base-rate or manipulated arousal differences lead to attention differences between introverts and extraverts.

Morgenstern, Hodgson, and Law (1974) found that extraverts actually performed better in the presence of distractions than they did in silence, whereas introverts showed a deficit in performance in the presence of distractions. Participants were asked to attend to, and remember, a number of words from a long list read to them while they were being read a passage by the same voice, both of which were recorded. Participants were given a means of controlling the balance of sound between the word list and the passage, but the greater this difference, the more the words to be remembered were distorted. This study posed three questions: Is the preference for distortion or distraction related to the personality dimension of introversion versus extraversion? Do the two groups of participants differ in their performance on the task? How did each participant arrive at his or her preferred balance? Morgenstern et al. found that extraverts made extravagant, sweeping movements in their efforts to find balance, whereas introverts made fewer, smaller adjustments. This finding was consistent with Eysenck's (1967) theory that the introvert's nervous system is overdamped. There was a trend for introverts to avoid distraction when the personality dimension was compared with choice of distortion versus distraction, and they did not perform the task as well; however, the effect was not statistically significant.

In an early experiment in this area, Daoussis and McKelvie (1986) found that although extraverts reported working with music twice as much as introverts (50% vs. 25% of the time), both groups reported playing music very softly. Both groups were given a reading recall test in which they were instructed to spend 10 min reading two passages (of about 900 words each) with the objective of answering specific questions immediately afterwards. Half of each group performed the task in silence and half with rock music played at low volume. Although there was no difference in the scores of extraverts, the scores of introverts were, as expected, significantly poorer in the presence of music. Daoussis and McKelvie concluded that this supported Eysenck's (1967) arousal and performance hypothesis.

Furnham and Bradley (1997) also found that in the presence of pop music songs separated by a male voice scores on a reading comprehension test and scores on a delayed-recall short-term memory test were significantly reduced for introverts and significantly increased for extraverts. In an investigation into the effects of complex and simple music (rated on such features as instrumental layering and tonal complexity) compared with silence, Furnham and Allass (1999) found that there was a marked (yet nonsignificant) trend for the performance of introverts to deteriorate with music and for their performance to deteriorate further as the complexity of the music increased. Extraverts, on the other hand, showed improvement in performance as the complexity of the music increased, with the most superior performance being seen in the complex music condition. They noted,

> However, data from the cognitive tests reveal that performance in the presence of simple music follows no systematic pattern. One explanation for this phenomenon may be that the variable of music has interacted with some other unspecified variable, such as musical preference or previous exposure. Indeed, these may be a complex set of interacting factors, such that introverts may find pop music more irritating, and hence distracting, than extraverts, play it less and be less familiar with it, and hence like it less. Alternatively, when the circumstances produced by simple music are examined, it is evident that this form of stimulation was unique in that the arousal it evoked could easily be tolerated by both subject groups, whilst it would not offer optimum conditions to any introvert or extravert. A state of mild dissatisfaction may be induced in all subjects; a state in which unanticipated factors (such as individual preference for a particular musical genre) may be more influential. It may be necessary in future studies to try to control for subjects' liking of, and previous exposure to, particular music chosen in the distraction task, as these factors may affect its ability to distract. (p. 36)

Not all studies have yielded predicted findings. Furnham, Trew, and Sneade (1999) examined the effects of vocal and instrumental music on the performance of introverts and extraverts on three cognitive tasks. In the presence of either vocal or instrumental music or in silence, introverted and extraverted school students completed a reading comprehension task, a logic problem, and a coding task. It was predicted that instrumental music would impair and enhance the test performance of introverts and extraverts, respectively, and that these effects would be magnified in the vocal music condition. No significant interactions were found, although introverts tended to be impaired by the introduction of music to the environment and extraverts tended to be enhanced by it, particularly on the reading and coding tasks. A main effect of extraversion was found in the reading comprehension task and nearly in the coding task.

There was a condition effect of the logic task, with participants performing best in the presence of instrumental music.

Television

Various studies have examined the distracting effects of television on cognitive processing. Armstrong and Greenberg (1990) reported significant performance decrements for several measures (i.e., spatial problem solving, mental flexibility, and reading comprehension) as a function of the distractor effect of television. These results were consistent with the idea that background television influences performance by causing cognitive processing limits to be exceeded for complex tasks. Although indicative of a television distraction influence on parallel cognitive activities, Armstrong and Goldberg's research did not investigate the possibility of individual differences among children in their parallel-processing capabilities. This point is particularly pertinent in light of research showing that personality factors such as introversion versus extraversion are important mediators of individual cognitive performance in the presence of distraction (Morgenstern et al., 1974).

In a series of programmatic studies Furnham and colleagues looked at how personality traits, specifically extraversion, interact with distractors to affect work performance. Furnham, Gunter, and Peterson (1994) examined the distracting effects of television on cognitive processing. Participants completed two reading comprehension tasks, one in silence and one in the presence of an operating television. As predicted, there was a significant interaction between personality type and condition: Extraverts and introverts both performed better in silence, but extraverts performed better than introverts in the presence of television distraction. This result was attributed to the television drawing on cognitive resources required for the reading comprehension task.

Summary

What this literature does indicate, however, is that three variables interact: (a) traits (e.g., extraversion); (b) situational distractors (e.g., type of music, presence of television); and (c) task outcome (e.g., test scores). Considering the relationship between any two and ignoring the third is likely to lead to artificial results. For example, looking at personality correlates of accidents without taking into consideration physical, group norm, and corporate cultural variables is to misunderstand what factors as main effects and interactions relate to work-related outcome variables. To put it into I/O terminology, the fit of the individual in the environment is the key moderator of the relationship among traits and work outcomes.

Why Personality Traits Predict Work Behaviors

A skeptic or pessimist could easily be persuaded by the somewhat mixed and equivocal literature that personality differences account for a very small percentage of the variance in explaining behavior at work. Work-related performance correlations of .2 to .4 suggest that about 10% of the variance can be accounted for, which leaves 90% unaccounted for.

On the other hand, one could easily make a strong case that effect sizes from .20 to .40 most often are the result of using single traits to predict single behaviors. Ahadi and Diener (1989) showed that, with this sort of data, the upper limit of .40 is what can be expected when using single predictors and single outcomes. Furthermore, effect sizes of .20 to .40 are comparable to most other predictors of work behavior, which themselves have problems. Cognitive ability tests are reasonably predictive, but issues regarding "adverse impact" make them difficult to use. Assessment centers probably yield the best data, but they are very expensive, and biodata is too job specific. One could argue in response that compared with other predictors of job success personality tests are relatively inexpensive yet effective.

The idea that if tests account for 10% to 20% of the variance the remaining 90% to 80% is accounted for by situational factors (e.g., supervising methods, corporate culture, technology) is simply not true. What robust evidence is available suggests that situational factors account for about the same amount of the variance as personality factors.

Finally, defenders of tests are also quick to point out that any statistic that focuses on "variance accounted for" is probably misleading (Ozer, 1985; Rosenthal & Rubin, 1982). For example, Rosenthal and Rubin (1982) considered how correlations improve predictability. With a correlation of .40 the hit rate improves from 50:50 to 70:30, a figure many social scientists (including economists) would be proud of.

However, there are ten well-researched reasons why studies fail to show the relevance or importance of personality traits in work-related outcomes:

1. *The personality theory is problematic.* There are a large number of personality theories derived from very different traditions. These change with fashion and may have little good theoretical support. A good current example is emotional intelligence, which is not yet based on sound, nonambiguous theoretical evidence (Petrides & Furnham, 2000). Hypotheses derived from weak or erroneous theories are rarely confirmed.

2. *The personality measure has not been sufficiently psychometrized.* Developing, piloting, and validating any measure is a long, difficult, and expensive process. It is often the case that test producers cut

corners, and the result is a so-called unidimensional scale that is in fact multidimensional (or the reverse) and has good face validity but is therefore very sensitive to dissimulation and impression management, and has scales that are badly skewed or have little evidence of predictive and construct validity. It is not surprising that measures of this type frequently are weakly associated with behavioral variables.

3. *The specific traits measured are not theoretically related to the particular work behavior specified.* Researchers too often use multidimensional personality tests that measure traits at the primary factor level rather than the superfactor level and relate these to a range of often unreliable work measures. The result is a large correlation matrix (often 30 primary traits [Big 5 × 6-Facet] and 10 work-related measures). They are then disappointed that so few correlations are significant. However, there often is no reason to suppose that a particular trait or factor (e.g., Openness to Experience) is related to a particular work-related behavior (e.g., absenteeism). When specific traits are thoughtfully and carefully related to well-measured outcome variables the results are much clearer.

4. *The measurement of work-related dependent variables is poor.* Getting sensitive, accurate, reliable, and robust work-related measures often is difficult because organizations may be unwilling to either collect or disclose them. Hence, it quite often is the case that researchers have only limited and poor-quality data (e.g., supervisor assessment ratings that are skewed, with restricted range, and with strong evidence of the halo effect). It is particularly important that work-related behaviors be aggregated to get a reliable measure and that, when possible, systematic errors be eliminated. A major problem lies in using single predictors of single outcome measures. Much research has shown that if multiple predictors of work behaviors are used, the magnitude of the validity coefficients often increases substantially (see Ones and Viswesvaran, chapter 4, this volume).

5. *The work behavior is shaped and constrained by other power factors.* Unknown restrictions, corporate cultural norms, changes in market conditions, team competence, and the power and reliability of new technology may artificially enhance or restrict work output. Work output is constrained by a large number of factors; this means that if there is a relationship between personality and work outcomes it may be significantly affected by poor or faulty

machinery, a sudden drop in demand for a product, or similar factors.

6. *Group norms and the tall-poppy syndrome affect work behaviors.* Employees are sensitive to the equity of input and output and, hence, group norms. There is a phenomenon known in Australia as the *tall-poppy syndrome.* This phrase refers to group sanctions aimed at curtailing highly effective performance. This leads to a severe restriction of range in the output variable that cannot be easily corrected statistically.

7. *Personality is a moderator variable and, if unmeasured, it remains unrecorded.* It is quite possible that many zero-order relationships at work are spurious in that the supposed causal link between them is affected by a personality variable. For example, it has been argued that the relationship between smoking and cancer is moderated by Extraversion and Neuroticism. Similarly, these same two fundamental personality factors probably moderate the relationship between job satisfaction and productivity (Furnham, 1997).

8. *Personality is a mediator variable.* It also is possible that personality traits are mediator variables in that the relationship between two variables (e.g., ability and sales) is mediated by personality. Although there may be a modest relationship between the two variables, it soon becomes abundantly clear that this is a strong relationship mediated by a particular trait. Therefore, measuring only ability and not personality, and vice versa, does not reveal the true nature of the causal path.

9. *Sampling problems have "washed out" or suppressed the relationship between variables.* The objective of the recruitment and induction process often is to select a particular type of individual who may or may not be productive in the workplace. As a consequence, organizations tend to show a generally consistent profile, which equally implies that many "types" are missing. This may mean that it is not possible to test particular hypotheses if, for example, all introverts or neurotics have been selected out. The same problem may be the result of a volunteer effect; it is well established that the personality profile of volunteers is different from that of nonvolunteers.

10. *Through resignation, firing, and promotion a chronic restriction of range develops.* Over time, the forces of the organizational culture can easily lead to significant staff homogeneity. That is, it is possible that most individuals with a particular personality profile

leave or get fired, whereas those with a somewhat different profile tend to get promoted. It thus can become particularly difficult to investigate the relationship between personality traits and outcome measures in an organization.

This list is more a condemnation of poor research than of personality traits. There is probably now sufficient good evidence from well-known studies for optimistic supporters of personality testing to seriously challenge the skeptics.

Conclusion

Applied personality researchers and I/O practitioners clearly need one another: the former to test and refine their theories regarding work behaviors and the latter to understand how personality processes affect work outcomes. There is now, mainly through meta-analytic work, much more evidence that personality traits account for significant amounts of the variance (i.e., 10%–30%) in work-related outcomes.

The rapprochement between these two branches of psychology will benefit both. To be able to test theoretically derived hypotheses in large adult working samples (instead of using college students) and have real-world yet robust and important cognitive and behavioral dependent measures can be a real benefit for most personality researchers, who often are restricted to using student samples and somewhat ecologically invalid outcome measures. I/O researchers and practitioners have a great deal to gain as well in helping explain the variation in their output measures. The neglect of the serious study and application of individual differences inevitably hampers the full understanding of work-related processes. Furthermore, personality theories offer not only a description but also an explanation of psychological process and often obvious implications for intervention. For example, Eysenck's (1967) arousal theory of extraversion has been profitably used to explain individual differences in speed–accuracy trade-offs, accidents, and training success (Furnham, 1997).

Personality variables inevitably influence the choice of, reaction to, and productivity at work. Vocational choice selection success, training efficiency, job satisfaction, and productivity are all related to personality traits. Thus, personality and ability variables are important at every stage of the job life cycle, from application to retirement. There is now evidence that, if appropriate tests are used, an important amount of the variance can nearly always be explained by trait variables for most, but not all, work outcomes.

However, it is most important to remember that personality variables act not only as main effects but often more powerfully in interaction with other variables. Three quite distinct types of variables can be distinguished: (a) individual-differences variables (e.g., abilities, beliefs, traits, values); (b) situational variables (e.g., corporate culture, group norms, physical context); and (c) work-outcome or task-related variables (e.g., productivity, satisfaction, supervisor ratings, absenteeism). The early literature focused on Person–Situation interactions but often did not take into consideration the possibility of three-way interactions.

Applied research often is more difficult than pure research because of the large number of confounding or uncontrollable variables that influence the relationship between what purists call the independent and the dependent variables. However, with more and better measures of work behaviors, the introduction of better appraisal systems and less expensive electronic monitoring of behaviors, and greater use of causal modeling statistics, the possibility of understanding how individual differences affect work behaviors has never been greater.

References

Ahadi, S., & Diener, E. (1989). Multiple determinants of effect size. *Journal of Personality and Social Psychology, 56,* 398–406.

Armstrong, L. R., & Greenberg, B. (1990). Background television as an inhibitor of cognitive processing. *Human Communication Research, 16,* 355–386.

Arvey, R., Bouchard, T., Segal, N., & Abraham, L. (1989). Job satisfaction: Environmental and genetic components. *Journal of Applied Psychology, 74,* 187–192.

Barrick, M. R., & Mount, M. K. (1991). The Big Five personality dimensions and job performance: A meta-analysis. *Personnel Psychology, 44,* 1–26.

Bass, B., & Barrett, E. (1981). *People, work and organizations: An introduction to industrial and organizational psychology.* Boston: Allyn & Bacon.

Blinkhorn, S., & Johnson, C. (1990). The insignificance of personality testing. *Nature, 348,* 671–672.

Bluen, S. J., Barling, J., & Burns, W. (1990). Predicting sales performance, job satisfaction, and depression using the achievement striving and impatient–irritability dimensions of Type A behaviour. *Journal of Applied Psychology, 75,* 212–216.

Campbell, J. B., & Hawley, C. W. (1982). Study habits and Eysenck's theory of extraversion–introversion. *Journal of Research in Personality, 16,* 139–146.

Campbell, J. P. (1990). Modeling the performance prediction problem in industrial and organizational psychology. In M. D. Dunnette & L. M. Hough (Eds.), *Handbook of industrial and organizational psychology* (2nd ed., Vol. 1, pp. 687–732). Palo Alto, CA: Consulting Psychologists Press.

Churchill, G. A., Ford, N. M., Hartley, S. W., & Walker, O. C. (1985). The determinants of salesperson performance: A meta-analysis. *Journal of Marketing Research, 22,* 103–118.

Cooper, R., & Payne, R. (1967). Extraversion and some aspects of work behaviour. *Personnel Psychology, 20*, 45–47.

Daoussis, L., & McKelvie, S. J. (1986). Musical preferences and effects of music on a reading comprehension test for extraverts and introverts. *Perceptual and Motor Skills, 62*, 283–289.

Digman, J. (1990). Personality structure: Emergence of the Five-Factor Model. *Annual Review of Psychology, 41*, 417–440.

Domanski, J. (1991). *Direct line to profits: The Canadian guide to telemarketing.* Toronto, Ontario, Canada: Grosvenor House.

Eysenck, H. (1967). *The biological basis of personality.* London: Hodder & Stoughton.

Fogelson, F. (1973). Music as a distractor on reading-test performance on eighth grade students. *Perceptual and Motor Skills, 36*, 1264–1266.

Freeburne, C. M., & Fleischer, M. S. (1952). The effect of music distraction upon reading rate and comprehension. *Journal of Educational Psychology, 43*, 101–110.

Funder, D., & Ozer, D. (1983). Behaviour as a function of the situation. *Journal of Personality and Social Psychology, 44*, 107–112.

Furnham, A. (1981). Personality and activity preference. *British Journal of Social Psychology, 20*, 57–65.

Furnham, A. (1992). *Personality at work.* London: Routledge.

Furnham, A. (1997). *The psychology of behaviour at work.* Hove, England: Psychology Press.

Furnham, A. (in press). Vocation preference of behaviour at work. *Applied Psychology: An International Review.*

Furnham, A., & Allass, K. (1999). The influence of musical distraction on the cognitive performance of extraverts and introverts. *European Journal of Personality, 13*, 27–38.

Furnham, A., & Bradley, A. (1997). Music while you work: The differential distraction of background music on the cognitive test performance of introverts and extraverts. *Applied Cognitive Psychology, 11*, 445–455.

Furnham, A., & Coveney, R. (1996). Personality and customer service. *Psychological Reports, 79*, 675–681.

Furnham, A., Forde, L., & Ferrari, K. (1999). Personality and work motivation. *Personality and Individual Differences, 26*, 1035–1043.

Furnham, A., Gunter, B., & Peterson, E. (1994). Television distraction and the performance of introverts and extraverts. *Applied Cognitive Psychology, 8*, 705–711.

Furnham, A., Jackson, C., & Miller, T. (1999). Personality, learning style and work performance. *Personality and Individual Differences, 27*, 1113–1122.

Furnham, A., & Miller, T. (1997). Personality, absenteeism and productivity. *Personality and Individual Differences, 23*, 705–707.

Furnham, A., & Steele, H. (1994). Measuring locus of control. *British Journal of Psychology, 84*, 443–479.

Furnham, A., Trew, S., & Sneade, J. (1999). The distracting effects of vocal and instrumental music on cognitive performance of introverts and extraverts. *Personality and Individual Differences, 27*, 381–392.

Furnham, A., & Zacherl, M. (1986). Personality and job satisfaction. *Personality and Individual Differences, 7*, 453–459.

Ghiselli, E. E., & Barthol, R. P. (1953). The validity of personality inventories in the selection of employees. *Journal of Applied Psychology, 37*, 18–20.

Gray, J. (1975). *Elements of a two-process theory of learning.* London: Academic Press.

Gunter, B., Furnham, A., & Drakeley, R. (1993). *Biodata.* London: Routledge.

Hakstian, A. R., Scratchley, L. S., Macleod, A. A., Tweed, R. G. & Siddarth, S. (1997). Selection of telemarketing employees by standardised assessment procedures. *Psychology and Marketing, 14*, 703–726.

Halverson, R. R., Behrens, G., & Nerad, A. (1990). *Telemarketing Applicant Inventory (TMAI) reliability and validity summary.* Rosemont, IL: McGraw Hill/London House.

Hertzberg, F., Mauser, B., & Snyderman, B. B. (1959). *The motivation to work.* New York: Wiley.

Hogan, J., Rybicki, S., Motowidlo, S., & Borman, W. (1998). Relations between contextual performance, personality, and occupational advancement. *Human Performance, 11*, 189–207.

Hogan, R. (1991). Personality and personality assessment. In M. D. Dunnette & L. M. Hough (Eds.), *Handbook of industrial and organizational psychology* (pp. 873–919). Chicago: Rand McNally.

Hogan, R., Hogan, J., & Roberts, B. (1996). Personality measurement and employment decisions. *American Psychologist, 51*, 469–477.

Hogan, R., & Shelton, D. (1998). A socioanalytic perspective on job performance. *Human Performance, 11*, 129–144.

Hough, L. M. (1992). The "Big Five" personality variable construct confusion: Description versus prediction. *Human Performance, 5*, 139–155.

Houston, B. K., & Jones, T. M. (1967). Distraction and Stroop colour-word performance. *Journal of Experimental Psychology, 74*, 54–56.

Hull, C. (1928). *Aptitude testing.* London: Harrap.

Kalechstein, A., & Nowicki, S. (1994). Social learning theory and the prediction of achievement in telemarketers. *Journal of Social Psychology, 134*, 547–548.

Kiger, D. M. (1989). Effects of music information load on a reading comprehension task. *Perceptual and Motor Skills, 69*, 531–543.

Kjellberg, A., & Skoldstrom, B. (1991). Noise annoyance during the performance of different non-auditory tasks. *Perceptual and Motor Skills, 73*, 39–49.

Konecni, V. (1982). Social interaction and musical preference. In D. Deutsch (Ed.), *The psychology of music*. New York: Academic Press.

Konz, S. (1962). *The effect of background music on productivity of two different monotonous tasks*. Paper prepared for Human Factors Society, New York.

Lee, C., & Gillen, D. (1989). Relationship of Type A behaviour pattern: Self-efficacy perceptions on sales performance. *Journal of Organizational Behaviour, 10,* 75–81.

Maslow, A. H. (1954). *Motivation and personality*. New York: Harper & Row.

Matteson, M. T., Ivancevich, J. M., & Smith, S. V. (1984). Relation of Type A behaviour to performance and satisfaction among sales personnel. *Journal of Vocational Behaviour, 25,* 203–214.

Mayfield, C., & Moss, S. (1989). Effect of music tempo on task performance. *Psychological Reports, 65,* 1283–1290.

McGraw-Hill/London House. (1989). *Telemarketing Applicant Inventory*. Rosemont, IL: Author.

Morgenstern, S., Hodgson, R. J., & Law, L. (1974). Work efficiency and personality. *Ergonomics, 17,* 211–220.

Mount, M., & Barrick, M. (1995). The Big Five personality dimensions. *Research in Personnel and Human Resources Management, 13,* 153–200.

Newman, R., Hunt, D., & Rhodes, F. (1956). Effects of music on employee attitude and productivity in a skateboard factory. *Journal of Applied Psychology, 50,* 493–496.

North, A., Hargreaves, D., & McKendrick, J. (1999). The influence of in-store music on wine selections. *Journal of Applied Psychology, 84,* 271–276.

Oldham, G., Cummings, A., Mischel, L., Schmidthe, J., & Zhan, J. (1995). Listen while you work? Quasi-experimental relations between personal-stereo headset use and employee work responses. *Journal of Applied Psychology, 80,* 547–564.

Ozer, D. (1985). Correlation and coefficient of determination. *Psychological Bulletin, 97,* 307–315.

Petrides, K., & Furnham, A. (2000). On the dimensional structure of emotional intelligence. *Personality and Individual Differences, 29,* 213–320.

Phares, E. J. (1976). *Locus of control in personality*. Morristown, NJ: General Learning Press.

Predmore, C. E. (1992). Relational communication and personality traits: Effects on telemarketing sales success [CD-ROM]. Abstract from: Dissertation Abstracts, Item 9207112.

Rauscher, F. H., Shaw, G. L., & Ky, K. N. (1993). Music and spatial task performance. *Nature, 365,* 611.

Robertson, I., & Kinder, A. (1993). Personality and job competency. *Journal of Occupational and Organisational Psychology, 66,* 225–244.

Rosenthal, R., & Rubin, D. (1982). A simple, general purpose display of magnitude of experimental effect. *Journal of Educational Psychology, 74,* 166–169.

Salamé, P., & Baddeley, A. (1989). Effects of background music on phonological short-term memory. *Quarterly Journal of Experimental Psychology, 41A,* 107–122.

Salgado, J. (1998). Big Five personality dimensions and job performance in army and civil occupations: A European perspective. *Human Performance, 11,* 271–288.

Schmidt, N., Gooding, R. Z., Noe, R. A., & Kirsch, M. (1984). Meta-analysis of validity studies published between 1964 and 1982 and the investigation of study characteristics. *Personnel Psychology, 37,* 407–422.

Singh, J., Goolsby, J. R., & Rhoads, G. J. (1994). The influence of market orientation of the firm on sales force behaviour and attitudes. *Journal of Marketing Research, 31,* 558–569.

Smith, B., Wilson, R., & Davidson, R. (1984). Extrodermal activity and extraversion. *Personality and Individual Differences, 5,* 59–65.

Sogin, D. (1988). Effect of three different musical styles of background music on coding by college-age students. *Perceptual Motor Skills, 67,* 275–280.

Spector, P. (1982). Behaviour in organisations as a function of employees; locus of control. *Psychological Bulletin, 91,* 482–497.

Squires, P., Torkel, S. J., Smither, J. W., & Ingate, M. R. (1991). Validity and generalizability of a role-play test to select telemarketing representatives. *Journal of Occupational Psychology, 64,* 37–47.

Staw, B., & Ross, J. (1985). Stability in the midst of change: A dispositional approach to job attitudes. *Journal of Applied Psychology, 70,* 469–480.

Stone, B. (1994). *Successful direct marketing methods.* Lincolnshire, England: Business Books.

Vermolayeva-Yomina, L. B. (1964). In J. A. Gray (Ed.), *Pavlov's typology.* London: Pergamon Press.

Vinchur, A. J., Schippmann, J. S., Switzer, F. S., & Roth, P. L. (1998). A meta-analytic review of predictors of job performance for sales people. *Journal of Applied Psychology, 83,* 586–597.

Vitulli, W. F., & McNeill, M. J. (1990). Short-term memory digit span performances under auditory and visual contexts as a function of rate digit presentation. *Perceptual and Motor Skills, 71,* 1131–1138.

Weitz, B. A. (1981). Effectiveness in sales interactions: A contingency framework. *Journal of Marketing, 45,* 53–62.

Williams, T. B. (1961). A study of the effect of music as a distractor on the mental test performance of certain eleventh grade students. *Dissertation Abstracts International, 22,* 168.

Wolfe, D. (1983). Effects of music loudness on task performance and self-report of college-aged students. *Journal of Research in Music Education, 31,* 191–201.

CHAPTER 11

Selecting the Right Stuff

Personality and High-Reliability Occupations

Rhona Flin

One of the goals of this book is to acquaint mainstream personality psychologists with the preoccupations of industrial and organizational (I/O) psychologists. My particular I/O preoccupation is the application of psychology to the management of safety and emergency responses in hazardous work settings (where errors can have life-threatening consequences). This is an increasingly important area of research for applied psychologists working in the fields of industry, aerospace, the military, medicine, and transportation, among others.

> Psychology in high hazard organizations is an unusual conception, a field which is only gingerly approached by our discipline. It requires a drastic expansion of received theoretical frameworks and demands incisive steps towards interdisciplinary cooperation. Barriers to more intensive involvement exist in- and outside psychology. Nevertheless enough theoretical and practical—even survival—reasons exist for psychologists not to pass up the challenge of helping to contribute to the safety and reliability of high hazard systems. (Wilpert, 1996, p. 78)

Organizations operating with good safety records in hazardous fields have been characterized as *high-reliability organizations* (HROs; Roberts, Rousseau, & La Porte, 1994; Rochlin, 1999; Weick, Sutcliffe, & Obstfeld, 1999). Such organizations include power generators, emergency services, nuclear plant operators, military units, medical surgical departments, and airlines. Their safety management systems are largely based on technical protection, although according to Kontogiannis (1999),

> The common response of the aviation, maritime, petrochemical and nuclear industries to introduce more advanced safety engineering devices has not managed to eliminate system accidents. The humans that operate these systems are increasingly taxed to make critical decisions under extreme time pressure and task demands. (p. 7)

In addition, if these protective safety systems fail, the quality of emergency management is dependent on those individuals holding key roles, who must be able to make critical decisions under stress. Therefore, for some HRO positions (e.g., control room operators, pilots, power plant directors, anesthesiologists, emergency commanders), stress resistance and decision-making and leadership skills are essential attributes. Given the importance of the human operators in such environments, significant effort is devoted to the selection of personnel for safety-critical positions. However, despite the interest of such organizations in identifying "the right stuff" and ensuring high-level performance, personality assessment appears to play a relatively minor role in selection procedures, and it has been infrequently incorporated into research studies of safety and emergency management.

This chapter reviews the extent to which personality theory and associated assessment techniques contribute to the selection of personnel for and the study of society in high-reliability occupations. A particular focus of the discussion of selection methods will be on incident commanders, that is, those who are responsible for taking charge in an emergency. Note that much of the material presented reflects European organizations, and there may be cultural differences.

Selection

> Whilst technology and legislation are progressively eliminating risks from many routine jobs such as farming, construction and transport, technological advances are also opening up new risks from working, for example in hostile environments or in situations where there is a concentration of energy. One way of attempting to manage these risks is to select individuals who are able to cope with the increased dangers. (Smith, 1996, p. 59)

To what extent does applied personality research enable I/O psychologists to offer advice to HROs regarding desired or undesired attributes for personnel? Smith (1996) pointed out that, "Selection in high-risk or high-stress occupations is a gray area which is attracting less attention from occupational psychologists. The difficulties are manifold." (p. 59). There are a number of reasons for this, including the following:

- Apart from aviation and the armed forces, the numbers of personnel involved usually are small; consequently, few large-scale validity studies are available.

- In military and commercial organizations, research material often is restricted, so the most interesting selection and performance data rarely reach the public domain.

- HROs may have a high level of security (e.g., military bases and nuclear plants) or may be very remote (e.g., offshore oil platforms, the space stations, Antarctic bases), and negotiating access to personnel for research purposes may be difficult.

- Once access to personnel has been obtained, the time allowed to conduct job analyses or to administer tests may be very limited.

- Criterion measures of performance under stress or in emergency conditions can be extremely difficult to obtain.

- The term *high-reliability occupation* covers an enormous range of jobs with the only common performance characteristics being (a) the ability to cope with stress and (b) decision-making skills.

In a review of methods for selecting personnel for hazardous occupations, J. Hogan and Lesser (1996) also acknowledged that there were difficulties in defining individual differences that predict job performance. To examine methods for selecting personnel for various HROs, they used the Big Five factors (McCrae & Costa, 1987) as a framework for considering psychological suitability (for both select in and select out characteristics). Their conclusion was that although surgency (Extraversion) and Agreeableness probably were inconsequential for hazardous work, Conscientiousness, Emotional Stability (i.e., Neuroticism), and Openness to Experience could be important predictors. Commenting on the role of measures of personality, they noted, "We suspect that gains in predicting effective performance will come from advances in understanding personality and personality disorders associated with persons who are attracted to hazardous work, but who are characterologically unsuited" (p. 218). Thus, there may be an opportunity to develop better methods of ab-initio selection (similar to those used in aviation and the military) through which individuals less suited for high-reliability occupations (i.e., who may be less safe, less careful workers) can be identified and "selected out" on the basis of such characteristics. For example, the European Joint Aviation Authorities' requirements for psychological fitness for pilots state that an applicant shall have "no established psychological deficiencies, particularly in operational aptitudes or any relevant personality factor, which is likely to interfere with the safe exercise of the privileges of the applicable license" (Pearson, 1995, p. 140; see also Goeters, 1998, and Johnston, 1996, who discuss issues relating to psychological assessment and pilot licensing). But what is known of predictor characteristics for high performance in high-reliability occupations? Do the validation studies of personality questionnaires present a coherent picture of select-in characteristics? This chapter examines this question for a sample of employment domains: aviation, the military, remote and hazardous work environments, and emergency services.

Aviation

> At every level in one's progress up that staggeringly high pyramid, the world
> was once more divided into those men who had the right stuff to continue
> the climb and those who had to be left behind in the most obvious way. (Wolfe,
> 1991, p. 30)

One high-reliability field with a long tradition of investment in personnel selection is aviation. The cost of training pilots—and the price of inadequate
operational performance—justifies intensive research programs to ensure that
the "right stuff" is sitting on the flight deck. Consequently, the national air forces
and the larger commercial airlines have devoted significant efforts and resources
to identifying the personal qualities desired in pilots (Hilton & Dolgin, 1991;
Hunter & Burke, 1995), and those selecting pilots appear to look for a fairly
consistent set of select-in characteristics. For example, Stead (1995), who has
performed research for Qantas Airways, suggested the following personal qualities for pilots: "Influence/Leadership; Communication Skills; Organizing/Plan-
ning; Motivation/Energy; Analytical; Empathy; Emotional Maturity; Decision
Making" (p. 177). British Airways regards the following characteristics as desirable in a pilot: (a) is competent, (b) is relaxed but alert, (c) involves and
listens to crew members, (d) influences behavior before using authority, (e) is
patient, (f) is sociable, and (g) is prepared to help (Flin & Slaven, 1994).

All of the major airlines use personality questionnaires as part of their
batteries of tests and procedures for pilot selection (Hunter & Burke, 1995).
British Airways has used the Jackson Personality Inventory (JPI; Jackson, 1994),
which assesses 15 dimensions of personality, including anxiety, responsibility,
risk taking, sociability, and empathy. The JPI was chosen as a suitable instrument following job analysis and critical incident analysis to identify defined job
requirements (Flin & Slaven, 1994). Cathay Pacific Airways has used the 16
Personality Factor Questionnaire (16 PF; Cattell, Eber, & Tatsuoka, 1970; Bartram & Baxter, 1996), Qantas has used the Occupational Personality Questionnaire (OPQ; Saville & Holdsworth, 1984; Stead, 1995), and Delta Air Lines has
used the NEO Personality Inventory (NEO; Costa & McCrae, 1991; Hoffmann,
1997). In a review of pilot selection measures, Hörmann (1998b) identified the
most commonly used commercially available personality instruments as the 16
PF, NEO, and OPQ. However, because the commercial airlines tend to protect
their validation data, there have been few meta-analyses of purely civilian pilot
training success or long-term job performance data. For the validity data that
are available, the predictive power (usually measured against training success
or job performance) has tended to be fairly low. Hörmann (1998a) referred to
personality tests as having mean validities for pilot selection (sample >22,000)
of 0.10–0.13 (from meta-analyses by Hunter & Burke, 1995, and Martinussen,
1996), compared with 0.15 for general selection (sample >20,000). He states

that, "in general, validation studies indicate that the personality profile of successful pilots is marked by high self confidence, emotional stability, and extraversion" (1998b, p. 59).

Although commercial airlines use personality tests for pilot selection, this generally is not the case in military aviation in the United Kingdom (K. Hazman, personal communication, March 1999). Ten years earlier, Hardinge, a Royal Air Force (RAF) psychologist explained,

> Most personality tests were produced for clinical use or as research tools rather than as purpose built tools for military selection. They present problems of faking and of adverse candidate reactions but foreign experience suggests that these are not insurmountable. The UK services do not use personality tests but rely on interview assessments, references, weighted application blanks, and, in the case of officer selection, group exercises. From time to time the Services try out new tests but so far personality tests have not been able to add anything useful to the predictive power of the selection process. (1989, p. 627)

In the United States, military pilot selection batteries have not routinely included commercial personality tests either (Damos, 1996; Hilton & Dolgin, 1991), but specific pilot personality questionnaires have shown that dimensions such as competitiveness can predict military performance (Street, Helton, & Dolgin, 1992). Personality assessment may be undertaken, but this often is done using structured interview techniques (Byrdorf, 1998) rather than questionnaires. However, it appears that personality questionnaires are sometimes used in air forces for research purposes. For example, Bartram and Dale (1982) assessed over 600 Army Air Corps and RAF pilots using the Eysenck Personality Inventory and found that those who were successful in training were more likely to be stable and extraverted than those who failed (see also Bartram, 1995). Stokes and Kite (1994) described personality measures that have been used in research with pilots, including behavioral tests such as the psychodynamic Defense Mechanism Test (DMT), which has been used by the Swedish Air Force. (But see Sjöberg, Kallmen, & Scharnberg, 1997, for a very critical review of the DMT, which has been advocated as an effective test for predicting ability to perform under stress.)

In summary, for civilian pilots, there is ample evidence that personality assessment is included in the ab-initio selection process, although it is used less often in selection for command, and some concerns about faking remain (Hörmann, 1998b). The meta-analyses that are available, which tend to be based on studies of military pilots (Hunter & Burke, 1995; Martinussen, 1996), have suggested that personality measures show an average validity coefficient of around 0.1.

In a review of military pilot selection, Hilton and Dolgin (1991, p. 95) had been fairly optimistic, "We conclude that activity in the personality/character area is likely to increase. It is possible that psychology may have been pursuing the right stuff but with the wrong scales." In fact, more recent research in military aviation seems to be moving away from the use of personality inventories to methods such as Situational Judgement Tests for the identification of key social and cognitive skills in aircrew (see Hedge et al., 2000). Sjöberg et al. (1997) were impressed by these validity scores and concluded,

> It is striking that the present situation when it comes to personality and pilot selection is not much different from the mid-century picture provided by McFarland (1953), and that validities appear to be dropping (Hunter & Burke, 1995). There is a challenge here for psychometrics, but not one likely to be quickly met with success. (p. 257)

Military (Army and Navy)

The armed forces also carefully monitor their procedures for officer selection and promotion to command ranks. They are particularly concerned with evidence of leadership potential and, according to Sale (1992), Field Marshall B. L. Montgomery's 1958 dictum on leadership is still stressed at the British Army Regular Commissions Board:

> The two vital attributes of a leader are: a) Decision in action; b) Calmness in crisis. Given these two attributes he will succeed; without them he will fail. Our great problem in peace is to select as leaders men whose brains will remain clear when intensely frightened; the yardstick of "fear" is absent. (p. 26)

In the United Kingdom, personality questionnaires generally have not been used for army or naval officer selection. More emphasis has been put on assessing cognitive skills than assessing personality (see Buck, 1999; Jeffrey, Lambe, & Bearfoot, 2000; Jones, 1991). According to Hardinge (1989), personality assessments are used for officer selection in Australia, Belgium, France, India, Israel, the Netherlands, and New Zealand. Sale (1992) points out that whereas the U.S. Army uses the Myers–Briggs Type Indicator (MBTI; Myers & McCauley, 1985) for up to very senior ranks, in fact, more recent research in aviation has moved away from the use of personality inventories to methods such as Situational Judgement Tests for the identification of key social and cognitive skills (see Hedge et al., 2000). I will discuss this further later in this chapter. There is an absence of objective personality measures in the selection of senior British army officers. Hedge performed a small study of 49 commanders (at brigade level) using a computerized battery of seven personality questionnaires (MANSPEC) that did not produce particularly conclusive results, although the author argued that the resulting psychometric profiles would be very useful in selection (see Milgram, 1991 for a more detailed account of personality factors which have been used in military selection).

There have been several studies of very demanding military occupations such as special forces (rarely published) and bomb disposal. Cooper (1982) used the 16 PF to study the personality characteristics of British Army bomb disposal experts, but this measure did not discriminate between those who were successful and a control group who were not so highly rated. However, J. Hogan and R. Hogan (1989) reported a study using the Hogan Personality Inventory (HPI; R. Hogan & Hogan, 1992) with U.S. naval bomb disposal trainees and found that the most effective were nonconforming but not reckless.

In summary, personality research into selection and job performance in army and navy occupations (certainly in the United Kingdom) seems to be rather limited. This may be partly due to research reports being classified, but the available evidence suggests that the military have traditionally paid more attention to measures of aptitude and of relevant cognitive skills than to personality characteristics.

Remote and Hazardous Work Environments

There are a number of occupations, both civilian and military, that are based in extremely remote and/or potentially dangerous work environments, such as space missions, Antarctic bases, oil exploration/production sites, and nuclear power plants. In the United States, the National Aeronautics and Space Administration (NASA) has funded extensive psychological research programs to define personality characteristics for use in selecting astronauts and commanders for space missions (Santy, 1994). Commanders must be able to deal effectively with emergencies in very remote environments to ensure the safety and survival of their crew and equipment. Studies of optimum leadership characteristics for commanders using comparable environments (e.g., remote Antarctic bases; Nesbitt, 1996; underwater simulations) have suggested that there may be certain behavioral attributes that characterize the leaders of effective and high-performing groups in confined or isolated environments (Penwell, 1990). These leaders tend to (a) be task and achievement oriented; (b) have a flexible, although primarily democratic leadership style; (c) work to maintain group harmony; and (d) be able to tolerate intimacy and status leveling without losing authority or the respect of the group. Effective leaders are described as having self-confidence, emotional control, self-reliance, and the strength of personality to maintain authority during both sustained intimacy and moments of crisis. In a discussion of leaders for Antarctic bases, Stuster (1997) reiterated the importance of social skills and decision-making ability: "The most effective leaders accomplish their objectives through consensus and skillful persuasion, but it is essential that the leader's role and authority be unambiguous and that the leader makes decisions as promptly and autocratically as necessary under the circumstances" (p. 945).

This research into leadership and command ability has produced some interesting although not necessarily definitive results. For example, according to Penwell (1990), it has not generated a definitive set of personality characteristics for the ideal space commander:

> While Kubis describes the effective space crew commander as technically competent, goal oriented and interpersonally sensitive, we have no direct data about the effectiveness of leadership styles in space environments. The Space Station Operations Task Force has recommended that only NASA career astronauts be eligible for the position of space station commander. While the selection criteria for the pool include physiological and psychological screenings to "select out" pathology, the selection criteria do not intentionally "select in" leaders. According to Cooper, except for the criterion of previous experience in space and the probable experience as a pilot of a previous shuttle mission, it is unclear, even to the astronauts, what methods are used to select mission commanders. (p. 2)

Personality is recognized as playing a significant role in success in remote work environments, but as Penwell (1990) pointed out, it may be most important to "select out" undesirable personality characteristics that make individuals unsuited to command positions. At NASA, psychiatrists tend to be responsible for determining and identifying these "select out" characteristics, which include anxiety, depression, and psychotic disorders and they use semistructured clinical interviews for this purpose rather than the standard questionnaire (Santy, 1994).

In high-reliability industrial settings (e.g., power plants), personality measures may be used in the selection process for key safety positions, such as site managers. Some offshore oil companies have used the 16 PF or the OPQ for the selection or development of managers of remote production platforms and drilling rigs located in the North Sea (Flin, Slaven, & Whyte, 1996). Williams and Taylor (1993) reviewed selection techniques used in the nuclear industry for process operators and found that very little validation research had been conducted because of complexity, access, and small sample sizes. Nuclear power companies tended to rely on traditional methods such as interviews and technical and cognitive tests to select out unsuitable applicants. There is some evidence that HROs are becoming more familiar with the concept of personality assessment, however. In an international survey of 34 nuclear companies in 13 countries, Stanton and Ashleigh (1996) examined the selection methods used for engineers and managers. They reported that personality tests were used by 86% of respondents to select managers and by 65% to select engineers, although they did not specify which instruments were used or supply any validation data.

Emergency Services

A number of investigations have examined the role of personality in emergency services occupations. The bulk of the research has been conducted with police officers (e.g., Cortina, Doherty, Schmitt, Kaufman, & Smith, 1992) but there are also some reports of validation studies with firefighters (e.g., Burke, 1997) and ambulance personnel (e.g., Tyler, 1999). One aspect of this work has examined whether or not there is a particular "police personality," that is, a personality type that is attracted to policing (Carpenter & Raza, 1987). The evidence is rather mixed, however there is suggestive evidence that police applicants are more extraverted than the general population (Khader, 1999). Of more relevance to this chapter are the studies which have used personality measures in the prediction of successful or unsuccessful performance in police service. These studies have tended to focus on screening or selecting-out individuals unsuitable for police work. For this purpose, scales such as the 16 PF and California Psychological Inventory (CPI) have been used as well as more clinical instruments such as the MMPI (see Blau et al., 1993) or the Inwald Personality Inventory (Inwald, 1982) which was specially designed for law enforcement occupations. For identifying select-in characteristics, a range of criterion measures has been used with police officers relating to training success, general job performance, or tenure. Salgado (1997) reported that extraversion is a valid predictor of police occupations and using the CPI (Gough, 1996), R. Hogan (1971) found that the performance of highly rated police officers in the U.S. could be predicted from self-control, responsibility, achievement through independence, and intellectual efficiency. In a later study, Quigely et al. (1989, cited in R. Hogan & Hogan, 1992) reported that the Managerial Potential scale of the HPI was associated with police officers' performance. The British Police Staff College has used the MBTI and the FIRO–B team roles questionnaire (Schutz, 1992) for self development purposes on senior officer training programs. British police forces have used 16 PF, OPQ, and the CPI for selection and development. Police psychologists are beginning to adopt the Big Five model as a theoretical basis for their validity studies. Khader (1999) looked at the relationship between personality and success in training of police recruits. He used a short form version of the NEO and reported that "successful police officers as defined in the training context, are likely to have higher Extraversion and Conscientiousness scores and lower Neuroticism scores" (p. 62).

The neuroticism factor may be related to the individual's ability to cope with the stress of dealing with traumatic events. Elliott and Smith (1993), discussing the selection of stress resistant individuals for firefighting and other emergency services, suggested that "A hardy personality, as measured by the Hardiness scale, appears to be more resilient to the effects of stressful life events. For fire service recruits, Elliott (1991) found a strong correlation between an anxious personality and a subsequent experience of stress during the basic training program." (p. 36). The Hardiness scale (Kobasa, 1982) focuses on commitment, control, and challenge in an individual's interpretation of stressful events and has also been used in research with police officers to study occupational stress (Tang & Hammontree, 1992). Tyler (1999) reported that the HPI scales of Adjustment and Stress tolerance were significant predictors of posttraumatic stress disorder and general well being scores in ambulance service staff. Several fire brigades are now testing the use of the HPI for personnel selection. For example, Shanks (2000) found that the HPI scale Ambition was the strongest predictor of rated command potential and overall job performance with the primary scale Adjustment and secondary scale Managerial Potential also showing significant prediction of fire service job performance. Personality instruments may also be used by the fire service for career development purposes. For instance, the British Fire Service College has used the MBTI in the development of self-awareness in senior officers being trained for command positions.

A few years ago, the London Fire Brigade revised its selection, training, and promotion procedures, placing particular emphasis on incident command. London has the largest fire brigade in the U.K., with 6,200 operational firefighters and officers who must deal with a high incident rate and difficult conditions resulting from the metropolitan environment. The brigade not only developed its own competence standards framework but also revised its selection procedures for its crew command, watch command, and junior-officer training programs, with selection criteria mapped from the standards (Burke, 1996, personal communication). At the junior-officer level, candidates for the Fire Service College course are selected using an assessment center that includes a personality questionnaire, the Business Personality Inventory (BPI; Feltham & Woods, 1995), aptitude tests, role play, and group exercises. The focus is on the candidate's ability to deal with situations, information, and with people. Burke (1997) also used the Big Five model (Digman, 1990) as a framework for categorizing junior-officers' critical operational activities, showing that Conscientiousness, Emotional Stability, and Openness to Experience related to assessing incident progress and Conscientiousness and Emotional Stability related to command and control. He commented "of note is the low weight given to Extraversion even though this has traditionally been a factor in the perceptions of officership both in the U.K. military and the U.K. fire service" (p. 122).

So, while the emergency services, especially the police, have a history of using personality instruments for research, selection, and development, the validation studies have not produced an entirely consistent set of predictive personality indicators. There is some evidence from the use of Big Five measures that higher Extraversion, higher Conscientiousness, and lower Neuroticism may be characteristics which predict success in training for emergency service recruits. The personality variables predicting success at later career stages (such as command positions) remain unknown. This may be partly due to the wide range of criterion measures employed across studies, especially in policing, where officers perform a number of very different duties.

One of the key roles in an emergency response organization is that of the on-scene commander who has responsibility for managing the event, be it a fire, a riot, a battle, or a nuclear plant emergency. Is it possible to define the "right stuff"—a set of generic characteristics and competencies for on-scene commanders? Does personality assessment aid this process? Organizations usually make midcareer appointments from within their staffs; thus, they have access to individuals' performance records for consideration. However, these records may reflect only performance in lower status positions, which may not always be directly relevant. Lines (1999) characterized the difficulty of assessing the qualities required for emergency management by police officers using standard selection procedures as follows: "Often officers will face having to make critical decisions with no assessments having been made of their suitability to do so and with little or no training to assist them" (p. 96).

The selection of individuals required to undertake the command role in an emergency is not only of relevance in the military and emergency services but also is pertinent to managers of hazardous industrial sites (e.g., petrochemical, nuclear, offshore oil) and transportation services (e.g., aviation, shipping), who may be called on to act as commanders should an incident occur. Selectors generally look beyond qualifications, training, and experience to find a particular type of individual or a certain leadership style. A survey of organizations employing emergency commanders identified a general consensus regarding the skills and personality characteristics desired, but it showed limited agreement as to the personality instruments most suited for selection or development purposes (Flin & Slaven, 1995). Certain personality characteristics are considered to be related to emergency command ability. These include willingness to take a leadership role, emotional stability, stress resistance, decisiveness, controlled risk taking, self-confidence, and self-awareness. The key dimensions (Flin, 1996) are as follows:

- *Leadership ability.* Inspires trust, commands respect, acts with authority and impartiality, is diplomatic, minimizes potential conflict across a multidisciplinary team, is a good communicator, shows integrity, directs and controls the efforts of others, and takes charge confidently and competently even when under pressure.

- *Stable personality.* Demonstrates emotional stability, maturity, steadiness, reliability, and balanced attitudes; is well adjusted and level-headed; and remains calm when under pressure.

- *Decisiveness.* Shows balanced analytical and sound judgment, demonstrates logical reasoning ability, can recognize and solve problems, is prepared to formulate and implement decisions when under pressure, and knows when to use authoritative or consultative decision-making style.

This list of characteristics also reflects the competencies identified as necessary for senior military commanders (Jeffrey et al., 2000, p. 367) and emergency services officers. For example, Brunacini (1985) noted,

> The Fireground Commander's [FGC's] personality is a big factor in the command system. The desirable traits for a FGC include the required knowledge of command and the inclination to command, control of temper, the ability to provide a positive example, psychological stability, physical fitness, fairness, being straightforward when communicating, a willingness to take reasonable risks without compromising safety, concern for all personnel, knowledge of limitations (self, personnel, apparatus, the plan), respect for command, being an organization person, and being disciplined and consistent. (p. 13)

Common to all lists of selection criteria is the requirement that an emergency commander be able to function well as a decision maker and leader when under stress. (See Breakwell, 2000, for a report on pressures experienced by British military commanders, and Flin and Arbuthnot, 2001, and McCann and Pigeau, 2000, for incident commanders' accounts of their experiences of command.)

Although selectors appear to be in reasonable agreement as to the "right stuff" and the "wrong stuff" in terms of personality characteristics, the relationship of these traits to incident command ability has been tested only rarely. There are very few validation reports. In one study of senior fire commanders, Burke (personal communication, May 1999) found that the group showing highest ratings for both general management skills and ability as an incident commander were characterized by open mindedness, extraversion, low neuroticism, and moderate structure (from the BPI).

As part of an investigation into crisis management in industry, a small-scale validation exercise was undertaken to assess whether a personality questionnaire could predict a manager's incident command performance in a simulated offshore emergency (Flin & Slaven, 1994). In the absence of formal job analysis data, the key characteristics were identified from a survey of 134 offshore installation managers (OIM), who mentioned (a) the ability to remain calm; (b) the ability to make decisions, particularly when under pressure; (c) leadership skills; (d) knowledge of the installation and its emergency procedures; and (e) the ability to assess the overall situation.

The search for a specific test of command characteristics to predict the "calm decision maker" was unproductive, and time constraints made it impossible to use a test battery (incorporating, for example, visuospatial reasoning, leadership style, anxiety). Because it was already being used by some oil companies for OIM selection, the OPQ was selected as the personality measure. The version used (Concept 5.2) contains 258 questions that provide scores on 30 dimensions of personality related to work. The objective of the study was to measure whether the OIMs' scores on any of the personality dimensions would predict their emergency command ability. Dimensions deemed relevant to incident command were preferred decision-making approach (fast vs. slow), propensity to worry, level of relaxedness, and preference for taking control. The OPQ was administered to 93 OIMs attending an offshore command center simulator. Ratings of each OIM's performance as commander during a simulated offshore emergency were obtained using a specially designed rating form with 16 scales based on the offshore oil industry's unit of competence, "Controlling Emergencies" (Offshore Petroleum Industry Training Organisation [OPITO], 1992). Two trainers rated the performance of each individual who played the role of the OIM in the 45- to 60-minute simulator exercise.

The personality scores were correlated with the uncorrected performance ratings, and few dimensions of the OPQ predicted command performance. The results of greatest interest were that the OIMs with higher performance ratings scored significantly higher on the *controlling* (likes to take charge), *outgoing* (sociable), and *decision making* (tends to make fast decisions) dimensions and significantly lower on the *conceptual* (prefers abstract thinking) and *behavioral* (likes to analyze the behavior of others) dimensions. Contrary to expectations, scores on the *worrying* and *relaxed* dimensions did not predict any aspect of command ability. Overall, the correlations were extremely modest and would require replication with a much larger sample. (It should be noted that the command performance scale had not been pretested for reliability or validity.)

Many emergency service organizations use personality instruments to develop self-awareness in senior officers with the goal of improving their performance as commanders but without precisely defining a single leadership style. But personality questionnaires seem to be rarely used in the selection process for senior command positions. This is understandable because in only a very few research studies has it been possible to determine whether a definitive set of personality factors can be identified as predictors for command. The problems of conducting validation research in this area have restricted opportunities to develop and test personality instruments for this purpose. For example, performance indicators (e.g., for emergency command) can be difficult to obtain; however, the introduction of command simulators may provide opportunities for more reliable performance measurement in the future.

Safety Research

It has been estimated that 70% to 80% of accidents in aviation and industrial environments can be attributed to human error (Wagenaar & Groeneweg, 1987). During the 1990s, interest in the potential contribution of psychology in the management of system safety in HROs increased (Fahlbruch & Wilpert, 1999; Misumi, Miller, & Wilpert, 1999; Stanton, 1996).[1] Personality is rarely discussed in this safety research literature (e.g., Reason, 1990; Wickens et al., 1997). One exception to this is the "accident-prone personality," which is now generally dismissed as unproven. In a 1998 review, Lawton and Parker failed to find sufficient evidence for an accident-prone personality type but acknowledged that methodological problems hampered much of the early research. For example, accidents as outcome measures are largely meaningless "being unreliable and stochastic in nature" (Lawton & Parker, 1998, p. 667). They advocated instead a multi-perspective approach focusing on the precursors to unsafe behaviors. However, they did suggest that personality factors may have some link to accidents but only through stress as a mediating variable. This multiperspective approach in current safety research encompasses behavioral modification programs, organizational culture, attitudes, risk perception, leadership style, and team working.

A major focus in safety research in HROs is on cognitive and social skills that have been shown to be linked to error management and high team performance (Kanas et al., 2000; King, Callister, & Retzlaff, 1998). These are often called *non-technical skills* (e.g., NOTECHS; van Avermaete & Kruijsen, 1988) or *crew resource management skills* (CRM; Wiener, Kanki, & Helmreich, 1993). These skills include leadership, communication, team working, decision making, situational awareness, and stress management. They were identified as safety-critical from simulator and flight observations, accident analyses (especially voice recordings), and confidential safety reports. Awareness of the importance of these skills is taught in CRM training courses that are now used by all major airlines (Flin & Martin, 2001), the military, air traffic control systems, nuclear power companies, offshore oil companies, and medical providers (see Edens, Salas, & Bowers, 2000). In addition, nontechnical skills are practiced and evaluated using simulators. The introduction of CRM (nontechnical) skills training to HROs represents one of the most significant applications of psychological research in industry.

The emphasis is on training these cognitive and interpersonal skills—the

---

[1] Although it may minimize managerial misconceptions to equate psychology with psychoanalysis, it has been unfortunate for psychology that this area has tended to be labeled under the all-encompassing heading of *human factors*.

role of personality has been deemphasized. Although personality measures were used during the early stages of CRM research (Kanki, 1996), there was a switch of focus away from personality to attitude measures by the late 1980s (Wiener et al., 1993). In fact, some of the systems for evaluating CRM skills state explicitly that they are not to be regarded as a method of judging personality (van Avermaete & Kruijsen, 1988, p. 29). However, there is little doubt that pilots, like any other workers, have different dispositional characteristics and may find the adoption of CRM skills (e.g., open communication) more or less difficult. Therefore, in some CRM courses, personality measures are used (e.g., the MBTI) with the purpose of raising awareness of the trainee's preferred behavioral or cognitive style. Hedge et al. (2000) have argued that while personality measures have generally been relatively poor predictors of pilot performance, the importance of CRM skills in aviation will require more sophisticated methods to select pilots with attributes associated with the ability to work effectively in teams. Similarly, some military researchers have begun to reexamine the relationship between personality and CRM skills, finding a significant correlation between the NEO Agreeableness scale and measures of CRM (Hoffmann, Hoffmann, & Kay, 1998). The general interest in high team performance in HROs has also directed attention onto "team styles" personality measures such as the FIRO–B (Dolgin, Wasel, & Langlelier, 1999; Kay & Dolgin, 1998). Although Hogan and Shelton (1998) have pointed out that, "As yet, we don't have a psychometric basis for assessing social skill and must rely instead on observer ratings" (p. 136).

In summary, while I/O psychologists studying safety have tended to ignore the personality literature, recognition of the importance of nontechnical skills in high-reliability occupations has produced some resurgence of interest in the role of personality characteristics related to team work.

Conclusion

Personality measures are widely used for the selection of personnel in some high-reliability occupations (such as commercial aviation) but are employed far less frequently in other sectors. Although the military and the emergency services undoubtedly recognize the importance of personality factors in job performance, they have not routinely used personality questionnaires for selection purposes. Interest in the psychological aspects of work performance is, however, increasing in high-reliability industries (Misumi et al., 1999), but the use of personality measures in the selection of key operating staff such as control room personnel, emergency managers, or incident response teams is still limited. The topic of personality has been regarded in some workplaces as problematic, raising contentious industrial relations issues about screening and selection (see Johnston, 1996 for an airline captain's view), rather than being seen as a valuable framework with which to understand individual differences.

As for the psychological research on industrial safety (e.g., Feyer & Williamson, 1998) and emergency management (e.g., Flin, Salas, Strub, & Martin, 1997), very few empirical studies have used personality theories as explanatory mechanisms or incorporated personality measures into their investigative designs. This work has tended to focus on motivational, attitudinal, cognitive, and behavioral variables with limited, if any, attention paid to personality constructs. This to some extent may have been a reaction against the historical concept of the accident-prone personality which has been generally discounted or, more simply, due to the general unfashionableness of personality as a research construct in the last decades of the 20th century (see Hogan & Roberts, chapter 1, this volume). Given the resources devoted in HROs to maximizing performance, it is surprising how little attention has been paid to personality research. From my own experience working with oil, nuclear, and aviation companies, I have identified several possible reasons personality theory may not be widely applied in relation to high-reliability occupations.

- Negative connotations of psychology (confusion with psychiatry and psychoanalysis) are still prevalent in the general population. (Psychologists working with pilots are warned to avoid psychobabble.)
- The literature on the subject of personality is often impenetrable for nonspecialists. Moreover, the labeling of personality factors can hardly be described as user friendly.
- Until the emergence of the Big Five model and associated meta-analyses, the multiplicity of measures and plethora of unreconciled findings only served to increase confusion.
- Critical reports of methodological weaknesses and low predictive validity for personality questionnaires received very wide coverage in the popular and managerial press, most notably Blinkhorn and Johnson's (1990) article in the journal *Nature*.
- Obtaining criterion measures of critical tasks (e.g., performance under stress) has been difficult as discussed above.
- Higher risk/responsibility operational positions (e.g., nuclear reactor desk engineer) are typically filled from within an organization, thus performance records are available to assist in selection.

These barriers appear to be present to a greater or lesser degree across the HRO domains I have reviewed in this chapter. A significant investment in psychometric research would be required before the requisite data sets could be produced to test whether or not personality measures can assist in selection decisions and in research models of safety behavior. This would also require a rather more sophisticated methodological approach, which has moved beyond a simple linear test to a more complex investigation incorporating mediating variables such as stress resistance, cognitive style, or organizational adjustment. It appears that such investment may be forthcoming as increasing attention from both regulators and the media are raising the stakes in terms of organizational accountability for safety and crisis management. Organizations' systems for selecting, training, and assessing the competence of personnel in safety-critical jobs are being more closely scrutinized. More attention is being paid to the selection of staff for high-reliability positions using behavioral observations from simulators and structured interviews. These techniques offer new possibilities for job analysis and the development of better criterion measures for critical skills.

To date, there has been more focus on identifying the psychopathology of those individuals unsuitable for high risk occupations (e.g., policing) than there has been for finding the factors to predict high performance. The existing validation studies for select-in characteristics do not present a coherent picture due to a wide range of instruments and of criterion measures, limited use of job analysis to delineate critical competencies, and few replications or meta-analyses. As both Burke (1997) and Hogan and Lesser (1996) have noted, the Big Five model may facilitate the reconciliation of scarce data sets and the building of a consensual picture of select-in and select-out characteristics for high-reliability occupations. The available evidence points to low Neuroticism as a core requirement, with indications that higher Extraversion, Conscientiousness, and Openness to experience may be useful predictors for some of these jobs. The growing emphasis on CRM skills for high-reliability operations (Edens et al., 2000) suggests that Agreeableness may play an important part, although Hogan & Lesser (1996) caution that for jobs involving rule enforcement (e.g., health security technician at a nuclear power plant), low Agreeableness may be the more relevant predictor.

Although the Big Five approach may provide a valuable starting point, its main limitation is the use of broad, generic factors (see Paunonen & Nicol, chapter 8, this volume). It seems likely that for specific high-reliability occupations such as control room operator, air traffic controller, anesthesiologist, or emergency team leader, specific, finer grained measures that reflect cognitive style preferences (e.g., rapid decision making, situational awareness) as well as key social behaviors (e.g., assertiveness) will need to be designed. Given the economic and strategic significance of these HROs, and in particular the costs of failure, it seems that the opportunity to develop specialist psychometric test instruments for high reliability occupations will not remain long unfulfilled.

References

Bartram, D. (1995). The predictive validity of the EPI and 16PF for military flying training. *Journal of Occupational and Organizational Psychology, 68*, 219–236.

Bartram, D., & Baxter, P. (1996) Validation of the Cathay Pacific Airways pilot selection program. *International Journal of Aviation Psychology, 6*, 149–169.

Bartram, D., & Dale, H. (1982). The Eysenck Personality Inventory as a test for military pilots. *Journal of Occupational Psychology, 55*, 287–296.

Blau, T., Super, J., & Brady, L. (1993). The MMPI good cop/bad cop profile in identifying dysfunctional law enforcement personnel. *Journal of Police and Criminal Psychology, 9*, 2–4.

Blinkhorn, S., & Johnson, C. (1990). The insignificance of personality testing. *Nature, 348*, 671–672.

Breakwell, G. (2000). Stressors faced by commanders in three operational environments. In C. McCann & R. Pigeau (Eds.), *The Human in Command*. New York: Plenum.

Brunacini, A. (1985). *Fire command.* Quincy, MA: National Fire Protection Association.

Buck, G. (1999). *The role of cognitive complexity in the management of critical situations.* Unpublished PhD Thesis, University of Westminster, London.

Burke, E. (1997). Psychological research and development in the London Fire Brigade. In R. Flin, E. Salas, M. Strub, & L. Martin (Eds.), *Decision making under stress: Emerging themes and applications* (pp. 116–125). Aldershot, England: Ashgate.

Burke, E. (2000, January). *Assessing and selecting decision makers for risk critical roles.* Paper presented at the British Occupational Psychology Conference, Blackpool, England.

Byrdorf, P. (1998). Military pilot selection. In K. M. Goeters (Ed.), *Aviation psychology: A science and a profession* (pp. 63–72). Aldershot, England: Ashgate.

Cattell, R., Eber, H., & Tatsuoka, M. (1970). *Handbook for the Sixteen Personality Factor Questionnaire (16 PF).* Champaign, Il: Institute for Personality and Ability Testing.

Cooper, C. (1982). Personality characteristics of successful bomb disposal experts. *Journal of Occupational Medicine, 24*, 653–655.

Cortina, J., Doherty, M., Schmitt, N., Kaufman, G., & Smith, R. (1992). The 'Big Five' personality factors in the IPI and the MMPI: Predictors of police performance. *Personnel Psychology, 45*, 119–140.

Costa, P., & McCrae, R. (1991). *NEO Five Factor Personality Inventory.* Lutz, Florida: Psychological Assessment Resources Inc.

Damos, D. (1996). Pilot selection batteries: Shortcomings and perspectives. *International Journal of Aviation Psychology, 6*, 199–209.

Digman, J. (1990). Personality structure: Emergence of the Big Five factor model. *Annual Review of Psychology, 41*, 417–440.

Dolgin, D., Wasel, B., & Langlelier, M. (1999, March). *Identification of cognitive, psycho-motor, and psychosocial skill demands of uninhabited combat aerial vehicle (UCAV) operators.* Paper presented at the Second Annual Unmanned Combat Air Vehicle Conference, London.

Edens, E., Salas, E., & Bowers, C. (Eds.). (2000). *Applying resource management.* Hillsdale, NJ: Erlbaum.

Elliott, D., & Smith, D. (1993). Coping with the sharp end: Recruitment and selection in the fire service. *Disaster Management, 5*(1), 35–41.

Fahlbruch, B., & Wilpert, B. (1999). System safety—An emerging field for I/O psychology. In C. Cooper & I. Robertson (Eds.), *International Review of Industrial and Organizational Psychology* (Vol 14, pp. 55–91). Chichester, England: Wiley.

Feltham, R., & Woods, J. (1995). *Business Personality Indicator. User's guide.* Windsor, England: ASE/NFER.

Feyer, A., & Williamson, A. (Eds.). (1998). *Occupational injury. Risk, prevention, and intervention.* London: Taylor & Francis.

Flin, R. (1996). *Sitting in the hot seat: Leaders and teams for critical incident management.* Chichester, England: Wiley.

Flin, R., & Arbuthnot, K. (Eds.). (2001). *Incident command: Tales from the hot seat.* Aldershot, England: Ashgate.

Flin, R., & Martin, L. (2001). Behavioural markers for crew resource management. *International Journal of Aviation Psychology, 11*, 1.

Flin, R., Salas, E., Strub, M., & Martin, L. (Eds.). (1997). *Decision making under stress: Emerging themes and applications.* Aldershot, England: Ashgate.

Flin, R., & Slaven, G. (1994). *The selection and training of offshore installation managers for crisis management.* Suffolk, England: HSE Books.

Flin, R., & Slaven, G. (1995). Identifying the right stuff: Selecting and training on-scene commanders. *Journal of Contingencies and Crisis Management, 3*, 113–123.

Flin, R., Slaven, G., & Whyte, F. (1996). Selection for hazardous occupations: Offshore oil installations. In M. Smith & V. Sutherland (Eds.), *International review of professional issues in selection and assessment, Vol. 1* (pp. 81–94). Chichester, England: Wiley.

Goeters, K. M. (1998). Standards of selection: Legal and ethical issues. In K. M. Goeters (Ed.), *Aviation psychology: A science and a profession* (pp. 97–101). Aldershot, England: Ashgate.

Gough, H. (1996). *California Psychological Inventory manual.* Palo Alto, CA: Consulting Psychologists Press.

Hardinge, N. M. (1989). Personnel selection in the military. In N. Anderson & P. Herriot (Eds.), *Assessment and selection in organizations: Methods and practice for recruitment and appraisal* (pp. 625–642). Chichester, England: Wiley.

Hedge, J., Bruskiewicz, K., Borman, W., Hanson, M., Logan, K., & Siem, F. (2000).

Selecting pilots with crew resource management skills. *International Journal of Aviation Psychology, 10*, 377–392.

Hilton, T., & Dolgin, D. (1991). Pilot selection in the military of the free world. In R. Gal & A. Mangelsdorf (Eds.), *Handbook of military psychology* (pp. 81–101). Chichester, England: Wiley.

Hoffmann, C. (1997). Pilot selection in Delta Air Lines. *Paper presented at the 9th International Symposium on Aviation Psychology.* Columbus, Ohio: Ohio State University.

Hoffmann, C., Hoffmann, K., & Kay, G. (1998, April). The role that cognitive ability plays in CRM. In *Proceedings of the RTO HFM Symposium on "Collaborative Crew Performance in Complex Operational Systems"* (MP-4). Neuilly-sur-Seine Cedex, France: NATO, RTO.

Hogan, J., & Hogan, R. (1989). Noncognitive predictors of performance during explosive ordnance training. *Journal of Military Psychology, 1*, 117–133.

Hogan, J., & Lesser, M. (1996). Selection of personnel for hazardous performance. In J. Driskell & E. Salas (Eds.), *Stress and human performance* (pp. 195–222). Hillsdale, NJ: Erlbaum.

Hogan, R. (1971). Personality characteristics of highly rated policemen. *Personnel Psychology, 24*, 679–686.

Hogan, R., & Hogan, J. (1992). *Hogan Personality Inventory manual* (2nd ed.). Tulsa, OK: Hogan Assessment Systems.

Hogan, R., & Shelton, D. (1998). A socioanalytic perspective on job performance. *Human Performance, 11*(2/3), 129–144.

Hörmann, H. (1998a). Basics of selection. In K. M. Goeters (Ed.), *Aviation psychology: A science and a profession* (pp. 47–53). Aldershot, England: Ashgate.

Hörmann, H. (1998b). Selection of civil aviation pilots. In K. M. Goeters (Ed.), *Aviation psychology: A science and a profession* (pp. 55–62). Aldershot, England: Ashgate.

Hunter, D., & Burke, E. (1995). *Handbook of pilot selection.* Aldershot, England: Avebury.

Inwald, R. (1982). *Inwald Personality Inventory technical manual.* Kew Gardens, NY: Hilson Research.

Jackson, D. (1994). *Jackson Personality Inventory.* Port Huron, MI: Sigma Assessment Systems.

Jeffrey, C., Lambe, D., & Bearfoot, J. (2000). Training of higher level commanders. In C. McCann & R. Pigeau (Eds.), *The human in command.* New York: Plenum.

Johnston, N. (1996). Psychological testing and pilot licensing. *International Journal of Aviation Psychology, 6*, 179–197.

Jones, A. (1991). The contribution of psychologists to military officer selection. In R. Gal & A. Mangelsdorf (Eds.), *Handbook of military psychology* (pp. 63–68). Chichester, England: Wiley.

Kanas, N., Salnitskiy, V., Grund, E., Gushin, V., Weiss, D., Kozerenko, O., Sled, A., & Maramar, C. (2000). Interpersonal and cultural issues involving crews and ground personnel during shuttle/Mir missions. *Aviation, Space, and Environmental Medicine, 71*(9 Suppl.), A11–16.

Kanki, B. (1996). Stress and aircrew performance: A team-level perspective. In J. Driskell & E. Salas (Eds.), *Stress and human performance* (pp. 127–162). Hillsdale, NJ: Erlbaum.

Kay, G., & Dolgin, D. (1998, April). Team compatibility as a predictor of team performance: Picking the best team. In *Proceedings of the RTO HFM Symposium on "Collaborative Crew Performance in Complex Operational Systems"* (MP-4) (pp. 6-1–6-7). Neuilly-sur-Seine Cedex, France: NATO, RTO.

Khader, M. (1999). *Police personality revisited with the Big Five.* Unpublished thesis, University of Leicester, Midlands, UK.

King, R., Callister, J., & Retzlaff, P. (1998, April). Assessing operators' potential for collaboration in complex systems. In *Proceedings of the RTO HFM Symposium on "Collaborative Crew Performance in Complex Operational Systems"* (pp. 91–93). Neuilly-sur-Seine Cedex, France: NATO, RTO.

Kobasa, S. (1982). The hardy personality: Toward a social psychology of stress and health. In G. Sanders & J. Suls (Eds.), *Social psychology of health and illness* (pp. 3–32). Hillsdale, NJ: Erlbaum.

Kontogiannis, T. (1999). Training effective human performance in the management of stressful emergencies. *Cognition, Technology, and Work, 1,* 7–24.

Lawton, R., & Parker, D. (1998). Individual differences in accident liability: A review and integrative approach. *Human Factors, 40,* 655–671.

Lines, S. (1999). Information technology multi-media simulator training: Outcomes of critical decision making exercises. *The Police Journal, 72,* 96–108.

Martinussen, M. (1996). Psychological measures as predictors of pilot performance: A meta-analysis. *International Journal of Aviation Psychology, 6,* 1–20.

McCann, C., & Pigeau, R. (Eds.). (2000). *The human in command.* New York: Plenum.

McCrae, R., & Costa, P. (1987). Validation of the Five Factor model of personality across instruments and observers. *Journal of Personality and Social Psychology, 52,* 81–90.

McFarland, R. (1953). *Human factors in air transportation.* New York: McGraw Hill.

Milgram, N. (1991). Personality factors in military psychology. In R. Gal & A. Mangelsdorf (Eds.), *Handbook of military psychology* (pp. 559–572). Chichester, England: Wiley.

Misumi, J., Miller, R., & Wilpert, B. (Eds.). (1999). *Nuclear safety: A human factors perspective.* London: Taylor & Francis.

Myers, J., & McCauley, M. (1985). *A guide to the Myers-Briggs Type Indicator.* Palo Alto, CA: Consulting Psychologists Press.

Nesbitt, K. (1996). Selection of Antarctic expeditioners. In M. Smith & V. Sutherland (Eds.), *International review of professional issues in selection and assessment, Vol. 1* (pp. 95–105). Chichester, England: Wiley.

Offshore Petroleum Industry Training Organisation (OPITO). (1992). *Units of competence governing the management of offshore installations.* Montrose, Scotland: Author.

Pearson, R. (1995). JAA psychometric testing: The reason. In N. Johnston, R. Fuller, & N. McDonald (Eds.), *Aviation psychology: Training and selection: Proceedings of the 21st Conference of the European Association for Aviation Psychology* (pp. 139–140). Aldershot, England: Avebury.

Penwell, L. (1990, September). *Leadership and group behaviour in human space flight operations.* Paper presented at the American Institute of Aeronautics and Astronautics Conference, Huntsville, Alabama.

Reason, J. (1990). *Human error.* Cambridge, England: Cambridge University Press.

Roberts, K., Rousseau, D., & La Porte, T. (1994). The culture of high reliability: Quantitative and qualitative assessment aboard nuclear-powered aircraft carriers. *Journal of High Technology Management Research, 5,* 141–161.

Rochlin, G. (1999). The social construction of safety. In J. Misumi, R. Miller, & B. Wilpert (Eds.), *Nuclear safety. A human factors perspective* (pp. 5–23). London: Taylor & Francis.

Sale, R. (1992). Towards a psychometric profile of the successful army officer. *Defense Analysis, 8,* 3–27.

Salgado, J. (1997). The Five Factor Model of personality and job performance in the European community. *Journal of Applied Psychology, 82,* 30–43.

Santy, P. (1994). *Choosing the right stuff: The psychological selection of astronauts and cosmonauts.* New York: Praeger.

Saville, P., & Holdsworth, R. (1984). *Occupational Personality Questionnaire.* Esher, Surrey: Saville Holdsworth.

Schutz, W. (1992). Beyond FIRO–B. *Psychological Reports, 70,* 915–937.

Sjöberg, L., Kallmen, H., & Scharnberg, M. (1997). Selection for stressful jobs: Is the defence mechanism test the solution? In R. Flin, E. Salas, M. Strub, & L. Martin, L. (Eds.), *Decision making under stress: Emerging themes and applications* (pp. 252–260). Aldershot, England: Ashgate.

Smith, M. (1996). Selection in high-risk and stressful occupations. In M. Smith & V. Sutherland (Eds.), *International review of professional issues in selection and assessment, Vol. 1* (pp. 59–80). Chichester, England: Wiley.

Stanton, N. (Ed.). (1996). *Human factors in nuclear safety.* London: Taylor & Francis.

Stanton, N., & Ashleigh, M. (1996). Selecting personnel in the nuclear power industry. In N. Stanton (Ed.), *Human factors in nuclear safety* (pp. 159–188). London: Taylor & Francis.

Stead, G. (1995). Personality on the flight deck. In N. Johnston, R. Fuller, & N. McDonald (Eds.), *Aviation psychology: Training and selection: Proceedings of the 21st Conference of the European Association for Aviation Psychology* (pp. 176–181). Aldershot, England: Avebury.

Stokes, A., & Kite, K. (1994). *Flight stress: Stress and fatigue in aviation.* Aldershot, England: Avebury.

Street, D., Helton, K., & Dolgin, D. (1992). *The unique contribution of selected personality tests to the prediction of success in naval pilot training* (Rep. No. NAMRL-1374). Pensacola, FL: Naval Aerospace Medical Research Laboratory.

Stuster, J. (1997). Human and team performance in extreme environments: Antarctica. In R. Jewer (Ed.), *Proceedings of the 9th International Symposium on Aviation Psychology.* Columbus, Ohio: Ohio State University.

Tang, T., & Hammontree, M. (1992). The effects of hardiness, police stress, life stress on police officers' illness and absenteeism. *Public Personnel Management, 21,* 493–501.

Tyler, G. (1999). Personality, general well being, and post-traumatic stress disorder in the ambulance service. *Occupational Psychologist, 37,* 30–34.

van Avermaete, J., & Kruijsen, E. (Eds.). (1988). *NOTECHS: The evaluation of non-technical skills of multi-pilot aircrew in relation to the JAR-FCL requirements.* Amsterdam, The Netherlands: National Lucht-en-Ruimtevaartlaboratorium.

Wagenaar, W., & Groeneweg, J. (1987). Accidents at sea: Multiple causes and impossible consequences. *International Journal of Man-Machine Studies, 27,* 587–598.

Weick, K., Sutcliffe, K., & Obstfeld, D. (1999). Organizing for reliability: Processes of collective mindfulness. *Research in Organizational Behavior, 21,* 81–123.

Wiener, E., Kanki, R., & Helmreich, R. (Eds.). (1993). *Cockpit resource management.* San Diego: Academic Press.

Williams, J., & Taylor, S. (1993). *A review of the state of knowledge and of current practice in selection techniques for process operators* (HSE Contract Research Rep. No. 58/1993). London: Her Majesty's Stationery Office.

Wilpert, B. (1996). Psychology in high hazard systems: Contributions to safety and reliability. In J. Georgas, M. Manthouli, E. Besevegis, & A. Kokkevi (Eds.), *Contemporary psychology in Europe: Proceedings of the IVth European Congress of Psychology.* Seattle, WA: Hogrefe & Huber.

Wolfe, T. (1991). *The right stuff.* London: Picador.

CHAPTER 12

Moral Integrity in Leadership

Why It Matters and Why It May Be Difficult to Achieve

Nicholas Emler

Tina Cook

The common belief is that who is in charge matters. It makes a difference who leads the army, the football team, the government, or the company. If the right person is in charge, the army will lose fewer battles, the football team will win more trophies, the nation's economy will improve, and the company will achieve higher profits. Conversely, if the army is regularly defeated in battle, if the football team loses all its matches, if the economy declines, or if company profits fall, we know who to blame and, more important, we know what to do: Change the leadership.

However, it also is generally recognized that the fortunes of such collective enterprises are not always entirely in the control of the leadership. For example, although well led, the Greek army in 1940 faced forces too numerous and too well equipped for it to defeat. Some English football teams have brilliant managers but too little money to recruit or hold onto the best players (Myers, 1955). And, when the world economy moves into recession, even the most exceptional politicians and gifted chief executive officers (CEOs) are hard-pressed to reverse it. We also know that an inept leadership will be all too willing to take refuge in such excuses, yet nonetheless will feel that a distinction can be made between the effects on group performance of factors beyond the control of the leadership and those effects for which the leadership is responsible. All of this suggests that we should take particular, even exceptional, care regarding our choices of leaders, for these choices are among the most significant decisions we are ever called on to make.

It therefore may come as a surprise to nonpsychologists that psychology does not share these commonsense beliefs about leadership. Within the psychology literature one could at various times find the following grounds for dissent: First, leaders are no different from those they lead. Second, leadership power is largely illusory—that is, what leaders are able to do depends substantially on what their followers will accept. Third, the quality of leadership makes little difference to the performance of an enterprise.

The first dissenting view, that leaders are no different from those they lead, was based on two highly influential reviews of research into the links between personality and leadership by Stogdill (1948) and Mann (1959). Both Stogdill and Mann were interpreted as concluding that, in terms of personality, there is very little to distinguish between leaders and others. Individuals chosen as leaders tend to be taller than average, a bit more self-confident, and a little more intelligent, but that is about all. The apparent finality of this conclusion and the implication that it would be fruitless to search further for the personality of the leader led research on leadership in other directions, toward a proliferation of contingency theories of leadership. These theories were essentially variations on the proposition that the kind of individual who will be selected or preferred as a leader will depend on various features of the context (e.g., the task at hand, the power available to the leader, and the composition of the group; cf. Fielder, 1978).

The second objection, that leadership power is largely illusory, was enunciated by Chester I. Barnard in his 1938 book *The Functions of the Executive* and summarized in his frequently repeated observation that a leader can exercise discretion only within the zone of indifference of his or her subordinates. In other words, the only choices available to leaders are among options about which their followers have no strong preference. In all other matters, leaders are constrained by what their followers will accept. There have been more elaborate versions of this argument. Sociological role theory, for example, is based on the premise that the performance of actors within social and organizational structures is a function of the roles they occupy within those structures rather than their own character or other personal qualities. Therefore, even in leadership roles, actors are largely constrained by the rules and norms that govern behavior in these positions.

As stated, the third objection was that even if leaders do systematically differ from followers in psychological characteristics, these differences have little, if any, bearing on the performance of the enterprise (Pfeffer, 1978). Advocates of this opinion have pointed to evidence such as that variations in sales, profits, and profit margins of large corporations owe little to variance in leadership (e.g., Lieberson & O'Connor, 1972) and that differences among city mayors have little effect on city budgets (Salancik & Pfeffer, 1977). They have argued that this is because collective performance is a function of factors primarily beyond the control of the leadership.

Finally, psychologists have turned their attention to the persistence of commonsense beliefs about the importance of leadership even though such beliefs are contrary to these compelling, scientifically based objections. The reason given for this is that the layperson, in contrast to the psychologist, clings tenaciously to his or her beliefs about leadership in an attempt to sustain an illusion of control. According to some authorities, leadership is romanticized out of proportion to its actual significance (Meindl, Ehrlich, & Dukerich, 1985), and the layperson's commitment to this romantic conception is an example of the fundamental attribution error, that is, the incorrigible gullibility and fallibility of the lay observer (Ross, 1977).

However, one can turn the question around and ask, What, apart from the scientific evidence, has attracted psychologists to study these contrary convictions? The following probably have played some part. First, in many branches of psychology, there was general hostility to the trait concept and to the idea that psychological differences among individuals were to any degree significant (cf. clinical and developmental psychology, Mischel, 1968; social attitudes, Wicker, 1969). For reasons to do both with the internal politics of psychology and methodological convenience, the preference was for explanations of behavior and its effects in terms of situational contingencies (Bowers, 1973). Second, the liberal leanings of many social scientists corresponded to egalitarian beliefs. Third, the Holocaust and later events (Stalin's regime in the post-war Soviet Union, the Communist regime in Romania, recent events in Kosovo, to name a few) seemed to justify extreme suspicion about the ways in which power could be exercised. The resulting antipathy to hierarchy was expressed in the belief that society actually could do quite well without power differences. That is, leaders were not necessary; instead, only individuals with a well-developed sense of fairness were needed (cf. Kohlberg, 1984).

This chapter advances the following arguments: (a) It does matter who is in charge, and the available evidence does not unequivocally support the objections to this view. (b) The personal qualities that matter in leaders include moral integrity. (c) Some of the processes that determine access to positions of leadership are insufficiently sensitive to relevant personal characteristics. (d) In particular, the top-down or bureaucratic processes that exist in many organizations are less likely than bottom-up processes to eliminate leadership candidates with moral flaws.

Why Leadership Matters

First, it is necessary to recognize that social organization (a) creates real power and (b) invariably gives this power to a minority of its members. Or, put another way, organizational functioning is based on control through a social hierarchy. In a famous series of experiments in social psychology, ordinary, average, decent people were brought to the point at which they gave powerful electric shocks to an innocent and unwilling victim, harmless shocks that, for all they knew, were lethal. They did this because someone in a position of authority instructed them to do so (Milgram, 1974). The point is that positions of leadership give their occupants the power to get people to do things they otherwise would not do, that is, things that are not within their zone of indifference. As a more dramatic example, it is difficult to imagine that the orders given to British infantry to attack German positions on the Somme in 1916, positions well defended and known by their putative attackers to be so, were within the British soldiers' zone of indifference.

The real power created by social–organizational hierarchies is also what Karl E. Weick (1969) called "power to" or decision-making discretion. An organizational role gives an individual the discretion to make decisions that he or she would not have outside that role. This discretion emerges in numerous small ways, often relating to apparently minor issues such as the timing of meetings, details of agendas, allocation of resources, dissemination or withholding of information, and so on. However, the cumulative effects of such discretion can be considerable.

But even if real power is concentrated in a few individuals, it still might be argued that it is of little consequence who has that power. An old sociological argument has it that the requirements of the role determine performance, not the character of its occupant. This could be true if all organizational roles, regardless of level in the organizational hierarchy, were always defined with equal precision and if the details of these role requirements were enforced with equal vigor and effectiveness. Then, those in those positions would need to bring to their positions only an ability to read the script; no idiosyncrasies of taste or temperament and no character flaws would make the slightest difference to performance. However, this is not the case. Along with other organizational theorists, Katz and Kahn (1978) observed that social organizations, or at least viable ones, are incomplete designs, and necessarily so. The actions of their members cannot be scripted down to the last detail. Organizations survive through their capacity to react flexibly to a changing and frequently unpredictable environment. Filling the resulting gaps in the script, that is, exercising judgment and discretion, is the function of organizational leadership.

Nor can we be confident that just anyone can do the job. Another infamous and dramatic example from social psychology illustrates that power cannot be allocated at random. In the early 1970s, Philip Zimbardo and colleagues at Stanford University attempted to simulate the conditions of a prison (Haney, Banks, & Zimbardo, 1973). The roles in this simulated social organization, those of guards and inmates, were assigned randomly to student volunteers. It is important to note that the participants knew this to be the case. Despite the fact that this was a role-playing exercise, a high degree of realism was achieved. Unfortunately, the arbitrary brutality of the "guards" and the distress of the "inmates" were so realistic that the experiment had to be abandoned only 6 days into a planned 2 weeks. Many reasons can be adduced for things going so wrong so quickly. For example, giving so much power so quickly to young people relatively inexperienced in handling responsibility and the lack of any training certainly would have been factors. Our opinion is that this study clearly illustrates the importance of appropriate selection in the allocation of organizational power.

Many social scientists (Box, 1983; Durkheim, 1898/1951) derived quite a different lesson from this study: Power corrupts. According to this line of thinking, leaders are not naturally corrupt; rather, they are corrupted by the opportunities and temptations of their positions. This in turn provided support for the liberal view that the dangers of corruption in the exercise of power can be eliminated only by the establishment of a different kind of social organization. In effect, this view is an argument to abolish hierarchy and strive instead for so-called "flat" social organizations and purely egalitarian arrangements in which each individual answers only to the imperatives of his or her conscience. It is interesting, however, that Milgram's (1974) own questions about his research concerned the subordinate: Why does this individual not act according to conscience? What would be necessary for him or her to resist authority and act autonomously?

We believe the weight of history is against this solution; it has yet to be shown to work. Instead, all of the available examples have demonstrated that beyond a very limited size and complexity, hierarchical control ceases to be an option and becomes inevitable. For example, in a survey of anthropological evidence on the social organization of nonindustrialized societies, Berry (1976) found that only the very simplest economies had no hierarchy or leadership. Similarly, in a discussion of the various mechanisms by which the activities of different people can be effectively coordinated to achieve particular goals, Mintzberg (1973) described only one that involved no hierarchy and therefore no power of one individual to direct the actions of others. Mintzberg also noted that this mechanism seemed to occur only in very small organizational units.

Even when organizations strive to be democratic and egalitarian, effective power ends up limited to a minority. Michels (1916/1949) described this as the "iron law of oligarchy." We work in an unusual institution, the University of Oxford, England. By any measure, it has been an extraordinarily successful social organization. It has survived for almost 800 years within a larger environment that has experienced dramatic change, moving from a kingdom, despite the surviving name, to a parliamentary democracy, from a feudal agrarian economy to an industrialized and highly urbanized society. Oxford's supporters probably would attribute this remarkable resilience to its form of governance. It is a highly democratic institution, much more so than most other universities. All of its leadership positions are filled by election for fixed terms. Instead of a CEO or university president with the power to hire and fire, the university has a vice principal who presides over ceremonial occasions but who has no genuine power to decide anything of consequence. Even the title of this position, which implies a higher office to which it is subservient, is an illusion. And yet the university is, as Michels predicted, run by a minority of its members, those with the time, inclination, and political skills needed to occupy positions at the top of a hierarchy of committees.

It seems that hierarchical control is also regarded by most people as a legitimate, if not natural, means of coordinating action. As an international study by Tannenbaum (1974) showed, hierarchical control in one form or another appears to be both a universal feature of social organization and accepted as necessary by those subject to it.

Finally, it should not be forgotten that collective action, hierarchically organized and directed, can result in extraordinary achievements and immense benefits, achievements and benefits far exceeding the capabilities of individuals acting independently and autonomously. Although not necessarily the best of examples, such achievements include the Great Wall of China and the Egyptian pyramids. However, in both cases, they were accomplished at immense costs to the builders and by regimes that were oppressive in the extreme and quite without regard for the welfare of their subjects. The modern nation of the Netherlands is a much better example. A large percentage of its land is below sea level; it was reclaimed from the sea and remains protected from inundation and therefore habitable through collective action (i.e., the country's famous network of dikes and dams). Better still is the daily collective achievement that underlies the feeding, clothing, housing, security, and health of billions of people throughout the world.

Organizational Failure

So, if people are dependent on forms of social organization in which a few individuals are responsible for managing and directing the actions of the many, what kinds of qualities are desired in these few, the occupants of the positions of organizational leadership? One way to try to answer this question is to consider the ways in which leadership can go wrong. Two broad kinds of failure can be identified. The first is illustrated by the examples given in this chapter's opening paragraph: The organization fails to achieve its goals to some degree. The army loses battles, the football team wins no trophies, the nation's economy declines, or the company produces losses rather than profits. These can be called *mission failures*. When an organization's leadership is implicated in such failures, suspicion tends to focus on its competence. For example, the leadership was just not smart enough to develop a winning strategy. Given this tendency, it seems reasonable to consider the intelligence, relevant experience, technical skills, professional expertise, and training of leaders. Leaders who are determined to be lacking in these areas by reason of senility, outdated knowledge or skills, or rising competitive standards, for example, would appropriately be removed from their positions, and candidates for their replacement would need to demonstrate superiority in these qualities. This, of course, is the primary focus of much effort in management selection. Organizations seek individuals possessing these qualities to fill management vacancies, and personnel psychologists offer guidance on their assessment.

Collateral Damage

We refer to this second kind of failure as *collateral damage*. Three points about collateral damage are significant. The first concerns its relative importance. The second relates to the qualifications for leadership, which the risk of collateral damage implies, and the third concerns its relation to mission failure.

By *collateral damage* we mean harm resulting from organizational action that is incidental to the organization's mission. This covers a wide spectrum of effects and includes such things as damage to the ozone layer or to the habitats of wildlife. However, to keep the discussion within manageable limits, this chapter focuses on harm done to people, particularly four kinds of harm: (a) stress, (b) damage to physical health and well-being, (c) death, and (d) financial loss. In addition, more subtle damage, such as effects on corporate reputation and collective confidence in the leadership will be considered as well.

Stress

It has long been recognized that the major source of stress in the workplace is the boss. In surveys of employee morale, between 60% and 75% of workers have reported that the worst or most stressful feature of their job is their immediate superior (Hertzberg, 1968). Almost all employed adults indicated that they had worked for an intolerable boss at some time. A recent British study of middle-level managers found that, among a number of factors contributing to stressful working conditions, one of the most consistent and powerful was supervision by a boss who was not supportive (Moyle, 1998). It may be that making conditions unpleasant for particular employees is an attractive goal for some individuals in supervisory positions, but it also seems likely that others regard this as a legitimate and effective management tool—in other words, a means to an end. Menzies (1980) quoted one corporate CEO as claiming that "leadership is confirmed when the ability to inflict pain is demonstrated." Whatever motivates such treatment, whether malice, misplaced optimism in punitive methods of control, or mere neglect, it is clear that it is a significant source of distress for employees. Consequently, both harsh methods of management and stress in the workplace are receiving greater attention.

Physical Health and Well-Being

Despite this, stress lies at the mild end of the collateral damage continuum. Employment is dangerous to workers' physical as well as mental health. In Britain between 1977 and 1979, an annual average of 330,000 nonfatal accidents occurred at the workplace. These unfortunate events were not the result of employee carelessness or ignorance, but rather of the conditions under which individuals were required by their employers to work (Box, 1983). To put this injury rate in perspective, it far exceeds the number of injuries suffered in criminal assaults. Adjusted appropriately for populations at risk, the ratio is about 7:1. Working conditions also pose long-term or cumulative risks, for example, from radiation, chemical contamination, and biological hazards.

Unfortunately, staying at home is not much safer. According to evidence from U.S. studies (e.g., American National Commission on Product Safety, 1971), about 20 million people are seriously injured each year by unsafe consumer products. For example, in the 1960s, a drug company marketed a product called MER/29, which was advertised as beneficial to heart sufferers, that had some rather unpleasant and injurious side effects, including cataracts and a variety of other eye disorders (Ungar, 1973). What is significant is that these effects were not unforeseen by senior leaders of the company; they had falsified the test results given to the Food and Drug Administration. Nor were the effects of another drug on the children born to some 8,000 mothers in the early 1970s, a drug called Thalidomide, entirely unanticipated by the company that produced and marketed it (Sunday Times Insight Team, 1979).

Death

Organizational action also can kill people on a grand scale. Such a result may be an explicit objective for some organizations, such as military forces involved in an armed conflict. But even in such a situation, an individual would not expect his or her own side, his or her own leaders, to expend lives carelessly. Sadly, however, military organizations seem to have been peculiarly inept in the selection of leaders and have put the wrong people in charge with unfortunate regularity. In an excellent book, *On the Psychology of Military Incompetence*, Dixon (1976) described the dreadful consequences of awarding power inappropriately. He illustrated these consequences by recounting a series of British military disasters, from the Charge of the Light Brigade at Balaclava in the

Crimean War, through the British retreat from Kabul, Afghanistan, in 1842, to the fiasco of Spion Kop in the Boer War, and culminating in the 1916 Somme offensive in World War I. In this last instance, the British Army command achieved what had never been done before (and since as well): 57,000 casualties on its own side in a single day. Dixon is clear that this was not just bad luck; it was a product of poor judgment that simply did not give sufficient weight to the risks.

One may feel that warfare is an inherently risky and lethal business and, moreover, that the pressure on subordinates to follow orders that put their lives at risk is very high. But, perhaps surprisingly, peacetime and civilian employment do not, by comparison, necessarily guarantee longevity.[1] It has been estimated, both for the United States (Reiman, 1979) and the United Kingdom (Box, 1983), that the ratio of avoidable deaths from occupational accidents and diseases to deaths recorded as homicides is between 5:1 and 7:1. Some deaths in the former category result from employees failing to observe safety regulations, but many more result from managerial policy (e.g., cutting corners on safety to improve profits).

In addition, employees are still in danger when they get home—from lethal consumer products—or perhaps even on the drive home. For example, the Ford Pinto was sold with a design fault that affected the integrity of its gas tank. This flaw made the tank likely to fracture and explode in the event of a rear-end collision, something revealed by the company's own product testing (Dowie, 1977). When this occurred, the consequences often proved fatal. Before the car finally was removed from the market, this known design flaw was responsible for the deaths of between 500 and 900 drivers and passengers. The company had judged any costs stemming from litigation over these deaths to be lower than the expense of redesigning the production line.

Financial Loss

In comparison with avoidable death, financial loss is a minor inconvenience, but it is important to appreciate its magnitude when it is a foreseeable effect of organizational action. It was estimated that for 1 year in the United States (i.e., Conklin, 1977, reviewed 1972) acts of robbery, theft, larceny, and automobile theft cost victims a total of between $3 and $4 billion. Costs in the same year

---

[1]An interesting, if depressing, statistic concerns the ratio of civilian to combatant deaths in warfare. In WWI, about 90% of deaths were suffered by service personnel. By WWII, that proportion had dropped to 50%. But in contemporary armed conflicts, chances of survival in the battle zone look to be much higher in the military than out of it: compared to WWI, the proportions are exactly reversed—90% of casualties are now civilians.

from consumer fraud, illegal competition, deceptive practices, and other corporate crime totaled $40 billion. Even a single corporation can produce huge losses for innocent victims. For example, the directors and executives of a company called Equity Funding fraudulently deprived policyholders and shareholders of between $2 and $3 billion dollars (Soble & Dallos, 1974), and it has been estimated that this single case represented losses greater than the total financial losses from all street crime in the United States in an entire year (Johnson & Douglas, 1978).

Summary

It might seem inappropriate to include the Equity Funding case under the heading of collateral damage. This and other instances of corporate fraud clearly had the objective of illegally depriving people of money. The other categories of harm and loss described above—stress, physical health and well-being, and death—seem for the most part to be more incidental to organizational activities, foreseeable and avoidable but not the primary goal of those activities. Nonetheless, two features unite all four categories: All are effects of the exercise of organizational power, and all result from the actions of organizations with entirely legitimate missions.

Moral Integrity

An additional point to be made concerns the personal qualities of those who exercise power in these negative ways. Collateral damage can occur because those individuals in positions of power are unable to determine the full effects of organizational action or lack the information needed to do so. However, the examples presented were of harm that was both foreseeable and avoidable, and for this reason we argue that they can more appropriately be attributed to insufficient moral integrity in organizational leadership.

Put simply, *moral integrity* is a matter of doing the right thing. Thus, moral integrity will be lacking to the extent that "the right thing" is not recognized or, if recognized, is not done. It therefore requires two distinctive qualities of the actor: (a) the ability to determine what is morally right in any situation and (b) the capacity to act in accordance with this judgment whatever the pressures or inducements to do otherwise. This brings us to what we regard as a fundamental point about the link between moral integrity and organizational leadership: Leadership requires extraordinary, not ordinary, moral virtue.

Little in the way of moral integrity is required of those toward the bottom of the hierarchy of a social organization. Right action is essentially guaranteed by a range of social control mechanisms. Opportunities for action are limited, and demands to make difficult moral choices are few. From an organizational perspective, it might seem that the most important virtue is what Durkheim (1925/1961) referred to as a sense of discipline or, in other terms, a conscientious willingness to follow instructions and abide by the rules (cf. Atwater & Yammarino, 1993). Durkheim also recognized that collectives function more effectively to the extent that their members strongly identify with the collective enterprise and its objectives. The contemporary equivalent is the recognition that organizational performance can depend on a spirit of mutual helpfulness among its members (Deutsch, 1991) or what Borman and Penner (chapter 3, this volume) labeled *contextual performance*. Nonetheless, the virtues required become more extensive the further an individual moves up the organizational hierarchy. It is not just that an individual's level of discretion—and with it opportunities for improper action—increases, but temptations and external pressures become greater as well. Moral problems to be solved also become more complex and demanding, and these problems are not merely occasional inconveniences. The point is, in quite a fundamental way, solving problems with a moral dimension constitutes the leadership role (see also Emler & Hogan, 1991).

Leadership matters because poor leadership can cause the enterprise to fail to achieve its mission, and high moral integrity in leadership matters because of the possibility of doing serious damage. However, lack of moral integrity also can threaten the organization's mission in a variety of ways. A leader who causes subordinates avoidable harm can undermine their confidence in the organization and their commitment to its mission. Morally flawed leaders also will erode this commitment in other ways, for example, by failing to be honest with the people they lead or by failing to deal with them fairly. At a minimum, the effects of a lack of moral integrity are likely to be seen in a decline in organizational performance (cf. Borman and Penner, chapter 3, this volume). At worst, disenchanted organizational members will end up sabotaging the organization and its mission (cf. Mars, 1982). Morally flawed leadership also can damage the reputation of the organization and, consequently, its relations with the external environment on which it depends, an environment made up of customers, clients, and other organizations. Survey evidence has routinely revealed a low level of trust in the honesty and integrity of politicians and tabloid journalists (Robinson, 1996). This distrust surely makes it more difficult for governments to secure popular support for policies that may actually serve the common good.

To summarize, social organizations can generate enormous power and will put control of this power in the hands of particular individuals. The manner in which this power is used can, and all too frequently does, result in significant damage. Because it can do so, power should be entrusted to individuals who will use it responsibly, not recklessly or carelessly, let alone selfishly or malevolently. Power should be given only to individuals with both moral integrity and technical competence. Because it so often results in so much damage, it is important to determine how power was put in the hands of unsuitable individuals, that is, those without sufficient moral integrity.

Difficulties in Ensuring Moral Integrity in Leadership

Moral Qualities Associated With Leadership Capacity

If you were to ask people which kinds of personal qualities they regard as important in an individual occupying a position of leadership in an organization, would they spontaneously mention moral qualities of any kind? Whenever managers have been surveyed about the qualities they would look for in a leader, moral integrity routinely appears at the top of the list. Kouzes and Posner (1987) found that trustworthiness was ranked highest among the traits that employees looked for and admired in their superiors. Conversely, lack of trustworthiness has been a common complaint leveled at those in positions of authority (Hertzberg, 1968), and senior British managers surveyed by Cox and Cooper (1989) all singled out integrity as a vital quality for leaders.

The same picture emerges from studies of electors' views of their political leadership, both actual and potential: character matters (Kinder, 1998). Moreover, the two traits that routinely emerge in voters' concerns about the character of politicians are competence and integrity. At this point, however, we need to consider a potential problem for our argument: There is surely no universal consensus about the meaning of moral integrity. This is particularly apparent in the realm of politics; differing political loyalties entail different views about the definition of the moral (e.g., Emler & Hogan, 1981). When Gary Hart's sexual misdemeanours came to light in the 1984 contest for the Democratic presidential nomination, his standing with Republicans suffered far more than it did with Democrats (Stoker, 1993). However, although such differences of view about the nature of moral integrity are not trivial they are also to some extent differences at the margins. In between are likely to be large areas of consensus (for a discussion of the pan-cultural reach of such a consensus, see Shweder, Mahapatra, & Miller, 1987).

So far, so good: People seem to recognize the importance of moral integrity. But do they follow through on this belief when making judgments about particular individuals as potential leaders? There are data on this question from experimental research on leadership. In a reanalysis of previously published evidence (Barnlund, 1962), Kenny and Zaccaro (1983) were able to show that some individuals are more likely than others to be chosen by their peers as leaderlike and to be chosen in this way consistently regardless of type of tasks or group composition. In other words, the kind of person to emerge as a leader in a group is not primarily a matter of the situation or group composition (as contingency theorists had claimed), but is a consequence of the personality of the individual concerned. What Kenny and Zaccaro could not determine from the data available to them were the distinguishing qualities of individuals identified as leaderlike. However, in a reexamination of the evidence reviewed by Stogdill (1948) and Mann (1959), Lord and his colleagues were able to answer this question (Lord, DeVader, & Alliger, 1986). Using statistical techniques not available to the earlier reviewers, Lord et al. were able to show that leadership potential was associated above all with perceived intelligence and to lesser extents with perceived masculinity, adjustment, extraversion, and conservatism. Therefore, it seems that when it comes to making actual choices, people pay little attention to the moral qualities of the candidates.

Although this conclusion looks to be clear, there are at least two reasons to doubt that it represents a general truth. The first is that much of the research evidence considered by Lord et al. came from a study of artificial situations. In the typical study of this type, an experimenter assembles an ad hoc group of participants who are unacquainted with one another. The participants perform some group task, then rate each other on various qualities, including leadership potential. The situation is artificial in several senses. For example, no real consequences flow from the ratings; the group is not in reality deciding to put its fate in the hands of one of its members by singling him or her out for a leadership role. It also is artificial because if the question of who would make a good leader arises, it tends to do so with respect to who are known and known well, not or very seldom with respect to individuals of such extremely short acquaintance. This relates to the second reason for doubting the wider significance or external validity of such research. Under the conditions in which such research is conducted it is very difficult for participants to make accurate judgments about others' moral qualities. Some qualities of personality and character are more visible than others (cf. Funder, chapter 6, this volume) and therefore are more accessible to the observer. This is true, for example, of extraversion and dominance, both of which can be judged very rapidly and with considerable accuracy on the basis of very small samples of an individual's behavior. Making a good assessment of someone's moral integrity requires a large sample of his or her behavior across a variety of relevant settings. It seems likely that given very limited time to make a judgment about someone's leadership potential, an observer would be most influenced by what is most accessible. Conversely, given more time and access to more behavioral evidence, such judgments would be influenced by qualities that are particularly relevant, such as moral integrity.

Some evidence for this latter expectation comes from a study we undertook with a sample of students (Emler, Soat, & Tarry, 1998). In this study, 43 acquainted groups of 4 students were asked to evaluate themselves and one another on a number of dimensions, including leadership and various moral qualities. This study allowed us to address a number of other relevant questions as well. For example, Do observers agree about a particular individual's leadership potential? Kenny and Zaccaro (1983) had answered this in the affirmative for ad hoc experimental groups, but it does not necessarily follow that observers who are well acquainted with the target would agree in their judgments. We found that observers do in fact agree and that this agreement is greater when they have more frequent contact with the target. This kind of agreement is important insofar as it suggests that collectives will be able to achieve a degree of consensus about who should lead them and also that informal encouragement to seek leadership positions will focus on the same candidates.

An equally important question concerns individuals' insight into their own leadership capacity, or at least into their reputation for leadership. Do individuals' self-appraisals agree with the assessments of others, and can they predict those others' assessments? This is important because an element of self-nomination is almost invariably involved in filling leadership positions: People need to apply for vacancies, put themselves forward for election, and accept nominations. Self-nomination can be regarded as a functional part of the process to the degree it is based on an accurate appraisal of one's leadership reputation. Again, it turns out that there is a fair degree of agreement between self-perceptions of leadership capacity and observers' perceptions. So, when people put themselves forward for a leadership role, more often than not their bid is likely to be supported by their acquaintances.

What perceived qualities are associated with leadership capacities? We considered three "moral" qualities (Emler et al., 1998), namely, responsibility, respect for authority, and kindheartedness. The only one of these to show a consistent pattern was responsibility. We found that the closer the acquaintance between target and observer, whether based on frequency of contact or warmth of the relationship, the greater the importance attached to moral responsibility. Participants also tended to give higher leadership ratings to people they liked. However, the more interesting result was that liking someone and getting along with him or her very well could be distinguished from recognizing whether or not they have the capacity for leadership.

Role of Moral Qualities in Career Progression

The Emler et al. (1998) study indicated that people would prefer in leadership positions those of their acquaintances whom they judged to be the most morally responsible. However, the question is, What kinds of individuals actually occupy such positions? Evidence from studies of managerial careers (e.g., Bentz, 1990; Howard & Bray, 1990) has not been encouraging. One major study (Jacobs, 1992) followed management recruits at AT&T through to several years into their careers, to a point at which some had progressed far up the corporate ladder so that effectively they were occupying leadership positions. Meanwhile, others had made much less progress. It was possible to link rate of progress and level achieved to the personality profiles of these individuals when they first joined the corporation. Several aspects of personality were very clearly related to managerial advancement. For example, the California Psychological Inventory (CPI; Gough, 1975) subscales that predicted promotion included Dominance, Sociability, Capacity for Status, Social Presence, and Achievement via Conformity. In contrast, the CPI subscales corresponding to moral qualities —the Socialization, Responsibility, Tolerance, and Self-Control Scales—did not predict promotion. In fact, their correlations with promotion were virtually zero. The implication is that moral flaws were no handicap whatsoever to advancement up the organizational hierarchy. Individuals who were bullies, bigots, or scoundrels were as likely to progress as those who were not. A similar British study, based on the careers of managers in a variety of organizations, also found no evidence that moral flaws negatively affected career progress (Dulewicz, 1997).

Selection Processes

The result is an odd paradox: People generally seem to want leaders who are honest, trustworthy, and of the highest moral integrity. When surveyed, they rank these qualities above all others. However, the people who actually lead them are no more likely to possess these qualities than anyone in the population at large. We believe an answer to this paradox may lie in the consequences of the different processes by which positions of leadership are filled. Self-nomination normally is a complement to one of two such processes. These processes are (a) top-down and (b) bottom-up selection. The first is demonstrated in a wide range of organizations as appointment and promotion. Typically, more senior position holders in the organization either appoint someone from outside the organization to a position below them in the hierarchy or promote a current more junior member of the organization to a higher position. (Only rarely are such appointments made by organizational members below the position being filled.) The most obvious real-world example of the second process is democratic election. (For the purposes of this article, we are ignoring the complex processes by which the range of options given to voters is decided.) The crucial difference between these two processes is the relationship of power between choosers and chosen. In the first, the choosers occupy a position of superior power, whereas in the latter, the choosers effectively decide who should have power over them. If the former process typifies the leadership selection process in most real-world social organizations, then the latter is implicitly— if not explicitly—the situation of participants in experimental research on leadership perceptions. We propose that these different processes produce different outcomes; that is, different types of individuals will emerge as the preferred candidates for leadership. Why might this happen?

Fiske and Depret (1996) offered three reasons why the perspective of the evaluator and, in particular, the power relationship between evaluator and the candidates evaluated could influence the evaluations made. One is that the powerful do not need to attend as carefully to information about subordinates as subordinates need to attend to information about those who have power over them. A second is that the powerful may be less able to attend carefully to such information because their attention would otherwise be overloaded. A third is that powerholders may have been selected for personality attributes associated with a low motivation to attend carefully to others. A fourth interesting possibility was suggested by Snodgrass, Hetch, and Ploutz-Snyder (1998): High-status individuals may be better at providing diagnostic information about themselves. However, the alternative we have considered in greatest detail is the motivation of the evaluator.

Superordinate and subordinate perspectives create different interests. Subordinates will not only be more motivated to be accurate in their assessment of candidates—given the capacity of the appointee to affect their interests—but will be particularly motivated to be accurate about the moral credentials of candidates, qualities having a determinate influence on their fate. But is there any evidence that perspective does make a difference, that it does result in candidate preference? We believe there is.

A hint can be found in work by Harris and Hogan (1992). They observed that the overall ratings of effectiveness that managers received from their superiors were related to their superiors' assessments of their technical competence. However, the equivalent overall ratings provided by their subordinates were more strongly predicted by the latters' evaluations of their moral integrity. In comparing subordinates' and superiors' judgments of a manager's leadership qualities, Morgan (1993) similarly found that subordinates' judgments were more strongly related to their assessments of the manager's ethical standards. Focusing more directly on the selection process, the following circumstances might be envisaged. In an ideal world, a candidate who is well qualified in every conceivably relevant respect would be found for every position of leadership or responsibility. In the real world, however, none of the available candidates may be perfect, but each may have different imperfections. In particular, some may have excellent technical qualifications but also various moral flaws, whereas others may be morally impeccable but lacking in technical competence. Given that a choice has to be made, which kind of flaw is more likely to be tolerated?

We explored this question first in a series of role-playing exercises with university students (Emler, 1993). In each exercise, participants played the role of either an individual in a position superior to the vacancy to be filled or an individual in a position subordinate to the vacancy. Participants were asked to evaluate candidates with contrasting qualifications: Candidates were either technically competent but morally suspect or morally competent but technically suspect. The vacant positions were of various kinds (e.g., the principal of a high school, a middle management position in a manufacturing company, the leader of a band of refugees). In each case, the role played had the predicted effect. Superior role players attached more weight to technical competence than to moral qualifications, whereas the reverse was true for those playing subordinate roles.

We then extended the research to individuals with more experience of organizational hierarchies (i.e., junior- and middle-level managers working in a range of public and private organizations; e.g., Cook & Emler, 1999). The judgments participants were asked to make were chosen to reflect as much as possible their own working experiences. The results were equally clear-cut. These experiments involved three judgment phases. In the first, individuals made private judgments of both the qualities needed for the job and the suitability of a group of short-listed candidates. In the second, participants met in small groups, discussed the candidates, and tried to reach consensus on their relative suitability. In the third phase, each participant recorded their private judgments about candidates' relative suitability. Figure 12.1 presents a summary of the final judgments for the two most relevant candidates (there were six in all). It can be seen that the perspective of the evaluator had only a modest effect on the evolution of technically flawed candidates; in fact, this effect was not statistically significant. However, perspective had a very marked effect on the evaluation of morally flawed but technically competent candidates. Perspective led to quite different candidate preferences. The candidate whose only evident flaw was moral in nature was actually the one most preferred by those judging from a superior perspective. For those evaluating from a subordinate perspective, this candidate was ranked fifth out of the six candidates.

It is not entirely clear why perspective produces this difference. Fiske and Depret (1996) may have been correct in their belief that because powerholders do not need to be accurate in their appraisal of subordinates they are less likely to search for, notice, or attend to diagnostic information. However, in our study (Cook & Emler, 1999) perspective had no influence on the qualities regarded as important for the job or on the things noticed about candidates. The effect of perspective seemed to be specific to the way that different bits of candidate information were combined to reach a summary judgment of suitability.

Conclusion

To summarize, we have argued that moral integrity in leadership matters because of the opportunities to do immense harm available to those who occupy leadership positions. Lack of moral integrity in a leader is thus of far greater

FIGURE 12.1

Summary of final judgments for the two most suitable candidates.

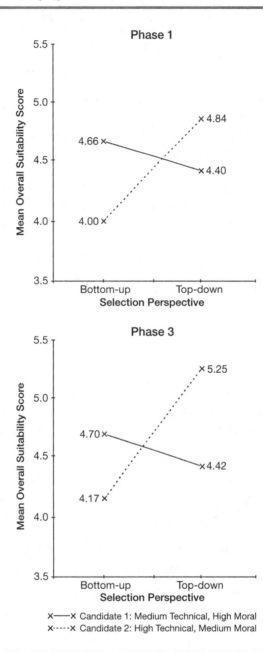

Phase 1

Phase 3

Mean Overall Suitability Score

Selection Perspective

×——× Candidate 1: Medium Technical, High Moral
×·····× Candidate 2: High Technical, Medium Moral

consequence than lack of conscience, self-control, or tolerance in any private citizen acting alone. We also have argued that individuals in leadership positions too frequently lack sufficient moral integrity and that one major reason for this lies in the effects of leadership selection processes.

Although moral integrity in leadership has so far proven difficult to achieve, the wholesale replacement of top-down selection processes with bottom-up mechanisms may not be the answer. Top-down processes could be enhanced by educating of selectors in the importance of moral credentials, for example. But as there already is evidence that employers look for integrity in potential employees (e.g., Dunn, Mount, Barrick, & Ones, 1995; Ones and Viswesvaran, chapter 4, this volume), there may be two additional problems to overcome: (a) recognizing that moral integrity is desirable not just in low-level employees (whose virtues may be primarily those of obedience, deference to authority, and conscientious execution of supervisors' instructions) and (b) developing procedures to appraise moral competence accurately (in our studies, the appraisals were provided; in reality, they are much harder to determine; Cook & Emler, 1999; Emler, 1993; Emler, Soat, & Terry, 1998). Nonetheless, the costs of failing to make these judgments and make them accurately are potentially so great that we cannot afford to abandon the challenge.

References

American National Commission on Product Safety. (1971). [Report]. Washington, DC: Government Printing Office.

Atwater, L. E., & Yammarino, F. J. (1993). Personal attributes as predictors of superiors' and subordinates' perceptions of military academy leadership. *Human Relations, 46,* 645–668.

Barnard, C. I. (1938). *The functions of the executive.* Cambridge, MA: Harvard University Press.

Barnlund, D. C. (1962). Consistency of emergent leadership in groups with changing tasks and members. *Speech Monographs, 29,* 45–52.

Bentz, V. J. (1990). Contextual issues in predicting high-level leadership performance: Contextual richness as a criterion consideration in personality research with executives. In K. E. Clark & M. B. Clark (Eds.), *Measures of leadership* (pp. 131–143). West Orange, NJ: Leadership Library of America.

Berry, J. W. (1976). *Human ecology and cognitive style: Comparative studies in cultural and psychological adaptation.* New York: Wiley.

Bowers, K. S. (1973). Situationism in psychology: An analysis and critique. *Psychological Review, 80,* 307–336.

Box, S. (1983). *Power, crime and mystification.* London: Tavistock.

Conklin, J. E. (1977). *Illegal but not criminal: Business crime in America*. Englewood Cliffs, NJ: Prentice-Hall.

Cook, T., & Emler, N. (1999). Bottom-up vs. top-down evaluations of candidates' managerial potential: An experimental study. *Journal of Occupational and Organizational Psychology, 72*, 423–439.

Cox, C. J., & Cooper, C. L. (1989). *High flyers: An anatomy of managerial success*. Oxford, England: Blackwell.

Deutsch, M. (1991). Egalitarianism in the laboratory and at work. In R. Vermunt & H. Steensma (Eds.), *Social justice in human relations. Vol. 1: Societal and psychological origins of justice* (pp. 195–209). New York: Plenum.

Dixon, N. (1976). *On the psychology of military incompetence*. London: Cape.

Dowie, M. (1977). Pinto madness. *Mother Jones, 2*, 18–34.

Dulewicz, S. V. (1997). *General management competences and personality: A 7-year follow-up study*. Unpublished manuscript, Henley School of Management.

Dunn, W., Mount, M., Barrick, M., & Ones, D. (1995). Relative importance of personality in managers' judgments of applicant qualifications. *Journal of Applied Psychology, 95*, 500–509.

Durkheim, E. (1951). *Suicide*. New York: Free Press. (Original work published 1898)

Durkheim, E. (1961). *Moral education*. New York: Free Press. (Original work published 1925)

Emler, N. (1993, September). *Evaluating candidates for leadership positions: The effects of evaluator perspective*. Paper presented at the British Psychological Society Social Psychology Section Annual Conference, Oxford, England.

Emler, N., & Hogan, R. (1981). Developing attitudes to law and justice. In S. S. Brehm, S. M. Kassin, & F. X. Gibbons (Eds.), *Developmental social psychology* (pp. 398–314). New York: Oxford University Press.

Emler, N., & Hogan, R. (1991). Moral psychology and public policy. In W. M. Kurtines & J. L. Gewirtz (Eds.), *Handbook of moral behavior and development* (Vol. 3, pp. 69–93). Hillsdale, NJ: Erlbaum.

Emler, N., Soat, C., & Tarry, H. (1998, September). *Peer-evaluations of leadership qualities*. Paper presented at the British Psychological Society Social Psychology Section Annual Conference, Canterbury, England.

Fielder, F. E. (1978). The contingency model and the dynamics of the leadership process. In L. Berkowitz (Ed.), *Advances in experimental social psychology, Vol. 11* (pp. 59–112). New York: Academic Press.

Fiske, S. T., & Depret, E. (1996). Control, interdependence and power: Understanding social cognition in its social context. In W. Stroebe & M. Hewstone (Eds.), *European review of social psychology* (Vol. 7, pp. 31–61). Chichester, England: Wiley.

Gough, H. (1975). *The California Psychological Inventory*. Palo Alto, CA: Consulting Psychologists Press.

Haney, C., Banks, C., & Zimbardo, P. (1973). Interpersonal dynamics in a simulated prison. *International Journal of Penology, 1*(1), 69–97.

Harris, G., & Hogan, J. (1992, April). *Perceptions and personality correlates of managerial effectiveness*. Paper presented at the 13th Annual Psychology in the Department of Defense Symposium, Colorado Springs, CO.

Hertzberg, F. (1968). One more time: How do you motivate employees? *Harvard Business Review, 46*, 53–62.

Howard, A., & Bray, D. W. (1990). Predictions of managerial success over long periods of time: Lessons for the Management Progress Study. In K. E. Clark & M. B. Clark (Eds.), *Measures of leadership* (pp. 113–130). West Orange, NJ: Leadership Library of America.

Jacobs, R. L. (1992). *Moving up the corporate ladder: A longitudinal study of motivation, personality and management success in men and women*. Unpublished doctoral dissertation, Boston University.

Johnson, J. M., & Douglas, J. D. (1978). *Crime at the top: Deviance in business and the professions*. New York: Lippincott.

Katz, D., & Kahn, R. (1978). *Social psychology of organization (2nd ed.)*. New York: Wiley.

Kenny, D., & Zaccaro, S. (1983). An estimate of variance due to traits in leadership. *Journal of Applied Psychology, 68*, 678–685.

Kinder, D. R. (1998). Opinion and action in the realm of politics. In D. Gilbert, S. Fiske, & G. Lindzey (Eds.), *The handbook of social psychology* (4th ed., Vol. 2) (pp. 778–867). New York: McGraw Hill.

Kohlberg, L. (1984). *The psychology of moral development. Vol. 2. Essays on moral development: The nature and validity of moral stages*. San Francisco: Jossey-Bass.

Kouzes, J. M., & Posner, B. Z. (1987). *The leadership challenge: How to get extraordinary things done in organizations*. San Francisco: Jossey-Bass.

Lieberson, S., & O'Connor, J. F. (1972). Leadership and organizational performance: A study of large corporations. *American Sociological Review, 37*, 117–130.

Lord, R., DeVader, C., & Alliger, G. (1986). A meta-analysis of the relation between personality traits and leadership perceptions: An analysis of validity generalization procedures. *Journal of Applied Psychology, 71*, 402–409.

Mann, R. D. (1959). A review of the relationship between personality and performance in small groups. *Psychological Bulletin, 56*, 241–270.

Mars, G. (1982). *Cheats at work: An anthropology of workplace crime*. London: Unwin.

Meindl, J., Ehrlich, S., & Dukerich, J. (1985). The romance of leadership. *Administrative Science Quarterly, 30*, 78–102.

Menzies, H. D. (1980). The ten toughest bosses. *Fortune, 101*, 62–69.

Michels, R. (1949). *Political parties: A sociological study of the oligarchical tendencies of modern democracy*. New York: Free Press. (Original work published 1916)

Milgram, S. (1974). *Obedience to authority*. New York: Harper & Row.

Mintzberg, H. (1973). *The nature of managerial work*. Englewood Cliffs, NJ: Prentice Hall.

Mischel, W. (1968). *Personality and assessment*. New York: Wiley.

Morgan, R. (1993). Self- and co-worker perceptions of ethics and their relationships to leadership and salary. *Academy of Management Journal, 36*, 200–214.

Moyle, P. (1998). Longitudinal influence of management support on employee well-being. *Work and Stress, 12,* 29–49.

Myers, E. C. W. (1955). *Greek entanglement.* London: Rupert Hall Davies.

Pfeffer, J. (1978). The ambiguity of leadership. In M. W. McCall, Jr. & M. M. Lombardo (Eds.), *Leadership: Where else can we go?* Durham, NC: Duke University Press.

Reiman, J. H. (1979). *The rich get rich and the poor get prison: Ideology, class, and criminal justice.* New York: Wiley.

Robinson, W. P. (1996). *Deceit, delusion, and detection.* London: Sage.

Ross, L. (1977). The intuitive psychologist and his shortcomings: Distortions in the attribution process. In L. Berkowitz (Ed.), *Advances in experimental social psychology, Vol. 10.* New York: Academic Press.

Salancik, G. R., & Pfeffer, J. (1977). Constraints on administrator discretion: The limited influence of mayors on city budgets. *Urban Affairs Quarterly, 12,* 475–498.

Shweder, R. A., Mahapatra, M., & Miller, J. (1990). Culture and moral development. In J. Kagan & S. Lamb (Eds.), *The emergence of morality in young children* (pp. 1–83). Chicago: University of Chicago Press.

Snodgrass, S., Hetch, M., & Ploutz-Snyder, R. (1998). Interpersonal sensitivity: Expressiveness or perceptivity? *Journal of Personality and Social Psychology, 74,* 228–249.

Soble, R. L., & Dallos, R. E. (1974). *The impossible dream: The Equity Funding scandal.* New York: Putnam.

Stogdill, R. M. (1948). Personality factors associated with leadership: A survey of the literature. *Journal of Applied Psychology, 25,* 35–71.

Stoker, L. (1993). Judging presidential character: The demise of Gary Hart. *Political Behavior, 15,* 193–223.

Sunday Times Insight Team. (1979). [Report] London: Times Publishers.

Tannenbaum, A. S. (1974). *Hierarchy in organizations: An international comparison.* San Francisco: Jossey-Bass.

Ungar, S. J. (1973). Getting away with what you can. In L. R. Heilbronner (Ed.), *In the name of profit.* New York: Doubleday.

Weick, K. E. (1969). *The social psychology of organizing.* Reading, MA: Addison-Wesley.

Wicker, A. W. (1969). Attitudes versus actions: The relationship of verbal and overt behavioral responses to attitude objects. *Journal of Social Issues, 25,* 41–78.

CHAPTER 13

Ego Depletion, the Executive Function, and Self-Control

An Energy Model of the Self in Personality

Roy F. Baumeister

elf-regulation refers to the processes by which the self alters or preserves its inner states so as to achieve various goals and meet certain standards. During the 1980s, many theorists began asserting that self-regulation is one of the centrally important processes that provide the essential keys to understanding the self (e.g., Carver & Scheier, 1981). Higgins (1996) spoke of the "sovereignty of self-regulation," (p. 1062) reflecting the greater importance of self-regulation compared with that of any other process in the self. My own work continues this approach.

The importance of self-regulation goes far beyond theoretical debates about the structure and functioning of the self. In fact, most of the major personal and social problems affecting modern Western citizens involve difficulties with or failures of self-control. For example, drug abuse, alcoholism, and other addictions all reflect some pervasive inability to control one's use of certain substances. This helps explain the link between addictions and personality patterns with weak self-control (Block, 1993). Teenage pregnancy, AIDS and other sexually transmitted diseases, and related problems stem from poor regulation of sexual behavior; most of the problematic consequences of sex could be avoided if people would control or moderate their behavior (e.g., by using condoms). Violent and aggressive behaviors often reflect impulsive responding. In fact, deficient self-control has been argued to be the conceptual key to understanding crime and criminality (Gottfredson & Hirschi, 1990). Excessive spending, gambling, and debt all can cause crushing financial difficulties; these behaviors reflect poor regulation of one's use of money. Similarly, underachievement in school and dropping out, as well as people's more general failures to perform to the potential defined by their abilities, often are the result of poor self-regulation (see also Baumeister, 1984). In addition, physicians have long advised that North Americans would live longer and healthier lives if they would quit smoking, eat properly, and exercise regularly. However, all of these require self-regulation; therefore, few people manage them as well as they should or would like.

Self-control may also be highly relevant to personality theory. Block (1993) found that ego-control (by which he meant the ability to regulate impulses) and ego-resiliency (the knowledge about when to exert control and when to let go) were consistent across personality from early childhood to adulthood. That is, people who were above average in these traits as children were still above average as adults, even though they naturally had somewhat more self-control as adults than as children. Mischel, Shoda, and Peake (1988) and Shoda, Mischel, and Peake (1990) showed that performance on a delayed-gratification task at age 4 predicted social and academic success more than a decade later as the participants entered college.

Self-Regulation in the Context of Self Theory

What is the nature of the self? To answer this question it is necessary to sift through the diverse manifestations of selfhood and even bypass the presumptive uniqueness of each individual self to identify some basic, universal phenomena that give rise to selfhood. There probably is no single experience or dimension that is the basis for all of selfhood. Instead, three basic phenomena appear to be universal and together constitute the basis for the self (Baumeister, 1998). These three phenomena also offer a framework that can encompass and organize the vast array of research findings regarding the self.

The first of these phenomena is *reflexive consciousness*. Human awareness is able to turn around on its source so that the subject also becomes the object of attention. Without this phenomenon, the very notion of selfhood would be incomprehensible and possibly incoherent. The human self forms an awareness of itself and gradually accumulates knowledge about itself. This dimension of selfhood has been studied in considerable depth, resulting in a large literature on self-awareness processes, self-knowledge, the so-called self-concept (or self-schemas), self-esteem, processes of self-deception, and so forth.

The second phenomenon is the *interpersonal aspect of self*. Selves do not exist in isolation, as if the human self were simply an isolated creature contemplating its own existence and nature. Instead, the self comes into being as a member of one or more groups and as part of various relationships. Moreover, relating to others is not simply something the self happens to do or as a means by which self-knowledge is acquired: It is an essential aspect of what the self is for. People are fundamentally motivated by a need to form and maintain relationships with at least a few other people (see Baumeister & Leary, 1995, for a review), and the self is a principal tool for accomplishing this. If a person cannot attract or keep friends, he or she is likely to alter his or her self to improve his or her chances of interpersonal success. This aspect of self has also been extensively studied, in processes such as self-presentation and adaptation to relationships as well as the reciprocal interactions between interpersonal or relationship contexts and views of the self.

The third phenomenon is the *executive function:* The self makes choices, initiates action, takes responsibility, exerts control over the environment, and regulates itself. Without this aspect, the self might know all about itself and might carry on long-term relationships, but it could not really do anything. Although this aspect seems crucial, it is understood far less than the other aspects. In fact, it is something of a cliché to remark on how relatively poorly this agentic, executive aspect of self is understood.

The purpose of this chapter is to offer one model of how the self's executive functioning operates. Specifically, it is argued that this functioning depends on a limited resource that is similar to strength or energy. Following exertion, the self is depleted and therefore less able to make choices or regulate itself until this resource can be replenished.

Energy models of personality have flourished at times, most notably in Freud's (1961/1923, 1961/1933) theorizing. These models, however, are far out of fashion now, and almost none of the currently influential theories about self or personality invoke an energy model. That these models are not currently in favor does not necessarily reflect any proven shortcoming or inadequacy. Indeed, it is quite conceivable that the current difficulty in understanding the self's executive function is partly attributable to the prevailing reluctance to use energy models. It may be no coincidence that psychology currently both lacks an adequate understanding of the self's executive function and eschews energy models in its theories.

Theories of Self-Control

How does the self actually regulate and change itself? Various conceptually plausible models have been proposed. These models can be characterized into three types: (a) strength, (b) schema, and (c) skill (e.g., Baumeister, Bratslavsky, Muraven, & Tice, 1998). These models deserve to be outlined briefly here because the attempt to distinguish among them empirically was what began my group's work on the executive function. In particular, these three models make conflicting predictions about how effective someone would be at a second act of self-regulation following a recent exertion.

The first model can be described by the traditional notion of "willpower" (see Mischel, 1996) because it depicts the self as using some kind of strength or power resource to effect change. This view probably derived from everyday experience with temptation. A tempting impulse is experienced as having a certain degree of strength, so resisting temptation (a familiar and important form of self-control) is presumed to require the self to bring the same amount of strength or more to bear to overcome the impulse. A willpower or strength model predicts that self-control would tend to be impaired after an initial exertion because some of the self's willpower or strength has been expended, leaving the person with a depleted resource.

The second model follows the currently more popular information-processing approach. In this view, self-regulation depends crucially on some accumulated store of self-knowledge and schematic representations of procedures as well as perhaps knowledge about environmental contingencies. In this model, self-regulation depends on having the self perceive and analyze its current situation, appraise its status, and then calculate the optimal line of behavior. A schema model predicts that a second consecutive act of self-regulation would be improved compared with the baseline because the first act of self-regulation primes the master schema, therefore facilitating subsequent work. This is consistent with well-established priming effects in the realm of social cognition (e.g., Higgins & King, 1981; Wyer & Srull, 1980). To use a computer analogy, the first act of self-regulation activates (loads) the relevant software; a second act of self-regulation would benefit from having the program already operating.

The third model depicts self-control as a skill. According to this model, people gradually learn how to control themselves better, and any individual act of self-regulation entails drawing on these skills to the extent that they have been mastered and even automatized. A skill model predicts that a given act of self-control would be unaffected by whether the person had recently performed some other act of self-control. Skill remains more or less constant on consecutive trials (although it does gradually improve over many trials).

Testing Theories of Self-Control

Thus, these models predict poorer, better, and unchanged performance, respectively, on a second act of self-regulation as a result of the first. Our initial series of studies investigated these conflicting predictions by having participants engage in two consecutive but seemingly unrelated acts of self-control.

Muraven, Tice, and Baumeister (1998) had participants engage in affect regulation, then they measured stamina. Physical endurance or stamina is a useful index of self-regulation because as the body becomes tired and wants rest, the self overrides these impulses and forces the body to continue its exertions. This study measured stamina with a handgrip task. Participants were instructed to squeeze the handgrip for as long as they could sustain their grip.

To control for individual differences in hand strength, participants performed this exercise twice. The first time served as the baseline, whereas the second constituted the main measure of self-regulatory performance.

In between the two handgrip exercises, all participants watched a disturbing video excerpt depicting horrific consequences of nuclear waste on wildlife. By random assignment, one third of the participants were instructed to stifle their emotional responses to the video, in terms of both not expressing emotion and trying to not even feel emotion. A second group was told to amplify their emotional responses (both feelings and expression) while watching the video. A third (control) group watched the video without trying to alter their feelings or expression in either direction.

The results of the study favored the strength or willpower theory. Both groups of participants who had tried to alter their emotional state, by either suppressing emotion or amplifying it, performed significantly worse on the second handgrip task. In contrast, participants in the control group showed no change in their performance. They had watched the same video and presumably had felt the same distress as participants in the other conditions, but they had not tried to regulate their feelings. Trying to alter their emotional state seemed to have consumed some resource that left participants less able to persevere on the physical stamina (handgrip) task.

Converging evidence was provided in a second study (Muraven et al., 1998). This experiment borrowed a thought-suppression procedure developed by Wegner, Schneider, Carter, and White (1987). According to this procedure, participants were instructed to avoid thinking about a white bear while recording their thoughts for 5 minutes. Control participants were instructed to simply record their thoughts for 5 minutes without trying to direct or regulate their thoughts in any way. Following this exercise in mental control, participants were set to work on anagrams that had been rigged to be unsolvable. Their persistence at these problems was measured. Persisting at such problems requires self-control because the repeated failure is disappointing and frustrating; people typically feel impulses to quit and do something more satisfying.

The strength or willpower model was supported again. Participants who had suppressed thoughts about a bear subsequently quit the anagram task faster compared with participants who had not attempted to regulate their thoughts. Thus, trying not to think of a white bear apparently consumed some resource that was then not available to enable participants to keep trying a task despite repeated failure.

A third experiment examined impulse control to determine whether it would produce similar decrements in subsequent self-control (Baumeister, Bratslavsky, et al., 1998). Under the guise of a research project on taste perception and memory, researchers contacted participants and asked them to skip a meal and not eat anything for 3 hours before the experiment, so most arrived hungry. On arrival, participants were seated in a room in which chocolate chip cookies recently had been baked and that therefore was full of the delicious, tempting aroma of chocolate and baking. In addition, a plate of these cookies and chocolate candies was located on the table in front of the participant. The table also contained a bowl of radishes. In the crucial condition, the experimenter told participants that they had been assigned to the radish condition, which would entail eating only radishes during the experiment. Participants were left alone for 5 minutes, ostensibly to allow them to eat radishes. Participants were left alone to maximize the temptation to eat from the tempting plate of cookies and chocolates. (Participants were surreptitiously observed to ensure that none actually ate the forbidden foods.)

Two comparison groups were included. Participants in one were instructed to eat the cookies and chocolates. No food was involved in the other condition. Neither of these conditions required participants to resist temptation.

All foods were removed, and participants were instructed to solve puzzles by tracing geometric figures with a pen. The puzzles required participants to trace each figure without retracing any lines and without lifting the pen from the paper. As in the first experiment (Muraven et al., 1998), the puzzles were rigged to be unsolvable (Feather, 1961; Glass & Singer, 1972). The measure used was how long participants persisted despite frustration and disappointment.

Again, the strength or energy model was supported. Participants in the radish condition, who had to resist eating the tempting cookies and chocolates, subsequently gave up on the unsolvable puzzles faster than participants in the other conditions. Even those participants who received nothing to eat were able to persist much longer than participants in the radish condition.

These studies converged to show that the capacity for self-control operates like a strength or muscle. Across several studies and different spheres of self-control, any exertion of control over the self was followed by impaired performance on a seemingly unrelated self-control task.

Additional studies were performed to rule out various alternative explanations (Baumeister, Bratslavsky, et al., 1998; Muraven et al., 1998). For example, the use of unsolvable problems raised the question of whether participants were actually regulating effectively by withdrawing effort rather than wasting it on impossible tasks. We repeated one study using solvable anagrams (which presumably also require self-regulation) and found that performance was still impaired (Baumeister, Bratslavsky, et al., 1998). Another question was whether the self-control manipulations were simply more mentally strenuous than the control tasks (i.e., in the first study, two groups had to try to change their emotions, whereas the control group did nothing, and doing nothing is presumed to be less exhausting or less strenuous). We assigned participants in the control group in one study a difficult and unpleasant task (i.e., solving three-digit multiplication problems by hand). The results were unchanged.

An additional concern was that the dependent variables tended to involve performance regulation, so we conducted one study in which the dependent variable was affect regulation. Participants were instructed to refrain from laughing or smiling while watching a video of a stand-up comedy routine, and judges (who did not know the experimental treatments or hypotheses) watched videotapes of participants' faces to code them for any expressions of mirth (Muraven et al., 1998). Not surprisingly, participants who had previously tried to control their thoughts (by suppressing thoughts of a white bear) were less able to inhibit their responses to the video than participants in the control conditions. Thus, the results were not limited to performance regulation. This study also helped rule out several alternative explanations based on possible affective consequences of self-regulation. For example, if the initial act of self-control induced a bad mood, then participants should have found it easier to refrain from laughing at the comedy video. Instead, they found it more difficult.

The implication of these findings is therefore that self-control involves the consumption of some resource that is similar to energy or strength. The self expends some of this energy each time it exerts control over itself to alter its thoughts or feelings, to manage its performance, or to control its impulses. Given the adaptive importance of self-regulation, this energy resource would have to be regarded as an important aspect of the self.

Two additional implications about this resource emerged from these studies. First, the same resource is used for very different acts of self-control. For example, it does not appear that controlling thoughts and controlling feelings are entirely separate processes. Rather, all acts of self-control seem to draw on a single, common resource.

Second, this resource appears to be quite limited. A mere 5 minutes of trying to avoid thinking about a white bear (which most people would not be thinking about anyway) or of making oneself eat radishes instead of chocolate chip cookies or chocolate candies was sufficient to produce substantial decrements in self-regulation on a subsequent task. If the capacity for self-control depends on the consumption of this energy resource, then that capacity appears to be quite severely limited.

Building and Recovering

The results discussed thus far suggest that the willpower concept (a) is quite viable and (b) describes an important component of personality. The concept of willpower resembles that of strength or muscle power, which tires after exertion. Before a strength model can be accepted, however, two other aspects need to be tested.

One of these is the notion that the self recovers its strength by resting, just as tired muscles regain their power during sleep and rest. Although there are no direct tests of this, there is ample evidence in the self-regulation literature that sleep is valuable for restoring the self's resources. In general, many patterns of self-control break down late in the day compared with in the morning, and it is reasonable to assume that most people have been sleeping more recently when it is morning than evening. Thus, diets are broken late in the day, addictive relapses occur in the evening, and even impulsive crimes are most common late in the evening (for reviews, see Baumeister, Heatherton, & Tice, 1994; Muraven & Baumeister, 2000). The implication is that sleep restores the self to its full resources, which are gradually expended during the course of wakeful activities, so that depletion becomes increasingly likely by the end of the day.

Periods of stress are associated by many with breakdowns in self-control. During examination periods, for example, university students often relinquish control over eating and smoking (poor impulse control), and they become irritable, grumpy, and prone to lash out at others (deficient affect regulation). Although these effects may be a direct result of the depletion of regulatory strength (i.e., during these periods the student is likely to be devoting his or her willpower to meeting deadlines and preparing for exams, thereby taking away from other areas requiring self-control), they also may be exacerbated by the lack of sleep that is common during these periods, when some students force themselves to stay up all night writing papers and studying.

Rest does seem to replenish the self. A second and more theoretically interesting issue is whether exercise can actually improve the capacity for self-control, just as a muscle gradually becomes stronger from regular exercise. In the studies described above, exertion resulted in a short-term drop in self-control. The question is, Is there also a long-term gain?

We conducted a longitudinal study to investigate this possibility (Muraven, Baumeister, & Tice, 1999). Participants were assigned various exercises of self-control (e.g., trying to improve their posture or regulate their moods) over a 2-week period. Their self-regulatory capacities were assessed both before and after, in laboratory sessions using thought-suppression (white bear) and handgrip procedures. The findings confirmed that, relative to the nonexercising control group, self-control did seem to gain in power from exercise. Although baseline levels of self-control did not change from before to after the 2 weeks of exercise, resistance to depletion did improve significantly. Moreover, examination of the logs kept by participants indicated that those who did the most exercise during the 2 weeks showed the greatest improvement. These results require further replication and confirmation, but they do provide initial evidence that self-control can be improved through exercise.

These findings about the improvement of self-control through exercise have practical as well as theoretical implications. Although unlikely, it is possible that someone might respond to these findings regarding depletion by concluding that they should refrain from exercising self-control to conserve the precious resource. This is hardly a socially desirable message for our research to convey. Fortunately, the improvement findings suggest that regular exercise of self-control is the best policy in the long run because it can increase an individual's capacity to regulate his or her behavior.

Meanwhile, questions remain about other possibilities for increasing the self's powers. One hypothesis is that positive emotional states may help replenish the self. Theorists have long suggested that emotions serve important functions by activating behavioral responses that can be adaptive (e.g., fear makes one flee from danger, thereby increasing one's chances of survival), but these arguments consistently seem to apply better to negative than positive emotions. The question of what functions positive emotions may serve thus remains unanswered. If positive emotions were determined to help replenish the depleted self, this would be a theoretically valuable and important contribution toward answering this important question.

We have conducted two preliminary studies that have indicated that positive emotions do help recharge the self (Baumeister, Dale, & Tice, 1998). Both studies began with a manipulation of ego depletion (in which participants had to cross out the letter *e*, then override that habit). After that, some of the participants were exposed to a stimulus designed to induce pleasant emotional states (i.e., a funny videotape), whereas others were given either a neutral affect induction or a negative emotional state (using a neutral or sad video clip). Subsequent self-control was measured by persistence at a difficult, frustrating task (Study 1) or success at solving anagrams (Study 2). The results from both studies suggested that the pleasant emotion helped reverse the effects of ego depletion. Although these results are subject to multiple, competing explanations, and further research is required, they do raise the possibility that the self's resources can be replenished by something other than rest.

Beyond Self-Regulation

The study findings discussed above indicated that self-regulation operates by consuming a common, limited resource. Given how important self-regulation is to successful human functioning, that resource would necessarily have to be regarded as one of the self's most important aspects and, indeed, as a vital aspect of personality. However, it was further plausible that this resource had applications even beyond self-regulation.

As noted earlier in this chapter, the executive function of the self (also known as the "agent") remains inadequately understood in current theory (see Baumeister, 1998). It seemed plausible that this energy resource might apply not only to the self but also to the other activities of the executive function, such as making choices, taking responsibility, and being active rather than passive.

To investigate whether the energy resource used for self-regulation is also used for responsible decision making, we investigated whether making such a decision would have effects on subsequent self-regulation similar to what we had observed for initial acts of self-regulation (Baumeister, Bratslavsky, et al., 1998). We borrowed a choice procedure from cognitive dissonance research (Linder, Cooper, & Jones, 1967). Participants were asked to record a speech advocating something contrary to their own attitudes and values (in this study, students were asked to make speeches in favor of large tuition increases). Participants in the high-choice condition were told that the final decision about whether to make the speech would be up to them and that they should make their own decision. In contrast, participants in the low-choice condition were instructed simply to make the speech without being asked or reminded that they had a choice or an implicit right to refuse.

Countless studies have used similar choice procedures to investigate the effects of making a deliberate choice on the relevant attitudes. This investigation was not concerned with the attitudinal consequences, however. We sought to determine whether participants would experience resource depletion after choosing to make the counterattitudinal speech. After the choice manipulation, participants performed the same persistence measurement task used in the radish/chocolate study. The main measure was how long participants kept trying to solve the unsolvable geometric puzzles.

The findings suggested that the same energy resource is used for both self-regulation and responsible decision making. Participants who chose to make the speech (and no one refused) subsequently gave up on the puzzles faster than participants in the low-choice condition. Apparently, the intrapsychic process of consideration and consent consumed some of the same resource that would have enabled participants to persist longer on the puzzle task.

Another experiment showed that exertions of self-control can impair decision making by making people become passive instead of active (Baumeister, Bratslavsky, et al., 1998). In this study, participants acquired a habit and then were required to break it, which is an important type of self-regulation. Specifically, participants first learned to proceed rapidly through a page of printed text and cross out all instances of the letter *e*. They then were given more printed text and instructed to cross out all instances of the letter *e* except those that were adjacent to or one letter removed from another vowel. The more complex instruction thus required the participant to override the habit of crossing out every *e*. Participants in the control condition worked on multiplication problems, which are difficult and unpleasant but do not require self-regulation (i.e., because multiplication requires the application of standard, well-learned procedures).

Following the exertion of self-regulation (or the multiplication task), passivity was measured by comparing the relative prepotency of passive versus active responses. Participants were instructed to watch a video for as long as they could, until they did not want to see it any more. The video was specially created to be as boring as possible: It simply showed the laboratory wall. Participants in one condition had to actively press a button to continue watching the film; if they passively did nothing, the film would automatically stop. In the other condition, the active and passive responses were reversed. Participants had to actively press a button to stop the film; if they did nothing, it automatically continued. By comparing the duration of film watching in the two conditions, it was possible to determine how passive participants were.

The findings from this study confirmed that the same resource that is used in other forms of volition is used in self-regulation. Participants who had performed the self-regulation exercise were more passive in their responses to the film than participants who had performed the multiplication task.

Additional evidence has been provided by more recent, still unpublished work (Twenge, Tice, Schmeichel, & Baumeister, 2000). In a pair of studies, participants were first asked to make a long series of choices between department store products. The choices were personally relevant, in that participants had been told (correctly) that they would eventually receive one of the items they selected. Participants spent about half an hour making dichotomous decisions (e.g., Would you prefer a red t-shirt or a green t-shirt? Would you prefer a vanilla-scented candle or an almond-scented candle?). Control participants completed a lengthy questionnaire reporting on their usage of various similar products, but they did not actually choose which among them they would prefer to have.

Following the product selection portion of the study, participants were asked to ingest an unpleasant-tasting liquid. Using a procedure developed by Muraven (1998), we offered participants $.25 for each ounce they could drink of a mixture consisting of half vinegar and half water plus unsweetened Kool-Aid flavoring. Forcing oneself to consume an aversive beverage requires self-regulation; therefore, the main measure was how much participants could make themselves drink. Participants who had made choices during the first part of the experiment drank significantly less of the vinegar–Kool-Aid mixture than the participants who had merely rated product usage. Thus, again, it appears that making choices consumes some resource that is then unavailable for self-regulation.

Taken together, these findings indicate that the same resource is used for all volitional activities of the self's executive function rather than being earmarked for self-regulation alone. Choice, initiative, active response, and self-control all draw on the same limited resource. Therefore, this resource must be regarded as one of the most important properties of the self.

The findings are reminiscent of Freud's (1961/1923, 1961/1933) theory that the ego (his term corresponding to the self) requires energy for its operation. In homage to Freud's seminal and prescient theorizing, we selected the term *ego depletion* to describe what happens to this resource after it is used (Baumeister, Bratslavsky, et al., 1998). Our initial work had suggested *regulatory depletion* as a characterization of what happens when the self-regulation resource has been consumed (Muraven et al., 1998), but given the broader application of this resource to activities beyond self-regulation, *ego depletion* seemed a more precise term.

Exhaustion or Conservation

Our studies showed the self's resources to be limited: Even a brief exertion depleted them and impaired subsequent performance. But how limited are they? The results of our experiments could well mean that the volitional resource is so limited that a single, brief exertion consumes most of it, leaving hardly any remaining. According to this view, the participants in our experiments might well have become seriously depleted, possibly even to the extent that they could experience difficulty functioning for the rest of the day (i.e., at least in terms of volition and self-regulation). The human capacity for volition would thus be almost dangerously small and, given this, requiring people to make decisions or exert self-control (even in our experiments) might be unethical.

On the other hand, the findings could indicate that when this resource is sufficiently depleted, the person seeks to conserve what is left. In this view, the depletion is genuine, but the person is not approaching genuine exhaustion after a brief decision or act of self-control such as in our experiments. The effects would be similar to the way muscles operate: Performance is impaired long before the muscle approaches true exhaustion, but some of the impairments reflect efforts to conserve the remaining strength. For example, an athlete does not typically put forth full, maximum effort until reaching the point of utter collapse. Rather, as an athlete begins to get tired, he or she will exert further effort judiciously, holding back at times to conserve energy for important points in the competition. This is adaptive for athletes, and a corresponding pattern of conserving the ego's resources would be equally, if not more, adaptive for people who might find themselves needing to make an important choice or inhibit some impulse.

The exhaustion theory holds that once the self has become depleted, it lacks the resources necessary for further exertion of volition. In contrast, the conservation hypothesis holds that depleted people may still use volition when they are sufficiently motivated (although the result would be more severe depletion). To distinguish between these two theories, therefore, it was necessary to put people through a depleting procedure and then determine whether they could exert volition if the incentive were substantial enough.

Muraven (1998) used such a design to investigate the conservation versus exhaustion views. The measure involved consuming the vinegar–Kool-Aid mixture, and people were offered either $.25 or $.01 per ounce. The higher incentive ($.25 per ounce, enough to allow participants to earn up to $10) eliminated the effects of ego depletion, and participants who had been depleted were able to consume as much as those who had not been depleted. In contrast, when the reward was low ($.01 per ounce), strong depletion effects were found. Depleted participants were unable to make themselves consume nearly as much as the nondepleted participants. In addition, the differences emerged only when self-control was required because the drink was foul tasting. In another condition, a pleasant-tasting drink was used, and no differences were found as a function of depletion or motivation.

Another study by Muraven (1998) investigated the conservation hypothesis directly. After the initial manipulation of depletion, but before the second and main measurement of self-control, one half of the participants were told that there was to be a third task that would require self-control: Specifically, they were told that they would have to suppress all laughter and smiling while watching a very funny video. These participants thus had an incentive to conserve. Not unexpectedly, these participants regulated less effectively on the second (main) task, as if to conserve their self-control resources for the anticipated third task.

Thus, people appear to conserve their volitional resources in ways similar to the ways in which athletes conserve their strength. They may put forth full effort initially, but after their resources become somewhat depleted, they expend them only reluctantly and warily. In particular, when they anticipate further demands on this resource, they hold back so as to be able to meet the anticipated future demands.

Similar patterns have been observed in other lines of research. In vigilance studies, for example, the progressive deterioration in performance is a well-established finding: People get progressively worse at vigilance as they continue to perform the task (e.g., Parasuraman, 1984). This does not appear to be due to declining motivation. In fact, such effects have been observed in sentries and sonar operators whose own lives are at stake. The progressive decline in performance is consistent with the view that some important resource is gradually depleted.

However, the decline in performance often is reversed as the end of the vigilant exercise approaches, provided the person knows that the end is coming. Thus, in a typical experiment, a participant will make more and more mistakes as the procedure continues but then will perform better again on the final trials. For most perception researchers, this reversal is simply an annoying source of variance that messes up their data, and they take various steps to prevent it (e.g., not telling participants how many trials will be involved or requiring participants to remove their watches during the experiment). For our purposes, however, it is a relevant and theoretically interesting sign that the decline in vigilance reflects the conservation of diminished resources rather than true exhaustion. When the end is in sight, and there is no further need to conserve, people put forth full effort again, and performance improves.

Implications

The research findings on ego depletion have potentially important implications for understanding human performance in industrial and organizational settings, as well as for the more basic understanding of personality. Indeed, they suggest that it may be useful to revive the approach to personality that invoked energy or other limited resources that can be expended, conserved, or depleted.

Undoubtedly there are important individual differences in this volitional resource. Some people may become depleted after any small act of volition or self-regulation, whereas others may be able to control themselves and make choices for long periods of time. Indeed, our findings that 2 weeks of regular exercise of self-regulation seemed capable of increasing participants' ego strength, at least in the sense of making them more resistant to the debilitating effects of ego depletion, indicates that individual differences can be created. Whether self-report measures can effectively assess the size of this resource is unclear. However, finding ways of assessing these differences in strength is a high priority for basic research. Such an assessment would be useful to organizations as well, because it could, for example, help identify leaders and workers who were capable of continuing to perform effectively under stress.

If people do indeed have a limited resource for self-regulation and volition, then work patterns are likely to be affected. Jobs that require initiative and decision making will deplete the people who hold these positions, and so some allowances or accommodations may be desirable. In particular, it may be better to spread such demands out over time rather than concentrating them. Someone who has just made a great many decisions is likely to be depleted and may begin to make poor decisions.

Decision making is hardly the only aspect of work that requires self-regulation. Many jobs require affect regulation, in which part of the job involves managing one's emotions (see Hochschild, 1983). Bill collectors, airline flight attendants, customer service representatives, complaint department workers, nurses, mental health workers, and others may become depleted simply through the demands of regulating their own emotions.

Lack of control and inability to make necessary decisions can contribute to the need for affect regulation. Karesek (1979) showed that workers with demanding jobs but little control (and little latitude for making important decisions) experienced the worst mental strain in their jobs, as shown by feeling exhausted after work, sleep disturbances, depression, anxiety, and chronic nervousness. It is not that power and authority are bad (see Zaleznik, Kets de Vries, & Howard, 1977), rather, having to cope with demands without having the autonomy to do so can leave a person feeling that he or she must deal with an impossible situation, and so the need for affect regulation would be frequent.

At the extreme, occupational burnout may consist of some form of lasting depletion (i.e., one that does not recover with a night's rest). Burnout arises in contexts in which workers feel that they have been exerting themselves in futility and in which the emotional demands are chronic and severe (see Maslach & Jackson, 1981). The very term *burnout* suggests that some resource has been fully consumed, and so it is at least plausible that ego depletion is a factor in burnout.

Interactions between home life and work performance also may involve ego depletion. Someone experiencing marital problems or parenting difficulties may have to devote considerable volition to these home demands and, as a result, their work performance may suffer in ways related to volition (e.g., task persistence, initiative, and responsible decision making). In contrast, such home problems may not interfere with other aspects of job performance, such as the ability to carry out instructions or perform routine, standardized duties. Meanwhile, depletion from work may interfere with a person's home life. A person may well come home in a depleted state, saying, "I don't want to make any decisions tonight!" More ominously, workers may manage their stamina to last for the duration of their workday and mistakenly think that life at home is simply a haven for recovery. However, particularly if a person's home life is stressful or family and marital problems exist, the person may have need of substantial resources at home. Meanwhile, depletion at work may lead to breakdowns in self-regulation in other areas, and the vulnerability of people in high-stress jobs to problems such as alcohol and substance abuse or sexual misconduct may well reflect the effects of ego depletion on subsequent self-regulation.

Routine is sometimes deplored as a symptom of soulless, inauthentic work, but our research findings on ego depletion suggest that routine can serve valuable functions. Because volitional resources are quite limited, people need to conserve them for when they are most needed. Routines minimize the role of volition, choice, and initiative. Following routines therefore enables a person to conserve these resources for use at other times.

Conclusion

The study of the self occupies an important niche in personality psychology, and our findings on ego depletion suggest that the self be reconceptualized in a way that harks back to Freud's (1961/1923, 1961/1933) thinking and other foundations of personality theory. Specifically, these findings indicate that the self has a single resource that resembles energy or strength. The same resource is used for a broad variety of seemingly quite different operations, including making choices, taking responsibility, exerting self-control, showing initiative, and avoiding passivity. All aspects of self-regulation (including regulating thoughts, controlling emotions, managing performance, and restraining impulses) use this resource.

Our work also suggests that this important resource is quite limited. A small or brief exertion of the self seems sufficient to cause subsequent impairments in the self's functioning. The depletion does not appear to be a full exhaustion, but even a small laboratory procedure can produce sufficient depletion to make people conserve their remaining resources. Undoubtedly there are cases in which the self actually does face a full exhaustion of its resources, such as might occur in cases of severe trauma or burnout. In any case, it seems necessary to revise the traditional views on human functioning so as to recognize that the self has a very limited capacity for volition, choice, and self-regulation. Although this capacity seems far beyond what other species have, and it is undoubtedly one of the most precious adaptations the human race has developed, it still is quite small compared with the potentially endless demands for choice and self-regulation that human life can pose.

References

Baumeister, R. F. (1984). Choking under pressure: Self-consciousness and paradoxical effects of incentives on skillful performance. *Journal of Personality and Social Psychology, 46*, 610–620.

Baumeister, R. F. (1998). The self. In D. T. Gilbert, S. T. Fiske, & G. Lindzey (Eds.), *Handbook of social psychology* (4th ed., pp. 680–740). New York: McGraw-Hill.

Baumeister, R. F., Bratslavsky, E., Muraven, M., & Tice, D. M. (1998). Ego depletion: Is the active self a limited resource? *Journal of Personality and Social Psychology, 74*, 1252–1265.

Baumeister, R. F., Dale, K. M., & Tice, D. M. (1998). *Replenishing the self: Effects of positive affect on performance and persistence following ego depletion*. Unpublished manuscript and research in progress, Case Western Reserve University, Cleveland, OH.

Baumeister, R. F., Heatherton, T. F., & Tice, D. M. (1994). *Losing control: How and why people fail at self-regulation*. San Diego, CA: Academic Press.

Baumeister, R. F., & Leary, M. R. (1995). The need to belong: Desire for interpersonal attachments as a fundamental human motivation. *Psychological Bulletin, 117,* 497–529.

Block, J. (1993). Studying personality the long way. In D. Funder, R. Parke, C. Tomlinson-Keasey, & K. Widaman (Eds.), *Studying lives through time* (pp. 9–41). Washington, DC: American Psychological Association.

Carver, C. S., & Scheier, M. F. (1981). *Attention and self-regulation: A control theory approach to human behavior.* New York: Springer-Verlag.

Feather, N. T. (1961). The relationship of persistence at a task to expectation of success and achievement related motives. *Journal of Abnormal and Social Psychology, 63,* 552–561.

Freud, S. (1961). The ego and the id. In J. Strachey (Ed. and Trans.), *The standard edition of the complete psychological works of Sigmund Freud* (Vol. 19, pp. 12–66). London: Hogarth Press. (Original work published 1923)

Freud, S. (1961). New introductory lectures on psycho-analysis. In J. Strachey (Ed. and Trans.), *The standard edition of the complete psychological works of Sigmund Freud* (Vol. 22, pp. 7–182). London: Hogarth Press. (Original work published 1933)

Glass, D. C., & Singer, J. E. (1972). *Urban stress: Experiments on noise and social stressors.* New York: Academic Press.

Gottfredson, M. R., & Hirschi, T. (1990). *A general theory of crime.* Stanford, CA: Stanford University Press.

Higgins, E. T. (1996). The "self digest": Self-knowledge serving self-regulatory functions. *Journal of Personality and Social Psychology, 71,* 1062–1083.

Higgins, E. T., & King, G. (1981). Accessibility of social constructs: Information processing consequences of individual and contextual variability. In N. Cantor & J. Kihlstrom (Eds.), *Personality, cognition, and social interaction* (pp. 69–121). Hillsdale, NJ: Erlbaum.

Hochschild, A. R. (1983). *The managed heart.* Berkeley: University of California Press.

Karesek, R. A. (1979). Job demands, job decision latitude and mental strain: Implications for job redesign. *Administrative Science Quarterly, 24,* 285–307.

Linder, D. E., Cooper, J., & Jones, E. E. (1967). Decision freedom as a determinant of the role of incentive magnitude in attitude change. *Journal of Personality and Social Psychology, 6,* 245–254.

Maslach, C., & Jackson, S. E. (1981). The measurement of experienced burnout. *Journal of Occupational Behavior, 2,* 99–113.

Mischel, W. (1996). From good intentions to willpower. In P. Gollwitzer & J. Bargh (Eds.), *The psychology of action* (pp. 197–218). New York: Guilford.

Mischel, W., Shoda, Y., & Peake, P. K. (1988). The nature of adolescent competencies predicted by preschool delay of gratification. *Journal of Personality and Social Psychology, 54,* 687–696.

Muraven, M. R. (1998). Mechanisms of self-control failure: Motivation and limited resources. Unpublished doctoral dissertation, Case Western Reserve University, Cleveland, OH.

Muraven, M. R., & Baumeister, R. F. (2000). Self-regulation and depletion of limited resources: Does self-control resemble a muscle? *Psychological Bulletin, 126,* 247–259.

Muraven, M. R., Baumeister, R. F., & Tice, D. M. (1999). Longitudinal improvement of self-regulation through practice: Building self-control through repeated exercise. *Journal of Social Psychology, 139,* 446–457.

Muraven, M. R., Tice, D. M., & Baumeister, R. F. (1998). Self-control as limited resource: Regulatory depletion patterns. *Journal of Personality and Social Psychology, 74,* 774–789.

Parasuraman, R. (1984). Sustained attention in detection and discrimination. In R. Parasuraman & D. R. Davies (Eds.), *Varieties of attention* (pp. 243–271). Orlando, FL: Academic Press.

Shoda, Y., Mischel, W., & Peake, P. K. (1990). Predicting adolescent cognitive and self-regulatory competencies from preschool delay of gratification: Identifying diagnostic conditions. *Developmental Psychology, 26,* 978–986.

Twenge, J. M., Tice, D. M., Schmeichel, B. J., & Baumeister, R. F. (2000). Decision fatigue: Making multiple personal decisions depletes the self's resources. Manuscript submitted for publication, Case Western Reserve University, Cleveland, OH.

Wegner, D. M., Schneider, D. J., Carter, S. R., & White, T. L. (1987). Paradoxical effects of thought suppression. *Journal of Personality and Social Psychology, 53,* 5–13.

Wyer, R. W., & Srull, T. K. (1980). Category accessibility and social perception: Some implications for the study of person memory and interpersonal judgments. *Journal of Personality and Social Psychology, 28,* 841–856.

Zaleznik, A., Kets de Vries, M. F. R., & Howard, J. (1977). Stress reactions in organizations: Syndromes, causes and consequences. *Behavioral Science, 22,* 151–162.

Author Index

Numbers in italics refer to listings in reference sections.

Subject Index

moral qualities associated with, 288–290

and organizational failure, 282–283

power of, 278, 280–282

psychological characteristics associated with, 278

selection processes in, 291–293

and those who are led, 278

Locus of control, 106, 232

and core-self evaluation, 96–97

research on, 93

MAB (Multidimensional Aptitude Battery), 170

MacKinnon, Donald W., 7

Managerial Potential scale (of Hogan Personality Inventory), 261, 262

MANSPEC, 258

MBTI. *See* Myers–Briggs Type Indicator

Megalomania, 212

MER/29, 284

Merit-based affirmative action, 35–37

MFS. *See* Multilinear formula scoring

Michels, R., 281–282

Milgram shock experiment, 279–281

Military psychologists, 223

Military services, officer selection in, 258–259

Minnesota Multiphasic Personality Inventory (MMPI), 6, 7, 200, 261

MIRT models. *See* Multiple IRT models

Mischel, Walter, 10, 124, 131

Mission failures, 282–283

MMPI. *See* Minnesota Multiphasic Personality Inventory

Montgomery, B. L., 258

Moral integrity, and leadership, 286–295

Moralistic bias, 199

Morey Narcissism Scale, 200

Motivation

for citizenship performance, 54–57

individual–job fit and work, 229–230

for self-enhancement, 196

Motivator factors/satisfiers, 230

Motivator needs, 230

Mozart, Wolfgang Amadeus, 238

MPD (multiple personality disorders), 149

Multidimensional Aptitude Battery (MAB), 170

Multilinear formula scoring (MFS), 146–148

Multiple IRT (MIRT) models, 147–148

Multiple personality disorders (MPD), 149

Music, effects of background, 238–242

Myers–Briggs Type Indicator (MBTI), 5, 258, 262, 267

NA. *See* Negative affectivity

Narcissism, 199–201, 204–205, 212

Narcissistic Personality Inventory (NPI), 200, 201, 204

National Aeronautics and Space Administration (NASA), 259–260

National Science Foundation, 4

Native Americans, 35

Negative affectivity (NA), 97, 98, 109 n.3

NEO Personality Inventory (NEO), 64, 100, 101, 105, 112, 165, 256, 261, 267

NEO Personality Inventory–Revised (NEO–PI–R), 166–168, 171, 173, 176–182, 184–188

Netherlands, 258

Neuroses, 5–6

Neuroticism, 236, 262

and core-self evaluation, 96, 100–108

and customer relations, 232

and job satisfaction/performance, 103

research on, 93

scope of, 101

and subjective well-being, 102–103

New Zealand, 258

Nominal models, 147

Non-technical skills, 266

NPI. *See* Narcissistic Personality Inventory

Nunnally, Jum C., 164–165

OAM. *See* Optimal appropriateness measurement

Observer harshness, 202

OCB. *See* Organizational citizenship behavior

About the Editors

Brent W. Roberts received his PhD from the University of California, Berkeley, in 1994. From 1994 to 1999, he was an assistant professor of psychology at the University of Tulsa in Oklahoma. Since 1999 he has been an assistant professor of psychology at the University of Illinois, Urbana–Champaign. He sits on the editorial boards of the *Journal of Personality and Social Psychology*, *Personality and Social Psychology Bulletin*, and the *Journal of Research in Personality*. In 1995, he was awarded the J. S. Tanaka award for outstanding dissertation in personality psychology. His research focuses on personality development, the relationship between personality and career development, and personality assessment.

Robert Hogan received his PhD from the University of California, Berkeley, in 1967. He was professor of psychology and social relations at Johns Hopkins University in Baltimore from 1967 to 1982 and McFarlin Professor of Psychology and chair at the University of Tulsa in Oklahoma from 1982 to 2001. He was editor of the *Journal of Personality and Social Psychology* from 1978 to 1984, and he is coeditor of the *Handbook of Personality Psychology* (with Johnson and Briggs, 1997). He is a Fellow of the American Psychological Association's Division 5 (Evaluation, Measurement, and Statistics), Division 8 (Society of Personality and Social Psychology), and Division 14 (Society for Industrial and Organizational Psychology). He has spent his career demonstrating the practical significance of well-validated measures of personality, especially for personnel selection and management development.